Dred Scott and the Dangers of a Political Court

Dred Scott and the Dangers of a Political Court

Ethan Greenberg

LEXINGTON BOOKS
A division of
ROWMAN & LITTLEFIELD PUBLISHERS, INC.
Lanham • Boulder • New York • Toronto • Plymouth, UK

Published by Lexington Books
A division of Rowman & Littlefield Publishers, Inc.
A wholly owned subsidiary of The Rowman & Littlefield Publishing Group, Inc.
4501 Forbes Boulevard, Suite 200, Lanham, Maryland 20706
http://www.lexingtonbooks.com

Estover Road, Plymouth PL6 7PY, United Kingdom

British Library Cataloguing in Publication Information Available

Library of Congress Cataloging-in-Publication Data
Greenberg, Ethan, 1957–
Dred Scott and the dangers of a political court / Ethan Greenberg.
p. cm.
Includes bibliographical references and index.
ISBN-13: 978-0-7391-3758-1 (cloth : alk. paper)
ISBN-10: 0-7391-3758-1 (cloth : alk. paper)
eISBN-13: 978-0-7391-3760-4
eISBN-10: 0-7391-3760-3
1. Scott, Dred, 1809–1858—Trials, litigation, etc. 2. Sanford, John F.A., 1806- or 7-1857—Trials, litigation, etc. 3. Slavery—Law and legislation—United States—History—19th century. 4. Political questions and judicial power—United States. I. Title.
KF228.S27G74 2009
342.7308'7—dc22

2009032656

The paper used in this publication meets the minimum requirements of American National Standard for Information Sciences—Permanence of Paper for Printed Library Materials, ANSI/NISO Z39.48-1992.

Printed in the United States of America

Dedication

For David and Marilyn, who came before;

For Eli and Ruby, who will go on after;

And for Marly,

The sweet heart of the heart of my life.

Contents

Acknowledgments

First and foremost, I wish to acknowledge and thank Fred Gilbert. He has been endlessly helpful (and endlessly patient) in putting this book together. Without Fred, this project could never have been finished.

Professor Philip Weinberg (of St. John's Law School) and Dean Evan Cornog (of Columbia Journalism School) read various drafts of this book; they provided valuable comments and welcome encouragement. So too did Ruth Greenberg and Jessica Levinson. Joyce Seltzer (of Harvard University Press) and Helen Tartar (of Fordham University Press) also helped to shape this book with their useful comments.

Bronx Supreme Court Librarian Margaret Beirne was able to locate even the most obscure sources, quickly and cheerfully.

It is customary for the author to acknowledge the people who helped along the way, and to take sole responsibility for any faults the book may have. That's certainly appropriate here. I thank all these people for their help. They could not have been kinder or more able. This book's flaws are purely of my own making.

* * *

I am also grateful to the following sources for permission to reprint excerpts of their work.

Alan M. Dershowitz, *America on Trial: Inside the Legal Battles That Transformed Our Nation* (New York: Warner Books, 2004), 118. Reprinted by permission.

Christopher Eisgruber, "The Story of Dred Scott: Originalism's Forgotten Past," in *Constitutional Law Stories*, ed. Michael C. Dorf (New York: Foundation Press, 2004), 155. Reprinted by permission.

Walter Murphy, James Fleming, Sotirios Barber, and Stephen Macedo, *American Constitutional Interpretation* (3d Ed.) (New York: Foundation Press, 2003), 218. Reprinted by permission.

Introduction

More than 150 years ago, in May of 1854, in a small and stuffy courtroom in St. Louis, Missouri, a jury returned a verdict for the defendant John Sanford in the federal court "freedom suit" of *Dred Scott v. Sanford*. The jury's verdict declared that the plaintiffs Dred Scott and his wife Harriet Scott (together with their two young daughters, Eliza and Lizzie) were still slaves who belonged to Sanford.

The Scotts had sued for their freedom on the grounds that their former owner—an obscure Army doctor named John Emerson—had taken the Scotts to live with him on free soil. Specifically, Dred Scott had served as Emerson's slave for roughly six years back in the 1830s at remote Army posts along the Indian frontier. Those posts were located in Illinois and the Wisconsin Territory. Slavery was illegal there (although Dr. Emerson and his fellow Army officers ignored that fact). Dred Scott therefore argued that he had become free by living in Illinois and in the Wisconsin Territory, and he based his lawsuit in large part on the legal doctrine "Once free, forever free." But the jury did not agree. Following the instructions on the law given by trial Judge Robert Wells, the jury found that Dred and Harriet Scott had not been emancipated, despite their extended residence on free soil.

The parties to the *Dred Scott* case were fairly ordinary people. By the time they brought their federal lawsuit against John Sanford, Dred and Harriet Scott had become household slaves in St. Louis. Dred Scott served mostly as a doorman and porter. Harriet Scott took in laundry. Their former master Dr. Emerson had passed away quietly in 1843, shortly after leaving the Army. Ownership of the Scotts later passed from Emerson's widow to her brother, John Sanford. Sanford was a wealthy but largely unremarkable New York City businessman who traveled frequently to St. Louis in order to look after his financial interests there. It seems likely that no one would remember any of these people today had the Scotts simply accepted the jury's verdict.

But the Scotts did not give up. They brought an appeal to the United States Supreme Court; and the decision of the Supreme Court in *Dred Scott v. Sandford*[1] in 1857 was a landmark in the history of the Court and of the United States.

The Opinion of the Court in *Dred Scott* was written by Chief Justice Roger Taney. It held that free Negroes (like Negro slaves) were not and could not be citizens of the United States. Even more important, *Dred Scott* declared that the Missouri Compromise of 1820 was unconstitutional. The Missouri Compromise had in substance forbidden slavery in all the U.S. territories north of Missouri.

Dred Scott was the very first case in American history where the Supreme Court set aside a substantive federal statute as unconstitutional. That was an historic and controversial development in itself. Moreover, the *Dred Scott* decision held that Congress had no power to prohibit slavery in any federal territory. That decision flew in the face of a long-established national understanding; from the very outset of U.S. history, Congress had passed numerous laws deciding which U.S. territories (and thus which future states) would be free, and which would have slavery.

The *Dred Scott* decision demonstrated to most neutral observers (although there were, admittedly, very few neutral observers at the time) that the Supreme Court was firmly committed to the defense of slavery. The decision appeared to be an attempt by the Court to resolve in favor of slavery the most hotly disputed political issue of the day—the future of slavery in the territories that made up the great American West. Not surprisingly, *Dred Scott* was met by a firestorm of criticism, protest and resistance. Many contemporaries believed, and most historians now agree, that the *Dred Scott* decision and its aftermath were important steps on the road that led to the Civil War.

History has not been kind to the *Dred Scott* decision. It is widely regarded as "the worst ever by the Supreme Court."[2] Yet, while there is general agreement that *Dred Scott* was a "ghastly mistake"[3] and a significant "self-inflicted wound"[4] for the Supreme Court, there remains widespread disagreement among legal scholars, historians and judges as to *why* the *Dred Scott* decision was so very bad.

That is somewhat surprising. American slavery ended in 1865. The great national controversy over slavery and its expansion into the U.S. territories that so deeply divided the nation in the 1850s is now a matter of historical interest only. No modern American favors slavery, or has much of a kind word for its antebellum defenders. Thus it seems strange that here in the twenty-first century there is still no general consensus as to why the *Dred Scott* decision was mistaken, or how the Supreme Court should have decided the case instead.

Most modern commentators tend to view *Dred Scott* through the prism of controversies over how the Constitution should be interpreted today. A number of "aspirationalist" or "liberal" legal thinkers have made the argument that *Dred Scott* is an example of how a "strict constructionist" or "originalist" philosophy can lead the Court to embrace and enforce gross injustice. Thus, for example, Professor Alan Dershowitz has asserted that *Dred Scott* fully embodies the "originalist methodology" favored by many modern-day political conservatives[5]; and a recent law journal piece describes *Dred Scott* as "a case of strict constructionism run amok."[6]

On the other hand, several legal scholars, public officials and pundits (including, most notably, Associate Supreme Court Justice Antonin Scalia and President George W. Bush) who favor interpreting the Constitution according to the "original intent" of the Framers take a very different view. They argue that the *Dred Scott* decision was wrong because the *Dred Scott* Court reached out to decide what was an essentially political and moral question as a matter of constitutional law. They see in *Dred Scott* a parallel to another decision that they disapprove of: *Roe v. Wade*[7]—the modern (1973) Supreme Court case that established a woman's right to obtain an abortion. Thus former federal Judge Robert Bork has written, "Who says *Roe*, must say . . . *Scott*"[8]; and noted conservative legal thinker Bruce Fein contends that "*Roe* is first cousin to *Dred Scott*."[9]

Neither of these schools of criticism is very illuminating or persuasive. Perhaps rigid "originalism" is a flawed philosophy of constitutional interpretation (as Professor Dershowitz, among many others, contends); perhaps not. But, in either case, the fault with *Dred Scott* lies elsewhere. The pro-slavery justices who made up the *Dred Scott* majority *and* the anti-slavery dissenters *all* employed an essentially "originalist" approach. They disagreed with each other chiefly because they drew different lessons from the Framers' ambivalent original legacy concerning slavery.

Looking to the other end of the modern-day political spectrum, many conservative legal thinkers (including, most notably, Justice Scalia) have argued that *Dred Scott*—like *Roe v. Wade*—was the work of an unduly "activist" or "liberal" court.[10] *Roe v. Wade* may or may not be good constitutional law. But, in either case, this criticism of *Dred Scott* also falls wide of the mark. True, slavery presented a great moral issue. However, the key legal issue that emerged in *Dred Scott* was whether Congress possessed the power to ban slavery in a U.S. Territory. That was a genuine legal question, and it could only be answered by reference to the Constitution. Accordingly, Chief Justice Taney and his colleagues cannot fairly be faulted merely because they looked to the Constitution in order to decide the real questions of law presented in *Dred Scott*.

Thus—despite the best efforts of modern commentators—*Dred Scott* cannot serve as an example of either "aspirationalism" or "originalism" gone wrong. The truth (as is often the case) is more complex. In truth, Chief Justice Taney and the pro-slavery majority in *Dred Scott* did not go wrong because they employed a faulty "methodology" or philosophy of constitutional interpretation. Instead, they deliberately and badly misread the law in order to reach a desired result. Along the way they distorted both legal precedent and the history of the era of the American Revolution almost beyond recognition. Moreover, they reached out over and over again to decide unnecessary and unpreserved issues, all in favor of slavery and slaveholders.

They did so because—like many white southerners in the period leading up to the Civil War—the *Dred Scott* majority was determined to safeguard slavery once and for all against what they saw as unwarranted and dangerous aggression by self-righteous northern abolitionists and Republicans. The *Dred Scott* majority feared (as Chief Justice Taney expressed it in a private letter) that "the power of the North will be exercised to gratify their cupidity and evil passions"[11]; and the majority therefore believed that the *Dred Scott* decision was necessary (in concurring Associate Justice Wayne's phrase) in order to restore "the peace and harmony of the country."[12]

Why study *Dred Scott* today? Why review a decision that deals chiefly with complex and arcane issues about the law of slavery in the 1800s—when, after all, American slavery ended more than a century ago?

There are many good reasons. To begin with, *Dred Scott* was a real case. Like most real cases, *Dred Scott* was about real people with real human stories. The tale of Dred Scott—his journey from Virginia, to Alabama and to St. Louis with his first master, Peter Blow; Scott's travels with Dr. Emerson and his service to Army officers engaged chiefly in fighting Indians (and disease) in the wilderness areas of Illinois and Wisconsin; Dred's legally recognized slave marriage (a rarity) to Harriet Scott; Scott's presence on the Rio Grande when the Mexican War broke out; and his lifelong friendly connection with the children of his original master, Peter Blow, who supported and helped to finance Scott's long legal struggle for freedom—is an odd and captivating one. Slavery was, of course, always a terrible form of oppression. But Dred Scott's strange and varied life story will surprise many modern readers because it illustrates how at least some slaves' lives contained some real, if limited, elements of autonomy and even adventure.

The stories of the lawyers, judges and political leaders who helped shape the *Dred Scott* decision are also interesting. Among other things, several of the concurring Justices in *Dred Scott* engaged in secret (and improper) correspondence with President-elect James Buchanan beforehand about how the case ought to be decided. Buchanan was a "dough-face"—a northern politician devoted to protecting the interests of the slave-holding South. Associate Justice John Catron of Tennessee was known by many as Buchanan's "wire-puller." With tact and secrecy, Buchanan and Catron together helped to construct a majority coalition of Supreme Court Justices who were willing to use the *Dred Scott* case as the occasion to strike down the anti-slavery provisions of the Missouri Compromise.

Chief Justice Roger Taney is an especially intriguing figure. As a young lawyer from the slave-holding border state of Maryland, Taney freed his own slaves, and on at least one occasion he publicly and passionately declared that all men who loved liberty must see that slavery violated the principles of the Declaration of Independence. But then time passed. Taney became a hard-headed, middle-aged politician, and then a brilliant judge who presided over the Supreme Court for nearly thirty years. Over the years Taney also became an ardent defender of slavery; and in *Dred Scott* Taney argued that it was the fixed and universal belief of the men who wrote the Declaration of Independence and the Constitution that the Negro race had been justly reduced to slavery, and that Negroes had no rights that a white man was bound to respect.

What happened to Taney? Why did he—like so many leading men of the South of his generation—move over time from a posture of mostly quiet regret over slavery to one of fierce defense of slavery as a just and essential institution? How did Taney square *Dred Scott* with his youthful vision of slavery as antithetical to the spirit of the Declaration of Independence?

It is thus worthwhile to study *Dred Scott* in order to learn more about Scott, Buchanan and Taney, about the other leading people involved in the case, and about the America they lived in.

Dred Scott was also an important event in the political history of the United States. The decision in essence attempted to outlaw as unconstitutional the central goal of the Republican party—to stop the expansion of slavery in the West. Republican opposition to and outrage over *Dred Scott* were immediate and powerful. Republican Abraham Lincoln became one of *Dred Scott*'s leading public critics. *Dred Scott* was a featured topic in many of the famed Lincoln–Douglas debates; and Lincoln's Cooper Union Address in February, 1860—which launched Lincoln as a serious presidential candidate—can be seen as an effort by Lincoln to rebut *Dred Scott* in a systematic fashion by demonstrating that America's Founding Fathers had favored the restriction and ultimate extinction of slavery. Thus *Dred Scott* is also worth study because the case plays an important part in the story of Lincoln's career and the story of the political and sectional crisis over slavery that led to the Civil War.

Perhaps most important—especially for students of the law—*Dred Scott* is indeed, as advertised, the very worst decision in the long history of the U.S. Supreme Court. So, when we study *Dred Scott*, we can also begin to answer the questions: What went wrong? Why was this great case so badly decided?

In brief, the answer that emerges is that the *Dred Scott* Court—motivated by sectionalism and racism—substituted what it considered to be an important and worthwhile political agenda for intellectually honest legal reasoning and for the disinterested application of neutral principles of law. The Supreme Court Justices who made up the *Dred Scott* majority wanted to preserve the Union by safeguarding the institution of slavery so thoroughly that it could no longer be a source of contention between the North and South. To that political end, they embraced whatever flimsy and faulty legal arguments they found at hand in order to justify the pro-slavery result that they had pre-determined.

In short, the *Dred Scott* Court gave into temptation: the temptation to subordinate law to politics. That is a temptation that calls to originalists and aspirationalists alike. And—given the overly political nature of legal debate in modern America—that temptation remains nearly as strong today as it was in pre–Civil War America. The story of *Dred Scott*, then, is the story of the dangers of a political court.

The first section of this book is mostly history—a review of the people and events involved in the *Dred Scott* case. The second is mostly law—a detailed examination of Chief Justice Taney's Opinion of the Court (together with a briefer look at the concurring and dissenting opinions). An effort is made not to simply condemn Taney's Opinion as contrary to modern thinking. Criticism based solely on the difference between the general beliefs of separate eras is probably not fair, and almost certainly not very useful. It is more helpful to evaluate both the strengths and weaknesses of the *Dred Scott* decision in the context of the law as it stood at that time. The third and final section of the book begins with a brief look at some modern analyses of *Dred Scott*, and then attempts to take a broader view and explain why the Court went wrong.

I am a lawyer, a judge, and a law school teacher, and I have enjoyed reading about American history since I was a boy. It is my hope that this book will be read and enjoyed by lawyers and judges, by legal historians and by American history scholars. But it is meant chiefly for students and for the serious general reader. Some of the legal principles involved in *Dred Scott* case are, of course, not immediately familiar to most non-lawyers. So those principles are introduced and explained here in a simplified, but not simplistic, fashion.

Notes

1. *Dred Scott v. Sandford*, 60 U.S. 393 (1857). John Sanford's last name was misspelled as "Sandford" in the U.S. Supreme Court reports. In the interest of brevity, references to "*DS*" hereinafter are to the *Dred Scott* decision.

2. Walter Ehrlich, "Scott v. Sandford," in Kermit L. Hall, ed., *The Oxford Companion to the Supreme Court of the United States* (New York: Oxford U. Press, 1971), 761.

3. Alexander Bickel, *The Supreme Court and the Idea of Progress* (New York: Harper & Row, 1970), 41.

4. Charles E. Hughes, *The Supreme Court of the United States: Its Foundations Methods, and Achievements* (New York: Columbia U. Press, 1928), 50.

5. Alan M. Dershowitz, *America on Trial: Inside the Legal Battles that Transformed Our Nation* (New York: Warner Books, 2004), 117–22.

6. Daniel Slater, Book Review, "Two Men Before the Storm: Arba Crane's Recollection of Dred Scott and the Supreme Court Case that Started the Civil War," *New York Law Journal*, March 17, 2006, 2.

7. *Roe v. Wade*, 410 U.S. 959 (1973).

8. Robert H. Bork, *The Tempting of America: The Political Seduction of the Law* (New York: The Free Press, 1990), 28–34.

9. Bruce Fein, "Pack the Supreme Court," *DC Bar*, Feb. 2005.

10. *Planned Parenthood v. Casey*, 505 U.S. 833 at 1001–1002 (Scalia, J., dissenting).

11. Carl B. Swisher, *Roger B. Taney* (New York: MacMillan, 1935), 492–93.

12. *DS* at 455 (Wayne, J., concurring).

HISTORY

Chapter 1
Preface—Dred Scott in a House Divided

Many modern Americans find it difficult to understand the *Dred Scott* case. The very idea of slavery is repulsive to virtually every American today. The idea of race-based slavery is even more disturbing, if that is possible. The *Dred Scott* decision countenanced African American slavery. Thus it is easy to simply condemn the *Dred Scott* Court and then quickly move on.

That gut reaction is not entirely wrong. The Opinions of Chief Justice Roger Taney and of the concurring Justices in *Dred Scott* are imbued with the idea that human slavery is acceptable, and even a positive moral good. Those Opinions thus exemplify a moral blindness that can indeed properly be condemned across the ages.

But that approach to *Dred Scott* is not particularly useful to the student of history, and it does little to advance the purpose of this book—to see *why* the Supreme Court went so terribly wrong in this landmark case. It is more useful to look at the question: Was the *Dred Scott* decision wrong given the law of that day, and if so, why?

A fundamental starting point in this inquiry is to recall two sad but important facts: a) prior to the Civil War, slavery was legal in the southern part of the United States; and b) slavery was tolerated by the original U.S. Constitution, albeit in indirect language.

In 1776 the Declaration of Independence proclaimed that all men are created equal and endowed by their Creator with an inalienable right to liberty. Yet slavery existed in all thirteen American colonies at that time. For a few years, it appeared that the generation who had made the American Revolution, inspired by the spirit of the age, was poised to bring American slavery to an end. Between 1776 and the adoption of the U.S. Constitution in 1789, five northern states prohibited slavery.

In 1789 the Constitution established our democratic system of government. But it did not further advance the cause of emancipation. Neither the Constitution nor the Bill of Rights freed or protected the slaves. To the contrary, it is clear from the text of the Constitution that the Framers envisioned that slavery would continue, at least for a time. Thus the original Constitution required that fugitive slaves must be returned from free states to their masters, and the Constitution counted slaves as three-fifths of a person for the purpose of determining how many representatives each state would be allotted in Congress.

Admittedly, the original Constitution did give Congress the limited power to end the importation of slaves from Africa beginning in 1808 (and thus halt the horrors of the dreaded "middle passage" from Africa to America during which so many slaves lost their lives). Moreover, the Constitution deliberately avoided the direct use of the word "slavery" because, as James Madison explained, the Framers did not want to give express approval to the idea that there could be "property in man." Nevertheless, the Constitution did not give the federal government the power to emancipate the slaves, or even to prospectively prohibit slavery, in the states where slavery existed.

Accordingly, when *Dred Scott* was decided in 1857, there was little doubt that slavery was legal and constitutional. This had led the prominent abolitionist William Lloyd Garrison, among others, to denounce the Constitution as a covenant with death and a compact with hell. But slavery was the law, and as a strictly legal matter the *Dred Scott* Court cannot be faulted for recognizing that to be the case.

After the adoption of the Constitution a few more northern states prohibited slavery. As a result, the Union exhibited a clear geographic division. Slavery was forbidden in the North and flourished in the South. As Lincoln memorably described it, America prior to the Civil War was a "house divided" between freedom and slavery.

For many years, most white Americans were able to overlook that division for most purposes. But there were at least four recurring circumstances that raised tensions between the North and South with regard to slavery. First, over the years there were always calls—often religiously inspired—from the North for the abolition of slavery in the South. Such calls caused fierce resentment, and they were sometimes met with violence, even in the North. (Thus, for example, a mob murdered Presbyterian minister and abolitionist publisher Elijah Lovejoy in Alton, Illinois, in 1837.)

Second, slaves sometimes escaped from the South to the North, only to be captured there. Many northern state citizens and courts were reluctant to return such fugitives to bondage in the South. Denunciation, counter-denunciation, and even armed resistance sometimes followed. (Thus, for example, in 1850 a Boston mob broke the fugitive slave Shadrach Minkins out of federal custody and helped him escape to freedom.)

Third, on occasion slaves traveled with their masters, or with the consent of their masters, from the South to the North for short or long periods of time. This presented an interesting "choice-of-law" or "conflict-of-law" problem as to whether the slave's status was controlled by the law of the southern slave state, or was instead controlled by the law of the northern free state in question. Such slaves sometimes sued and won their freedom on the ground that their residence on free soil had emancipated them. Dred Scott's case began as such a lawsuit in Missouri state court.

Fourth, and most important, vast tracts of land were added to the Union by the Louisiana Purchase from France, by treaties with Spain and England, and through the Mexican War. There was deep and continuing disagreement and acrimony between the North and South over whether slavery would exist in the those new territories and in the new states later created out of those territories. That disagreement reached a violent peak during the 1850s in the struggle over the future status of slavery in "Bleeding Kansas."

The crucial question decided in *Dred Scott* was not whether slavery was right or legal or constitutional. The question decided was a significantly narrower one. It was the same question that had deeply divided the nation during the periods leading up to the Missouri Compromise of 1820, the Compromise of 1850, and the Kansas-Nebraska Act of 1854.[1] The crucial question was this: What should be done about slavery in the territories that made up the great American West? And who would choose between slavery and freedom there?

These were the burning political issues that the North and South had struggled with throughout the antebellum era. These were the intractable issues that made it appear to many Americans in the 1850s that the "house divided" was about to fall. And these were the issues that the *Dred Scott* Court reached out to decide, with terrible results.

Notes

1. Each of these federal laws attempted to resolve the question of slavery in the territories by designating certain areas where slavery would be permitted and certain areas where it would be prohibited.

In briefest form, the Northwest Ordinance of 1787 (re-enacted in 1789) provided that slavery would be forbidden in the old Northwest Territory (now Indiana, Ohio, Michigan, Wisconsin, Illinois and part of Minnesota). Slavery was not prohibited south of the Ohio River (now Tennessee and Kentucky).

The Missouri Compromise of 1820 dealt chiefly with the territory acquired under the Louisiana Purchase. Slavery was forbidden north of the line of 36°30' north latitude (with the exception of Missouri), and permitted south of that line.

The Compromise of 1850 was more complex. It dealt chiefly with the territory acquired through the Mexican War. The Compromise of 1850 provided, among other things, that: California was admitted as a free state; the territories of New Mexico and Utah were created with no restriction on slavery; slave-trading was prohibited in Washington, D.C.; and a more severe Fugitive Slave Act replaced the prior one of 1793.

Finally, the Kansas-Nebraska Act of 1854 left it to the (white male) settlers of those two territories to decide whether or not slavery would be permitted there.

Chapter 2
A Slave's Life

Slavery deprived a man of his freedom. In a sense, it also deprived the slave of much of his history and his posterity. Dred Scott is probably one of the most famous slaves in American history, and even so, very little is known about him.[1]

To begin with, no one knows who Dred Scott's parents were, and no one knows for certain where or when he was born. It appears that he was born in Southampton County, Virginia, in or around the year 1800. It is not even clear that his name was always Dred Scott. There is some indication that his original name may have been Sam. (One story has it that while Sam was a slave to Army physician John Emerson, Sam's name was changed in honor of Army General Winfield Scott; "Dred Scott" may have been a variation of General Scott's nickname "Great Scott."[2])

There is no surviving written description of Scott's physical appearance as a boy or young man. Contemporary newspaper stories about Scott's 1857 Supreme Court case describe the middle-aged Scott as a very small and serious-looking man. The only known portrait of Scott tends to confirm that impression.[3]

Newspaper interviews with Scott from this same period indicate that when Scott was much younger Scott had a wife who was "sold away" from him.[4] No one now knows that woman's name or what happened to her.

Still, it seems likely that Scott mourned the loss of his first wife, and this loss may have helped to strengthen Scott's resolve to win freedom for himself, for his second wife Harriet, and for their children.

Very little is known about Dred Scott's character, apart from the obvious fact that Scott pursued his freedom with remarkable determination through state and federal courts for more than ten years. (There was for many years one school of historical writing that persistently described Scott as "shiftless" and lazy. However, upon examination, this oft-repeated description appears to have grown largely out of the fanciful racist musings of one old woman who may have met Scott in person; her credibility was substantially undermined because she also appears to have thought that Scott was still alive nearly twenty years after his death.[5])

It is clear that Dred Scott was born a slave. He belonged to a man named Peter Blow. Blow's path in life followed the westward path of settlement of the nation. Blow was a farmer. He owned a plantation in Southampton County, Virginia, alongside the Nottoway River, near several other plantations owned by family relations. Peter Blow had difficulty making his plantation profitable, in part because the soil had been farmed so heavily by several preceding generations.

Blow heard reports that many farmers were making a fortune in cotton in Alabama. In 1818 Blow pulled up stakes, and with his wife, children and slaves made a slow trek west over the Alleghenies to land that Blow had purchased near Huntsville, Alabama. (It may have been at this time that Blow "sold away" Dred Scott's first wife.) There Blow became a cotton farmer.

Blow's timing was bad, however. With the end of war in Europe, cotton prices dropped dramatically. Blow accumulated debt, rather than a fortune, in Huntsville. In 1821, Blow decided to move again, this time to Florence, Alabama; and Blow gave up farming. He opened up an inn in Florence and called it the Peter Blow Hotel.

Blow's new career probably brought about a dramatic change in Dred Scott's life. Scott no longer worked regularly in the fields. Now he worked at the hotel, helping with guests' luggage and taking care of horses (although he may still have been "hired out" from time to time to work on nearby plantations). Scott (now in his early twenties) also probably helped to take care of the Blows' growing children.

Peter Blow kept on moving. In or about the year 1830, Blow, his wife Elizabeth, their children and their slaves left Florence and came to live in St. Louis, Missouri, on the banks of the Mississippi River. The Mississippi then marked the edge of the settled United States, and St. Louis was one of the great bustling jumping-off places for those who wanted to explore and settle the West. Blow rented a large boarding house and opened it as the Jefferson Hotel. Dred Scott lived and worked at the hotel, and was sometimes hired out to work as a roustabout on steamboats that plied the Mississippi.[6]

The hotel business probably seemed like a good idea in a town like St. Louis filled with travelers headed west. Yet the Blows again encountered financial difficulties. Then Elizabeth Blow died in 1831, and Peter followed in 1832. And so, at around this date, Dred Scott was sold to Dr. John Emerson.[7] (Scott retained a degree of connection with the Blow family for the rest of his life; Peter Blow's son, Taylor Blow, and other relatives later provided important financial support for Scott's legal struggle for freedom, and it was Taylor Blow who ultimately bought and then freed Scott after that struggle failed.)

John Emerson was a physician. He received his degree from the University of Pennsylvania in 1824. In 1832 he got work as a temporary replacement for the Army Medical Officer at Jefferson Barracks near St. Louis. Emerson developed a taste for Army life very quickly. By 1833 he had secured his own appointment as an assistant surgeon in the Army.

Throughout his military career, Dr. Emerson maneuvered to be assigned to what he thought were better posts—often claiming convenient illnesses in order to bolster his requests for new assignments. Over the years in the course of applying for new posts, Dr. Emerson complained of (among other things) rheumatism, liver disorder, respiratory illness, an unspecified foot ailment that never quite required surgery, and "syphiloid disease." Emerson was transferred frequently over the course of his Army career, and he usually took his slave Dred Scott with him to each new post. The fact that some of these posts were in slave states and some not is the historical accident that made possible Dred Scott's long legal struggle for emancipation.

The details of Emerson and Scott's travels are a bit complex.[8] Scott and Emerson first lived at Jefferson Barracks near St. Louis, Missouri. Missouri was a slave state. For about two years (from 1834 to 1836), they lived a short distance up the Mississippi at Fort Armstrong (on Rock Island) in Illinois, a free state. (Fort Armstrong was evacuated in 1836, in part because of the Indian situation on the frontier, and in part because of difficulties controlling cholera outbreaks that were frequent in the rough conditions there.) From 1836 through 1840 (with one interruption for a trip to Louisiana), Scott lived at Fort Snelling near the site of what is now St. Paul, Minnesota. (During this period Scott either worked directly for Emerson, or was hired out to other Army officers while Emerson was away.)

Fort Snelling was part of the Wisconsin Territory. Slavery was forbidden there. Nevertheless, there was a small community of slaves who, like Dred Scott, had been brought to serve some of the officers stationed at Fort Snelling. (Indeed, it appears that throughout the pre–Civil War era Army officers often brought their slaves with them to frontier Army posts located on free soil, and simply disregarded local laws forbidding slavery.[9])

Within a year or so of arriving at Fort Snelling with Dr. Emerson in 1836, Dred Scott met and then soon married young Harriet Robinson. Harriet was the slave of the Fort's resident Indian agent, Major Lawrence Taliaferro. (Taliaferro regularly brought slaves up to Fort Snelling from Virginia to be hired out there; it appears he first brought the teenaged Harriet up to Fort Snelling between 1833 and 1835.) Taliaferro performed the wedding himself, and informally "gave" Harriet to Emerson.

Dred and Harriet Scott's marriage was unusual. Legal marriages between slaves were a rarity. The general rule in most American states prior to the Civil War was that slaves could not marry because they were not competent to enter into any contract. (The Scotts' lawyers later argued —without success—that the Scotts' marriage demonstrated that Dr. Emerson and Major Taliaferro had intended that Dred and Harriet Scott be free. This argument was, however, less than persuasive in view of the fact that Emerson continued to treat the Scotts as slaves long after their wedding.[10])

In the fall of 1837 Dr. Emerson was assigned to Fort Jessup in western Louisiana. He hired out Dred and Harriet Scott to serve other officers at Fort Snelling, and made the long trip down the Mississippi alone, arriving in Louisiana in November. There Emerson met Eliza Irene Sanford, the twenty-three-year-old daughter of a St. Louis manufacturer. Miss Sanford was at Fort Jessup visiting her sister Mary, who was married to Colonel Henry Bainbridge. Like Dred Scott, Dr. Emerson moved quickly when it came to matrimony. John Emerson married Eliza Sanford just a few months later, in February of 1838.

Dred and Harriet Scott were summoned to Fort Jessup to serve Dr. Emerson and his new wife. They traveled together, unaccompanied by any white overseer, to join the Emersons in Louisiana (and made no effort to escape anywhere along the way). The Scotts' stay in Louisiana was brief, however. (Indeed, their stay in Louisiana was so brief that the lawyers for both sides in the *Dred Scott* case simply skipped over this period of time in their recitation of the facts.[11]) Dr. Emerson did not like Fort Jessup. He began a campaign of letter writing, seeking a new assignment from the Army. He claimed that a post in a cooler climate would help him deal with his own many and varied medical problems.

In the fall of 1838 Dr. Emerson was reassigned back to Fort Snelling. He, Mrs. Emerson and the Scotts traveled north together. While on the steamboat *Gypsy* headed up the Mississippi River, Harriet Scott gave birth to a baby girl. Dred and Harriet Scott named their daughter Eliza, after Mrs. Emerson. (In the years that followed, Dred and Harriet had two sons who did not survive infancy, and a second daughter, named Lizzie.)

From 1838 to 1840 the Scotts served the Emersons at Fort Snelling. Not much is known about this period of their lives, but Dr. Emerson does appear as a signatory for the Army to one treaty with the Chippewa Indians. In the spring of 1840 Dr. Emerson was reassigned again, this time to Florida. (According to some accounts, Dr. Emerson was transferred in part because he got into a serious fist fight with a Quartermaster at Fort Snelling who refused to supply Dred Scott with a stove to warm his hut for the winter. Dr. Emerson's nose was bruised and his eyeglasses were shattered during the fight, and afterward Dr. Emerson was briefly arrested for threatening the Quartermaster with a pistol.[12]) The Seminole War was underway, so Emerson went to Florida alone. His wife and slaves moved to St. Louis, and took up residence there in a home owned by Mrs. Emerson's father.

Emerson was unhappy in Florida too. He wrote many letters seeking reassignment, again claiming that his bad health required that he be moved to a cooler place. Apparently, Emerson's constant complaints proved too much for the Army. Rather than transfer Emerson again, the Army discharged Emerson in 1842. (The discharge was labeled "honorable" but was not amicable; there was a rumor that Emerson had embezzled some hospital funds.[13])

Emerson returned to St. Louis for a time. He tried without success to secure a new appointment in the Army. He also began work on building a house in Davenport, Iowa, on land that Emerson had acquired while serving at nearby Fort Armstrong.

In November of 1843 Mrs. Emerson gave birth to a daughter, Henrietta. Less than a month later, Dr. Emerson died. He was only forty years old. As a physician, Emerson understood that he was near his end. He prepared and signed his will just a few hours before he passed away.

Emerson's will left his estate (including his slaves, the Scotts) to his wife for her lifetime, and after that to their infant daughter, Henrietta. Mrs. Emerson's father Alexander Sanford was named as one of the Missouri executors of Dr. Emerson's will. Her brother John Sanford was named as one of the Iowa executors. John Sanford lived in New York. However, Sanford was the widower of Emily Chouteau, originally from St. Louis, and he was an important agent for his former father-in-law's fur trading company, the Pratte-Chouteau Company; for those reasons, Sanford traveled frequently throughout the West (and especially to St. Louis) on business.

It becomes more difficult to follow Dred and Harriet Scott in the period immediately following Dr. Emerson's death. It appears that Harriet Scott and the children stayed with Mrs. Emerson at Mrs. Emerson's father's house in St. Louis, and that Dred Scott was informally "loaned" to Mrs. Emerson's brother-in-law Henry Bainbridge.[14]

Bainbridge was now an Army Captain. In 1843 he was assigned to Jefferson Barracks in St. Louis. In 1844 he was sent once again to Fort Jessup in Louisiana. In 1845 Bainbridge was assigned to serve in Texas, which had just been annexed to the United States and which was in the midst of a significant military build-up. In all likelihood Dred Scott traveled with Bainbridge to each of these posts. In 1846 the Mexican War broke out. Captain Bainbridge joined General Zachary Taylor's forces and marched on Mexico City. At the outset of the war, Dred Scott was sent back to St. Louis.

There Dred Scott sought to purchase freedom for himself and his family from Mrs. Emerson.[15] Over the course of his many years of service to Dr. Emerson, to Captain Bainbridge, and to others Army officers, Scott had somehow managed to accumulate some money. He offered Mrs. Emerson to make a down payment on the purchase price for his family's freedom, and to give security for the remainder. Mrs. Emerson refused the offer.

A few weeks later Dred and Harriet Scott sued Mrs. Emerson in Missouri state court, seeking their freedom on the ground that their extended residence on free soil had emancipated them. The suit also alleged that Mrs. Emerson had beaten, bruised and "ill-treated" Dred Scott.

This was the beginning of Dred Scott's long legal struggle for freedom. He had lived a slave's life. Like most slaves in pre–Civil War America, Dred Scott was never permitted to learn to read or write; and none of his masters cared enough to write much of anything about him. Thus many of the facts of Dred Scott's life as a slave were never recorded and cannot now be reconstructed. Yet Dred Scott soon became famous because of his suit for freedom–far more famous than any of those who had held him in bondage. The facts of his life story that were most important for legal purposes were those that showed where and when he had lived on free soil, and those facts therefore remain fairly clear to history.

They can be summarized as follows. Scott had lived and served as Dr. Emerson's slave: a) in the slave state of Missouri (from 1832 to 1834); b) in the free state of Illinois (from 1834 to 1836); c) in the free territory of Wisconsin (from 1836 to 1840); and d) once again in the slave state of Missouri.

Notes

1. The known facts of Scott's life are set forth in a number of books.

Don E. Fehrenbacher, *The Dred Scott Case: Its Significance in American Law and Politics* (New York: Oxford U. Press, 1978) is brilliant, exhaustive and authoritative on all matters relating to the *Dred Scott* case.

Paul Finkelman, *Dred Scott v. Sandford: A Brief History with Documents* (Boston: Bedford/St. Martin's, 1997) is also excellent, is much more compact, and, as the title indicates, includes excerpts from many relevant documents. Professor Finkelman has written widely about *Dred Scott* and related topics and is today's leading scholar in the field. Along with Jack Balkin and Sanford Levinson, Professor Finkelman is the editor of the very useful "Symposium: 150th Anniversary of Dred Scott," 82 *Chicago-Kent Law Review* (2007). The symposium was conducted at the University of Texas Law School in March 2007, and many of the presentations are available in video form online through the law school's web-site.

Walter Ehrlich, *They Have No Rights: Dred Scott's Struggle for Freedom* (Westport, CT: Greenwood Press, 1979) is also well written, and is especially valuable because of its use of Missouri sources, including previously unavailable Missouri State Court records and local histories.

Remarkably, all the remaining Missouri State Court records from the case are now available online (both in original handwritten form and in transcript form) through a website created by Washington University in St. Louis.

Vincent C. Hopkins, *Dred Scott's Case* (New York: Fordham U. Press, 1951) is not always as reliable as the later books. But it includes some details that do not appear in the other books listed above, and gives an interesting and somewhat more sympathetic reading to the Supreme Court's decision in *Dred Scott*.

Earl M. Maltz's *Dred Scott and the Politics of Slavery* (Lawrence: U. of Kansas Press, 2007) provides a good compact review of the case and its place in the pre–Civil War era.

2. Hopkins takes it as a given that Dred Scott's original name was Sam. Hopkins, *Dred Scott Case*, 1–3 and 7, n.13. However, the assertion that Peter

Blow's slaves Dred Scott and Sam were one and the same person is probably inaccurate conjecture, and the speculation that the name "Dred Scott" derived from "Great Scott" is even more doubtful. *See* Ehrlich, *They Have No Rights*, 12–15; Fehrenbacher, *The Dred Scott Case*, 239–41.

Lea Vander Velde, *Mrs. Dred Scott* (New York: Oxford U. Press, 2009) takes the view that the name "Dred" was a variation on the name "Etheldred." The book is based on impressive extensive research in previously obscure documents. It reaches many new and surprising conclusions—such as the "Etheldred" hypothesis—some of which are less firmly grounded than others.

3. Following the Supreme Court's *Dred Scott* decision in 1857 denying Scott his freedom, Taylor Blow purchased and then freed Dred Scott. A short time later, photographs of Dred Scott, Harriet Scott and their children were taken for *Frank Leslie's Illustrated Newspaper*. Hopkins, *Dred Scott's Case*, 176.

4. Interviews with Dred Scott were featured in the *Washington Union* of April 11, 1857, and *Frank Leslie's Illustrated Newspaper* of June 27, 1857.

5. Fehrenbacher, *Dred Scott Case*, 570–71. As detailed by Fehrenbacher, the myth that Dred Scott was "shiftless" and a "no-account nigger" ultimately worked its way (without the racist epithet) into the 1935 Edition of the *Dictionary of American Biography*.

6. Fehrenbacher, *Dred Scott Case*, 239–41; Ehrlich, *They Have No Rights*, 9–11; Hopkins, *Dred Scott's Case*, 2–3.

7. It is unclear whether Peter Blow himself sold Dred Scott before Blow's death, or whether Scott was instead sold by the executors of Blow's estate. It is also unclear whether Scott feared or instead welcomed his purchase by Dr. Emerson. One account held that Dred Scott at first ran away and hid in the swamp when sold by Blow; another account, however, asserted that Scott begged to be purchased by Emerson after receiving a cruel beating from Blow. Fehrenbacher, *Dred Scott*, 242, and n. 8; Ehrlich, *They Have No Rights*, 15.

8. A full narrative of Scott's life with Dr. Emerson is given in Fehrenbacher, *Dred Scott*, 242–48; Ehrlich, *They Have No Rights*, 16–25; and in Hopkins, *Dred Scott's Case*, 5–7. Gwenyth Swain, *Dred and Harriet Scott: A Family's Struggle for Freedom* (St. Paul: Borealis Books, 2004) is intended for younger readers, but is also quite good and contains some especially valuable detail about Dred Scott's years in Virginia and Alabama at 5–25.

9. Associate Supreme Court Justice John Catron, for one, was apparently surprised to learn during oral argument in Dred Scott's case in 1856 that Army officers often brought along slaves to serve them on Army posts situated on free soil. He dashed off a quick letter of inquiry to Secretary of War (and later Confederate President) Jefferson Davis about the subject. Davis replied and confirmed that Army officers had always "been in the habit" of taking their servants and slaves with them to "Indian Country," whether or not slavery was legally permitted there. Hopkins, *Dred Scott's Case*, 52.

10. *See*, Finkelman, *Scott v. Sanford*, 15–17. *See also* L. Vander Velde and S. Subramanian, "Mrs. Dred Scott," 106 *Yale L.J.* 1033 (1997).

11. Thus none of the nine Opinions rendered by the Supreme Court's nine Justices in *Dred Scott* made any reference to Dred Scott leaving free soil at Fort Snelling for Fort Jessup in Louisiana.

12. Fehrenbacher, *Dred Scott*, 246–47.

13. Ehrlich, *They Have No Rights*, 11.

14. Fehrenbacher, *Dred Scott*, 249; Ehrlich, *They Have No Rights*, 26–29; Hopkins, *Dred Scott's Case*, 6–7.

15. Scott described his offer to purchase himself and his family to a reporter in an interview conducted in 1857. *See St. Louis Evening News*, April 3, 1857; Hopkins, *Dred Scott's Case*, 20 and n. 8.

Chapter 3
False Promise of Freedom—Scott's State Court Trials

—The Decision to Sue—

Historians (and others) have sometimes wondered why Dred and Harriet Scott chose to sue for their freedom when they did—that is, in 1846, after Dred Scott completed his service to Captain Bainbridge in Texas and returned to Mrs. Emerson's home in St. Louis. It seems almost certain that Dred Scott would have had a better chance to win his case if he had brought his suit in the "free-soil" jurisdictions of Illinois or the Wisconsin Territory when he served Dr. Emerson there during the 1830s.

It may be that Scott was concerned that as an isolated black slave at a remote Army fort he would have been vulnerable to retaliation for bringing such a suit. Perhaps Scott had no white friends to help him with such a lawsuit in Illinois or Wisconsin (as several members of the Blow family later helped the Scotts in Missouri). Or perhaps Scott was, relatively speaking, content to serve Dr. Emerson (and Captain Bainbridge thereafter) on military posts, and decided to sue only when confronted with the prospect of working directly for Eliza Emerson as a house slave in St. Louis.[1]

The most likely explanation, however, is that Dred and Harriet Scott did not learn that it was possible for a slave to sue for freedom till shortly before they actually brought suit. The connections between the Scotts and their first lawyer lend support to this relatively simple explanation.

Over the years, a number of lawyers came to represent the Scotts, at least briefly.[2] But Francis Murdoch was the Scotts' first lawyer, and Murdoch also posted a bond accepting personal financial responsibility for the Scotts' legal costs.

Murdoch had come to St. Louis from Alton, Illinois. He had served as Alton's City Attorney. In that job he had prosecuted many of the men who participated in the infamous 1837 Alton riot. During that riot, a mob surrounded the Alton office of an abolitionist newspaper published by Elijah Lovejoy, a young minister and anti-slavery activist. When Lovejoy refused to surrender his printing press, the mob murdered Lovejoy and destroyed his press.

A black man named John Anderson was one of Lovejoy's typesetters. Anderson was a former slave who had purchased his own freedom. He survived the Alton riot, and Lovejoy's death helped inspire Anderson to pursue further anti-slavery activism. Anderson became a minister. Like Murdoch, Anderson later moved from Alton to St. Louis. There Anderson became the pastor of Harriet Scott's church, the Second African Baptist Church of St. Louis. Anderson helped many St. Louis area slaves to achieve their freedom. On occasion, he also loaned money to help keep some slaves from being sold to toil on the cotton plantations of the deep South.[3]

There is no proof that Murdoch knew Reverend Anderson from Alton, but it seems likely that they would have met during Murdoch's investigation of the Alton riot. Thus it may well have been that it was the former slave Reverend John Anderson who in 1846 introduced Harriet and Dred Scott to their first lawyer Francis Murdoch, and that it was Anderson, Murdoch and the Scotts who together first set in motion the Scotts' historic case.[4]

—The *Somerset* Principle—

The Scotts' lawsuit against Mrs. Emerson was not a novel one. Such cases were often called "freedom suits." Missouri's Slave Code (like that of several other southern states) expressly provided for such suits. More generally, there was a long tradition of such suits for freedom in both American and English law that dated back at least as far as the *Somerset* case in 1772.

By way of background, James Somerset was born free in Africa, captured, and sold into slavery in colonial Virginia. His master Charles Stewart (a British customs official) brought Somerset from Virginia to London in 1769. In 1771 Somerset ran away, but he was soon captured by Stewart's agents and then locked in chains aboard a ship bound for Jamaica. Stewart planned to resell Somerset there as punishment for his effort to escape. (The life of a slave on a Jamaican sugar plantation was usually an especially hard and cruel one.)

Sympathizers (including British abolitionist Granville Sharp) obtained a writ of habeas corpus for Somerset. His case was heard by Lord Chief Justice Mansfield of the King's Bench. Mansfield ruled that Somerset was entitled to his freedom because there was no English law that affirmatively authorized his imprisonment. It was widely understood that Mansfield's opinion (which was delivered orally, but restated in detail in several legal treatises) had further declared that the institution of slavery was so "odious" and contrary to nature that it could only be enforced where positive law expressly supported it.

Somerset was an English case decided prior to American independence. After the American Revolution, American courts for the most part accepted English common law decisions from the pre-Revolutionary period as part of American law, unless they were displaced by a new American statute or constitutional provision. Thus the *Somerset* case was part of American law.

Lord Mansfield himself may have intended that *Somerset* be construed relatively narrowly.[5] Nevertheless, as the U.S. Supreme Court explained in the 1841 case of *Prigg v. Pennsylvania,*[6] in American law *Somerset* came to stand for the broad general principle that slavery was contrary to natural law and therefore could exist only where expressly provided for by local law. Thus, for example, the slave state of Kentucky's highest court declared in the 1820 freedom suit *Rankin v. Lydia*: "[F]reedom is the natural right of man, although it may not be his birthright. By the municipal laws of government it may be taken away . . . ."[7]

Taking *Somerset* as a starting point, a body of law developed in American courts to deal with the situation where a slaveholder from a slave state brought a slave into a free state. Courts in both the North and South held that pursuant to the *Somerset* principle a slave brought to live in a free state became free because there was no free state law that expressly authorized his continued bondage.[8]

This *Somerset* principle doctrine of emancipation by residence on free soil was often summarized by the oversimplified, but nevertheless inspiring, phrase, "Once free, forever free." In many instances, courts who granted freedom in such cases also cited the ancient Roman legal maxim "In favorem liberatis."[9] (This maxim provides in full: "In favorem vitae, liberatis, et innocenciae omnia praesumptur"; the maxim means that every presumption should be made in favor of life, liberty and innocence.)

There was, however, at least one very important qualification to the *Somerset* principle. Where a slaveholder and his slave were merely "sojourning" in a free state, the slave would remain a slave. "Sojourning" meant that the slaveholder's presence in the free state was temporary, and the slaveholder did not intend to make the free state his new home (or "domicile"). (The reasons usually given by antebellum courts for this qualification were derived from international law, or—as it was often called—the "law of nations." The general rule of international law as explained by these American courts was that a traveler or sojourner must obey the laws of the place he visits, but his property rights are still governed by the laws of his home country.[10]) On the other hand, if the slaveholder did intend to make the free state his new domicile, then the slave would be emancipated.[11]

The rule distinguishing between sojourning and domicile for *Somerset* purposes was subject to increasing pressure in the 1840s and 1850s as the national conflict over slavery escalated. On the one hand, some northern states, either as a matter of case law or statute, began to define "sojourning" quite strictly, so that even a brief presence by a slave in a free state might lead to emancipation.[12] On the other hand, some southern courts began to follow the lead of the 1828 English case *The Slave, Grace* and hold that when a slave who had been sojourning in a free state returned to a slave state, the slave's legal status "reattached" so that he became a slave once again.[13] Nevertheless, in spite of these pressures, the *Somerset* principle and sojourning/domicile rule were generally followed in most American courts up till the time of Civil War.

The *Somerset* principle does not itself appear in the Constitution. But, as the Supreme Court explained in *Prigg v. Pennsylvania*, the language of the Constitution reflects the Framers' assumption that the *Somerset* principle was law. Specifically, as Justice Story explained in his Opinion of the Court in *Prigg*, the Fugitive Slave Clause was included in the Constitution in part because the Framers recognized the *Somerset* principle, and wished to limit it.

The Fugitive Slave Clause provides:

> No person held to service or labor in one State, under the laws thereof, escaping into another, shall, in consequence of any law or regulation therein, be discharged from

such service or labor; but shall be delivered up, on claim of the party to whom such service or labor may be due.

A person "held to service" under the laws of "one State" meant a slave, because, according to *Somerset*, slavery was created by local law—which, in America, meant state law. Under the *Somerset* principle, a slave who escaped into a free state might automatically become free because there was no free state law authorizing his continued enslavement. The Fugitive Slave Clause was therefore included in the Constitution, Justice Story explained, in order to carve out an exception to *Somerset* for runaway slaves, and thus ensure that the free states would return fugitive slaves to their masters in the slave states.[14]

Thus the *Somerset* principle of emancipation by residence on free soil—and the exceptions to that principle for fugitive slaves and for sojourners—were central elements of the American law of slavery from the very outset of U.S. history. Dred Scott's "freedom suit" broke no new legal ground.

—The *Somerset* Principle in Missouri's Courts—

Accordingly, there had been many lawsuits like Dred Scott's where a slave demanded freedom because his (or her) master had taken the slave to live on free soil for an extended period of time. (By way of illustration, St. Louis reached a population of slightly over twenty thousand people by the year 1840; it has been estimated that in the years 1824 through 1844, 127 "freedom suits" were filed in St. Louis County Court, with the slave winning freedom in sixty–five of those cases.[15])

Indeed, Missouri's highest court had decided a case very similar to Scott's in favor of emancipation less than a decade earlier. In *Rachael v. Walker*[16] (decided in the year 1836) the Missouri Supreme Court held that a slave named Rachael was entitled to freedom because her former master, an Army officer named Stockton, had taken her to live at Army posts on free soil in Illinois and the Wisconsin Territory, much like Dr. Emerson and Dred Scott. The Missouri court acknowledged that Stockton had been required to serve on these Army posts, but ruled that Rachael was nevertheless entitled to emancipation because the Army had certainly never compelled Stockton to bring Rachael with him to live there.

The *Rachael* case followed the rule of an earlier Missouri case called *Winny v. Whitesides.*[17] In that case the defendant Mrs. Whitesides and her husband had brought their slave Winny with them from the Carolinas to live in Illinois for three or four years. Illinois was then a free territory. The Whitesides next moved with Winny to Missouri. Winny sued for her freedom in Missouri state court, arguing that she had become free when she was brought to live in Illinois. Winny prevailed at trial and was declared free. Mrs. Whitesides appealed to Missouri's Supreme Court.

In 1824 that court agreed that Winny was free. Judge Tompkins' Opinion of the Court noted that slavery was forever prohibited in Illinois by virtue of the Northwest Ordinance of 1787. In passing, Judge Tompkins explained the purpose of that Ordinance in plain language, stating that when the United States became independent "they found their citizens claiming a right of property in a miserable portion of the human race. Sound national policy required that the evil should be restricted as much as possible. What they could, they did. They said, by their representatives, it shall not vest within these limits . . . ."[18]

The Missouri Supreme Court then found that the Whitesides had given up their right to hold Winny as a slave by bringing her to live in a free territory. The Court also firmly rejected the idea that once Winny became free in Illinois she could nevertheless become a slave once again simply because the Whitesides later brought her to the slave state of Missouri: "If by a residence in Illinois [Mrs. Whitesides] lost her right to the property in [Winny], that right was not revived by a removal of the parties to Missouri."[19]

—Trial and Retrial in Missouri State Court—

Based on *Winny*, *Rachael* and a long line of similar Missouri cases,[20] it appeared that Dred Scott's[21] lawsuit against Mrs. Emerson had a fair chance for success.

The case proceeded in an ordinary manner for some time, without any reference to the controversial issue of Congressional authority over the territories for which the case later became famous. Depositions were collected, and the case then went to trial in St. Louis County Court in June of 1847 before Judge Alexander Hamilton and a jury. At first, the case went smoothly for the Scotts. Deposition testimony was introduced to show that Dred Scott had served as Dr. Emerson's slave on free soil in Illinois and the Wisconsin Territory during the 1830s.

But Scott's case then hit a snag. In order to make his case against Mrs. Emerson, Dred Scott had to prove that Mrs. Emerson now held Dred and his wife Harriet as slaves. By the time of trial, however, Dred and Harriet Scott had been hired out by Mrs. Emerson to a family named Russell. The Scotts therefore called Mr. Samuel Russell as a witness to testify that he had hired out the Scotts from Mrs. Emerson, thus proving Mrs. Emerson's ownership. But upon cross-examination it became clear that it was the witness' wife, Mrs. Adeline Russell, who had actually conducted the hiring transaction with Mrs. Emerson, and that Mr. Russell could provide only inadmissible hearsay evidence. Mr. Russell candidly acknowledged that he knew "nothing of the hiring but what I have been told by my wife." Thus when the time came to decide the case, the jury returned a verdict for Mrs. Emerson, in essence because the Scotts had not provided admissible proof that Mrs. Emerson was in fact their owner.[22]

In December of 1847, Judge Hamilton granted a motion by Dred Scott for a new trial. Mrs. Emerson appealed that order to Missouri's Supreme Court, but in June 1848 the Missouri Supreme Court dismissed Mrs. Emerson's appeal. The Scotts' second trial was delayed for almost a year and a half for a number of reasons, including a major fire that swept through St. Louis in May of 1849 and was then followed by a cholera epidemic. The second trial finally began in January of 1850, once again before Judge Hamilton and a jury.

This time all went well for the Scotts. They provided essentially the same evidence as at the first trial, and they also presented a deposition given by Mrs. Russell. Mrs. Russell's deposition testimony furnished the missing proof that it was Mrs. Emerson who owned and hired out the Scotts as slaves. To drive the point home, Mrs. Russell testified, "I heard Mrs. Emerson say that they were her slaves."[23]

Mrs. Emerson's lawyers tried to argue that the Scotts had not been emancipated by their residence in Illinois and the Wisconsin Territory because the Scotts were working for an Army officer (Dr. Emerson) and therefore were subject to military, rather than civil, law. (Notably, Mrs. Emerson's lawyers still did not raise any challenge to the Missouri Compromise or to the principle of Congressional authority over slavery in the territories.) But the jury followed Judge Hamilton's instructions on the law, and found that the Scotts had indeed been freed because Dr. Emerson had voluntarily brought them to live on free soil.

Mrs. Emerson appealed the verdict. Pending appeal, the Scotts continued to be held as slaves hired out under the supervision of the St. Louis County

Sheriff. But the jury's verdict promised freedom to Dred and Harriet Scott and their two daughters, after a lifetime of slavery. That promise proved false.

Notes

1. Mrs. Emerson's father Colonel Alexander Sanford may have played a part in the Scotts' thinking. In 1846 Mrs. Emerson lived on her father's St. Louis estate (called "California"). Sanford was becoming an increasingly prominent pro-slavery activist. He was elected a vice president of St. Louis' new Anti-Abolitionist Society, which was dedicated to protecting slave property from the "evil designs" of abolitionists. (Among the Society's favored legislative proposals was a law prohibiting African Americans churches, unless their services were conducted by an ordained white minister.) *See* Kenneth C. Kauffman, *Dred Scott's Advocate: A Biography of Roswell Field* (Columbia, Mo.: U. of Mo. Press, 1996), 144–45. Upon returning to St. Louis from Texas, Dred Scott may well have found the prospect of working in Colonel Sanford's home especially difficult to tolerate.

2. One of them—Arba Crane—in later years rather dramatically overstated his role in the case, and as a result he is one of the protagonists of the recent historical novel, Gregory Wallance, *Two Men Before the Storm: Arba Crane's Recollection of Dred Scott and the Supreme Court Case That Started the Civil War* (Austin: Greenleaf Press, 2005).

Crane claimed that as a young lawyer working in Roswell Field's office he met Dred Scott (who was cleaning up), and that it was Crane who then first conceived the idea of Scott bringing his freedom suit.

The chief difficulty with this colorful claim was that Crane did not graduate Harvard Law School and arrive in St. Louis to work for Field till 1856. Scott commenced his first State court freedom suit in 1846 (when Crane was only twelve years old), and commenced his later federal suit in 1854 (when Crane was still a student at Harvard). *See* Fehrenbacher, *Dred Scott*, 661, n. 7. *See also* Kauffman, *Dred Scott's Advocate*, 212–13 and notes 16–17.

3. *See* Kauffman, *Dred Scott's Advocate*, 142–43.

4. Finkelman, *Scott v. Sanford*, at 19, and Ehrlich, *They Have No Rights*, 36–38, each similarly speculate that Harriet Scott first learned about the possibility of a freedom suit through Reverend Anderson and/or his church.

5. *See* Paul Finkelman, *Slavery in the Courtroom* (Washington, D.C.: Library of Congress, 1985), 19–20.

6. *Prigg v. Pennsylvania,* 16 Peters 539, 611–612 (1841).

7. *Rankin v. Lydia*, 9 Ky. 467 at 470 and 475 (1820).

8. *See e.g.*, cases cited in Fehrenbacher, *Dred Scott*, 612–13, notes 17 and 19. Some of the heroes of the American Revolution had personal experience dealing with the *Somerset* principle. For example, President Washington took pains to rotate his

slaves back and forth between Philadelphia (the new nation's capital) and his Mount Vernon plantation so that they would not become free under Pennsylvania law. (A Pennsylvania statute provided that a slave who resided in the State for six months or more became free.) *See* Henry Wiencek, *An Imperfect God: George Washington, His Slaves and the Creation of America* (New York: Farrar Straus, 2003), 315–16.

Similarly, when Thomas Jefferson served in the American embassy in Paris, he tried to prevent his slaves from learning that they might be entitled to seek their freedom under French law. *See* Joseph J. Ellis, *American Sphinx: The Character of Thomas Jefferson* (New York: Alfred Knopf, 1997), 88. (The French followed a rule similar to *Somerset*, holding that slaves brought from the colonies to France became free according to the "l'ancienne et bonne coutume" of France. *See* Paul Finkelman, *An Imperfect Union: Slavery, Federalism and Comity* (Chapel Hill: U.N.C. Press, 1981), 37–39.

9. *See e.g., Harry v. Decker & Hopkins*, 1 Miss. 36 (1818).

10. *See e.g., Rankin v. Lydia*, 9 Ky. 467 at 477–79.

11. The case of *Butler v. Hopper*, 4 F. Cas. 904 (1806), provides a noteworthy example of how the *Somerset* principle and the sojourning/domicile rule worked in practice. In that case a jury found that the slave Ben had been emancipated because his master Pierce Butler (a Framer of the Constitution, and once a U.S. senator from South Carolina) had brought Ben to live for several years in Philadelphia.

Butler contended that he was a mere "sojourner" in Pennsylvania, because he still owned and visited plantations in the South (and even served in South Carolina's State Legislature). If Butler were considered a mere "sojourner" in Pennsylvania, then Ben would remain his slave. But the jury found that Butler had made Philadelphia his and Ben's permanent domicile, and that Ben was therefore entitled to his freedom. Judge Bushrod Washington (who was a slaveholder, a nephew of George Washington, and a U.S. Supreme Court Justice sitting in his capacity as a circuit court judge) affirmed the jury's verdict.

12. *See e.g., Commonwealth v. Aves*, 18 Pick. 193 (Mass. 1836), discussed in Chapter 14.

13. *See e.g., Graham v. Strader*, 44 Ky. 173 (1844) discussed in Chapter 8.

14. *Prigg v. Pennsylvania*, 41 U.S. at 611–12.

15. Kauffman, *Dred Scott's Advocate*, 96, 108–9.

16. *Rachael v. Walker*, 4 Mo. 350 (1836). Some scholars speculate that Harriet Scott may have known Rachael because both were slaves at Fort Snelling at about the same time. *See* L. Vander Velde and S. Subramanian, "Mrs. Dred Scott," 106 *Yale L.J.* 1033 (1997).

17. *Winny v. Whitesides*, 1 Mo. 472 (1824).

18. *Winny v. Whitesides*, 1 Mo. 472 at 476.

19. *Winny v. Whitesides*, 1 Mo. 472 at 475.

20. *See e.g., John Merry v. Tiffin and Menard*, 1 Mo. 725 (1827); *Tramel v. Adam*, 2 Mo. 157 (1829); and cases cited in Ehrlich, *They Have No Rights*, 41.

21. Dred and Harriet Scott filed separate but identical lawsuits against Mrs. Emerson. By agreement of the parties, however, it was Dred Scott's case that went forward, with the understanding that the result in Dred Scott's case would also govern Harriet Scott's case. *See* Ehrlich, *They Have No Rights*, 43.

As noted, all the surviving records of Dred Scott's state court trials are available online on a website maintained by Washington University. In addition, select records from both Scott's state and federal trials are reprinted in John Lawson, Ed. *American State Trials*, Vol. 13 (St. Louis: Thomas Law Book, 1921), 220–255.

22. *See* Ehrlich, *They Have No Rights*, 51–54. *See also* Kauffman, *Dred Scott's Advocate*, 157–60.

23. Kauffman, *Dred Scott's Advocate*, 160.

Chapter 4
"A Dark and Fell Spirit"—
The Missouri Supreme Court Reverses

—Time Marches Against the Scotts—

Time and its passage are factors in most serious litigations. For example, most lawyers think that delay is good for a defendant in a criminal case up until the time of trial, and bad for the defendant thereafter. That is so because the prosecution in a criminal case bears the heavy burden of proof beyond a reasonable doubt. The more time that passes prior to trial, the more difficult it becomes to meet that burden—because the memory of witnesses may fade, and because some witnesses may move away, or pass away, or lose interest in the case, or otherwise lose contact with the prosecution. However, once a defendant is convicted and sentenced after a trial, the calculus of delay changes. Usually such a defendant is sitting in jail, and every day's delay in having his appeal heard is a day that he can never truly recover.

In some cases, the passage of time brings with it an important change in the cast of characters, or in the political or legal climate. Two corporations may wage an expensive legal battle for many years; but when new corporate executives (who had no personal involvement in the original disputed transaction, and thus no emotional stake in the outcome of the case) take over, a reasonable settlement may quickly follow. Or, for another example, one president may direct his Justice Department to pursue an aggressive anti-trust policy. When a new president with different priorities assumes office, however, the Department of Justice may quickly settle or drop anti-trust cases initiated during the prior administration.

Time impacted the Scotts' case in several ways. Once the Scotts filed their suit against Mrs. Emerson, they were placed under the supervision of the St. Louis County Sheriff and were hired out to serve various masters on an interim basis. Missouri law provided that if the Scotts ultimately won their freedom, then they would receive the money they had earned; otherwise, the money would go to Mrs. Emerson. More important, Mrs. Emerson was not allowed to sell the Scotts while the case was pending. Thus, for as long as Dred Scott's case was undecided, there was little danger that Dred Scott would lose his wife Harriet (or vice versa), or their children, as he had lost his first wife when she was "sold away" from him many years before. So time and its passage helped the Scotts in this way.

On the other hand, the passage of time hurt the Scotts' chances to win their freedom because the legal and political climate of Missouri and of the United States concerning slavery changed dramatically over the years. Dred Scott began his lawsuit in 1846, when Captain Bainbridge marched off to war with Mexico. The Mexican War ended in 1848. Even before the war was over, Americans began to disagree passionately about the status of slavery in the territory that was to be taken from Mexico. The U.S. Congress was rocked by heated debates over this issue. Those debates ultimately led to the Compromise of 1850, but not before southern advocates of slavery adopted a new, far more strident tone. They hinted broadly that the South might secede from the Union if northern "free-soil" men continued to challenge the South's asserted rights to maintain and expand slavery. Thus, for example, in 1849 Congressman Robert Toombs of Georgia thundered:

> I do not hesitate to avow before this House [of Representatives] and country, and in the presence of the living God, that if, by your legislation, you seek to drive us from the territories of California and New Mexico, purchased by the common blood and treasure of the whole people, and to abolish slavery in this District [of Columbia], thereby attempting to fix a national degradation upon half the States of this Confederacy, I am for disunion.[1]

Missouri state politics went through significant transformation too, as the longtime political powerhouse Senator Thomas Hart Benton was defeated and replaced by Henry Geyer. Benton (nicknamed "Old Bullion") was a moderate on the slavery issue, and in the debates surrounding the Compromise of 1850 Benton stood firm for the proposition that Congress possessed the power to prohibit slavery in the U.S. Territories. Geyer supported slavery, and like the South's leading pro-slavery political thinker, Senator John Calhoun of South Carolina, Geyer denied that Congress possessed such power. To a large degree, Geyer defeated Benton by appealing to Missouri voters on the issue of slavery in the territories. Geyer's election also foreshadowed the election of "anti-Benton" Democrats to the Missouri Supreme Court, Missouri's highest state court.

Looking at the situation more broadly, as a practical matter Dred Scott brought his freedom suit just a few years too late. Had Dred Scott brought his case back in 1836, for example, he probably would have quietly won his freedom—much like the slave Rachael did in the nearly identical 1836 Missouri case of *Rachael v. Walker*.

But time changed everything. Dred Scott had the misfortune to bring his suit just as the sectional conflict between North and South over slavery began to build quickly and steadily, until it culminated in the crisis of the Civil War. At first, the future of slavery in the territory taken from Mexico was the central divisive issue in this conflict. A few years later, the future of slavery in the Kansas and Nebraska Territories entered the debate as well.

Other events also seemed to conspire to ratchet up the tension between North and South. Abolitionist speeches and pamphlets denounced slavery as a terrible sin; they excited great anger in the South. Southern state governments sought to suppress such literature because they claimed it might provoke slave rebellions; that effort in turn excited anger in the North as a denial of freedom of speech and of the press. Many southerners believed (often with good cause) that runaway slaves were being harbored illegally by northern anti-slavery men. Many northerners in turn believed (also often with good cause) that southern "slave-catchers" were kidnapping free Negroes, rather than reclaiming fugitive slaves. The rhetoric of the conflict escalated too, and ugly appeals to explicit racism became more common.

In short, all the compromises—legal and cultural, express and implied—over slavery that had held North and South together since the formation of the American republic were beginning to unravel.

Time had marched against the Scotts. In an earlier era, their freedom suit would have evoked little interest and little controversy. But Mrs. Emerson's appeal of the jury verdict that had declared the Scotts free reached Missouri's Supreme Court's for decision in 1850; and, by then, the politics of slavery had become supercharged, and had begun to distort the legal process as well.

—The Missouri Supreme Court Reverses—

Nearly two years went by before the Missouri Supreme Court ruled on Mrs. Emerson's appeal.

Meanwhile, Mrs. Emerson met and married another physician, Dr. Calvin Chaffee of Massachusetts. (Chaffee later became a Republican congressman and an opponent of the expansion of slavery; his indirect connection with Dred Scott led Chaffee to be charged with hypocrisy, and it also led some people to suspect—with little basis—that Mrs. Emerson was actually colluding with Scott in Scott's suit for freedom.) Mrs. Chaffee moved from St. Louis to Massachusetts; and so some time around the year 1851 Mrs. Chaffee—apparently by informal agreement—gave the Scotts to her brother, John Sanford.

In March of 1852, the Missouri Supreme Court issued a 2–1 decision reversing the verdict at trial for the Scotts, and holding that they were still slaves. The Court's Opinion in *Scott v. Emerson* (written by Justice William Scott) acknowledged that based on past Missouri precedents Dred and Harriet Scott might well have won their freedom. But the Court explained that the case was governed by the principles of conflict of laws, the issue being the degree to which Missouri's courts should honor the laws of Illinois and of the Wisconsin Territory that prohibited slavery.

In the past, the Court explained, the Missouri courts had given effect to such out-of-state laws in appropriate cases as a matter of "comity" between the states. But comity is a discretionary doctrine, the Court reasoned, and assumes that all states will respect each others' laws. The Missouri Court heatedly declared that it was no longer willing to extend such respect as a matter of comity because, the Court said, the free states were now embarked on a course of hostility toward the slave states:

> It is a humiliating spectacle to see the courts of a State confiscating the property of her own citizens by the command of a foreign law . . . . Times are not now as they were when the former decisions on this subject were made. Since then not only individuals but States have been possessed with a dark and fell spirit in relation to slavery, whose gratification is sought in the pursuit of measures whose inevitable consequences must be the overthrow and destruction of our government. . . . We will not go to them to learn law, morality or religion on the subject.[2]

Thus the Missouri Supreme Court found that it had no obligation to give effect to either Illinois or Wisconsin law. Missouri law governed, and Missouri law said that Dred Scott was still a slave.

The Opinion then went further, going beyond legal matters in order to give the Court's own general views on issues of race and morality. Expressing a perspective that may shock many modern readers, the Court praised American slavery as an institution intended by God as the means by which the "miserable" African race could be lifted to a place "within the pale of civilized nations."[3] The Missouri Supreme Court's Opinion in *Scott v. Emerson* was thus a far cry from its own Opinion in *Winny v. Whitesides*, written less than thirty years earlier, which had declared that slavery was an "evil [that] should be restricted as much as possible."

Justice Hamilton Gamble dissented. Like Justice Scott, Gamble noted that under prior Missouri precedents the Scotts would have been entitled to their freedom. Gamble then focused his dissent on the majority's assertion that Missouri's rule should now change because "times are not now as they were."

Justice Gamble did voice some sympathy with the resentment expressed by Justice Scott on behalf of slaveholders who had been vilified by northern anti-slavery advocates. (And Justice Gamble added a not-too-subtle criticism of self-righteous abolitionists by noting that many of them possessed inherited wealth that had in part been created by the slave system.) It was only natural, said Gamble, that southerners "when denounced, in terms that would be appropriate, if they had actually kidnapped the slaves from the coast of Africa, or had inherited the fortunes accumulated by such iniquitous traffic, should feel exasperated by such wanton and unfounded attacks . . . ."[4]

But Gamble nevertheless insisted that the recent dramatic change that had taken place in the political and social climate concerning slavery did not justify a change[5] in Missouri law: "Times may have changed, public feeling may have changed, but principles have not and do not change; and, in my judgment, there can be no safe basis for judicial decisions, but in those principles, which are immutable."[6] Thus Gamble maintained that Missouri should continue to give effect to Illinois and Wisconsin law, and that the Scotts should be declared free.

Despite Justice Gamble's eloquent dissent, Justice Scott's Opinion of the Court in *Scott v. Emerson*—declaring that Dred and Harriet Scott were still slaves—became Missouri law. Dred and Harriet Scott's case was remanded to the trial court for further proceedings.

The Missouri Supreme Court's Opinion in *Scott v. Emerson* brought to an end Dred Scott's six–year struggle to win his freedom through Missouri's state courts. Soon he would take his cause to federal court.

Notes

1. *Congressional Globe*, 31 Cong., 1 Sess., 27–28 (1849).
2. *Scott v. Emerson*, 15 Mo. 576, 585–87 (1852).
3. *Scott v. Emerson*, 15 Mo. 576 at 587.
4. *Scott v. Emerson*, 15 Mo. 576 at 590 (Gamble, J. dissenting).
5. Gamble had good personal reason to know that prior Missouri law favored Dred Scott's claim to freedom. In 1836 Gamble represented the losing slaveholder in the quite similar case of *Rachael v. Walker*. Dennis K. Boman, *Lincoln's Resolute Unionist: Hamilton Gamble, Dred Scott Dissenter and Missouri's Civil War Governor* (Baton Rouge: L.S.U. Press, 2006) is an engaging biography of Gamble.
6. *Scott v. Emerson*, 15 Mo. 576 at 591–92 (Gamble, J. dissenting).

Chapter 5
New Trial and Defeat in St. Louis Federal Court

— The Scotts' Predicament—

The 1852 decision of Missouri's Supreme Court in *Scott v. Emerson* left the Scotts in a very dangerous position. The Court had declared that they were still slaves who belonged to Mrs. Emerson (now Mrs. Chaffee). But Mrs. Emerson had moved to Massachusetts. Her father, Colonel Alexander Sanford, had died in 1848, and his St. Louis home had been sold shortly thereafter. Mrs. Emerson had informally given the Scotts to her brother, John Sanford. Although it was unclear whether legal title to the Scotts had formally passed to John Sanford, all concerned recognized Sanford as the Scotts' new owner.[1]

John Sanford lived in New York City, although he did travel to St. Louis regularly on business. He probably had little use for Dred and Harriet Scott, or for their two young daughters. (Indeed, Sanford had already sold the slaves he had inherited as a part of his father's St. Louis estate four years earlier.)

Thus there was a real danger that Sanford might sell the Scotts, or (even worse) sell them away from each other, destroying the Scott family.[2]

Based on John Sanford's family connections, it also did not seem likely that Sanford would be kindly disposed to the Scotts in the wake of their lawsuit. Sanford's father, Colonel Sanford, had been a prominent St. Louis pro-slavery activist, and John Sanford had married into the Chouteau family. The Chouteaus owned many slaves, and the Chouteau family was exceptionally tenacious in resisting freedom suits brought by their own slaves.[3]

While the Scotts' case against Mrs. Emerson was pending, the Scotts had been hired out by the St. Louis County Sheriff to Charles LaBeaume (for five dollars a month). Charles LaBeaume was a St. Louis lawyer. His sister Eugenie was married to Peter Blow, one of the sons of Dred Scott's original master, Peter Blow.

LaBeaume's ties to both Dred Scott and Peter Blow were no coincidence; they reflected the fact that Dred Scott had reconnected with the Blow family after his return to St. Louis. In the years that followed the elder Peter Blow's death in 1832, his children enjoyed personal and financial success in the St. Louis area. In particular, Henry and Taylor Blow did well as partners in a wholesale paint and drug business. (Henry Blow later became a congressman and U.S. ambassador to Venezuela, and his daughter Susan went on to found America's first kindergarten.)

The Blows and their in-laws formed a close-knit family; and, over the many years during which Dred Scott's freedom suit slowly dragged through the court system, the Blow family provided important support to the Scotts. On occasion various family members posted bond for the Scotts, and it appears that they paid some of the Scotts' legal fees. For a time, attorney Charles Drake represented the Scotts; he had married Martha Ella Blow, one of the elder Peter Blow's daughters. And the younger Peter Blow's brother-in-law Charles LaBeaume hired Dred and Harriet Scott from the Sheriff in order to make sure that they would be treated well.

The Blow family did all this for the Scotts chiefly out of affection and kindness. Some of the older Blow children had likely once worked beside Dred Scott on their father's farm from time to time, and Dred had probably helped care for some of the younger Blow children when they were small. They formed a lasting bond with him. Indeed, Dred Scott himself once referred to Taylor Blow as "one of the those boys" he had been "raised with."[4]

Following the Missouri Supreme Court's decision against the Scotts, Mrs. Emerson's lawyers made a motion before the trial judge, Judge Alexander Hamilton. The motion requested an order directing that the Scotts be returned by the St. Louis Sheriff to Mrs. Emerson's control. Had Hamilton granted that motion, the Scotts would have been in serious jeopardy.

However, in June of 1852, Judge Hamilton issued a brief order denying Mrs. Emerson's motion, without explanation. Thus, at least for the short term, the Scotts continued to be hired out to Charles LaBeaume.[5]

Hamilton's decision gave the Scotts some additional time to decide what to do next. The Scotts were determined to continue to seek their freedom through the courts. With the help of Charles LaBeaume and others, they hit upon a new legal strategy.

—*Scott v. Sandford*—

LaBeaume consulted with Roswell Field concerning the Scotts' legal predicament. Field (originally from Vermont) was also a St. Louis lawyer. Field was morally opposed to slavery, although he also disapproved of abolitionist "agitation" of the slavery question. More to the point, as a lawyer Field was troubled by the Missouri Supreme Court's decision denying the Scotts their freedom. Field believed in the principle of "Once free, forever free" that had previously been Missouri law—that is, that once a slave was domiciled in a free state, he became free forever. Field thus disagreed with *Scott v. Emerson* and with other recent southern state court decisions that had held (in line with the British *Slave, Grace* case) that if such a slave later returned to a slave state, then the slave might once again be treated as a slave.[6]

LaBeaume may have chosen to approach Field in part because Field was friendly with both Missouri Supreme Court Justice Hamilton Gamble (who had written the Missouri Supreme Court dissenting Opinion favoring the Scotts) and with Judge Alexander Hamilton (who had presided over the Scotts' state court trials).[7] Field also knew Dred Scott personally because one of Scott's duties while he was hired out to LaBeaume was to clean up Field's law office.

After talking the Scotts' case over with LaBeaume, Field suggested that the fact that the Scotts' new owner John Sanford was a New Yorker might give Dred Scott a second opportunity to pursue his legal claim to freedom, this time in federal court.[8]

Scott's lawsuit against Mrs. Emerson had been brought in Missouri state court because they both lived in Missouri. But because Sanford was a citizen of New York, Field saw that Scott had, at the very least, a good argument that Scott was entitled to sue Sanford in federal court on the ground of diversity of citizenship.

By way of background, many kinds of lawsuits must be brought in state court and cannot be brought in federal court. Federal courts—that is, courts run by the United States government and not by the government of an individual state—are courts of limited jurisdiction. This means that a person who wants to bring a federal lawsuit must show that his case falls within a recognized category of cases that are appropriate for federal court. (This is probably where the expression "You don't have to make a federal case out of it" comes from.) To use legal terminology, the person who brings the federal lawsuit—the plaintiff—must show that there is a basis for federal jurisdiction.

The two major bases for federal jurisdiction are federal question jurisdiction and diversity jurisdiction. Federal question jurisdiction exists where the lawsuit is based on a federal law or the U.S. Constitution. Diversity jurisdiction exists where the plaintiff and the defendant are citizens of different ("diverse") states. The idea behind diversity jurisdiction is the expectation that a federal court will be less likely than a state court to unfairly favor the citizens of a particular state.

Roswell Field thus believed that Dred Scott could bring a lawsuit against John Sanford in federal court on the basis of diversity of citizenship on the theory that Scott was a citizen of Missouri and Sanford a citizen of New York.

The chief difficulty with Field's legal strategy was fairly easy to see: True, Sanford was plainly a citizen of New York; but was Dred Scott really a citizen of Missouri? Obviously, slaves are not citizens. Thus, if Scott were a slave, it did not seem that he could bring a federal lawsuit on the theory that he was a citizen of Missouri. On the other hand, if (as Scott contended) Scott had been emancipated because he had lived in Illinois and Wisconsin where slavery was illegal, then Scott had a much better chance to argue that he was a Missouri citizen who could bring suit in federal court. In other words, Scott's procedural argument—as to why he could bring suit in federal court—and his substantive argument—as to why he was entitled to freedom—were thoroughly intertwined, if not somewhat circular.

Field and Scott decided to pursue Field's new legal strategy. In November, 1853, Field (who served without pay) filed suit on behalf of Dred and Harriet Scott against John Sanford in the federal circuit court for Missouri. This second Dred Scott case was officially titled *Dred Scott v. Sanford.* (Sanford later became "Sandford" through a clerical error.) *Dred Scott v. Sandford* is the case that ultimately went to the United States Supreme Court and led to what is perhaps still the most controversial court decision in American history.

—The Plea in Abatement—

Prior to trial, Sanford filed a motion (called a plea in abatement) challenging Scott's theory of federal diversity jurisdiction. In the motion Sanford argued that Scott, as a Negro, was not a citizen of Missouri and therefore could not rely on diversity of citizenship as a basis for federal court jurisdiction.

The motion and Dred Scott's case were referred to St. Louis' new federal circuit court judge, Judge Robert Wells. (Wells had been Missouri's State Attorney General. He was a slaveholder, but favored gradual emancipation for Missouri.) After hearing oral argument, Judge Wells denied Sanford's motion. He held that a free Negro—while not necessarily entitled to all the rights of a white citizen—could nevertheless be considered a citizen for purposes of bringing a lawsuit in federal court on the ground of diversity of citizenship.

Wells acknowledged that some slave states granted free Negroes the right to sue, while others did not. He pointed out that if a free Negro could not sue in federal court because he was not a citizen, he also could not *be* sued there—and that would give free Negroes an unfair advantage over white citizens. Judge Wells further noted that a Negro who was a citizen of a foreign country could bring suit in the United States courts, and Wells asked why a native-born free Negro should not have that same right. Wells concluded that if Scott were free, then he had the right to sue in federal court.[9]

—Trial and Defeat—

The case came to trial in May 1854. (Sanford failed to raise the issue of federal jurisdiction again at trial; later on down the road, when the case reached the U.S. Supreme Court on appeal, this failure by Sanford created an issue as to whether the question of federal jurisdiction was properly brought before the Supreme Court for review.)

The parties did not call any live witnesses at trial. Instead they presented an Agreed Statement of Facts to the jury, and they then based their arguments to the jury on that Agreed Statement. Judge Wells instructed the jury on the law that applied to the case. His instructions substantially mirrored the legal reasoning set out by the Missouri Supreme Court in *Scott v. Emerson*. Among other things, Judge Wells instructed the jury that the removal of a slave by his master to Illinois did not free the slave; it only suspended the condition of slavery temporarily, and the master's dormant ownership of the slave was revived as soon as they returned to Missouri.[10]

In view of these instructions,[11] it was not surprising that the jury returned a verdict for Sanford, finding that the Scotts were still slaves. Notably, the issue for which the *Dred Scott* case later became most famous when it reached the Supreme Court—the constitutionality of the Missouri Compromise—was not raised or even hinted at during the Scotts' trial. (As detailed later, an issue must ordinarily be raised at trial in order to be taken up on appeal.)

A short time later, Roswell Field filed the papers to begin Dred Scott's appeal to the United States Supreme Court.

Notes

1. *See* Ehrlich, *They Have No Rights*, 73; Fehrenbacher, *Dred Scott Case*, 270–75.

2. *See* Kauffman, *Dred Scott's Advocate*, 178–79.

3. The Chouteau family probably owned more slaves than any other St. Louis family. Perhaps the most noteworthy "freedom suit" involving the Chouteau family was that of *Pierre v. Gabriel Chouteau*. In that case two slaves named Pierre and

Mary Charlotte sued for their freedom in Missouri state court on the ground they had once lived in Canada. Their owner Gabriel Chouteau's reaction was so violent that the slaves were placed in jail for their protection. That case dragged on for twenty years, from 1843 till 1863, by which time Pierre had died in jail.

4. *See* Fehrenbacher, *Dred Scott*, 240–41 and 653 notes 4,6; Ehrlich, *They Have No Rights,* 10–12; *St. Louis Daily Evening News*, May 26, 1857.

5. *See* Kauffman, *Dred Scott's Advocate*, 179, and notes 54 and 55.

6. *See* Kauffman, *Dred Scott's Advocate*, 52–54; 182–83.

7. *See* Kauffman, *Dred Scott's Advocate*, 111–12, 124–25, 181–82. (Field named Hamilton as guardian of his youngest son; and Gamble once recommended Field for appointment to St. Louis Circuit Court.)

8. *See* Fehrenbacher, *Dred Scott*, 270–71; Ehrlich, *They Have No Rights*, 73–81; Kauffman, *Dred Scott's Advocate*, 181–183.

9. Ehrlich, *They Have No Rights*, 83–84.

10. Ehrlich, *They Have No Rights*, 86.

11. As a personal matter, Judge Wells was sympathetic to the Scotts, but he felt that the law clearly required that he instruct the jury in Sanford's favor.

Wells later entered into a correspondence about the case with Montgomery Blair, who represented the Scotts before the U.S. Supreme Court. In a letter to Blair, Wells confessed that "my feelings were deeply interested in favor of the poor fellow [Dred Scott], and I wish the law was in favor of his freedom." But Wells explained that in his view the federal court was required to follow the Missouri Supreme Court's interpretation of Missouri state law in *Scott v. Emerson*.

Chapter 6
At the Summit—
Argument and Reargument
Before the Supreme Court

—New Lawyers—

The first problem that confronted Dred and Harriet Scott in pursuing their appeal to the U.S. Supreme Court was a prosaic one—finding a good lawyer. Roswell Field was a very able St. Louis attorney. However, then as now, the job of arguing a case before the U.S. Supreme Court was one usually best left to a member of a select group of exceptionally talented lawyers accustomed to appearing before the nation's highest court. The Scotts' problem was made more difficult because the Blow family did not appear willing to pay a lawyer to handle their appeal. The Scotts' friends made both public and private appeals for help. Among their efforts, they published a brief pamphlet in July of 1854. The pamphlet took the form of a plea for assistance made in Dred Scott's own words. (This was probably intended as a mere literary device, however; it was understood that, like most slaves, Dred Scott could not read or write.) The pamphlet asked plaintively:

> My fellow-men, can any of you help me in my day of trial? Will nobody speak for me at Washington, even without hope of other reward than the blessings of a poor black man and his family? I do not know. I can only pray that some good heart will be moved by pity to do that for me which I cannot do for myself. . . .[1]

For quite some time it appeared that in fact no one was willing to speak for the Scotts before the Supreme Court in Washington. But in December of 1854 Roswell Field wrote a letter to Montgomery Blair asking him to take on the Scotts' case. Field appealed to Blair, stating that by helping the Scotts Blair would also aid the "cause of humanity."

As a legal matter, Field highlighted for Blair what Field saw as the two key issues in the case. First, Field believed in the principle of "Once free, forever free" and disagreed with the doctrine of "reattachment" that some southern courts had adopted from the British *Slave, Grace* case. Thus Field urged Blair to challenge the rule laid down by the Missouri Supreme Court in *Scott v. Emerson* (and followed by Judge Wells at the Scotts' federal trial)—namely, that when a slave who had been domiciled in a free state returned to a slave state, he should once again be treated as a slave.[2] Second, Field noted Judge Wells' pretrial ruling that a Negro could be a citizen for purposes of bringing a federal court lawsuit. Field thought that this holding might be useful as a basis for Negroes to insist on a trial by jury when claimed as fugitive slaves. (Many anti-slavery activists thought the Fugitive Slave Act of 1850 unjust precisely because it prohibited jury trials in such cases.[3])

After consideration, Blair agreed to represent the Scotts. Blair provided his services for free, and Gamaliel Bailey (editor of the abolitionist newspaper *The National Era*) agreed to pay the Scotts' court costs. (*The National Era* had gained great public attention because Harriet Beecher Stowe's 1852 anti-slavery novel *Uncle Tom's Cabin* first appeared there in serial form; the novel caused a sensation, winning many new adherents to the cause of abolition and embittering southern defenders of slavery.)

Montgomery Blair was already an important public figure. He had served as the U.S. Attorney for Missouri, and was once mayor of St. Louis. Blair had moved to Washington, D.C., in 1853, and as the first solicitor general of the U.S. Court of Claims, Blair appeared often before the Supreme Court. (His father-in-law, Levi Woodbury, had been a U.S. Supreme Court Justice until his death in 1851.) Blair took up residence in a mansion located across the street from the White House, and his home (today's Blair House) became a center of Washington society and politics.

Blair's father, Francis Preston Blair, had been a publisher and an important political advisor to Presidents Andrew Jackson and Martin Van Buren. The Blairs remained politically active. Both Montgomery Blair and his brother Frank Blair were regarded as political lieutenants to longtime Missouri Senator Thomas Hart Benton. Like Jackson, Van Buren and Benton, the Blairs had been Democrats; but the Blairs were now key figures in what was to become the national Republican party. (Montgomery Blair later served as Republican President Abraham Lincoln's Postmaster General.)

Blair was thus well suited to serve as the Scotts' lawyer. He was an accomplished litigator, with U.S. Supreme Court experience; and, based on his reputation and connections, Blair's clients could expect that their lawyer would be heard with respect by any court. Moreover, while Blair was firmly and publicly opposed to the expansion of slavery, he was a former slaveholder and opposed to abolition. Accordingly, Blair could not easily be written off as a mere ideologue or extremist.

John Sanford also brought in new lawyers better qualified than his St. Louis counsel to argue before the nation's highest court. He retained Reverdy Johnson and Henry Geyer. Johnson had served as a U.S. senator, and as United States Attorney General under President Zachary Taylor. (In later years, Johnson was instrumental in keeping Maryland in the Union during the Civil War, served another term in the U.S. Senate, and served as U.S. Ambassador to Great Britain.) Johnson was close to U.S. Supreme Court Chief Justice Roger Taney, and he enjoyed a reputation as perhaps the leading constitutional lawyer of his day. Henry Geyer was the man who had defeated and replaced Thomas Hart Benton as Senator from Missouri, and Geyer also appeared frequently as an attorney before the Supreme Court.

The involvement of these high-powered lawyers reflected the fact that Dred Scott's case was no longer chiefly a private matter, or even an important matter of Missouri law. The *Dred Scott* case was becoming a case of national importance because it touched upon the hottest political issues of the day. Dred Scott's appeal to the Supreme Court was soon to become intertwined with the national debate over slavery in the federal territories, and in particular in "Bleeding Kansas."

—"Bleeding Kansas"—

The Compromise of 1850, carefully crafted by elder statesman like Senators Henry Clay of Kentucky and Daniel Webster of Massachusetts, had been intended to put the national controversy over slavery to rest for at least a generation. It failed.

In 1854, following the lead of the "Little Giant," Senator Stephen Douglas of Illinois, Congress reopened the slavery controversy by passing the Kansas-Nebraska Act. (Douglas later defeated Abraham Lincoln in the

Illinois senatorial campaign of 1858—famed for the Lincoln-Douglas debates—and was in turn defeated by Lincoln in the presidential campaign of 1860.) Douglas had been a key player in pushing the Compromise of 1850 to passage. But now he hoped that the first transcontinental railroad would run from his home state of Illinois though the Nebraska Territory and on to the far West. Douglas needed the support of southern Democrats to get his railroad bill passed, and Douglas also believed that it would be helpful to his railroad proposal for the Nebraska Territory to be organized. Douglas therefore decided to promote the Kansas-Nebraska Act and what Douglas termed the "great principle of popular sovereignty."

The Kansas-Nebraska Act divided the Nebraska territory into two territories, Kansas and Nebraska. The Act then left it to the (white male) settlers of those two territories to decide whether slavery would be permitted there. Previously, slavery had been barred from this area by the Missouri Compromise of 1820. Douglas argued that the doctrine of "popular sovereignty" required that the people of a territory must be allowed to decide their own future as a free or slave state. The Act won southern support for Douglas (and for his railroad bill) because it created the possibility that slavery might be allowed to enter into territory where it had previously been prohibited.

Opponents of the Kansas-Nebraska Act derided it as establishing a system of "squatter sovereignty": they argued that the Act would in effect invite zealots and ruffians to come into the Kansas Territory solely in order to promote or oppose slavery there, and thus invite discord and conflict. More generally, many of the Act's opponents saw it as a pro-slavery betrayal of the long-standing Missouri Compromise.

The heated and acrimonious Congressional debate over the Kansas-Nebraska Act effectively began in January of 1854 with the publication in the *National Era* of the "Appeal of the Independent Democrats."

In that "Appeal," a number of anti-slavery congressmen denounced Douglas' proposal "as a gross violation of a sacred pledge, as a criminal betrayal of precious rights, as part and parcel of an atrocious plot" to make Nebraska "a dreary region of despotism," all allegedly in service to Douglas' presidential ambitions. Over the next few months "America's fiercest Congressional battle" was waged until finally, in May of 1854, the Kansas-Nebraska Act became law.[4]

Douglas' critics were certainly right that the Act promoted the possibility of disorder and conflict. Northern abolitionists instituted various programs to encourage anti-slavery men and women to settle in Kansas. Brooklyn's celebrated minister Henry Ward Beecher was involved in these efforts, and some of the anti-slavery settlers were provided with guns that were nicknamed "Beecher's Bibles." Some pro-slavery men in Missouri (sometimes called "Border Ruffians") rode over the border en masse in order to cast illegal votes in Kansas elections and intimidate anti-slavery voters. Rival pro-slavery and anti-slavery Kansas "governments" were set up at Lecompton and Topeka, Kansas. Pro-slavery and anti-slavery zealots in Kansas and neighboring Missouri armed and organized themselves into competing private military forces. Violence flared up in Kansas, particularly near the Missouri border.

The rhetoric employed by many political leaders was far from helpful in quelling this violence. For example, pro-slavery Missouri Senator David Atchison proclaimed that the anti-slavery settlers were "Negro thieves" and "abolitionist tyrants"; he urged Missourians, if necessary, "to kill every God-damned abolitionist in the District."

Slavery's opponents were outraged by the Kansas-Nebraska Act. The national Republican Party was formed largely in response to the Act. The new party's chief organizing principle was opposition to the expansion of slavery in the territories. By the time the Supreme Court conducted oral arguments in the *Dred Scott* case in February 1856, a presidential election year was under way. In fact, one of the Supreme Court Justices—John McLean of Ohio—was thought to be a leading contender for the Republican Party's presidential nomination. The issue of slavery in the territories, and especially in "Bleeding Kansas," had become by far the leading political issue in the nation.

—First Oral Argument—

At oral argument before the Supreme Court in February of 1856, Sanford's lawyers Henry Geyer and Reverdy Johnson injected that issue directly into the *Dred Scott* case. They were not content to rest Sanford's defense on the grounds upon which Sanford had prevailed at trial, namely that Missouri law governed and provided that Scott remained a slave. Instead, Geyer and Johnson reached out for a new argument, even though that argument was seemingly extraneous to Sanford's personal interests in the case.

Specifically, Geyer and Johnson focused on Scott's assertion that his residence at Fort Snelling in the Wisconsin Territory had emancipated him because slavery was forbidden there. Geyer and Johnson noted that Wisconsin was a free territory because the U.S. Congress had so provided in the Missouri Compromise in 1820. But Geyer and Johnson argued that, under the U.S. Constitution, Congress (and the federal government) had no power to pass such a law prohibiting slavery in a territory.

This was a bold step by Sanford's lawyers. True, there was a growing chorus of pro-slavery advocates, particularly in the South, who questioned whether Congress had the authority to legislate against slavery in the territories. (Indeed, President Franklin Pierce's December 1855 Annual Message to Congress—the equivalent of our modern day "State of the Union" speech—questioned the constitutionality of the Missouri Compromise.) But Congress had in fact passed laws regulating, and in some instances limiting, slavery in the territories throughout the nation's history, beginning with the Northwest Ordinance of 1787, and continuing through the Missouri Compromise of 1820, the Compromise of 1850, and the Kansas-Nebraska Act of 1854. Thus Sanford's lawyers were setting Sanford up in opposition to long-standing practice and tradition.

Moreover, the issue was not particularly important to the case directly at hand. After all, Dred Scott had claimed freedom based on his residence in both the Wisconsin Territory *and* the *state* of Illinois. The Missouri Compromise plainly had nothing to do with the Illinois state law forbidding slavery. Accordingly, a declaration by the Supreme Court that the Missouri Compromise was unconstitutional, or even a more general declaration that Congress had no power to legislate against slavery in any of the federal territories, would not really do much to advance John Sanford's chances of winning the lawsuit brought against him by Dred Scott. Even with such a declaration, Sanford would still have to deal with Scott's claim to freedom based on Scott's residence in Illinois.

Thus the decision by Sanford's lawyers to nevertheless direct a large part of their argument to the constitutional issue of Congressional authority over slavery in the territories signalled that they wanted the Supreme Court to treat the *Dred Scott* case as a "test case" of sorts—a chance to make law and decide issues that may have been of only tangential importance to John Sanford and Dred Scott, the actual people involved in the case. (Sanford's lawyers' decision may also have reflected the fact that Sanford himself was losing personal control over the case; Sanford was already suffering from mental illness by February 1856, and was placed in an institution a short time later.)

The emphasis placed by Sanford's lawyers on the territorial issue may have somewhat surprised the Scotts' lawyer, Montgomery Blair. Blair's brief had not even mentioned that question. Instead, it was divided into two roughly equal parts that focused on the same two points that Roswell Field had highlighted for Blair, namely: a) asserting that Negroes should be regarded as citizens for purposes of bringing a federal court lawsuit on the ground of diversity of citizenship; and b) arguing that the "reattachment" rule of *Scott v. Emerson* was wrong, and that the U.S. Supreme Court should instead follow older Missouri precedents such as *Winny v. Whitesides* that acted on the principle of "Once free, forever free."

Blair's initial decision not to discuss the territorial issue was logical; the issue had never been raised before in the litigation and seemed largely irrelevant. However, Blair's decision to give so much emphasis to the issue of diversity jurisdiction and Negro citizenship was an odd one. After all, Blair represented Dred Scott, and the citizenship issue had been decided in Dred Scott's favor by the court below. Presumably, the trial court's pre-trial ruling on citizenship would stand undisturbed unless someone affirmatively asked the Supreme Court to review it on appeal. Accordingly, one would expect that if any one were to raise the citizenship issue before the Supreme Court, it would be John Sanford—not Dred Scott.

Perhaps Blair chose to emphasize the citizenship question because he thought the principle might be helpful in future fugitive slave cases. (If so, Blair was also treating the Scotts' case as something of a "test case.") On the other hand, it may be that Blair was instead merely trying to anticipate and defuse a potential troublesome issue that he thought Sanford's lawyers would likely raise.

In any event, the U.S. Supreme Court heard argument on the *Dred Scott* case from Blair, Johnson and Geyer for twelve hours over the course of four days in mid-February 1856. The parties then settled in to wait for the Court's decision.

—Order for Reargument—

In May of 1856, however, the Supreme Court—acting on its own initiative—ordered a second round of oral argument in the *Dred Scott* case. The Court's terse Order indicated that it wanted the lawyers to further address two issues: 1) whether the question of federal court diversity jurisdiction was properly preserved for the Supreme Court's review by Sanford's pre-trial motion on that subject; and 2) if so, whether Dred Scott was indeed a "citizen" of Missouri for purposes of diversity jurisdiction.

Both contemporary observers and historians have speculated and disagreed as to why the Supreme Court ordered further oral argument. (One anti-slavery newspaper, the *New York Daily Tribune*, ran a series of articles that purported to describe in detail the Supreme Court's confidential internal discussions about the case; those reports were close enough to the mark to lead Justice John Catron, for one, to believe that one of his fellow Justices was actively leaking information to the *Tribune*.[5])

It is , of course, not possible to know with any certainty what took place during the Court's private deliberations. However, it appears that Blair had been more successful than Sanford's lawyers in drawing the Court's attention to the issues that he wanted addressed. Thus, despite the efforts by Sanford's lawyers to obtain a ruling on the constitutionality of the Missouri Compromise, at this point the Justices did not intend to make such a ruling.[6] On the other hand, the Court's Order indicated that at least some of the Justices were interested in the citizenship issue that Blair had highlighted.

The obvious effect of the Order was to delay a decision in the case till after the 1856 presidential election, and that may well have played some part in the Court's thinking.[7] If, however, the Court privately hoped that the issue of slavery in the territories might somehow cool off and grow less controversial after a period of delay, that hope was almost immediately disappointed. During that summer of 1856, Kansas erupted in widespread violence. First, pro-slavery men rode into the town of Lawrence, burned the Free State Hotel down, destroyed anti-slavery printing presses, and ransacked stores and homes all around Lawrence. Then abolitionist John Brown led a raid on Pottawatomie Creek; Brown's ragtag "army" dragged five pro-slavery settlers from their homes and hacked them to death. Pro-slavery raiders retaliated by burning the free-state town of Osawatomie to the ground.

Back in Washington, D.C., anti-slavery Senator Charles Sumner of Massachusetts gave a long inflammatory speech on the Senate floor, denouncing the "Crime Against Kansas" as the "rape of a virgin territory, compelling it to the embrace of slavery." In the course of his speech, Sumner directed a number of harsh remarks at pro-slavery Senator Andrew Butler of South Carolina. Some of those remarks appeared to mock the "loose expectorations" of the aged Butler's impaired speech. A few days later, Congressman Preston Brooks (a cousin of Senator Butler) walked into the Senate and beat Sumner unconscious with a cane. Sumner was unable to return to the Senate for several years because of his injuries.

In November of 1856 Democrat James Buchanan—a northerner with strong ties to pro-slavery southerners—was elected President. The debate over "Bleeding Kansas" continued unabated. The outgoing President Franklin Pierce delivered his final Annual Message to Congress. In his prior Annual Message Pierce had expressed serious doubts as to the constitutionality of the Missouri Compromise. In his final message—perhaps embittered because his own party had refused to renominate him for the Presidency—Pierce let loose. No longer merely doubtful, he categorically asserted that the Missouri Compromise was wholly unconstitutional, "a mere nullity . . . a monument of error . . . a dead letter in law." Those who opposed slavery in the territories, President Pierce further declared, were trying to lead Americans down a "path of evil."

—Second Oral Argument—

Thus when the Supreme Court conducted a second round of oral argument in the *Dred Scott* case beginning on December 15, 1856, the issue of Congressional authority over slavery in the territories remained the most controversial issue in the country. And even though the Supreme Court's Order directing re-argument had not asked the lawyers to address that issue again, that is where both Scott's and Sanford's lawyers directed much of their effort during the second round of oral argument.[8]

Remarkably, even though the issue of the Missouri Compromise's constitutionality had not played any part in either the first *Dred Scott* case before the Missouri state courts, or in the federal court case of *Scott v. Sandford* that was before the Supreme Court on appeal, the lawyers involved (especially John Sanford's lawyers) and at least some of the Supreme Court Justices now seemed eager to take that issue head on. Moreover, there was a growing sense among the national press and politicians that the decision in Dred Scott's case might deal with the issue of Congressional authority over slavery in the territories. (Of course, not everyone was pleased with the prospect of leaving that issue to the U.S. Supreme Court; Horace Greeley, the anti-slavery editor of the *New York Daily Tribune*, quipped that he would sooner trust a dog with his dinner.)

In all likelihood, that was the reason why several prominent members of Congress and many reporters attended the second round of oral argument before the Supreme Court.

For the same reason, Scott's lawyer, Montgomery Blair, was joined at the very last minute (that is, on either the first or second day of the December argument) by a new co-counsel, George Curtis. Curtis had long been associated with Senator Daniel Webster of Massachusetts, and was a brother of Supreme Court Justice Benjamin Curtis. George Curtis was both a lawyer and a scholar; he wrote a well-received *Constitutional History of the United States* (and a biography of James Buchanan). George Curtis did not attempt to master all the intricacies of Dred Scott's case; he limited his role at oral argument to elaborating Scott's position concerning Congressional authority over slavery in the territories.

Neither Blair nor George Curtis were outright abolitionists.[9] Consistent with both their own personal views and with Dred Scott's best chances for victory, Blair and especially Curtis attempted for the most part to cast Scott's legal claim to freedom in a conservative light. They did not pursue a rhetorical crusade on behalf of African Americans. (However, the politically ambitious Blair did expound during oral argument on the anti-democratic effects of the institution of slavery.) Instead Scott's lawyers attempted to argue that even in the context of the existing legal system which thoroughly protected slavery in the South, Scott was still entitled to freedom under a long-standing line of precedents dating back to the *Somerset* case.

Blair and Curtis's argument for Scott regarding the Missouri Compromise followed naturally along these conservative lines. They pointed out that Article IV of the Constitution gives Congress the power to admit new states into the Union, and further expressly grants Congress the "Power to dispose of and make all needful Rules and Regulations respecting the Territory or other property belonging to the United States . . . ." (The former provision is sometimes referred to as "the Statehood Clause," and the latter as "the Territory Clause.") Pursuant to this authority and to the inherent power of any sovereign nation over its own territory, Blair and Curtis argued, the United States Congress had the power to make laws for the U.S. territories, including laws either forbidding or permitting slavery. And, in point of fact, Congress had since the beginning exercised that authority over and over again, with little constitutional controversy, in the Northwest Ordinance, in the Missouri Compromise, in the Compromise of 1850 and in the Kansas-Nebraska Act. (Blair's brief further methodically demonstrated this point by citing thirteen different Acts of Congress which had, over the years, either authorized or prohibited slavery in various federal territories.) Thus Blair and Curtis argued that Sanford's lawyers were advocating a radical departure from a long-settled common national understanding of the Constitution.[10]

Sanford's lawyers, Geyer and Johnson, took on the tougher job of arguing that Congress had no power to legislate over slavery in the territories, even though Congress had done so for more than sixty years. They argued that the Constitution's grant to Congress of the power to make needful rules and regulations respecting the territory of the United States referred only to the power to make such rules as were necessary to govern the disposal of land; the Constitution did not confer upon Congress a general power to legislate for the territories.

Sanford's lawyers further asserted that it must be up to the people of the territories (and, after the territories become new states, to the people of the new states) to decide for themselves whether or not to permit slavery. Otherwise, Geyer and Johnson argued, democracy and the will of the people would be thwarted, and Congress would in essence be acting like an imperial ruler over the U.S. territories. Moreover, Sanford's lawyers asserted that a Congressional ban on slavery in a federal territory violated the principle that all states were equal. Such a ban, they argued, discriminated against the citizens of the slaveholding states of the South by discouraging them from moving into the territories—which, Geyer and Johnson argued, should properly be regarded as the common property of all Americans, both North and South.

Sanford's lawyers conceded (as they had to) that over the years Congress had in fact passed several laws forbidding slavery in various federal territories, but they noted that those laws had never before been brought to the Supreme Court for constitutional review. Thus Johnson and Geyer argued the Court could and should strike down the Missouri Compromise as unconstitutional.

Following oral argument in December of 1856, Dred Scott's case awaited the Supreme Court's decision. Over the next two months the Justices began to discuss, debate and shape the Court's decision. Soon a powerful outside party—President-elect James Buchanan—also became involved in the Court's deliberative process.

Notes

1. Quoted in Fehrenbacher, *Dred Scott,* 280. Strangely, the only known surviving copy of the pamphlet went missing from the University of Missouri Law School Library in 1988. Kauffman, *Dred Scott's Advocate,* 196 and note 17. Fortunately, it was quoted extensively in many earlier works. *See e.g.,* Lawson, *State Trials,* 243–45.

2. The July 1854 pamphlet appealing for help for Dred Scott was probably written by Field or by Charles LaBeaume. It too challenged the rule of *Scott v. Emerson*, this time from the perspective of Dred Scott himself. The pamphlet stated:

> [The] judge [Wells] said that as soon as my master got me back this side of the line of Missouri my right to be free was gone. . . . I thought it hard that white men should draw a line . . . on one side of which a black man was to become no man at all, and never say a word to the black man about it until they got him on that side of the line.

3. *See* Kaufman, *Dred Scott's Advocate,* 200–202 for a fuller description of Field's correspondence with Blair.

4. *See* David M. Potter, *The Impending Crisis* (New York: Harper & Row, 1976) 145–76, and 163.

5. *See* Carl B. Swisher, *Roger B. Taney* (New York: MacMillan, 1935), 488–89; Ehrlich, *They Have No Rights*, 99. The contemporary newspaper speculation (much of which was contradictory) about the Court's deliberations following the first round of oral argument in *Dred Scott* is summarized in Ehrlich, *They Have No Rights*, 98–103.

6. Justice Benjamin Curtis wrote a private letter to his uncle George Ticknor on April 8, 1856, stating that the Court "will not decide the question of the Missouri Compromise line, a majority of the Judges being of the opinion that it is not necessary to do so."

7. Supreme Court Justice John McLean may have been disappointed that the decision in *Dred Scott* was put off. The delay deprived McLean of the chance to use *Dred Scott* as a means to publicize his anti-slavery views in advance of the 1856 Republican national convention, where McLean was a contender for the presidential nomination.

However, in June of 1856, McLean did decide to write a "private" letter (quickly reprinted in newspapers) to Joseph Hornblower (retired Chief Justice of New Jersey). In that letter McLean stated that while he could not comment on the pending case of *Dred Scott*, McLean still adhered to his previously stated view that Congress did indeed possess the power to prohibit slavery in the territories.

McLean's public comments on an issue before the Court were not proper. And they did him little political good. The Republicans chose John Charles Fremont over McLean as their presidential candidate in 1856.

8. The oral argument before the Supreme Court in the *Dred Scott* case is described at length in Fehrenbacher, *Dred Scott*, 293–302, and Ehrlich, *They Have No Rights*, 117–21. The Supreme Court briefs in the *Dred Scott* case are available in their original form online at curiae.law.yale.edu. These include briefs filed for Dred Scott before the February and December 1856 arguments and for John Sanford before the December 1856 argument. There is no brief for Sanford prior to the February argument. Either Sanford's lawyers Geyer and Johnson did not submit a brief then or (more likely) it has since been lost. For both the briefs and a portion of the oral argument *see* Paul Finkelman, Ed. *Slavery, Race and the American Legal System 1700–1872*, Vol 3, 17–179 (New York: Garland, 1988).

9. To the contrary, both George and Benjamin Curtis had gained a degree of fame in part by insisting—despite the more fervent anti-slavery sentiments of their Boston community and their own moral opposition to slavery—that the legal rights of slaveholders must be honored. *See* Stuart Streichler, *Justice Curtis in the Civil War Era* (Charlottesville: U. of Va. Press, 2005); Paul Finkelman, *Slavery in the Courtroom* (Washington, D.C.: Library of Congress, 1985) 25, 27–8, 47–53, 87–94, and 115–17. For a good brief description of the division in Boston society over the issue of slavery, including the Curtis brothers' role, *see* Louis Menand, *The Metaphysical Club: A Story of Ideas in America* (New York: Farrar, Straus, 2001), 2–23.

Specifically, George Curtis had once served as a U.S. commissioner charged with enforcing the Fugitive Slave Law. Benjamin Curtis had presided as judge at a celebrated trial of a group of Boston anti-slavery men who had allegedly broken an imprisoned slave named Shadrach out of federal prison. *See* Chapter 14.

10. Blair and Curtis' argument emphasized that leading pro-slavery men of the South (including John Calhoun, subsequently the leading theoretician of the pro-slavery "states'-rights" school of constitutional law) had supported the Missouri Compromise of 1820. However, even as far back as 1820 there were many southern senators and representatives who challenged Congress' right to legislate against slavery in the federal territories. *See* Mark A. Graber, *Dred Scott and the Problem of Constitutional Evil* (New York: Cambridge U. Press, 2006), 120–24.

The Congressional debate over the constitutionality of the Missouri Compromise is discussed in a more old-fashioned literary style in Hopkins, *Dred Scott*, 112–116.

Chapter 7
The President-Elect Secretly Intervenes

—Speculation Abounds—

The second round of oral argument before the Supreme Court in the *Dred Scott* case ended one week before Christmas in 1856. Once again the Scotts and all concerned had to wait for the Court's decision.

As often happens when a case becomes the focus of public attention, quite a few people claimed to know what the Court would likely decide. There was a great deal of newspaper coverage about the oral argument, and a great deal of editorial comment about the case as well. Most of the newspapers took the view that the Court was likely to take the important step of ruling on the constitutionality of the Missouri Compromise. The *New York Courier* was typical in this regard; in its December 18 edition it declared the Missouri Compromise issue "the most important [question] that has ever been brought before that tribunal."[1]

The anti-slavery and Republican press for the most part expressed the fear that the Court, with its southern and pro-slavery majority, would declare the Missouri Compromise unconstitutional. On the other hand, Democratic and pro-slavery newspapers were generally more guarded, and usually expressed the hope that the Justices would not decide the *Dred Scott* case along sectional lines.[2]

Dred Scott's lawyer, Montgomery Blair, came away from the December 1856 oral argument with the discouraging feeling that things would not go well for his client. In early February of 1857 Blair wrote to former President Martin Van Buren, a longtime political ally. (Van Buren had sent Blair a note congratulating Blair for the job he had done at oral argument.) Blair promised to send Van Buren a copy of Chief Justice Taney's Opinion when it was rendered. Blair also stated that the general sense in Washington was that the Court would deny Scott his freedom and would declare the Missouri Compromise unconstitutional. Blair—who was a seasoned and skillful practitioner of both law and politics—added that he thought this sense was probably correct, and noted that he believed the Court was being subjected to considerable outside pressure to reach just such a decision.[3]

Blair's educated guess was right. Congressman Alexander Stephens of Georgia (future vice president of the Confederate States of America), for one, was actively lobbying for a decision that would declare the Missouri Compromise invalid. On December 15, 1856 (while oral arguments were still being conducted), Stephens wrote his brother about the *Dred Scott* case, saying: "I have been urging all the influences I could bring to bear upon the Supreme Court . . . to decide [on the constitutionality of the Missouri Compromise]. . . . I have reason to believe they will [decide] that the restriction was unconstitutional." On New Year's Day 1857, Stephens again wrote to his brother, updating him on "the great case," as Stephens now termed it. Stephens reported that based on what he had heard "sub rosa . . . [t]he restriction of 1820 [the Missouri Compromise] will be held to be unconstitutional. The judges are all writing out their opinions, I believe, seriatim.[4] The Chief Justice will give an elaborate one."[5]

Given the importance of the issues raised by *Dred Scott*, it seems likely that other people were also frantically attempting to lobby various Supreme Court Justices during this time period. The Court itself moved very slowly. The Justices did not even meet as a group to discuss the case until early February of 1857. (This delay came about in part because Justice Peter Daniel's wife died after a terrible accident in which her calico bathrobe caught fire. Daniel himself was burned in a failed effort to rescue his wife and was therefore absent from the Court for a time.)[6] Meanwhile, President-elect James Buchanan decided to weigh in on the *Dred Scott* case.

—James Buchanan—

James Buchanan of Pennsylvania entered the Presidency in 1857 with an exceptionally broad and strong background in public service. He had served in Pennsylvania's State Legislature and in the U.S. House and Senate. He had been appointed American Minister to Russia and to England. He was Secretary of State to President Polk. Presidents Tyler and Polk each offered Buchanan a seat on the U.S. Supreme Court. Buchanan's austere personality[7] was such that few members of the public referred to him by any nickname; but his experience over nearly forty years in government service was so great that some politicos and members of the press dubbed Buchanan the "Old Public Functionary." Buchanan was a contender for the Democratic Party's presidential nomination in 1844, 1848 and 1852. Finally, in 1856 the Democratic Party chose Buchanan as its candidate after eighteen ballots.[8]

Most historians consider Buchanan to be among America's worst presidents. During his single term in office, the sectional crisis over slavery spun completely out of control. The southern states began to secede from the Union during Buchanan's final months as president, setting the stage for the Civil War. Buchanan's handling of the Kansas controversy and of the sectional conflict was indeed remarkably inept and did contribute significantly to the strife between North and South.[9] But criticism of Buchanan in this regard is usually appropriately tempered by the recognition that by Buchanan's time the divide between the two sections had grown so deep that it may have already been impossible for any president—no matter how skillful—to lead the nation to reconciliation, and that the secession crisis was perhaps inevitable.

For many years history books (especially those written for younger students) credited Buchanan with the distinction of being America's only "Bachelor President." In more recent years (as discourse about such subjects has become considerably freer), many scholars have openly speculated that Buchanan was homosexual. (Some of Buchanan's coarser contemporaries had few qualms about raising the subject, at least in private. President Andrew Jackson derisively referred to Buchanan as "Aunt Nancy," and others referred to Buchanan's rumored longtime boyfriend, Senator William King of Alabama, as "Aunt Fancy.") A strong case can be made for the more remarkable proposition that Buchanan never had any sex life at all, and thus might properly be regarded as America's only "Virgin President."

It is clear that as a somewhat lonely bachelor Buchanan adopted a distinctive style of social life while in Washington. As President, he insisted that the members of his (almost exclusively southern) cabinet be his close personal friends. They spent time and shared meals with Buchanan, and—when their wives were out of town—they slept at the White House. Similarly, most members of Congress either established a home with their wife in Washington, or boarded with members of their home state's Congressional delegation; but when Buchanan was in Congress, he roomed either with Senator King of Alabama or (on occasion) with other congressmen from the South.

Buchanan, a Pennsylvanian, was drawn both socially and politically to southern politicians. His closest friends included King, Jefferson Davis of Mississippi (future president of the Confederate States of America), and Senator Howell Cobb of Georgia. Buchanan admired the aristocratic culture of southern gentlemen, and to some degree he modeled "Wheatland"—a manorial estate Buchanan purchased near Lancaster, Pennsylvania—after a southern plantation. More important, Buchanan was what many called a "dough-face"—a northern public official friendly to the South's political aspirations, especially the protection of slavery.[10] (Critics charged that the faces of northern slavery-friendly politicians like Buchanan were made of "dough" that southerners could reshape at their pleasure.)

As far back as 1826 Buchanan conceded that as a theoretical matter slavery might be regarded as an evil; but he asserted that it was an evil that could not be remedied without the "introduction of evils infinitely greater." Abolition, he declared, would turn slaves into masters and would lead to "the massacre of the high-minded, and the chivalrous race of the men of the South . . . ." In such a case, Buchanan proclaimed, he would "without hesitation, buckle on my knapsack, and march . . . in defense of their cause."[11] For Buchanan (like many southerners), the fear of slave rebellion always lurked in the background, and was sometimes linked with lurid fears of sexual aggression. Thus Buchanan once exclaimed, "Many a mother clasps her infant to her bosom when she retires to rest, under dreadful apprehensions that she may be roused from her slumbers by the savage yells of the slaves by whom she is surrounded."[12]

Buchanan was a Democrat. By 1856, when Buchanan was elected President, the Democratic Party was the only American political party that still enjoyed significant support in both the North and South. In that presidential election year, Buchanan and the Democrats ran on a platform endorsing "popular sovereignty" or "Congressional non-intervention"—the idea that the people of each federal territory (rather than Congress) should decide whether or not to permit slavery there. Democrats both North and South came together to endorse Buchanan and the principle of popular sovereignty, but their joint support masked an ambiguity in that doctrine.

Specifically, not all advocates of popular sovereignty agreed as to *when* it was that the people of a territory would decide between slavery and freedom. On the one hand, most southern Democrats contended that the decision between freedom and slavery should be made only when the territory applied for statehood, and that there could be no prohibition against slavery while the territory remained a territory. Many northern Democrats, however, believed that even before applying for statehood, the people of a territory could prohibit slavery through legislation enacted by their territorial legislature.

The question whether a territorial government could prohibit slavery in the pre-statehood period was thought to be very important. Most observers believed that if slavery were permitted to gain a foothold in a territory during the territorial period, then it was inevitable that the new state to be created from that territory would ultimately choose to permit slavery, rather than deprive its own citizens of their already existing property.[13]

The question whether a territorial legislature could properly ban slavery was also a very hot one in 1856; it was at the heart of the struggle over Bleeding Kansas. Yet throughout the 1856 presidential campaign Buchanan avoided taking a clear stand on that question. By carefully straddling the issue, Buchanan was able to gain enough support from both North and South to win the presidency.[14]

This was not merely a matter of political expediency. To some degree, Buchanan thought that the entire national debate over slavery in the territories was something of a waste of time and effort—an abstract dispute about a small number of slaves in a few remote places, and a dispute that threatened to distract America from what Buchanan viewed as the far more important business of expansion into Cuba and Mexico.

Nevertheless, Buchanan took a very one-sided view of the national controversy over slavery. Republicans and abolitionists were not only wrong; they were dangerous. Anti-slavery agitation was dangerous because it might lead to slave insurrections; and the Republican Party was also dangerous because it was a "sectional" or "geographical" party[15] that threatened the integrity of the Union.[16] (Buchanan did not admit that the intensification of the national conflict over slavery during the 1850s was in important part the result of southern and Democratic "agitation" demanding that slavery be permitted where it had previously been barred by the Missouri Compromise.) Accordingly, just a few weeks after the election, Buchanan declared in a private letter to Supreme Court Justice Robert Grier: "The great object of my administration will be if possible to destroy the dangerous slavery agitation and thus restore peace to our distracted country."[17]

Buchanan saw the *Dred Scott* case as a means to accomplish those purposes. A decision by the Supreme Court declaring the Missouri Compromise unconstitutional because Congress had no power to limit slavery in the territories would, Buchanan hoped, bring to an end the destructive and seemingly interminable political conflict between North and South over slavery. It could also put an end to the Republican Party—whose central purpose was to support federal legislation banning the expansion of slavery into the territories. Such a decision by the Supreme Court would have special value because it would put the imprimatur of the Constitution and of the Court—a body thought to be above partisan politics—on Buchanan's policy of Congressional "non-intervention."

—Buchanan Enlists Catron—

In Buchanan's era, the new president was inaugurated in March (rather than in January). Accordingly, there was a period of several months following Buchanan's election before he assumed the presidency, following Franklin Pierce. During that time Buchanan assembled his cabinet and prepared to take office. He also began work on his Inaugural Address. He used his Address as the occasion to begin a secret correspondence with friendly members of the Court about *Dred Scott.*[18]

On February 3, 1857, Buchanan wrote first to longtime friend Associate Supreme Court Justice John Catron and asked whether the *Dred Scott* case would be decided before Inauguration Day. It was natural for Buchanan to turn to Catron with this delicate inquiry. Over the years, Catron had performed many political tasks for Buchanan ably and with great tact. (For this reason, Andrew Jackson Donelson—nephew and personal secretary to President Andrew Jackson—regarded Catron as Buchanan's "wire-puller"; and Francis Preston Blair once commented that

Catron and his wife were "the right and left hands of Old Buck [Buchanan]."[19])

On February 6, Catron replied, stating that the Court had not met to discuss the case since the December argument. Catron explained that Chief Justice Taney would decide when the Court would take the case up in conference. Taney, along with Catron, remained resentful that the substance of the Justices' confidential discussions about *Dred Scott* had been leaked to the *Tribune* the previous spring. Catron explained that, along with Justice Daniel's absence, this lingering resentment was the reason why Taney was now proceeding slowly and carefully. Catron promised to try to get Buchanan the information he wanted about *Dred Scott*. He then closed his letter by adding a not-too-subtle request that Buchanan appoint former Governor Aaron Brown of Catron's home state of Tennessee as Buchanan's postmaster general; Buchanan took Catron's hint and named Brown to that patronage-rich post just a few days later.[20]

On Tuesday, February 10, Catron wrote a follow-up letter to Buchanan, as promised. Catron reported that all nine Justices would meet in formal conference to discuss the *Dred Scott* case that coming Saturday, February 14. Catron's letter also made it evident that individual Justices were already talking fairly extensively with each other about the case because Catron was able to venture some very concrete predictions for Buchanan's benefit.

First, Catron reported that the case would not be decided before the end of February. (Inauguration Day was set for Wednesday, March 4.) Second, Catron stated that the decision would probably not help Buchanan with his Inaugural Address. The Court, Catron indicated, would not pass upon the question of constitutionality of the Missouri Compromise,[21] although some of the Justices might comment on that issue: "Some of the Judges will not touch the question of power, and others may, but that it will settle nothing is my present opinion."[22]

—A Narrow Decision Proposed—

The Justices did meet in conference that Saturday to discuss *Dred Scott*. Justice Catron's prediction that the Court would decide not to determine the Missouri Compromise issue appeared correct. By the end of the February 14 meeting it was tentatively agreed that Justice Nelson would draft an Opinion of the Court that would deny Dred Scott his freedom based upon essentially the same relatively narrow grounds previously relied upon by

Judge Wells and by the Missouri Supreme Court before that; the Nelson Opinion would not pass upon the question of Negro citizenship or upon the constitutionality of the Missouri Compromise.[23]

The citizenship issue had been the focus of the Court's prior Order in May 1856 directing reargument. At that time the Justices had been evenly divided (with Justice Nelson uncertain) as to whether the citizenship issue was properly preserved for Supreme Court review.[24] Now, Nelson had also come around to the view that it was not necessary (and perhaps improper as well) for the Supreme Court to deal with the citizenship question.

The Missouri Compromise issue was more sensitive. At the February 14, 1857 conference, all five southern Democratic Justices (Taney, Campbell, Catron, Daniel and Wayne) expressed the view that the Missouri Compromise was unconstitutional, and two of the northern Justices (the Republican McLean and the Whig Curtis) took the opposite position. Justices Nelson and Grier—both northern Democrats—advocated the idea that the Court should issue a narrow Opinion that would avoid the Missouri Compromise issue altogether. For the moment, Nelson and Grier carried the day, in all likelihood because one or more of the southern Justices were reluctant to declare the Missouri Compromise unconstitutional by a slim five-to-four majority composed entirely of southerners.

Justice Nelson set to work drafting a proposed Opinion of the Court. Nelson's draft (which later served as the basis for his Concurring Opinion) traced the history of Dred Scott's travels with Dr. Emerson. It then reasoned that once Scott returned to Missouri it was up to Missouri's courts when determining Scott's legal status to decide whether or not to apply Illinois or Wisconsin's law prohibiting slavery. Nelson continued by saying that Missouri's highest court had properly decided in *Scott v. Emerson* to apply Missouri law (rather than Illinois or Wisconsin law), and that Scott was still therefore still a slave. Nelson's draft Opinion of the Court further expressly declined to reach both the Missouri Compromise issue and the Negro citizenship issue on the ground that those admittedly important and controversial issues were not necessary to decide the case before the Court.[25]

It thus appeared that Dred Scott would lose his appeal, that the doctrine of "reattachment" as embodied in *Scott v. Emerson* would effectively be endorsed by the Supreme Court, and that the Court would not attempt to decide the far larger and more controversial issue of Congressional authority over the territories.

—The Court Shifts to a Broad Decision—

But then things changed, and history was made. There were and are conflicting versions of what followed. That should not be surprising, for several reasons. To begin with, there is of course no record of the Court's internal discussions; to the contrary, those discussions are supposed to be kept confidential. Thus whatever is "known" about the Court's internal decision-making process is really at best a deduction derived from several sources—including the Justices' published Opinions, a few private letters from and to various Justices (sometimes self-serving, and sometimes written long after the fact), the occasional memoir, and contemporary gossip as reported by the press.

Indeed, not even all of the Justices were themselves aware of all the Court's internal discussions about *Dred Scott.* That is so because (as happens with most cases) some of the Justices spoke with each other about *Dred Scott* outside of the Court's formal conference, either individually or in small groups. Moreover, we now know that at least two or three Justices were secretly corresponding about the case with President -elect Buchanan, and sharing the substance of those communications with some Justices but not with others.

In other words, none of the nine Justices—indeed, no single person—really knew all that was going on as the Court finally moved to decide *Dred Scott*. It should therefore come as no surprise that historians today cannot fully reconstruct with any certainty what happened inside the Supreme Court 150 years or so ago.

It is clear that within a few days of the February 14 conference the Justices discussed the case as a group again (although it appears that not all nine Justices were present as at a formal conference). This second meeting grew quite heated. Years later, Justice Curtis recalled that at one point Chief Justice Taney rebuked the squabbling Justices "like schoolboys," reminding them they were members of the Supreme Court and directing them to be seated. Justice Wayne proposed that the Court issue a broader opinion that would rule upon the Missouri Compromise issue, and that Chief Justice Taney be assigned to draft the Opinion of the Court. Ultimately, Wayne's proposal was approved.[26]

Different reasons were given for this shift by the Court. In private correspondence Justices Grier and Catron asserted that the Court changed its mind and decided to take up the Missouri Compromise issue when it became apparent that Justices McLean and Curtis intended to express the view in their dissents that the Missouri Compromise was constitutional. Thus Grier and Catron claimed that the issue of the Missouri Compromise was in a sense "forced" upon the Court for decision by the two dissenters.[27] (Catron, of course, never acknowledged that either President-elect Buchanan's secret letters to Catron or Buchanan's appointment of Aaron Brown as postmaster general played any part in Catron's decision to vote for Wayne's proposal.)

This was an odd way of looking at things, and suggests a strained effort by Grier and Catron to rationalize a questionable decision. After all, laws are usually presumed to be constitutional and valid. (Indeed, until *Dred Scott* was decided, no substantive federal law had ever been declared unconstitutional.) Thus it should not have been all that remarkable for McLean and Curtis to opine in their dissents that the Missouri Compromise was constitutional. More important, a majority opinion is not, of course, required to rebut every point offered up in a dissenting opinion. Thus—regardless of what McLean or Curtis wrote in dissent—it was still appropriate and natural for the majority to follow the approach originally advocated by both Nelson and Grier. In other words, whatever the dissenters' intentions were, Nelson's draft Opinion of the Court—which expressly declined to pass either way upon the constitutionality of the Missouri Compromise because that momentous issue was not necessary to decide Dred Scott's case—was still a perfectly good way for the Court to go.

Wayne himself did not argue that the anticipated dissents were the reason why the Court should write a broader Opinion. Rather, in putting forward his proposal, Wayne pointed out to his fellow Justices that the case had created great public interest, that the issue of the Missouri Compromise had been fully argued to the Court twice, and that the public expected a decision on that issue. Wayne asserted that the Court would be evading its responsibility to the nation if it chose not to pass upon the Missouri Compromise. Years later, Justice Campbell recalled that it was chiefly these considerations—that is, meeting public expectations and resolving an important national controversy—that led the Court to take up the Missouri Compromise issue: "[T]he apprehension had been expressed by others of the Court, that the Court would not fulfill public expectations or discharge it duties by maintaining silence on these questions."[28]

Chief Justice Roger Taney is usually regarded as the chief architect of the *Dred Scott* decision because he ultimately wrote the Opinion of the Court striking down the Missouri Compromise. Yet it appears that it was not until this second February 1857 meeting of the Court concerning the

Dred Scott case that Taney made up his mind and cast the deciding fifth vote in favor of Wayne's proposal to issue a broad decision in *Dred Scott*. Wayne, Daniel, Campbell and Catron were already to some degree favorably disposed toward such a broad decision, but Taney had previously held back.

Taney's support for a broad opinion was thus crucial, and it appears that it was Wayne who convinced Taney to take that path. On the very day that Wayne's proposal passed, Wayne exulted to Senator David Yulee of Florida that he had "gained a triumph for the southern section of the country, by persuading the Chief Justice that the Court could put an end to all further agitation on the subject of slavery in the territories."[29] Wayne had persuaded Taney that *Dred Scott* was the proper means by which to strike a decisive blow for the South and against the anti-slavery movement.

—Buchanan "Speeds" Grier—

On February 19 Catron wrote to Buchanan again in order to report the good news about the shift in the Court's thinking. Catron then went two steps further.

First, Catron suggested that in his Inaugural Address Buchanan should note that the issue of the constitutionality of the Missouri Compromise was before the Supreme Court, and then declare that based on the Court's "high and independent character" Buchanan expected that the Court would soon settle that controversy which had "so long and seriously agitated" the country. Catron went so far as to draft a flowery paragraph[30] along these lines for Buchanan's use. (The hypocrisy of these proposed remarks is almost comical; Catron was urging the president-elect to speak to the nation of the Court's "high and independent character," while at the very same moment Catron was leaking confidential information about the Court's deliberations to Buchanan and suggesting tactics by which Buchanan could further influence the Court's decision. Yet neither Buchanan nor Catron appeared to experience any discomfort over this contradiction.)

Second, Catron focused Buchanan's attention on Justice Grier. Grier was important to Buchanan and Catron because Grier was a northern Democrat; the *Dred Scott* decision would likely have much greater weight if at least one northern Justice joined in its pro-slavery result. Catron reported that Grier privately agreed that the Missouri Compromise was unconstitutional. However, Grier still preferred to avoid deciding that inflammatory issue in *Dred Scott*, and to join instead in a narrow Opinion along the lines of the draft Opinion prepared by Justice Nelson. Thus, said Catron, Grier had been "persuaded to take the smooth handle for the sake of repose."[31] Catron therefore suggested that Buchanan write directly to Grier and urge Grier to join the pro-slavery majority in declaring the Missouri Compromise unconstitutional. A few days later, Catron repeated his request that Buchanan lobby Grier; in a remarkably blunt letter, Catron reported to Buchanan that most of the Justices had nearly completed writing their opinions, and Catron flatly told Buchanan: "I want Grier speeded. I think whatever you wish may be accomplished."[32]

Buchanan took Catron's advice and went to work "speeding" Grier. In that process, Buchanan cast off any last remaining pretense of respecting the Court's independence. On February 23 Buchanan wrote to Grier and frankly urged Grier to rule that the Missouri Compromise was unconstitutional.[33]

Grier described what happened next in a reply written to Buchanan later that same day.[34] Grier took Buchanan's letter and showed it to their "mutual friends" Justices Taney and Wayne. Taney, Wayne and Grier together discussed Buchanan's letter, and they all agreed with Buchanan that the Court should rule on the constitutionality of the Missouri Compromise. Taney and Wayne had, of course, already taken that position by voting for Wayne's proposal that the Court issue a broad decision. Now Buchanan's letter had also won Grier over to the pro-slavery majority that was determined to strike down the Missouri Compromise; Buchanan had successfully "speeded" Grier.

With Taney and Wayne's concurrence, in his reply letter to Buchanan Grier recited in considerable detail the history of the Court's confidential discussions about *Dred Scott* to date. Grier then stated two concerns. First, Grier thought it important that he join the pro-slavery majority so that it would include at least one northern Justice. He stated: "I am anxious that it should not appear that the line of latitude should mark the line of division of the Court."

Second, Grier thought that the *Dred Scott* decision would be far less effective if it were based on inconsistent or clashing individual Opinions rendered by the concurring pro-slavery Justices. Thus, Grier told Buchanan that he had agreed to concur in Taney's opinion, and that Wayne would try to persuade Campbell, Daniel and Catron to do the same. Grier added that he, Taney and Wayne had agreed not to reveal to their fellow Justices "the true cause of their anxiety to produce this result"—that is, presumably, to help Buchanan achieve his objectives—but that the three Justices thought that they should tell Buchanan in confidence "the real state of the matter." (Apparently, neither Grier, Taney nor Wayne had any qualms about plotting strategy concerning a pending case with the president-elect, or about keeping secrets from their fellow Justices in order to further that strategy.[35]) Finally, Grier advised Buchanan that (because of Chief Justice Taney's frail health) the *Dred Scott* decision would be announced on Friday March 6, at the earliest—that is, after Buchanan's Inauguration.

—Toward Decision—

On March 4, the Justices all attended Buchanan's Inauguration. Chief Justice Taney administered the oath of office. (Some critics of *Dred Scott* later theorized that during the ceremonies Taney secretly whispered to Buchanan what the result of the *Dred Scott* case would be[36]; the specific rumor was silly, but the general suspicion that there were secret communications between Buchanan and the Court was ultimately vindicated.)

In his Inaugural Address Buchanan lauded the principle of "popular sovereignty" in the territories as the only sound basis for resolving the national conflict over slavery. Popular sovereignty, said Buchanan, embodied the "simple rule, that the will of the majority shall govern." He then referred directly to the *Dred Scott* case, declaring:

> A difference of opinion has arisen in regard to the point of time when the people of a Territory shall decide this question [between slavery and freedom] for themselves.
>
> This is, happily, a matter of but little practical importance. Besides, it is a judicial question, which legitimately belongs to the Supreme Court of the United States, before whom it is now pending, and will, it is understood, be speedily and finally settled. To their decision, in common with all good citizens, I shall cheerfully submit, whatever this may be.

Buchanan's words were remarkable in several respects. First, Buchanan's professed open-minded willingness to cheerfully submit to the Court's *Dred Scott* decision "whatever this may be" was something of a sham. Buchanan already knew full well that the Court was about to render a pro-slavery decision because he had been so advised in his secret and improper correspondence with Catron and Grier; indeed, Buchanan had to some degree helped to shape that decision himself.

Second, it might have appeared to an outside observer that Buchanan was somewhat confused as to what precise legal question was before the Supreme Court in *Dred Scott*. Most people anticipated that the Court might rule on the question whether Congress possessed the power to legislate against slavery in the territories, and thus whether the Missouri Compromise was constitutional. Yet Buchanan's Inaugural remarks had identified a related, but distinct, issue. Buchanan's remarks indicated that he expected that the Court was about to resolve the ambiguity inherent in the doctrine of popular sovereignty—namely, at what point the people of a territory where there was no federal law prohibiting slavery (such as Kansas) could choose between freedom and slavery. In other words, Buchanan's Address indicated that he expected that the *Dred Scott* decision would rule on the question whether a territorial legislature could prohibit slavery in the pre-statehood period.

This was odd, because the *Dred Scott* case plainly had nothing to do with the act of any territorial legislature. There was thus little apparent reason for Buchanan to think that the *Dred Scott* decision would deal with the precise legal question that he identified in his Inaugural Address.

Yet—just as Buchanan predicted—Chief Justice Taney's Opinion of the Court did indeed briefly assert that a territorial legislature could not pass a law forbidding slavery in the pre-statehood period. It thus seems exceedingly likely that (unless Buchanan was clairvoyant) Taney (or someone acting at Taney's direction) had secretly revealed the substance of Taney's Opinion in considerable detail to Buchanan in advance. Accordingly, it appears that there were secret communications about the *Dred Scott* case between Buchanan and the Court beyond those already reflected in the secret correspondence that has been discovered between Buchanan, Catron and Grier.

The importance of these secret communications between Buchanan and the pro-slavery Justices in *Dred Scott* should not be overstated. It may well be that even if Buchanan had never intervened in the Court's decision-making process the Justices would ultimately have followed the same course of action. There is no way to know for sure. What is certain is that Buchanan's efforts to influence the Court's decision were grossly improper. They should have been firmly rebuffed. They were not.

All in all, the manner in which the Supreme Court handled the *Dred Scott* case prior to decision was most unusual. The Court took a long time to first hear the case. Then it did not do anything for a substantial period of time. Following the first round of oral argument, at least one of the Justices leaked detailed confidential information about the Court's decision-making process to the *Tribune*. The Court then ordered a second round of oral arguments that no one had asked for. While awaiting the second round of argument, one anti-slavery Justice (McLean) wrote a letter publicly stating his position on the most important potential issue in the case—the constitutionality of the Missouri Compromise—in order to bolster his presidential hopes. During both rounds of oral argument the Court entertained extended presentations on that same issue, even though it had never been raised before or considered by the court below. Following the second round of oral argument, at least two of the Court's Associate Justices secretly corresponded and strategized about the case with President-elect Buchanan while the Court was in the process of deciding what to do. And the Chief Justice of the Supreme Court and the President-elect secretly communicated with each other about the case so that the President-elect could make political use of his advance knowledge of the decision's contents in his Inaugural Address.

Clearly, the political pressures of the day and the importance of the issues before the Court were leading the Court to treat the *Dred Scott* case like no other.

—The Decision Announced—

On March 6—just two days after Buchanan's Inauguration—the Court announced its decision in the *Dred Scott* case. Chief Justice Taney read his Opinion of the Court aloud to the crowded courtroom. This took about two hours. Taney was just two weeks shy of eighty years old and his voice was hard to hear, but everyone present nevertheless immediately understood that the *Dred Scott* case would be a landmark in history. The Supreme Court had held that the Missouri Compromise was unconstitutional, and that black people were not, and could not be, citizens of the United States. The Court also declared that Dred and Harriet Scott were still the slaves of John Sanford—although neither the Court nor the public seemed to really care very much what happened to the Scotts themselves.

Once Taney was done, Associate Justices Nelson and Catron read their briefer concurring Opinions aloud. The next day Justices John McLean and Benjamin Curtis read their dissenting Opinions aloud in court. The other Justices filed their written concurring Opinions and dispensed with an oral reading. Each one of the nine Justices filed his own separate Opinion; *Dred*

Scott was one of a handful of cases prior to the Civil War where that was so.[37]

McLean and Curtis published their Opinions and released them to the press immediately. Taney continued to revise his written Opinion of the Court until it was published in late May. This delay occasioned a mean-spirited correspondence between Taney and Curtis that was surprisingly[38] ungentlemanly for two judges on the same court. Curtis accused Taney of withholding and revising Taney's written Opinion so that Taney could answer certain points made by Curtis in his dissent. Taney in turn accused Curtis of playing to the public by rushing to publish his dissent. (In retrospect, both men's accusations seem correct.) Curtis resigned from the Supreme Court that fall, in large part because he was resentful over this exchange with Taney.[39]

In the immediate aftermath of the *Dred Scott* decision there was an avalanche of newspaper coverage and public pronouncements either praising or damning the decision. As time went on, Republicans opposed to the expansion of slavery spent a great deal of effort trying to minimize the impact of *Dred Scott*. To that end, some Republicans argued that much of the Opinion of the Court was mere "dicta"—that is, discussion of legal points not essential to the actual decision in the case, and therefore arguably not legally binding.[40] Somewhat similarly, some Republicans also argued that not all of the Justices agreed with Taney on all the points made in his Opinion of the Court, so that Taney's Opinion was not necessarily a definitive statement of the law.

But no matter how one parses the Opinions of the other Justices, Taney's Opinion was the official Opinion of the Court. Moreover, Taney and five other Justices all concurred in the central and most controversial holding in *Dred Scott*—that Congress had no power to limit slavery in the territories, and that the Missouri Compromise was therefore unconstitutional. Thus, in the end, Taney's Opinion of the Court was, for better or worse, the *Dred Scott* decision, and it is chiefly that Opinion by Taney that should be analyzed in order to evaluate what the Supreme Court did in *Dred Scott*. It is therefore worthwhile to first look briefly at the life of Chief Justice Roger Taney.

Notes

1. Kauffman, *Dred Scott's Advocate*, 211.

2. Ehrlich, *They Have No Rights*, 122–27 summarizes the newspaper coverage during this period and quotes extensively from leading papers. On New Year's Day, 1857, the *New York Herald* made a surprisingly specific prediction—it reported that the Court had decided by a vote of seven to two (with Justices Curtis and McLean dissenting) to rule in *Dred Scott* that the Missouri Compromise was unconstitutional. The very next day the *Herald* retracted the story. Whether the author of the *Herald* article had genuine "inside information" or was instead merely a good analyst of Supreme Court trends is not clear. In either case, his prediction was premature but ultimately proved essentially correct, both as to the Court's holding and as to the alignment of the Justices. The *Herald* story inspired many other pundits to speculate at length about how the *Dred Scott* case would soon be decided. *See* Ehrlich, *They Have No Rights*, 126.

3. Hopkins, *Dred Scott's Case*, 52–53; Fehrenbacher, *Dred Scott*, 688, note 5.

4. "Seriatim" means individually, or one by one. No one knows who was providing Stephens with this confidential information "sub rosa." (Some have speculated that it was Associate Justice James Wayne, from Stephens' home state of Georgia.) But Stephens' source—whoever it was—was very, very good.

Stephens' predictions proved uncannily accurate. The Court did indeed rule that the Missouri Compromise was unconstitutional, and Chief Justice Taney did write an elaborate Opinion. Most remarkably, Stephens was also right in predicting that each of the nine Justices would write a separate Opinion. *Dred Scott* was the first (or arguably, second) U.S. Supreme Court decision where that was so.

5. *See* Ehrlich, *They Have No Rights*, 125–26; Hopkins, *Dred Scott's Case*, 52–53.

6. John P. Frank, *Justice Daniel Dissenting* (Cambridge: Harvard U. Press, 1964), 257–58.

7. *See* Allan Nevins, *The Emergence of Lincoln (Vol.1)* (New York: Charles Scribner's, 1950), 63:

> No electric spark, no glow of genius ever lighted up his mind. He had never coined an epigram or written an eloquent passage; he could not even quote aptly, for he had no interest in literature. "I do not think he ever uttered a genuine witticism in his life," stated his intimate friend Henry S. Foote.

8. Jean H. Baker, *James Buchanan*, (New York: Times Books, 2004) is an excellent short biography. Elbert B. Smith, *The Presidency of James Buchanan* (Lawrence: U. of Kansas Press, 1975) is also valuable and more detailed. A briefer sketch of Buchanan's life and politics by Professor Smith is available online at

www.presidentprofiles.com/Washington-Johnson-Buchanan-James.html, hereinafter "Smith, *Buchanan.*"

9. *See* Kenneth M. Stampp, *America in 1857: A Nation on the Brink* (New York: Oxford U. Press, 1990), 282, 330–31.

10. Baker, *James Buchanan*, 22–26, 56; Smith, *Buchanan*, 3–6.

11. Baker, *James Buchanan*, 30–33; Smith, *Buchanan*, 2–3.

12. *See* Nevins, *Emergence of Lincoln*, 66.

13. *See* Arthur Bestor, "State Sovereignty and Slavery: A Reinterpretation of Pro-slavery Constitutional Doctrine, 1846–1860," *Journal of the Illinois State Historical Society* (Summer, 1961), LIV, 148, reprinted in Kutler, ed., *Dred Scott Decision,* 164, at 165–166: "To opponents and defenders of slavery alike, it seemed clear that the first decisions made in the territories would be the determining ones. . . . Long before a state attained full standing, its social system could have been irrevocably fixed by decisions already made."

14. Potter, *The Impending Crisis,* 259–65; Fehrenbacher, *Dred Scott,* 199–201, 205–208.

15. Thus in his Inaugural Address Buchanan proclaimed that twenty years of antislavery agitation had not accomplished any good for the slave, master or country and might "endanger the personal safety of a large portion of our country-men where the institution exists"; and Buchanan expressed the "hope that the long agitation of this subject is approaching an end, and that geographical parties to which it has given birth . . . will speedily become extinct."

16. Thus Buchanan wrote to a friend in the summer of 1856: "The Union is in danger and the people everywhere begin to know it. Black Republicans must be, as they can be with justice, boldly assailed as diunuionists and this charge must be reiterated again and again." Baker, *James Buchanan*, 71.

17. *See* Baker, *James Buchanan*, p. 80; Walker Lewis, *Without Fear or Favor: A Biography of Chief Justice Roger Brooke Taney* (Boston: Houghton, Mifflin, 1965), 389; Carl B. Swisher, *The Taney Period: 1836–64* (The Oliver Wendell Holmes Devise, History of the Supreme Court of the United States, Vol. V) (New York: Macmillan, 1974), 610.

18. This correspondence was first published many years later in Phillip Auchimpaugh, "James Buchanan, the Court and the Dred Scott Case," *Tennessee Historical Magazine*, IX (1926).

19. *See* Swisher, *The Taney Period,* 563 and 627.

20. Auchimpaugh, "Buchanan," 234.

21. Catron then added his own view that the Missouri Compromise was invalid because it conflicted with the treaty with France for the Louisiana Purchase—which promised that the property rights of the inhabitants of the acquired territory would be protected.

Catron, however, rejected the suggestion made by Sanford's lawyers that the Territory Clause did not confer power upon Congress to legislate for the territories. Catron thought that such a holding would contradict both the recent decision of the Court in *Cross v. Harrison*, 16 How. 164 (1854), and the practice of sixty-eight years of history under the Constitution. Denying Congressional authority over the territories would, Catron told Buchanan, "subject the Court to ridicule."

22. Auchimpaugh, "Buchanan," 234–35.

23. Swisher, *Roger B. Taney*, 496–98; Ehrlich, *They Have No Rights*, 126–27.

24. Swisher, *The Taney Period*, 606–8.

25. *See* Fehrenbacher, *Dred Scott*, 307–8.

26. Swisher, *The Taney Period*, 618–20, Ehrlich, *They Have No Rights*, 128–30, and 226, n. 23.

27. Thus Catron stated in his February 19 letter to Buchanan: "A majority of my brethren will be forced up to this point by the two dissentients." Auchimpaugh, "Buchanan," 236.

Similarly, Grier's letter of February 23 to Buchanan indicated that those Justices who disagreed with McLean and Curtis' intended dissents "feel compelled to express their opinions on the subject." Auchimpaugh, "Buchanan," 237.

Contrary evidence suggesting that it was in fact Wayne's proposal to issue a broad pro-slavery opinion that first moved McLean and Curtis to touch upon the Missouri Compromise issue is summarized in Ehrlich, *They Have No Rights*, 128–29 and 226, n. 32, and Fehrenbacher, *Dred Scott*, 309 and 669, n.11.

28. *See* letter of John A. Campbell to Samuel Tyler, *Memoir of Roger Brooke Taney, LLD* (Baltimore: John Murphy & Co. 1872), 384. *See also* Swisher, *The Taney Period*, 619; Ehrlich, *They Have No Rights*, 129.

29. Lewis, *Without Fear or Favor*, 392; Ehrlich, *They Have No Rights*, 128.

30. Auchimpaugh, "Buchanan," 236.

31. Auchimpaugh, "Buchanan," 236.

32. Auchimpaugh, "Buchanan," 238.

33. Buchanan's February 23 letter to Grier no longer exists, but its essential contents can be readily deduced from Grier's reply of the same day.

34. Set out in full in Lewis, *Without Fear or Favor*, 393–95 and in Auchimpaugh, "Buchanan," 236–37.

35. As late as 1870, Campbell and Nelson's correspondence indicates that they had no idea about Buchanan's communications with their fellow Justices concerning *Dred Scott*. *See* Tyler, *Memoir of Roger Brooke Taney*, 382–85.

36. One variation of the theory of secret Inaugural Day "whisperings" carried on between the President and the Chief Justice was elaborated by Senator William Seward of New York—a leading Republican and Presidential hopeful—in a memorably vituperative Senate speech on March 3, 1858. Reprinted in Kutler, *Dred Scott Decision*, 60–63. Taney was said to have been so angry over Seward's speech that Taney vowed to refuse to administer the oath of office to Seward if Seward were elected President.

37. *See* Paul Finkelman, "*Scott v. Sanford*: The Court's Most Dreadful Case and How it Changed History," 82 *Chicago Kent Law Review* Vol. I, 3 and note 4.

38. The exchange was particularly surprising because Curtis had previously been especially impressed by Taney's courteous nature and unfailing dignity. The

respectful relationship that had existed between Curtis and Taney before *Dred Scott* is evidenced by a touching exchange of letters between Curtis (who had also lost a wife and children) and Taney on the occasion of the death of Taney's wife and daughter. *See* Tyler, *Memoir of Roger Brooke Taney, LLD*, 326–28.

39. Streichler, *Justice Curtis*, 145–48, attributes Curtis' resignation both to his resentment over his correspondence with Taney and to Curtis' desire to silently protest the *Dred Scott* decision.

40. Ironically, Congressman Calvin Chaffee—Eliza Sanford Emerson's second husband—was one such Republican. In 1858 Chaffee asserted with regard to *Dred Scott*: "The dictum of the Court is a very different affair from a decision." Fehrenbacher, *Dred Scott*, 473.

Chapter 8
"The South Is Doomed"—Roger B. Taney

Roger Taney's long tenure as Chief Justice of the Supreme Court both began and ended in political controversy and exceptionally bitter feelings. When Taney (pronounced "tawny") was appointed to the Court in 1836, one New York newspaper wrote: "The pure ermine of the Supreme Court is sullied by the appointment of that political hack, Roger B. Taney." When Chief Justice Taney died in 1864, several years after the *Dred Scott* decision, George Templeton Strong wrote in his diary: "The Hon. old Roger B. Taney has earned the gratitude of his country by dying at last. Better late than never." In 1865, Congress considered but then rejected a proposal to pay for a marble bust of Taney to be placed with the busts of all the prior Chief Justices of the Supreme Court. In the course of the debate, Senator Sumner declared that Taney's name should be "hooted down the pages of history." Sumner's colleagues in the Senate who voted "no" on Taney's bust apparently agreed; Senator Benjamin Wade even volunteered that the people of his state of Ohio would rather pay twice as much in order to hang Taney in effigy.[1] Clearly, the principal author of the *Dred Scott* decision was not forgiven, even after his death.

Roger Brooke Taney was born on his family's plantation on the Patunxet River in Maryland in 1777.[2] Taney was the product of a close-knit rural society. Taney's father, Michael Taney V, and mother, Monica

Brooke Taney, grew up on plantations that faced each other across the Patunxet. Like many of the area's other leading families, the Taneys farmed (chiefly) tobacco and owned slaves.

Michael Taney V was a vigorous outdoorsman who had an explosive temper; local lore had it that he once killed a man in a knife fight. It was expected that Michael Taney V would leave his estate to his eldest son Michael VI. Roger Taney was tall, frail and bookish. Fairly early on, Roger and his family decided that Roger would become a lawyer.

Roger Taney entered Dickinson College in Carlisle, Pennsylvania, at the age of fifteen; he graduated as his class valedictorian. He moved to Annapolis, where he studied law with Judge Jeremiah Chase; Taney was admitted to the bar in 1799. Soon thereafter he began a successful legal practice in Frederick. Taney also became active in Maryland politics, initially winning election to the state legislature as a member of the Federalist Party. (Taney later broke with the Federalists because he felt they gave inadequate support for the War of 1812; as the Federalist Party faded into obscurity, Taney became a Democrat.)

Perhaps Taney's quirkiest claim to fame was that he was a brother-in-law of Francis Scott Key, the author of "The Star–Spangled Banner." Key (also a lawyer) was Taney's good friend, and Taney married Key's sister, Anne.

In 1823, Taney moved his law practice to Baltimore. By this time he was recognized as one of Maryland's leading lawyers. Taney was no great orator, and confessed that he found courtroom work nerve-wracking and therefore exhausting. But the legal community understood that Taney possessed an exceptional intellect; he was able to make clear the most difficult and complex points of law. One colleague—William Wirt, later U.S. Attorney General—called Taney a man "with a moonlight mind"; like the "moonlight of the arctics" said Wirt, Taney "gave all the light of day without its glare."[3]

In 1827, Taney was appointed Maryland's State Attorney General. At about the same time Taney became very active in supporting Andrew Jackson's successful campaign for the presidency. In 1830 Jackson became so dissatisfied with the squabbling within his own cabinet that he demanded and received resignations from most of its members. Jackson accepted the resignation of U.S. Attorney General John Berrien and appointed Roger Taney in his stead. In the years that followed, Taney became a fierce political partisan for President Jackson and Jackson's strongest ally in the

President's long and difficult struggle to defeat the Bank of the United States.

Taney paid a heavy price for being considered Jackson's political "hatchet man." In 1834 the Senate refused to confirm Taney as Secretary of Treasury. He was the first man in American history to be rejected by Congress for a Cabinet post. In 1835 the Senate rejected Taney's nomination as an Associate Justice of the Supreme Court. But in March of 1836 Taney won Senate confirmation to be Chief Justice of the Supreme Court, succeeding the great John Marshall.

Taney served as Chief Justice for nearly thirty years. For the most part, he surprised even those who had opposed his appointment by steering a fairly moderate course. During his tenure the last remnants of the old Federalist Party of Chief Justice Marshall were swept away. By the time *Dred Scott* was decided in 1857, seven of the nine Justices on the Court were Democrats. One of the other two (John McLean) was previously a Democrat who had only recently converted to the new Republican Party. The Taney Court was thus a Democratic Court, and many of the Justices were (like Taney) devoted to the political legacy of Andrew Jackson.[4] The Taney Court was true to its Jacksonian origins in that it did issue a number of decisions that moved away to a degree from the ultra-nationalist and pro-business line of the Marshall Court in favor of state regulation and agrarian interests; but the shift was slow and by no means extreme.[5]

As Chief Justice, Taney won praise even from many of his early detractors for his moderation, for the intellectual quality of his work, and for his integrity. For example, by the year 1850, both Senator Henry Clay, the great Whig leader from Kentucky, and President John Tyler—each avowed enemies of Taney during the Bank War of the 1830s—had expressed the view that Taney had been a great Chief Justice and that they regretted[6] their earlier opposition to his appointment.[7]

Among other accomplishments, Taney was credited for developing what is now called the "political question" doctrine. In the case of *Rhode Island v. Massachusetts,*[8] Taney wrote: "The powers given to the courts of the United States by the Constitution, are judicial powers and extend to those subjects only which are judicial in character; and not to those which are political." In *Luther v. Borden,*[9] the Court refused to decide which of two competing factions was the true government of Rhode Island; this was a "political question," said Taney, that was for Congress and not the Court to decide. To this day, *Luther v. Borden* is cited for the general proposition that the Court should avoid deciding political questions. These "political question" cases had little to do with the specific issues that later presented themselves in *Dred Scott*, but they did help to give Taney a reputation for exercising judicial restraint and giving appropriate deference to other branches of government.

There were, however, two issues that stood in dramatic contrast to this general picture of Chief Justice Taney as a restrained and moderate judge—the Bank of the United States and slavery. In a sense, Taney's long and generally placid career in national life was bracketed by the heated controversy over the Bank near the beginning, and the even more acrimonious dispute over *Dred Scott* and slavery near the end.

—Taney and the Bank—

Taney first became an important—and in many circles, despised—figure in national politics because he and President Andrew Jackson were devoted to dismantling the Bank of the United States, despite great opposition.

In the 1819 landmark case of *McCullough v. Maryland*[10] the U.S. Supreme Court had decided that under the Constitution's "necessary and proper" clause the federal government could properly charter a national bank. But Taney supplied Jackson with a legal memo that argued that Jackson could veto as unconstitutional a new law rechartering the bank; and Jackson (whose veto message paraphrased Taney's memo at length) went ahead and vetoed the law, thus commencing what became known as the "Bank War."

As the Bank War progressed, Jackson was forced to dismiss two Treasury secretaries who refused to obey Jackson's directive to remove federal deposits from the Bank of the United States and to place those funds in a number of smaller state banks instead. But Acting Treasury Secretary Taney did the job more than willingly.

Taney explained the decision to remove the federal deposits from the Bank in a report to Congress that declared: "It is a fixed principle of our political institutions to guard against the unnecessary accumulation of power over persons in any hands." Taney anticipated and appeared to relish the coming political fight over the Bank's future. In a letter to the Speaker of the House, Taney wrote "We have a fiery contest before us, but we shall conquer the mammoth, with all of the allies that are coming to its aid."[11]

Taney was subject to personal, as well as political, attacks because of his role in the Bank controversy. Senator Daniel Webster of Massachusetts, for example, publicly denounced Taney as a mere "pliant instrument" of Jackson, and Webster (not too) privately dismissed the legal arguments devised by Taney as "trash."[12]

The personal attacks came about in part because Taney was formerly a director of, and was still a large shareholder in, the Union Bank of Maryland. The Union Bank was one of the state banks that received the federal funds withdrawn from the Bank of the United States. (Indeed, one of the many connections between Taney and Reverdy Johnson, one of the attorneys for John Sanford in *Dred Scott*, was that Johnson had assisted Taney back during the Bank controversy by investigating and quieting allegations that the Union Bank's president had misused some of the federal funds for personal stock speculations.)

Taney's resentment over the Bank controversy remained with him always. As Chief Justice he properly recused himself in the case of *Bank of the United States v. United States*.[13] (In non-legal language, this means that Taney did not participate in deciding the case because he recognized that he had a potential conflict of interest.) But then, apparently unable to restrain himself, Taney wrote a lengthy essay disagreeing with the Court's decision in the case anyway, and he had it published as an "Appendix" to the Court's decision. Clearly, Taney's rancor toward the Bank overcame his better judgment and his judicial duty to truly recuse himself.

Taney himself saw the parallel between the controversy over the Bank in the 1830s and that which followed *Dred Scott* in the 1850s. In August of 1857 he wrote to former President Franklin Pierce about the stormy reaction to his *Dred Scott* decision. His words revealed an abiding taste for political warfare that seems most unjudicial:

> You see I am passing through a conflict, much like the one which followed the removal of the deposits, and the war is waged upon me in the same spirit and by many of the same men who distinguished themselves on that occasion by the unscrupulous means to which they resorted.
>
> At my time of life when my end must be near, I should have enjoyed to find that irritating strifes of this world were over, and that I was about to depart in peace with all men and all men in peace with me. Yet perhaps it is best as it is. The mind is less apt to feel the torpor of age when it is thus forced into action by public duties.[14]

In the same combative[15] vein, in a letter to former Attorney General Caleb Cushing, Taney said of the public reaction to *Dred Scott*, "I have thought all along that this wrath and fury was strong, proof that I was right."[16]

—Taney and Slavery—

Taney's attitudes toward slavery seem to have changed over time, and to have paralleled to some degree those of the South as a whole. Taney was born during the American Revolution. The leaders of the South in that generation maintained slavery; but many of them expressed quiet regret about the institution at times, and some even made occasional token gestures toward emancipation. As a young man, Taney too made some gestures against slavery. He freed most of his own slaves, and he was a member of an organization dedicated to the colonization of freed slaves.[17]

In 1818 the up-and-coming attorney Roger Taney defended Jacob Gruber. Gruber was a Methodist minister from the free state of Pennsylvania who visited Maryland and gave a strong anti-slavery sermon there. He was indicted for inciting slaves to rebel. Taney secured an acquittal for Gruber. In his opening statement, Taney (a Catholic) invoked the principles of freedom of speech and of religion, arguing, "No man can be prosecuted for preaching the articles of his religious creed, unless his doctrine is immoral, and calculated to disturb the peace and order of society."[18]

Taney's passionate summation was filled with anti-slavery sentiments, and some of his words associated the Declaration of Independence with the cause of freedom for the slaves. Taney declared:

> A hard necessity, indeed, compels us to endure the evil of slavery for a time . . . . Yet while it continues it is a blot on our national character and every real lover of freedom confidently hopes that it will be effectually, though it must be gradually, wiped away . . . until the time shall come when we can point without blush to the language held in the Declaration of Independence, every friend of humanity will seek to lighten the galling chain of slavery . . . .[19]

This language later proved embarrassing to Taney because it certainly seemed to conflict with the view he expressed in *Dred Scott* that the Declaration had nothing to do with Negroes.

Like many men, as Taney grew older and more successful in professional life, he grew more conservative; and like many southerners in the pre–Civil War era, Taney moved from a posture of mostly quiet regret over slavery to one of active, aggressive defense of slavery.

An early indication of this shift came in 1832, shortly after Taney first became U.S. Attorney General. A question arose concerning North Carolina's Negro Seaman Law. That law was similar to laws passed in several other southern states in the 1820s and '30s. It required that free black sailors serving on any ship that came into port in North Carolina must be held in jail until the ship departed. The law was a reflection of the fact that concern over "agitation" by free Negroes was on the rise in the South, especially after the Nat Turner slave revolt of 1831.

Taney produced a draft Attorney General's Opinion approving North Carolina's Negro Seaman Law. The Opinion was circulated but never officially published. It stated a harsh and uncompromising view—that Negroes were members of a degraded race that had lawfully been reduced to slavery, and that neither Negro slaves nor free Negroes (such as free black sailors) were citizens of the United States, or entitled to any rights as such.[20] Taney expressed much the same view (in nearly the same language) twenty five years later in *Dred Scott*.

As Chief Justice, Taney seldom dealt directly with the issue of slavery. But when questions related to slavery did arise, Taney was always solidly in the pro-slavery camp. For example, in *Groves v. Slaughter*,[21] Taney concurred with the conclusion that the provision of the Mississippi State Constitution, which barred the importation of slaves from out of state, did not justify setting aside the sale in 1836 of certain slaves from out of state; the sale was still valid, said the Court, because it was made before implementing legislation was passed by Mississippi's State Legislature in 1837.

Similarly, in the 1841 case of *Prigg v. Pennsylvania*,[22] Taney concurred with the conclusion that the Pennsylvania conviction of a Maryland slave catcher for kidnapping was unconstitutional. The slave catcher had been charged with kidnapping because he recovered a fugitive slave without first getting a required certificate from the Pennsylvania state authorities. But the Supreme Court set aside the conviction because the Pennsylvania statute requiring the slave catcher to get a certificate from the state government improperly interfered with the enforcement of the federal Fugitive Slave Act. (Taney's Concurring Opinion was in fact even more strongly pro-slavery than Justice Story's Opinion of the Court in *Prigg*. The Opinion of the Court upheld the federal Fugitive Slave Act and forbade state officials to interfere with its enforcement. Taney's Opinion went even further and declared that state officials had the power and the *affirmative duty to assist* in securing the return of fugitive slaves.)

One of the very first cases that Taney decided as Chief Justice dealt with some of the same issues of slavery, sojourning, comity and "reattachment" that later figured prominently in *Dred Scott*. The 1837 case of *United States v. The Garronne*[23] concerned (among other questions) the fate of a slave named Priscilla. In 1835 Priscilla's owner (a widow named Smith) traveled to Havre in France for health reasons, taking Priscilla with her. In 1836, at Priscilla's request, Mrs. Smith sent Priscilla home to New Orleans aboard the ship *Garronne*. Since 1808, federal law had prohibited the importation of slaves into the United States; it provided that any ship importing slaves was forfeited, and that slaves illegally imported became free. Accordingly, upon Priscilla's return to New Orleans, it was argued that the *Garronne* was illegally importing slaves, and that Priscilla should go free.

Taney, however, made quick work of the argument. First, he declared that the law forbidding the importation of slaves referred to slaves newly imported from Africa, and not to American slaves returning from travel abroad. Second, Taney noted that it was possible that under French law Priscilla had become free upon arriving in France (where slavery was illegal). Nevertheless, Taney said that—regardless of French law—Priscilla remained a U.S. resident while sojourning in France; and so, once Priscilla returned to the U.S. she would still be regarded as a slave.

—*Strader v. Graham*—

Taney's most important contribution to the law of American slavery prior to *Dred Scott* came in the case of *Strader v. Graham*. That case originated in the border state of Kentucky, where the Underground Railroad from the South to Ohio, and then on to Canada and freedom, operated frequently.

Christopher Graham was a Kentucky physician. He owned three slaves named George, Henry and Rubin. Beginning in 1837 Dr. Graham permitted

Henry and Rubin to be hired out to a man named Williams. Williams ran a "minstrel" show. Henry and Rubin performed as musicians in the show, which traveled widely. The show played frequently in Ohio, among many other places. In 1841, Henry, Rubin and George escaped from Kentucky to freedom in Canada. They were carried across the Ohio River from Kentucky to Ohio by the steamboat *Pike*. The *Pike* was owned in part by a man named Jacob Strader. Dr. Graham therefore sued Strader under a Kentucky statute that made a boat owner liable in damages if his boat assisted a slave to escape.

Strader asserted a novel defense. He argued that he was not liable because Henry and Rubin were already legally free at the time of their escape; specifically, Strader claimed that Henry and Rubin had been emancipated because their owner had previously allowed them to travel in Ohio, a free state. After many ups and downs through the Kentucky state court system, Dr. Graham won a judgment for $3,000 in damages against Strader. The Kentucky Court of Appeals followed the rule of *The Slave, Grace* case and held that once Henry and Rubin returned to Kentucky after their travels with the minstrel show in Ohio, their status as slaves reattached; thus they were still slaves in Kentucky, and Strader *was* liable for helping them to escape.[24]

Strader appealed to the U.S. Supreme Court. Strader's appeal faced an important hurdle at the outset: namely, the question of jurisdiction in the Supreme Court. Strader was attempting to appeal the decision of Kentucky's highest *state* court about a question of Kentucky *state* law—that is, the law providing that the owner of a boat used in a slave's escape could be liable for money damages. The U.S. Supreme Court is a *federal* court, and thus a part of the federal government of the United States. It is not a *state* court. Ordinarily, the Supreme Court has no jurisdiction to hear an appeal from a state court decision that is based on state law. The only bases for the Supreme Court to exercise jurisdiction over such an appeal are that either: a) the state court's decision conflicts with the U.S. Constitution or with federal law; or b) the state court's decision is based on a mistaken view of the U.S. Constitution or federal law.

In order to appeal to the Supreme Court, Strader therefore had to argue that the decision of Kentucky's state court against him conflicted with some *federal* law. So Strader argued that the decision conflicted with the Northwest Ordinance of 1787. That Ordinance provided, among many other things, that there would be no slavery in the old Northwest Territory. The old Northwest Territory included the area that later became the state of

Ohio. Strader therefore argued that the Northwest Ordinance—a *federal* law—had been violated by the Kentucky court's refusal to recognize that Rubin and Henry had been freed by virtue of their travels in Ohio as part of their minstrel band. Thus, said Strader, the U.S. Supreme Court did have jurisdiction over his appeal.

Chief Justice Taney wrote the Opinion of the Court in *Strader*. His *Strader* Opinion foreshadowed his much more famous Opinion in *Dred Scott* in at least two ways. First, and most obvious, his *Strader* Opinion came to a pro-slavery result. Second, and perhaps more interesting, Taney structured his *Strader* Opinion so that he could express a pro-slavery view on a question that was not really necessary to the resolution of the *Strader* case; this was a strategy that Taney repeated on a much grander scale in *Dred Scott*.

Specifically, Taney's *Strader* Opinion *ended* with the seemingly obvious point that the federal Northwest Ordinance of 1787 providing for the government of the old Northwest Territory had ceased to operate in Ohio long ago once Ohio adopted its own state Constitution and joined the Union as a free state. Thus, Taney pointed out, there was no genuine issue of federal law involved in the *Strader* case, and the Supreme Court therefore was required to dismiss Strader's appeal for lack of jurisdiction.

This *final* section of Taney's Opinion was fairly clearly correct and unremarkable. The Supreme Court did not in fact have jurisdiction over Strader's appeal because no question of federal law was truly presented. But *before* reaching that final point, Taney first went out of his way to state that the legal status of the slaves Rubin and Henry "depended altogether upon the laws of that State [Kentucky], and could not be influenced by the laws of Ohio."

This statement by Taney was clearly unnecessary. Since the Supreme Court had no jurisdiction over Strader's appeal, the Supreme Court had no business commenting on the merits of the case—that is, as to whether Ohio's laws forbidding slavery should be given effect in Kentucky's state courts. But Taney nevertheless did express a view on the merits, saying that Kentucky was not required to give effect to Ohio's anti-slavery laws. Taney's statement was a bit vague; but he certainly seemed to be saying that he agreed with the decision of the Kentucky Court below—that once Rubin and Henry returned from Ohio to Kentucky their status as slaves under Kentucky law reattached.

Thus, as a formal matter, Taney's Opinion of the Court in *Strader v. Graham* did not adopt the doctrine of "reattachment," because the Court found that it had no jurisdiction to decide the merits of the case. But Taney's Opinion nevertheless went out its way to hint very, very strongly that the doctrine of "reattachment" was indeed correct. (This position was also consistent with Taney's prior Opinion in the *Garronne* case.) In the years that followed, a number of southern state courts took this rather broad hint, and applied the principle of reattachment in order to deny freedom in similar cases.

—Taney's Private Views on Race—

Taney discussed his general views on race and slavery and their role in southern society more frankly in a few of his private letters. In a letter to Massachusetts clergyman Samuel Nott, Taney touched upon his feelings toward blacks. Negroes, he said were a "weak and credulous race." Their life in slavery was "usually cheerful and contented." Immediate emancipation would mean "absolute ruin to the negroes, as well as to the white population." In most cases, said Taney, "freedom has been a serious misfortune to the manumitted slave."[25]

In the fall of 1856 (while the Supreme Court was awaiting the second round of oral argument in *Dred Scott*), Taney wrote a letter to his nephew in which Taney talked about the upcoming presidential election. He expressed the grim view that, regardless of the results of the election, the North would inevitably dominate and oppress the South:

> The South is doomed to sink into a state of inferiority, and the power of the North will be exercised to gratify their cupidity and their evil passions, without the slightest regard to the principles of the Constitution . . . . I grieve over this condition of things, but it is my deliberate opinion that the South is doomed, and that nothing but a firm united action, nearly unanimous in every State, can check Northern insult and Northern aggression.[26]

In a private letter written to his son-in-law as the 1860 presidential election approached, Taney expressed an even bleaker view. Taney correctly predicted that the Republican Lincoln would win; according to Taney, this meant that "the knife of the assassin" was at the South's throat. Thus Taney saw even a moderate Republican like Lincoln (who had repeatedly pledged to make no effort to disturb slavery in the states where it already existed) as a mortal enemy of an embattled South. And Taney's letter further appeared to indicate that Taney feared that Lincoln's election would inspire slave rebellions and race war in the South—somewhat like the massive slave rebellion in Santo Domingo during the 1790s:[27]

> My thoughts have been constantly turned to the fearful state of things in which we have been living for months past. I am old enough to remember the horrors of Santo Domingo, and a few days will determine whether anything like it is to be visited upon any portion of our own Southern countrymen. I can only pray that it may be averted . . . .[28]

Taney was not the only southerner who remained mindful of the "horrors of Santo Domingo." Actual slave rebellions were extremely rare in the antebellum South. But the danger of slave insurrection was a common (and often luridly played) theme in southern politics and literature prior to the Civil War. Rumors of planned slave rebellions and occasional "panics" were common, and some white southerners lived in almost constant fear of "servile insurrection." For these reasons, as historian David Potter has written, the oft-invoked history of the Santo Domingo slave rebellion "lived as a nightmare in the mind of the South."[29]

Like many people from the slave-holding states, Taney further believed that—even in the absence of general emancipation—the mere presence of free Negroes in a slave state enhanced the risk of slave rebellions and racial violence. In the *Passenger Cases*[30] of 1849 Taney dissented from the Court's decision striking down certain state laws that placed a tax on immigrants coming into port. For Taney, it was of paramount importance that a state be able to protect its citizens from foreigners; and Taney's Dissenting Opinion made it clear that the foreigners he most feared were free blacks.

Thus Taney asserted (with apparent dread) that if the majority Opinion prevailed "then the emancipated slaves of the West Indies have at this hour the absolute right to reside, hire houses, and traffic and trade throughout the Southern States, in spite of every State law to the contrary; inevitably producing the most serious discontent and ultimately leading to the most painful consequences. . . . I cannot imagine any power . . . more dangerous and full of peril to the States."[31]

This, then, was the mind-set of the Chief Justice who wrote the Opinion of the Court in *Dred Scott*. Taney believed that Negroes, whether free or enslaved, were members of an inferior and degraded race that had no rights under the Constitution, and that Negroes were far better off as slaves. Taney further believed that the North was engaged in an aggressive campaign to oppress the South[32] and to deny the South its constitutionally protected right to maintain the institution of slavery; and Taney feared that this campaign and the ascension of the Republican Party might soon touch off massive slave rebellions and a horrible race war in the South.

These views all came to the fore as Taney looked at the seemingly simple case of Dred Scott, a powerless slave whose master Dr. Emerson had taken him to live for six years at remote military posts on free soil in Illinois and the Wisconsin Territory.

Notes

1. *See* Fehrenbacher, *Dred Scott*, 227, 577–78; and Finkelman, *Scott v. Sandford*, 220–26.

2. There is room for a good modern biography of Taney. Walker Lewis' *Without Fear or Favor* is not always factually reliable and evidences some bias. Carl Swisher's *Roger B. Taney* is the work of a great scholar and is very useful. However, the subjects of race and slavery are, of course, important to any study of Taney. Unfortunately, Swisher's book sometimes takes on the same benevolent, yet offensively paternalistic, racial attitudes that Swisher attributes to Taney. *See e.g.* Swisher, *Roger B. Taney*, 93: "Taney . . . had been brought up in the midst of slaves, with pickaninnies as playmates. . . . (He) recognized the restlessness among slaves caused by the presence of free negroes, and the difficulty of free negroes in maintaining themselves in a white man's society."

Bernard C. Steiner, *Life of Roger Taney* (Baltimore: Williams & Wilkins, 1922) is also useful, albeit dated. The very recent James F. Simon, *Lincoln and Chief Justice Taney* (New York: Simon & Schuster, 2006) is excellent and includes a fine brief biographical sketch of Taney at 5–44.

3. Simon, *Lincoln and Taney*, 13.

4 Austin Allen, *Origins of the Dred Scott Case: Jacksonian Jurisprudence and the Supreme Court 1837–1857* (Athens: U. of Ga. Press, 2006) is a scholarly and intelligent study of the Taney Court. It makes an effort to connect the *Dred Scott* decision with certain prior decisions made by the Taney Court in areas of the law that had little to do with slavery. Allen argues that the *Dred Scott* decision was, in a sense, compelled by those prior decisions because they made it untenable for the Taney Court to pursue what Allen terms a strategy of "evasion" in the *Dred Scott* case. (Professor Allen revisits these themes in Allen, "Rethinking Dred Scott: New Context for an Old Case," 82 *Chicago Kent L. Rev.* 1, 141 (2007)).

In Allen's terminology, a narrow Opinion (like Justice Nelson's original draft Opinion of the Court) that denied Dred Scott his freedom based on Missouri state law as set out in *Scott v. Emerson* without reaching the Missouri Compromise or Negro citizenship issues would have constituted an "evasion" by the Supreme Court of the larger questions in the case.

Allen argues that by virtue of its past decisions—especially *Swift v. Tyson*, 16 Pet.1 (1842) and *Pease v. Peck*, 18 How. 595 (1856)—the Taney Court was effectively foreclosed from adopting a narrow Opinion along the lines of Justice Nelson's original draft.

By way of background, *Swift v. Tyson*—much later overruled by the 1938 decision in *Erie Railroad v. Tomkins*, 304 US 64 (1938)—indicated that in a federal diversity case (like *Dred Scott v. Sanford*) involving a commercial dispute, a federal court should apply general federal common law principles, rather than follow the substantive law of the particular state involved in the case. *Pease v. Peck* held that in a diversity case where the federal court did apply state substantive law, the federal court was not always required to accept the most recent decision of that state's highest court as an authoritative statement of state law on the subject in question.

Allen argues that these two prior Taney Court decisions made it virtually impossible for the *Dred Scott* Court to adopt Justice Nelson's approach—that is the *Dred Scott* Court could not "evade" the Missouri Compromise issue by saying first that Dred Scott's status was controlled by Missouri state law, and second that Missouri state law as set forth in *Scott v. Emerson* provided that Scott remained a slave. According to Allen, *Swift v. Tyson* instead suggested that federal common law, rather than Missouri state law, might govern; and *Pease v. Peck*, suggested that if Missouri law still did apply, then the Supreme Court was nevertheless permitted to look beyond *Scott v. Emerson*. Allen, *Origins*, 133–59.

There are many important problems with Allen's thesis. First (and most obviously), in *Dred Scott* Justice Nelson did in fact follow the line of reasoning that Allen characterizes as a "strategy of evasion." Plainly, Nelson did not see either *Swift v. Tyson* or *Pease v. Peck* as presenting any significant obstacle to adopting a narrow Opinion in *Dred Scott*. And none of the other majority Justices in *Dred Scott* appeared to disagree with Justice Nelson on this score; they simply chose to go on and give additional reasons for denying Scott his freedom.

Indeed, as a historical matter, it appears that (as Professor Allen acknowledges) up until the Court's second internal conference about *Dred Scott*, five or six Justices were fully prepared to join in Nelson's narrow Opinion; but they were then persuaded by the political pressures of the day (including President-elect Buchanan's secret lobbying) to issue a broader Opinion. None of the majority Justices ever stated, or appeared to believe, that *Swift v. Tyson* or *Pease v. Peck* foreclosed a narrow Opinion like Justice Nelson's.

Second, as a legal matter, suppose that the *Dred Scott* majority did believe that *Swift v. Tyson* required the Supreme Court to fashion or follow a general federal common law rule (rather than Missouri law) in the *Dred Scott* case. In all likelihood, the Taney Court would then have found that the general federal rule should be the same as that utilized in *Scott v. Emerson*. More specifically, based on precedents like the *Garronne* case, *Strader v. Graham* and *The Slave, Grace*, the Taney Court would likely have found that the general federal rule was that once Scott returned to Missouri his status as a slave "reattached." Thus—even if *Swift v. Tyson* ruled out *Scott v. Emerson* as controlling precedent—there would still be no reason to go further and write a broad Opinion dealing with the Missouri Compromise issue.

Similarly, suppose the Court thought that *Pease v. Peck* applied to Dred Scott's case. *Pease v. Peck* merely *permitted* a federal court to look beyond the most recent decision of a state's highest court if the federal court wished; but *Pease v. Peck* did not *require* the federal court to do so. Thus, it was perfectly consistent with *Pease v. Peck* for the *Dred Scott* Court to accept *Scott v. Emerson* as a correct statement of Missouri law, and then deny Scott his freedom without going into larger issues such as the Missouri Compromise.

In short, the traditional view—that the *Dred Scott* decision striking down the Missouri Compromise was largely motivated by the desire of the Court to settle the national political controversy over slavery—still seems correct; and Professor Allen's thought-provoking thesis, linking *Dred Scott* to prior Taney Court decisions unrelated to slavery, is ultimately unpersuasive.

5. The best history of the Taney Court is Carl B. Swisher, *The Taney Period 1836–64* (Oliver Wendell Holmes Devise, History of the Supreme Court, Vol. V) (New York: MacMillan, 1974). David P. Currie, *The Constitution in the Supreme Court: The First Hundred Years 1789–1880* (Chicago: Chicago Press, 1985) covers a longer period, brings a more modern perspective and is also excellent.

6. However, not all of Taney's adversaries from the Bank War shared this forgiving perspective. Senator Daniel Webster—who appeared with Taney as co-counsel before the Supreme Court in the 1820s, and argued before the Court with Taney as Chief Justice in the 1830s and '40s—declared (with more than a hint of anti-Catholic prejudice): "Taney is smooth and plausible, but cunning and jesuitical, and as thorough going a party judge as ever got onto a bench of justice. He is a man who wears his robe for the purpose of protecting his friends and punishing his enemies." *See* Simon, *Lincoln and Taney*, 33–34.

7. Swisher, *Roger B. Taney*, 449–50.

8. *Rhode Island v. Massachusetts*, 12 Peters 657, 752 (1838).

9. *Luther v. Borden*, 48 U.S. 1 (1849)

10. *McCullough v. Maryland*, 17 U.S. 316 (1819).

11. *Congressional Globe*, 23 Cong., 1Sess., 59 (1833); Simon, *Lincoln and Taney*, 23.

12. *See* Simon, *Lincoln and Taney*, 24–25.

13. *Bank of the United States v. United States*, 2 Howard 711 (1844).

14. Fehrenbacher, *Dred Scott*, 319.

15. Some historians have theorized that the death of Taney's wife, Anne, and daughter Alice in 1855 helped to turn Taney into a harder and more bitter man. Taney may have felt some degree of responsibility for their death. His daughter Alice wanted to summer in Newport, Rhode Island, in 1855, but Taney insisted that Alice and Anne summer at Old Point Comfort in Virginia instead. Taney believed that Alice's desire to go to Newport reflected an "unfortunate feeling of inferiority in the South." Anne and Alice were killed that summer at Old Point by a yellow fever epidemic that also swept through the southern ports of New Orleans, Norfolk and Portsmouth. *See* Swisher, *Roger B. Taney*, 464–70.

16. Fehrenbacher, *Dred Scott*, 428.

17. It should be noted, however, that support for colonization did not necessarily imply liberality toward African Americans. To the contrary, some slaveholders supported colonization efforts precisely because they feared that the presence of free Negroes constituted a threat to white slave-holding society.

For example, Taney's brother-in-law Francis Scott Key was a prominent member of the American Colonization Society. He also served as the prosecutor in a celebrated Washington, D.C., case brought against one Reuben Crandall. Crandall was charged with conspiring to incite slave insurrections because he possessed abolitionist literature.

In his summation, Key forcefully (and at great length) contrasted the goals of abolitionists with those of the Colonization Society. Key conceded that slavery was an evil. However, Key asserted that the very presence of "colored" people in America was a far greater evil. Accordingly, Key argued that the colonization of freed slaves was sensible, but that emancipation without colonization was a dangerous program that could lead to slave rebellions and racial violence. *See* Paul Finkelman, *Slavery in the Courtroom* (Washington, D.C.: Library of Congress, 1985), 167–70.

Similarly, in the wake of Virginia's 1831 Nat Turner slave uprising, Taney's younger brother Dr. Octavius Taney (a Maryland state senator) proposed legislation calling for the removal of all free blacks from Maryland and from the United States. *See* Swisher, *Roger B. Taney*, 147–49.

18. Simon, *Lincoln and Taney*, 10–11.

19. Swisher, *Roger B. Taney*, 97–98.

20. Taney wrote:

> The African race in the United States even when free, are everywhere a degraded class, and exercise no political influence. The privilege they are allowed to enjoy are accorded to them as a matter of kindness and benevolence, rather than of right. They are the only class of persons who can be held as mere property, as slaves . . . . They were never regarded as a constituent portion of the sovereignty of any State . . . . They were not looked upon as citizens by the contracting parties who

> formed the Constitution. They were evidently not supposed to be included by the term citizens and were not intended to be embraced in any of the provisions of that Constitution, but those which point to them in terms not to be mistaken.

Fehrenbacher, *Dred Scott*, 70; Swisher, *Roger B. Taney*, 154.

21. *Prigg v. Pennsylvania*, 16 Peters 539 (1842).

22. *Groves v. Slaughter*, 15 Peters 449 (1841).

23. *United States v. The Garronne*, 11 Pet. 73 (1837).

24. *Strader v. Graham*, 44 Ky. 173 (1844).

25. Swisher, *Roger B. Taney*, 517–18; Simon, *Lincoln and Taney*, 130–31.

26. Swisher, *Roger B. Taney*, 492–93.

27. During the 1790s, the slave and free black population of Santo Domingo (under the leadership of Toussaint L'Ouverture, among others) rose up and overthrew their colonial masters. In the process, however, horrible atrocities—such as murdering white men by burying them alive or sawing them in two—were committed, and virtually all the island's white people were killed or driven off. These were the kind of "horrors" that Taney believed might follow Lincoln's election.

28. *See* Fehrenbacher, *Dred Scott*, 553.

29. David M. Potter, *The Impending Crisis: 1848–1861* (New York: Harper & Row, 1976), 452–54.

30. *Smith v. Turner*, 48 U.S. 283 (1849)

31. *Smith v. Turner*, 48 U.S. 283, 430 (Taney, dissenting).

32. Taney's sectional loyalty became increasingly evident during the Civil War. *See* Simon, *Lincoln and Taney*, 177–99, 220–32, 245–46, 263–65. Taney did not resign his post and join the Confederacy as many of his colleagues did, but he privately sympathized with the Confederacy. He expressed pride that one of his sons-in-law served in the Confederate Army, and Taney once told a young Confederate Army recruit that the recruit would perform a patriotic service like that rendered by the recruit's grandfather during the American Revolution.

More important, Taney opposed virtually every Union war measure that came before him while on the Court. Sometimes Taney's opposition could at least arguably be attributed to genuine principle; in *Ex Parte Merryman*, 17 Fed.Cas.144 (CC Md. 1861), for example, Taney proclaimed that only Congress—and not President Lincoln—could suspend *habeas corpus* during time of war.

But Taney's true purpose—to obstruct the Union war effort—became transparent in other cases. Thus for four years (until Taney's death) Taney personally prevented *any* person from being tried in Maryland for treason or sabotage.

Taney's presence was required for such a trial because of his role as a circuit court judge. But Taney always fell "ill" just in time to prevent any such trial from actually going forward. (This included the trial of John Merryman himself; Merryman was charged with blowing up railroad lines in order to prevent the movement of Union troops through Maryland.)

LAW

Chapter 9
Taney's Opinion of the Court: An Overview

Chief Justice Taney's Opinion of the Court in *Dred Scott* is a long, rambling and sometimes repetitious essay. It roams far and wide in search of legal and historical precedent. At times it is sharp and insightful; at other times its logic is rather obviously muddled. Even worse, Taney's recitation of history and his treatment of certain legal precedents are often blatantly dishonest.

In the immediate aftermath of *Dred Scott*, Republican critics of the decision attempted to argue that much of Taney's Opinion consisted of non-binding dicta and emphasized that not all the concurring Justices adopted all of Taney's reasoning. ("Dicta" or "obiter dicta" is a disparaging legal term. It expresses the concept that some comments made in the course of a judicial opinion are not essential to the holding in the case, and therefore constitute mere words—or "dicta"—that are not binding as law in future cases.) The evident political purpose of this approach was to allow Republicans to continue to adhere to their central goal—to stop the expansion of slavery into the U.S. territories—without appearing to directly defy the Supreme Court's pronouncement that this goal was unconstitutional.

For many years thereafter, historians and legal scholars concentrated on the same two themes. Until quite recently, much of the scholarly commentary about *Dred Scott* focused on the question how much of the *Dred Scott* decision was mere dicta, and scholars devoted a great deal of attention to a kind of judicial "head-counting" in which they analyzed and sometimes debated the question which Justices had joined in which aspects of Taney's Opinion.

For present purposes, however, those issues are largely besides the point. Slavery was, of course, abolished at the close of the Civil War. Thus it now matters very little whether the points of law made about slavery in *Dred Scott* were binding law, or were instead dicta.[1]

The more interesting and important questions today are: What did Taney's Opinion of the Court decide, and why?

In essence, the Opinion makes five central points, as follows:

First) **Jurisdictional Issue Preserved**—As a technical matter of the rules of pleading, the question whether the federal courts had jurisdiction over the Scott lawsuit was indeed properly presented for review by the Supreme Court.

Second) **No Negro Citizenship**—Neither a slave nor a free black man could be a citizen of the United States entitled to bring a lawsuit in federal court; accordingly, the Scott lawsuit should have been dismissed by the federal court below for lack of jurisdiction.

Third) **Slavery in the Territories Protected by the Constitution**—The provisions of the Missouri Compromise (enacted by Congress in 1820) that barred slavery in the western territories of the United States north of Missouri were unconstitutional and void; Congress had no power to bar slavery from any territory or state.

Fourth) **Missouri Law Controls Case**—Dred Scott's status was governed by the law of Missouri—where he lived and brought suit—and not by Illinois law or Wisconsin's territorial law. Under Missouri law, Scott remained a slave.

Fifth) **Prior Missouri Decision Controls Case**—Scott's federal lawsuit was an improper attempt to re-litigate the prior decision of Missouri's highest state court, which had already finally determined that Scott was not emancipated by virtue of having lived in Illinois and the Wisconsin Territory. Accordingly, the federal courts should never have entertained Scott's lawsuit in the first place.

The relative amount of space devoted by Taney to each of these five points is surprisingly uneven, and this uneven treatment to some degree betrays the political nature of Taney's true concerns. The overwhelming bulk of Taney's Opinion was devoted to the second and third main points listed above—that is, the politically charged declarations that black people could not be United States citizens and that the Missouri Compromise was unconstitutional. The fourth and fifth points listed above—that Missouri's law governed over that of Illinois or Wisconsin, and that the verdict in Scott's prior state court case could not be overturned by a federal court—were each more than sufficient to decide the entire *Dred Scott* case. But they largely involved rather dry matters of law that had only limited political impact. And so Taney devoted only a few paragraphs out of his otherwise laboriously long Opinion to those points.

In the course of his Opinion Taney made two other subsidiary points, seemingly almost in passing, that were also intensely controversial. First, Taney opined that—like the U.S. Congress—a territorial legislature was also powerless to prohibit slavery in a U.S. territory prior to the territory becoming a state.

Second, Taney intimated—but did not clearly state—that the Fifth Amendment's guarantee that no person be deprived of his property without due process of law might operate to invalidate any law that restricted a slaveholder's right to bring his slaves to live with him on free soil. This point was stated in a vague and somewhat confusing manner. But many people—including both supporters and critics of the *Dred Scott* decision—understood Taney's Opinion to at least suggest that a slaveholder would retain ownership of his slave despite bringing the slave to live in a free territory, or even in a free *state*. This suggestion was viewed with considerable alarm by Republican critics of *Dred Scott* (including Lincoln), and it was often woven into Republican accusations that there was a vast conspiracy afoot to nationalize slavery.

Each of Taney's points is summarized and analyzed directly below. In the end, what emerges is an Opinion that attempted to decide virtually every issue in the national debate over slavery in the pre–Civil War era in favor of slavery, without regard to whether those issues were genuinely relevant to the case of *Dred Scott v. Sandford.*

Notes

1. Indeed—political considerations aside—the distinction drawn between holding and dicta in *Dred Scott* was of limited significance even at the time. Admittedly, classical legal training teaches that when a lawyer is confronted by a court decision that makes points of law that are bad for a lawyer's client, the lawyer should try (if possible) to argue that those points were mere dicta—that, is a discussion in passing of legal issues not essential to the court's decision—and thus not binding on other courts later confronted with the same question.

But that classical strategy has only limited value when the decision at issue is made by the Supreme Court, the highest court in the land. When the Supreme Court makes a considered pronouncement about an important point of law, it will usually be followed in all subsequent cases by all lower courts—whether or not the point might technically be regarded as dicta. That is so because everyone expects that (absent some significant change in the make-up of the Supreme Court) should the same issue arise again, the Supreme Court would rule the same way.

Thus, the Supreme Court's declaration in *Dred Scott* that the Missouri Compromise was unconstitutional may arguably have been "dicta" as a formal matter. But six Justices concurred on that vitally important and highly controversial point after exceptionally thorough consideration. Thus after *Dred Scott* there was little doubt that as a legal matter the Missouri Compromise was indeed void. *See* Edgar S. Corwin, "The Dred Scott Decision in Light of Contemporary Legal Doctrines" (1911) reprinted in S. Kutler, Ed., *The Dred Scott Decision: Law or Politics?*, 123–38, at 125.

Chapter 10
Can a Black Man Be a True American?—Taney on Negro Citizenship

John Sanford's plea in abatement—questioning whether Missouri's federal circuit court could properly entertain Dred Scott's case pursuant to the federal court's diversity jurisdiction—presented a seemingly dry, even dull, legal issue. But, as detailed below, in Roger Taney's hands this dull legal issue of federal court jurisdiction was transformed into one that touched upon fundamental questions of race, justice and the nature of American society. For Taney, the *Dred Scott* case ultimately presented the question: Can a black man be a true American?

(A) Preservation of the Jurisdictional Issue

At the outset of the Opinion of the Court, Taney addressed the question whether the defendant John Sanford had waived—that is, given up—his right to challenge the issue of jurisdiction before the Supreme Court. The jurisdictional issue was whether Dred Scott truly was a "citizen" entitled to bring a lawsuit in federal court on the ground of diversity of citizenship.

Scott's lawyers had argued that when Sanford contested Scott's lawsuit on the merits at trial without bringing up the jurisdictional issue, Sanford had waived the right to raise the jurisdictional issue on appeal. Sanford's lawyers in response had argued that the jurisdictional issue had been raised by Sanford's pre-trial plea in abatement and therefore could now properly be reviewed by the Supreme Court.

Taney found that it was proper for the Supreme Court to rule on the jurisdictional question. A federal court, Taney explained, is a court of limited jurisdiction. It is therefore up to the plaintiff in every case to show that the federal court has jurisdiction over that case. If the federal court lacks jurisdiction, any judgment it renders is a nullity. Accordingly, if the federal circuit court did not in fact have jurisdiction over *Dred Scott v. Sanford*, Taney reasoned, then the Supreme Court could set aside the judgment reached by the circuit court below after trial as null and void, and then return the case to the circuit court with the instruction to dismiss Scott's lawsuit outright for lack of jurisdiction. As long there was sufficient material in the record to decide the question of jurisdiction, said Taney, then the Supreme Court was empowered to examine that question. And there was sufficient evidence in the *Dred Scott* case to make that determination, said Taney, because of the pre-trial plea in abatement[1].

Taney's reasoning seems sound as far as it goes—the Court could properly examine the issue of Negro citizenship *if it wanted to*. But the important question that Taney's Opinion logically leads up to, but does not even attempt to answer, is this: Why did the Supreme Court *want* to look at the issue of Negro citizenship?

After all, Taney's Opinion gave at least two other completely independent and completely sufficient bases for the Supreme Court to rule for Sanford and against Scott's claim for freedom. Specifically, the Supreme Court could have found for Sanford without ever touching the question of Negro citizenship by holding either: a) that Missouri law governed and provided that Scott was still a slave; *or* b) that Scott's claim had already been rejected in *Scott v. Emerson* and could not be litigated again.

Plainly then, the Supreme Court did not *need* to look at or decide the issue of Negro citizenship in order to resolve the *Dred Scott* case. Instead, the Court could have much more easily affirmed the decision of the circuit court below for essentially the same narrow reasons relied upon by the circuit court. In point of fact, that was the approach that Associate Justice Nelson had taken in his original proposed draft Opinion of the Court (which later served as the basis for Nelson's concurring Opinion).

Indeed, by reaching out to also decide that the federal courts had no jurisdiction over the *Dred Scott* case, Taney unintentionally undercut all the other points made in his own Opinion; for Taney's critics could and did argue with some logic that since the Supreme Court had found that it lacked jurisdiction, all the rest of the Court's findings were mere non-binding dicta. (For example, Justice McLean's dissent declared: "Nothing has been said by them (the majority) which has not a direct bearing on the jurisdiction of the court, against which they decided, that can be considered as authority. I shall certainly not regard it as such. The question of jurisdiction . . . was decided by them authoritatively, but nothing beyond that question."[2])

Perhaps Taney was concerned that an Opinion that did not discuss the issue of Negro citizenship might later be misread as an implicit approval of Negro citizenship. But, as Taney must have known, such a concern could have easily been overcome by simply adding a few cautionary sentences in the Opinion to the effect that the Court was not expressing any view either way on that issue.

Notably, even though six other Justices voted with Taney to affirm the verdict for Sanford, only two others—Justices Wayne and Daniel—concurred in Taney's conclusion that even free Negroes could not be citizens. So the question presents itself again with even greater force: *Why* did Taney want so badly to discuss the issue of Negro citizenship in the *Dred Scott* case, when that issue was plainly not the focus of the Circuit Court proceedings below, and was not necessary in order for the Supreme Court to decide the case? Taney never directly answered this question. But the answer becomes apparent as one analyzes the rest of his Opinion of the Court.

(B) Negro Citizenship and the Jurisdiction of the Court

—Taney's Fear of Negro Equality—

With regard to Negro citizenship, the legal question actually presented by the *Dred Scott* case as a matter of logic ran along these lines. The Constitution provides that federal courts shall have jurisdiction over cases between "citizens of different States." This is the constitutional basis for what is called federal diversity jurisdiction. Scott claimed that he was a citizen of

Missouri, that Sanford was a citizen of New York, and that the federal courts therefore had diversity jurisdiction over Scott's case against Sanford. If Scott were still a slave, obviously he was not a citizen of Missouri. But if, as Scott contended, Scott were a free Negro, was Scott a "citizen" of Missouri entitled to bring a federal diversity lawsuit against Sanford?

The federal circuit court judge below, Judge Wells, had said yes. Specifically, Judge Wells ruled on Sanford's pre-trial plea in abatement by holding that a free Negro was a citizen of Missouri, at least for the purpose of bringing a federal lawsuit.

There was more than a little logical force to the circuit court's holding. After all, there was no doubt that Scott could bring a suit for freedom in Missouri *state* court against a fellow resident of Missouri under Missouri law; that was how Scott had previously sued Mrs. Emerson. Thus it could well be argued that in a case where the defendant happened to be a non-Missouri citizen (like John Sanford), Scott should be allowed to bring his claim in federal court as a diversity case for the very same common-sense reason that any plaintiff is permitted to bring a federal diversity action against a citizen of another state—namely, that a federal court is less likely to unfairly favor one state's citizens over another's. (Indeed, as Scott's lawyer, Montgomery Blair, pointed out, Taney himself had once participated in a federal diversity suit that had proceeded on the theory that a free Negro was a citizen for diversity jurisdiction purposes; specifically, back in 1829, when Taney was still a practicing lawyer, in *LeGrand v. Darnall*,[3] Taney had represented a white plaintiff who sued a black man in federal court on the basis of diversity of citizenship.)

Whether Circuit Judge Wells' ruling on the diversity jurisdiction was correct or not, it is important to note how narrow the issue he saw was. The question that Wells saw was this: Is a free Negro a "citizen" *for the purposes of federal court diversity of citizenship jurisdiction*? Wells did *not* attempt to either ask or answer questions about whether a free Negro was a citizen for other purposes. Thus, for example, Wells did not ask: Is a free Negro a "citizen" for the purpose of voting, or paying taxes, or serving on a jury? (The distinctions between these different kinds of citizenship can be important; for example, corporations are recognized as "citizens" for the purpose of federal diversity jurisdiction, but corporations are not "citizens" who are entitled to vote in elections.)

Chief Justice Taney saw the jurisdiction issue and the issue of Negro citizenship much, much more broadly than did the circuit court below. Indeed, as soon as Taney formulated the issue at the outset of his Opinion, the reader could see where Taney was headed and why it was that Taney thought it appropriate to reach out to decide the question of jurisdiction.

Specifically, Taney formulated the question presented as follows:

> The question is simply this. Can a negro, whose ancestors were imported into this county, and sold as slaves, become a member of the political community formed and brought into existence by the Constitution of the United States, and as such *entitled to all the rights and privileges and immunities guaranteed by that instrument to the citizen*? One of which rights is the privilege is suing in a court of the United States in the cases specified in the Constitution.
>
> It will be observed, that the plea [in abatement] applies to that class of persons only whose ancestors were negroes of the African race and imported into this country, and sold and held as slaves. The only matter in issue before the court, therefore, is whether the descendants of such slaves, when they shall be emancipated, or who are born of parents who became free before their birth, are citizens of a state, in the sense in which the word citizen is used in the Constitution of the United States.[4] (Emphasis added.)

In this brief melodramatic passage Taney radically redefined the legal question presented, and he did so in a way that revealed his true concerns. The redefinition is obvious. The question for Taney was not the dry and narrow legal question: Should a free Negro be regarded as a citizen for purposes of federal court diversity jurisdiction? The question for Taney was a much grander one: Can any free Negro ever be a member of the "political community formed and brought into existence" by the United States Constitution? In other words, Taney saw the question as: Can a black man be a true American?

Taney's real concerns were also revealed in this passage. Taney did not express any concern that the federal courts would somehow be flooded by diversity lawsuits involving free Negroes. In deciding the *Dred Scott* case, Taney apparently gave little or no thought to practical concerns about the scope of federal court diversity jurisdiction. Taney's eye was on a much bigger prize. Taney was concerned that if the Court held that a free Negro could be a "citizen" for purposes of diversity jurisdiction, then it might be argued that free Negroes were also entitled to all the other rights guaranteed to white citizens by the U.S. Constitution.

In a word, Taney was worried about the possibility of Negro equality. He was not content that Negro slaves would remain in bondage. Taney also wanted to make sure that free Negroes would never come close to attaining citizenship or equality, no matter what the northern states might do. (Thus it can be said that in one sense Taney in 1857 anticipated and dreaded the demands for true equality for African Americans that were raised a century later by the Civil Rights movement.)

In particular, Taney was worried about the "privileges and immunities" clause of the Constitution. That clause provides: "The Citizens of each State shall be entitled to all privileges and immunities of Citizens in the several States." Taney was concerned that if a free Negro could be regarded as a "citizen" for purposes of federal court diversity jurisdiction, then it might further be argued that a free Negro who was regarded as a "citizen" by the Negro's home state in the North would also be entitled to *all* the privileges and immunities enjoyed by that northern state's white citizens, even when that free Negro was visiting the South.

This idea was anathema to Taney. He could not bear the thought that there might be a class, however small, of free Negroes who were entitled to be treated as true citizens in the South. Moreover, Taney believed that the presence of truly free Negroes in the South would inevitably break down the southern system of slavery and pervasive legal racial discrimination, and would probably lead to racial violence. Thus Taney stated in no uncertain terms that the Constitution could not possibly mean that free Negroes could ever be "citizens," for the South would never have accepted the Constitution on those terms:

> [I]t cannot be believed that the large slaveholding States regarded them [Negroes] as included in the word citizens or would have consented to a Constitution which might compel them to receive them in that character from another State. For if they were so received, and entitled to the privileges and immunities of citizens, it would exempt them from the special laws and from the police regulations which they [the slave States] considered necessary for their own safety. It would give to persons of the negro race, who were recognized as citizens of any one State in the Union, the right to enter every other State whenever they pleased, singly or in companies, without pass or passport, and without obstruction, to sojourn there as long as they pleased, to go where they pleased at every hour of the day or night without molestation . . . and it would give them the full liberty of speech in public and in private upon all subjects upon which its own citizens might speak; to hold public meetings upon political affairs, and to keep and carry arms whenever they went. And all of this would be done

> in the face of the subject race of the same color, both free and slaves, and inevitably producing discontent and insubordination among them, and endangering the peace and safety of the State.[5]

—Taney Employs Faulty History in Order to Deny Negro Citizenship—

Fearful of these potential consequences of Negro citizenship, Taney set himself to the task of demonstrating that the Framers of the Constitution never intended that Negroes could be regarded as "citizens." Taney did so by putting together a strange brew: one part sound logic, one part faulty reasoning, one part historical truth and one part historical fiction.

The central logical flaw that runs through much of Taney's discussion of citizenship is his refusal to distinguish between slaves and free Negroes. The central twin historical falsehoods that run through that same discussion are a) Taney's sweeping overstatements of the degree to which the Founding Fathers embraced slavery, and b) Taney's categorical (and obviously false) denials of the fact that many of the Founders were deeply troubled by the existence of slavery in the land of the free, and hoped that American slavery would one day come to an end.

Taney's analysis began with the assertion that the terms "citizens" and "people of the United States" were synonymous and meant the same thing. The question then, as Taney redefined it yet again, was whether Negroes were a part of the people of the United States who had declared independence from Great Britain in 1776, established the Constitution in 1789, and who were thereafter governed by their elected representatives. Accordingly, Taney (serving as his own historian) summarized "the state of public opinion in relation to that unfortunate race which prevailed in the civilized and enlightened portions of the world at the time of the Declaration of Independence, and when the Constitution . . . was framed and adopted."[6]

According to Taney, during the age of the American Revolution, Negroes had:

> For more than a century before been regarded as beings of an inferior order, and altogether unfit to associate with the white race, either in social or political relations; and so far inferior, that *they had no rights* which the white man was bound to respect; and that the negro might justly and lawfully be reduced to slavery for his benefit. He was bought and sold, and treated as an ordinary article of merchandise and traffic, whenever a profit

> could be made by it. *This opinion was at that time fixed and universal in the civilized portion of the white race.* It was regarded as an axiom in morals as well as in politics, which no one thought of disputing, or supposed to be open to dispute; and men in every grade and position of society daily and habitually acted upon it in their private pursuits, as well as in matters of public concern, without doubting for a moment the correctness of this opinion.[7] (Emphasis added.)

The men who wrote the Declaration of Independence and proclaimed that all men are created equal, said Taney, never supposed for a moment that Negroes were included in that proclamation; for if Negroes were men, then the conduct of the Founding Fathers "would have been utterly and flagrantly inconsistent with the principles they asserted . . . they would have received and deserved universal rebuke and reprobation."[8] Instead, Taney argued, the men who wrote the Declaration knew that no one would understand the Declaration to embrace "the negro race which, by common consent, had been excluded from civilized Governments and the family of nations, and doomed to slavery."[9] (This argument incidentally showed that Chief Justice Taney had personally changed a great deal since he, as a young lawyer, had defended abolitionist minister Francis Gruber and passionately declared that only when slavery had come to an end could lovers of freedom look at the Declaration of Independence "without blush.")

Similarly, said Taney, the Framers of the Constitution did not regard Negroes as forming any part of the people of the United States or as citizens. (Here, Taney reiterated the same view he had expressed back in 1832 as Attorney General when reviewing North Carolina's Negro Seaman law.) The Framers' view, said Taney, was demonstrated by the Constitutional provisions a) permitting the African slave trade to continue through the year 1808, and b) requiring the return of fugitive slaves.[10] Furthermore, Taney pointed out that there were many instances of state and federal legislation enacted both shortly before and after the adoption of the Constitution that discriminated against Negroes, even in states that had abolished slavery. For example, there were state laws that prohibited white people to marry or have sex with Negroes, or to provide schooling to Negroes. Other state laws barred Negroes from serving in the state militia. Taney argued that such legislation further demonstrated the "fixed and universal" view of the Founding Fathers' era that Negroes were not citizens.[11]

Taney's arguments from history had both some obvious strengths and some obvious flaws. His central point is painful, but undoubtedly true—the generation that made the Revolution and the Constitution did indeed tolerate Negro slavery on a massive scale in the South and further discriminated against free Negroes in both the North and South. It thus made good sense to question, as Taney did, whether the Framers regarded Negroes as "citizens" in any sense.

But Taney's historical claims were plainly overstated and proved too much. Admittedly, the fact that the Constitution tolerated slavery does prove that the Framers did not regard Negro *slaves* as citizens. Sadly, it also proves that the Revolutionary generation was pervaded by terrible racism. But the real question presented by the jurisdictional issue in *Dred Scott* was not about Negro *slaves*. The real question was whether *free* Negroes could be regarded as "citizens" for purposes of federal court jurisdiction based on diversity of citizenship: Did the Framers envision that *free* Negroes were "citizens" for this purpose?

In point of fact, as Justice Curtis pointed out in dissent in *Dred Scott,*[12] at the time of the adoption of the Constitution free Negroes *were* regarded as citizens in at least four or five states and were permitted to vote in those states. True, even in those states free blacks were subject to extensive legal discrimination; so it is perhaps more accurate to say that free blacks were treated as second-class citizens there. Nevertheless, there was solid historical evidence to support the proposition that at the time of the adoption of the Constitution there was a small but recognizable class of free blacks who were regarded as citizens, at least in their own states. Thus there was, at the very least, an open and debatable question as to whether the Framers intended that free Negroes might be "citizens" for purposes of federal court diversity jurisdiction—to the extent that the Framers ever consciously considered that question at all.

Taney avoided grappling with this genuinely debatable historical question. For Taney, the undoubted fact that the Framers accepted Negro slavery was sufficient in itself to prove that the Framers did not intend that *any* class of Negroes—free or slave—could be entitled to any form of citizenship. In essence, Taney got the answer he wanted by largely ignoring the real question presented.

—The Framers and Slavery: A More Balanced View—

On a broader level, Taney's history of the Revolutionary era was profoundly dishonest. Taney repeatedly and categorically asserted that the "fixed and universal" view of the generation who produced the Declaration of Independence and the Constitution was in favor of African slavery. Taney further asserted that the progress of abolition in the North after the Revolution (and the ban on slavery in the Old Northwest enacted in the Northwest Ordinance of 1787) were solely the result of economic considerations, and had nothing to do with moral opposition to slavery.[13]

These assertions were false, and Taney had to know it. Many—indeed most—of the Founding Fathers were troubled by the institution of slavery and looked forward to its eventual demise. The attitudes of the Revolutionary generation toward slavery is a complex and broad field of historical study in itself.[14] But two leading examples—those of Thomas Jefferson and James Madison—should be sufficient to make the general point that Taney's version of American history was plainly wrong.

Jefferson was the principal author of the Declaration of Independence and America's third president. America's fourth president, James Madison, is often regarded as the Father of the Constitution because he was, more than any other man, the leading actor at the Constitutional Convention of 1787. Jefferson and Madison can thus fairly serve as representative of the men who made the Declaration and the Constitution.

It was Thomas Jefferson who wrote:

> The whole commerce between master and slave is a perpetual exercise of the most . . . unremitting despotism on the one part, and degrading submissions on the other. . . . Nothing is more certainly written in the book of fate than that these people are to be free. Indeed I tremble for my country when I reflect that God is just, [and] that his justice cannot sleep forever . . . .[15]

It was Jefferson who in his first draft of the Declaration of Independence asserted that one of the great injustices done to America by the King of England was the imposition of African slavery on the American colonies: "He [the King] has waged cruel war against human nature itself, violating its most sacred rights of life and liberty in the persons of a distant people who never offended him . . . ."[16] Similarly, it was Jefferson who proposed a plan in his *Notes on the State of Virginia* whereby all slaves born after the year 1800 would eventually become free. In 1784 Jefferson proposed Congressional legislation prohibiting slavery in all the western territories; that proposal failed by a single vote, but it became the basis for the similar Northwest Ordinance of 1787.

Jefferson thus saw slavery as a terrible wrong. For him the great difficulty was finding a practical way to manage emancipation, which Jefferson believed would require compensation for slave owners and resettlement of the freed slaves abroad. Jefferson foresaw a race war if the freed slaves remained in America. Jefferson therefore believed that slavery was both unjust and dangerous, but that ending slavery was perhaps even more dangerous: "We have the wolf by the ears; and we can neither hold him, nor safely let him go. Justice is in one scale, and self-preservation in the other."[17]

In retrospect, Jefferson can fairly be charged with hypocrisy. He verbally condemned slavery, but he *did* almost nothing (including freeing his own slaves) to end it. (Modern science has further shown that Jefferson was also a hypocrite in a very different sense; although Jefferson took the view that Negroes were inferior and publicly denounced the mixture of the races, modern DNA testing seems to show that Jefferson fathered a number of children with his slave Sally Hemings.) Nevertheless, it is clear that Jefferson, the author of the Declaration of Independence, saw American slavery as an evil institution that should be brought to an end—albeit in a very distant future.

Like Jefferson, James Madison was a Virginian and slaveholder. And, like Jefferson, Madison saw slavery as an evil; at the Constitutional Convention in 1787 Madison termed slavery "the most oppressive dominion ever exercised by man over man." Similarly, at the Constitutional Convention Madison argued at length that the importation of slaves from Africa should be banned at the earliest possible date, and Madison opposed deriving tax revenues from the importation of slaves as dishonorable to the national character. When he lost on these points, Madison did successfully argue that the Constitution should at least not refer to the slave trade directly by name because he "thought it wrong to admit in the Constitution the idea that there could be property in man."[18]

But Madison never thought that the time was right to *do* much about slavery. Thus, for example, in 1790 the Pennsylvania Abolition Society—with the endorsement of the great Revolutionary leader Benjamin Franklin—presented an anti-slavery petition to the first Congress. In response, Madison wrote that slavery "is a Moral and political Evil, and . . . .Whoever brings forward in the Respective States, some General, rational and liberal plan, for the Gradual Emancipation of Slaves will deserve well of his Country—yet I think it was very improper, at this time, to introduce it in Congress." [19]

Obviously, the Revolutionary generation—in which Jefferson and Madison played such important parts—did not abolish slavery in the South; to the contrary, as Taney pointed out at great length in *Dred Scott*, slavery was to a degree affirmatively protected by the Constitution. But as the examples of Jefferson, Madison and Franklin (and those of Washington, Adams, Hamilton and Jay, among many others) prove, Taney's broad and categorical assertions that the men who made the Revolution all supported slavery and did so without question were blatantly false. Apparently, Taney felt that in order to defend slavery and the southern way of life in 1857 in *Dred Scott* it was necessary to rewrite and falsify the history of the era of the American Revolution and Constitution.[20]

C) Excluding Negroes from Citizenship and the American People

Taney concluded that the entire history of the era of the Founding Fathers, together with discriminatory legislation passed both before and after the adoption of the Constitution, made it clear that the Framers did not intend that Negroes—free or slave—should be regarded as citizens for purposes of federal court diversity jurisdiction, or for any other purpose.[21]

Accordingly, Taney held (with an accompanying annoyingly overblown assertion of certainty) that Negroes were not and could not be "citizens" or part of the American "people," that the federal circuit court therefore lacked jurisdiction over Dred Scott's diversity lawsuit, and that the circuit court should have dismissed that suit outright prior to trial:

> [I]f anything in relation to the construction of the Constitution can be regarded as settled, it is that which we now give the word "citizen" and the word "people."
>
> And upon a full and careful consideration of the subject, the Court is of the opinion that, upon the facts stated in the plea in abatement, Dred Scott was not a citizen of Missouri within the meaning of the Constitution,

and not entitled as such to sue in its courts; and, consequently, that the Circuit Court had no jurisdiction of the case . . . .[22]

Notes

1. *Dred Scott*, 60 U.S. at 401. In the interest of brevity, references hereinafter to "*DS*" are to the *Dred Scott* decision.
2. *DS* at 549–50 (McLean, J., dissenting).
3. *LeGrand v. Darnall*, 29 U.S. 664 (1829).
4. *DS* at 403.
5. *DS* at 416–17.
6. *DS* at 410.
7. *DS* at 407.
8. *DS* at 410.
9. *DS* at 410.
10. *DS* at 411.
11. *DS* at 407.
12. *DS* at 573.
13. *DS* at 412.
14. See, for example David Brion Davis, *The Problem of Slavery in the Age of Revolution* (New York: Oxford U. Press, 1999); Duncan J. Macleod, *Slavery, Race and the American Revolution* (Cambridge: Cambridge U. Press, 1974); Paul Finkelman, *Slavery and the Founders: Race and Liberty in the Age of Jefferson* (Armonk: M.E. Sharpe, 1996). Chapter Three ("The Silence") in Joseph J. Ellis, *Founding Brothers: The Revolutionary Generation* (New York: Alfred A. Knopf, 2001) is a wonderfully written short treatment of the subject.
15. Thomas Jefferson, *Notes on the State of Virginia* in *The Life and Selected Writings of Thomas Jefferson*, Adrienne Koch and William Peden, Eds. (New York: Modern Library, 1944).
16. *The Papers of Thomas Jefferson*, Julian P. Boyd, et al. Eds, Vol. 1, 426 *et seq.* (Princeton: Princeton U. Press, 1950).
17. Letter from Jefferson to John Holmes, April 22, 1820, printed in Vol. 12, 159 *The Writings of Thomas Jefferson*, Paul Leicester Ford, Ed. (New York and London: G.P. Putnam & Sons, 1905).
18. *The Life and Writings of Thomas Jefferson*, 279.
19. Thus, for example, the Fugitive Slave Clause of the Constitution refers to slaves not as "slaves," but as persons "held to service or labor."

Paul Finkelman, "The Founders and Slavery: Little Ventured, Little Gained," 13 *Yale Journal of Law and the Humanities* 413, 425–26 (2001), details the discussions at the Constitutional Convention about the conscious decision to avoid the direct use of the words "slave" and "slavery."

20. Not all of slavery's defenders felt, as Taney did, that they had to falsely claim that the Founders favored slavery. Alexander Stephens, the vice president of the Confederate States of America, was much more honest in his "Cornerstone Speech" in 1861. Stephens declared:

> The prevailing ideas entertained by him [Jefferson] and most of the leading statesmen at the time of the formation of the old Constitution, were that the enslavement of the African . . . .was wrong in principle, socially, morally and politically. It was an evil they knew not well how to deal with, but the general opinion of the men of that day was that somehow or other in the order of Providence, the institution would . . .pass away.

Reprinted in Paul Finkelman, *Defending Slavery: Proslavery Thought in the Old South* (New York:Bedford/St. Martin's, 2003), 89–96.

21. *DS* at 413.

22. *DS* at 426–27.

Chapter 11
"Upon These Considerations"—Taney Strikes Down the Missouri Compromise

Chief Justice Taney's discussion of the Missouri Compromise issue is at the very heart of the *Dred Scott* decision. Striking down the Missouri Compromise was (and still is) the most remarkable and the most controversial aspect of the *Dred Scott* decision. *Dred Scott* represented the very first time in the history of the nation that the Supreme Court declared a substantive federal law to be unconstitutional.[1]

In one bold stroke, the *Dred Scott* decision set aside the legal framework that had been created by Congress pursuant to which a large portion of the American West had been settled and organized over the course of more than thirty years. And more controversial (at least at the time), the *Dred Scott* decision appeared to be an effort by the Supreme Court to decide as a matter of constitutional law the most important and most divisive political issue of the age—namely, whether the federal government should prohibit slavery in the West.

The Republican party was one of only two major parties at that time. It was founded and based on the principle that slavery should not be allowed to expand into the West. Thus the *Dred Scott* decision, in a sense, attempted to outlaw as unconstitutional the Republican party's core principle. The predictable political firestorm of dissent that followed the *Dred Scott* decision was probably the most dramatic and most widespread instance of opposition to "judicial activism" in American history (with the possible exception of resistance to *Brown v. Board of Education*, the school desegregation case, in the 1950s and '60s).

Unfortunately for the modern reader, Taney's discussion of the Missouri Compromise issue is long, labored, difficult to follow, and difficult to summarize. That is no coincidence. The disorganization of Taney's writing reflects the disorganization of his legal thinking in this area. In tracing Taney's argument, it is useful to start with and keep in mind the following outline of the key elements in that argument.

First, as detailed (in Section A) later, Taney began his discussion of the Missouri Compromise by attempting to justify the Court's momentous decision to address the Missouri Compromise issue at all, since it did not seem necessary to reach that issue in order to decide the *Dred Scott* case.

Second (as detailed in Section B), Taney entered into a lengthy, rambling analysis of possible sources for Congressional authority over the U.S. territories. In the course of that analysis, Taney attempted to meet and defeat two arguments from precedent. Those arguments had been raised by Dred Scott's lawyers in order to support the proposition that, by virtue of the Constitution's Territory Clause, Congress did possess the power to limit slavery in the territories. Specifically, Taney attempted to discredit both the Northwest Ordinance and the case of *Atlantic Insurance Co. v. Canter* as relevant precedent. In that process, Taney came to the conclusion that the Constitution's Territory Clause applied only to those U.S. territories that existed at the time the Constitution was adopted in 1789.

Third, having decided that the Territory Clause did not confer upon Congress any power to govern the many U.S. territories (extending from the Mississippi to the Pacific) acquired since the adoption of the Constitution in 1789, Taney found (as detailed in Part C) that the Constitution's Statehood Clause (which empowered Congress to admit new states into the Union) by implication did grant Congress a limited power to govern the territories in order to prepare them for statehood; but, said Taney, that limited power did not extend so far as to authorize Congress to pass laws regulating slavery in the territories.

Moreover, in a confusing and still exceptionally controversial passage, Taney invoked the Fifth Amendment and at least appeared to suggest that to grant freedom to a slave (like Dred Scott) because the slave had been brought to live in a federal territory where slavery was prohibited would be to deprive the slave's master of his property without due process of law.

Taken as a whole, Taney 's discussion of the Missouri Compromise issue did make some good points that were difficult (but not impossible) for anti-slavery advocates to answer (see Section D); but ultimately Taney's analysis of the Missouri Compromise was simply wrong as a matter of both law and logic (Section E).

A) Taney Strains to Reach the Missouri Compromise Issue

Having concluded that the circuit court had no jurisdiction to hear Dred Scott's lawsuit in the first place because Scott was not a citizen, Taney might well have stopped right there. He could have directed the circuit court to dismiss Scott's suit for lack of jurisdiction, noted that the Supreme Court was not expressing any view on any other issue raised by the case, and let it go at that.

Taney and his fellow Justices did not take that course. Instead, Taney moved on to find that Congress had no power to legislate against slavery in the territories, and that the Missouri Compromise was therefore unconstitutional.

Taney of course knew that he would be criticized for this. In particular, he was sensitive to and concerned about the argument that any point he made in *Dred Scott* beyond the jurisdictional issue should be considered mere dicta.

Thus Taney wrote:

> But before we proceed to examine this part of the case, it may be proper to notice an objection taken to the judicial authority of this court to decide it; and it has been said, that as this court has decided against the jurisdiction of the Circuit Court on the plea in abatement, it has no right to examine any question presented by this exception; and that anything it may say upon that part of the case will be extra-judicial and mere obiter dicta.[2]

Accordingly, Taney spent several pages of argument trying to justify the Supreme Court's decision to go beyond the jurisdictional issue in order to consider the merits of the case. In this connection, Taney boldly asserted that there "can be no doubt as to the jurisdiction of this court to revise the judgement of a Circuit Court, and to reverse it for any error apparent on the record . . . . [I]f it appears upon its face that any material error or errors have been committed by the court below, it is the duty of this court to revise the judgement and remand the case."[3]

This was a most unusual assertion. There was and is no "duty" for the Supreme Court, or for any appeals court, to examine *any* errors made by a trial court.[4] To the contrary, there is a large and sophisticated body of law elaborating the general principle that an appellate court should ordinarily consider *only* those issues that were properly raised and argued at the trial level and thereby preserved for appeal.

Moreover, even Taney himself seemed to be saying that the Supreme Court should be concerned with "material" errors—that is, in plain language, errors that made a real difference. Yet Taney conceded that Scott's suit against Sanford would be dismissed whether or not the Supreme Court moved beyond the citizenship issue, and that there would thus be "very little, if any, difference in a pecuniary or personal point of view to either party"[5] regardless of whether or not the Court looked at the Missouri Compromise question. But, said Taney, this fact would not "justify this court in sanctioning an error in the judgement which is patent on the record and which, if sanctioned, might be drawn into precedent and lead to serious mischief and injustice in some future suit."[6]

This too was a very doubtful point. Taney ignored the obvious. There was no *real* danger that the *Dred Scott* decision would be seen as "sanctioning" any error committed by the circuit court that the Supreme Court did not comment on. All that was necessary to avoid this supposed "danger" was for the Supreme Court to state in its Opinion that its decision did not reach or decide any issue beyond the threshold jurisdictional issue of citizenship.

As far as Taney's Opinion of the Court indicates, it also appears that Taney gave little consideration to the concept that a court should avoid deciding cases on constitutional grounds—and should in particular avoid striking down legislation—where a case can instead be fairly decided without reaching such constitutional issues. (This subject will be returned to in greater depth.) Nor did Taney give any consideration to the idea that the Missouri Compromise issue might be a "political question" best avoided by the courts.

To the contrary, the structure that Taney gave to his discussion of the territorial question indicated that Taney was *determined* to rule on the constitutionality of the Missouri Compromise, even though that question had very little to do with the real issues in *Dred Scott*.

Taney began that discussion of the territorial question by briefly setting out the history of Dred Scott's travels with Dr. Emerson—beginning in Missouri, then to the free state of Illinois, next to the free territory of Wisconsin, and then finally back to the slave state of Missouri again.[7]

Taney then framed his analysis by asking *first* whether Scott was free by virtue of his residence in the Wisconsin Territory, and then asking *second* whether Scott was free by virtue of his residence in Illinois. Taney then moved directly to consider the question of the constitutionality of the Missouri Compromise:

> [T]wo questions arise: a) Was he [Scott] together with his family, free in Missouri by reason of his stay in the territory of the United States herein before mentioned [Wisconsin]? And b) If they were not, is Scott himself free by reason of his removal to . . . the State of Illinois . . . ?
>
> We proceed to examine the first question. The act of Congress upon which the plaintiff relies declares that slavery and involuntary servitude . . . shall be forever prohibited . . . in all that . . . territory . . . which lies north of thirty six degrees thirty minutes north latitude, and not included within the limits of Missouri. And the difficulty which meets us at the threshold of this part of the inquiry is whether Congress was authorized to pass this law under any of the powers granted to it by the Constitution; for if the authority is not given by that instrument, it is the duty of this court to declare it void and inoperative, and incapable of conferring freedom upon anyone who is held as a slave . . . .[8]

This arrangement of the order of questions made little sense. Since Scott lived in the state of Illinois first, it made more sense to examine the effect of his Illinois residence first. After all, if the Court found that Scott had become free by virtue of his residence in Illinois, then there would be no point to going on to discuss the effect of his later residence in the Wisconsin Territory.

Moreover, Taney in fact ultimately agreed with the circuit court below (and with the Missouri Supreme Court before that) that since Scott now lived in Missouri his case was governed by Missouri law (rather than either Illinois or Wisconsin law), and Missouri law provided that Scott was still a slave. Thus if Taney had examined Scott's residence in Illinois first, then as a matter of logic Taney could and should have found: a) that since Missouri law governed over *any* other jurisdiction's law, Scott would remain a slave; and b) as a result, there was no need to go on to look further at Scott's residence in Wisconsin, or to inquire into the constitutionality of the Missouri Compromise's ban on slavery in the Wisconsin Territory.

Thus Taney had a definite, but unexpressed, purpose when he decided to look at Wisconsin first and Illinois second, even though Scott lived in Illinois first and Wisconsin second. It was only by looking at Scott's travels out of chronological order and out of logical order that Taney was able to reach the issue of the Missouri Compromise. Taney's determination to make law on this subject—even though it was extraneous to the case before him—was becoming more and more apparent.

B) Taney on Possible Sources of Congressional Authority over the Territories

Since the beginning of the nation's history Congress had passed legislation for the United States territories, including legislation that dealt with slavery. Taney set out to examine the possible bases for Congress's authority to do so, with view to proving in particular that Congress did not have the power to enact the Missouri Compromise.

Scott's lawyers had laid out two possible theories for such authority. First, the Territory Clause of the Constitution expressly grants Congress the power to make all needful rules and regulations for the territory of the United States, and that power (said Scott's lawyers) included the authority to either bar or permit slavery. Second, the United States government, and thus the Congress, had the inherent power to make laws for the United States territories.

Scott's lawyers had at least one past Supreme Court case on their side in this area. The case of *American Insurance Co. v. Canter*[9] decided in 1828 did not deal with slavery, but it did explore the nature and extent of Congressional authority over the territories.

The *American Insurance* case grew out of the wreck of the ship *Point a Petre* off the coast of Florida. Florida was at that time still a U.S. territory, having been acquired from Spain by treaty in 1819. The ship carried a large quantity of cotton. The cotton was saved and then auctioned (under a principle of maritime law known as "salvage") by the order of a court at Key West. That court had been established by Florida's territorial legislature pursuant to authority granted by an Act of Congress. The central legal question, then, in the *American Insurance* case was: Did Congress have the authority to set up a territorial court with maritime jurisdiction like that exercised by the Key West court?

Chief Justice Marshall's Opinion of the Court found that Congress did have such authority. Marshall explained that by virtue of the U.S. treaty with Spain the inhabitants of Florida had become U.S. citizens. But, he said, they did not:

> participate in political power; they do not share in the government till Florida shall become a State. In the mean time, *Florida continues to be a territory of the United States, governed by virtue of that clause in the Constitution which empowers Congress to make all needful rules and regulations, respecting the territory, or other property belonging to the United States.*
>
> Perhaps the power of governing a territory belonging to the United States . . . may result necessarily from the fact that it is not within the jurisdiction of any particular State and is within the jurisdiction of the United States. The right to govern may be the inevitable consequence of the right to acquire territory. Whichever may be the source whence the power is derived, the possession of it is unquestioned . . . .
>
> *In legislating for them (the territories), Congress exercises the combined powers of the general [federal], and of a State government.*[10] (Emphasis added.)

Accordingly, said Marshall, Congress did have the power to set up a territorial maritime court, and the Key West court's order directing an auction of the salvaged cotton was valid.

Dred Scott's lawyers could and did point to this portion of the *American Insurance* case as support for the proposition that Congress could make laws for the U.S. territories. Marshall's Opinion certainly seemed to say that this power to make laws for the U.S. territories came chiefly from the Territory Clause, and might also come from other sources, but that the power itself was beyond question. Marshall's Opinion also clearly said that when Congress did make laws for the territories it exercised the combined powers of both the federal and a *state* government. There was, of course, no question that a *state* government could prohibit slavery. Thus, Scott's lawyers argued, the *American Insurance* case helped make it clear that, like a state government, Congress *did* have the power to exclude slavery from the territories.

—Taney Discounts the Territory Clause—

Taney attempted to dismiss the Territory Clause in a novel way. Sanford's lawyers had argued that the Territory Clause of the Constitution only granted Congress the power to make rules and regulations about the disposal of land in the territories, and not laws about slavery. Taney ignored that pro-slavery argument, and came up with one of his own instead.

Taney argued that the power granted by the Constitution to make rules and regulations for the territory of the United States applied only to the territory of the United States *that existed at the time the Constitution was adopted in 1789*: "The power is given in relation only to the territory of the United States—that is, to the territory then in existence, and then known or claimed as the territory of the United States."[11] The Wisconsin Territory and the other territories that were the subject of the Missouri Compromise had been added to the United States by the Louisiana Purchase from France in *1803*—fourteen years after the adoption of the Constitution. Thus, said Taney, the Territory Clause gave Congress no power over any of the lands acquired by the Louisiana Purchase, including the Wisconsin Territory.

This was a remarkable leap of law and logic. Taney could not and did not cite (that is, point to) any previous case or any evidence from the period in which the Constitution was written (such as comments from the *Federalist Papers*, or materials from the debates at the Constitutional Convention) to support his theory. It seemed to be drawn out of thin air, or, at best, out of Taney's imagination.

True, it does seem likely that the Framers would naturally be thinking chiefly about the existing territory of the United States when they wrote the Territory Clause. (However, they were probably also thinking about that western portion of Georgia which everyone at the Constitutional Convention correctly anticipated was soon to be ceded to the United States, and that ultimately became part of the states of Alabama and Mississippi.) But was there any good reason to suppose that the Framers intended to treat any territories that might later be added to the United States differently than the territory that already existed in 1789? And, if they did, why then didn't they just say so in the Territory Clause?

Taney did try to offer up a reason why the Framers might have intended that the Territory Clause be limited solely to the United States territory that existed in 1789. His explanation was so labored and muddled, however, that it is difficult to follow, let alone summarize. In essence, Taney argued that the original territory of the United States was unique in that it had been ceded (given) to the U.S. government by some of the states during the period prior to the Constitution when the country was governed under the Articles of Confederation. Taney noted that during this Articles period Congress passed the Northwest Ordinance which established a government and laws for the Northwest Territory. Accordingly, said Taney, when the Constitution was adopted there was a pressing need to give the new Congress the limited authority to pass rules and regulations in order to implement the territorial government and laws that had already been created by the Articles Congress. The Territory Clause, said Taney, was written solely to meet that pressing need. And the power conferred by the Territory Clause to make "rules and regulations," he added, was far more limited than a general power to make laws.[12]

Taney's excursion into the history of the Articles period did little to advance his argument. The Territory Clause of the Constitution still plainly gave Congress the authority to make *all* needful rules and regulations for the territory of the United States, and the Territory Clause simply did *not* include any limitation to the territory that existed as of 1789. No one had perceived any such limitation prior to Justice Taney. (Thus, for example, the Supreme Court's Opinion in the *American Insurance* case took the view that the Territory Clause applied to *Florida*, which was not added to the United States until 1819; and just three years prior to *Dred Scott* in the case of *Cross v. Harrison*[13] the Supreme Court had held that Congress possessed the authority through the Territory Clause to govern California, which was acquired by the U.S. in 1848.)[14] The Framers never expressed any intention to create such a limitation. This supposed limitation was a rather transparent invention by Justice Taney, and little more.

Nor was there any reason to think that the power given to Congress to make "all needful rules and regulations" for the territories was more limited than the power to make laws. The Constitution uses the terms "rules and regulations"[15] and "laws" substantially interchangeably at several points. For example, the Constitution gives Congress the power to "regulate" interstate commerce, and that power has always been understood to include to power to pass laws. Perhaps more important, the *American Insurance* case had already made it clear that Congress had the power to make *laws* for a territory, just as a state government could.

—Taney Discounts the Northwest Ordinance—

The Northwest Ordinance banning slavery in the old Northwest Territory was particularly troublesome to Taney in several respects. First, it certainly seemed to evince a general feeling against slavery during the age of the Revolution and Constitution—yet Taney denied that any such feeling existed.

Second, and more important, the original Northwest Ordinance was passed by Congress under the Articles of Confederation in 1787, while the Constitutional Convention was under way. The Ordinance was then reenacted in substantially the same form in August 1789 by the first Congress organized under the new Constitution, within a few weeks of the adoption of the Constitution. A large number of the Framers participated in that first Congress and voted for the Ordinance, and none ever seemed to question its constitutionality.

Those who favored federal legislation preventing the expansion of slavery into the territories thus had at their disposal a very powerful argument to show that such legislation was indeed constitutional, namely: 1) the Northwest Ordinance banned slavery in the old Northwest Territory; 2) the Framers of the Constitution who sat in Congress themselves approved the Northwest Ordinance within a few weeks of the adoption of the Constitution; 3) it was therefore clear that the Ordinance did not violate the Constitution or the intention of the Framers; and 4) accordingly, subsequent similar federal legislation (such as the Missouri Compromise) banning slavery in other territories was also constitutional.

Taney therefore felt that he needed to discredit the Northwest Ordinance as relevant constitutional precedent. But the reasoning he put forward on this point was especially weak. Why, in Taney's view, did the first Congress organized under the Constitution have the power to enact the Northwest Ordinance in 1789 and ban slavery in the Northwest Territory? According to Taney, Congress had such power in 1789 only because it was merely confirming the action that had already been taken in 1787 by a prior Congress (operating under the Articles of Confederation) in passing the original Northwest Ordinance.[16]

This made little sense, and seemed especially hypocritical coming from Taney. Taney was a "strict constructionist." Thus he was ordinarily quite insistent that Congress and the federal government possessed only those powers that were expressly granted to them by the Constitution; indeed, Taney forcefully made that very point several times in the course of his

Dred Scott Opinion.[17] Yet the Constitution plainly did *not* give Congress a power to pass laws that would otherwise be unconstitutional just because previous Congresses operating under the Articles of Confederation had once passed similar laws. Accordingly, the power of the first Congress operating under the Constitution to pass the Northwest Ordinance banning slavery in the Northwest Territory *had* to come from the Constitution itself. It was almost silly for Taney to pretend otherwise.

Moreover, it was hard to swallow Taney's explanation of why he believed that, on the one hand, the Articles Congress could properly legislate against slavery in the Northwest Territory, yet, on the other, Congress operating under the Constitution could not pass a law like the Missouri Compromise.

As a general matter, the widely understood central purpose of the Constitution was to *strengthen* the federal government, a government which was thought to be far too weak under the Articles. So how did Taney explain why it was that the weak Articles Congress could supposedly do what the stronger Constitutional Congress could not—that is, ban slavery in a federal territory?

Taney answered by asserting that the United States under the Articles of Confederation was not really a government at all; it was instead more like a league of independent sovereignties, namely, the independent states. Furthermore, according to Taney, Congress under the Articles was not really a legislature either; it was instead a sort of conference of ambassadors from the independent states. Thus, said Taney, when Virginia and several other states gave to the United States the land that became the Northwest Territory, they were free to make it a condition of their gift that slavery must be banned there; and the independent states were similarly free to accept that condition:

> They had no power to accept it under the Articles of Confederation. But they had an undoubted right as independent sovereignties to accept any cession of territory for their common benefit, which all of them assented to . . . . [They] had a right to establish any form of government they pleased, by compact or treaty by themselves.[18]

The chief and most glaring defect of this theory of Taney's was that the Northwest Ordinance of 1787 was, of course, not a compact or a treaty. It was a law enacted by Congress under the Articles in largely the same form and in the same manner as all the other laws passed by that body.[19] Moreover, it was a law passed by a vote of eight states only, and not a compact assented to by "all" thirteen states as Taney misleadingly suggested. Taney's discussion of the Northwest Ordinance thus served only to demonstrate that he was again willing to deny the most obvious historical truths in order to further his cause.

(C) The Statehood Clause and the Fifth Amendment

Having dismissed (at least in his own mind) the Territory Clause as a possible source for Congressional authority to legislate for the territories beyond the original territory of the United States, and having eliminated (to his own satisfaction) the Northwest Ordinance as a useful precedent, Taney still had a problem. Obviously, Congress had passed all sorts of unremarkable laws for the territories over the years that had nothing to do with slavery. Taney wanted to develop a theory that would both justify Congress's power to make those ordinary laws, yet deny that Congress had the power to legislate against slavery in the territories.

Taney began by asking where the power to acquire territories came from. The Constitution does not speak directly about any power for the federal government to add territory to the United States. It was for this reason that at the time of the Louisiana Purchase in 1803 some people questioned whether such a power existed. But the United States did grow anyway—taking in vast portions of the West extending all the way to the Pacific through the Louisiana Purchase and the Mexican War. Most legal thinkers of the time took the view that the power to add new territories to the United States was authorized as ancillary to or implied by the constitutionally recognized powers of the federal government to make treaties and to make war.

Taney took a different view. He asserted that the power to add territories was implicit within the Constitution's Statehood Clause.[20] That clause provides:

> New States may be admitted by the Congress into this Union; but no new State shall be formed or erected within the jurisdiction of any other State, nor any State be formed by the junction of two or more States, or parts of States, without the consent of the Legislatures of the States concerned as well as of the Congress.

This was an odd assertion. After all, new states could come from the existing states or from the already existing territory of the United States. Accordingly, the power granted by the Statehood Clause to create new states did not necessarily imply the power to *add* new territories from which new states would then be created. But Taney claimed it did.

Taney further reasoned that since the power to acquire territory came from the Statehood Clause, the only proper purpose for acquiring territory was to create new states to be admitted on an equal footing with the original states.[21] For Taney, this meant that the people who settled in the territories were Americans and enjoyed the same rights as other Americans, even before the territories became states.

Taney insisted that people who moved to the territories "cannot be ruled as mere colonists, dependent upon the will of the General Government, and to be governed by any laws it may think proper to impose . . . . A power . . . in the General Government to hold colonies and dependent territories over which they might legislate without restriction, would be inconsistent with its own existence in its present form . . . ."[22]

In particular, Taney argued that the federal government could not deprive the inhabitants of a territory of any of their rights under the Constitution. For example, Congress could not pass a law depriving a territory's inhabitants of their freedom of speech or religion, or of their right to a jury trial in an appropriate case.[23]

Then Taney made another great leap in logic. From the rather bland general proposition that Congress could not violate the Bill of Rights in the territories, Taney moved to the Fifth Amendment's guarantee that the federal government can not deprive any person of life, liberty or property without due process of law. Taney then boldly declared (without citing any authority) that any "Act of Congress which deprives a citizen of the United States of his liberty or property, merely because he came himself or brought his property into a particular Territory of the United States and who had committed no offense against the laws, could hardly be dignified with the name of due process of law."[24]

In other words, Taney's thesis at least seemed to be this: a) Congress's power over the territories came from the Statehood Clause, and was limited by the Bill of Rights, including the Fifth Amendment; b) the Statehood Clause did confer on Congress a limited power to make laws for a territory in preparation for statehood; c) the Statehood Clause did not, however, confer any power on Congress to legislate against slavery in the territories; and d) the Fifth Amendment would not permit any law that would deprive a master of his slave just because the master brought the slave into a free territory. Moreover, Taney volunteered, a territorial legislature could not pass such a law either. (There was a national ongoing debate as to whether a territorial legislature, like that of Kansas, could ban slavery; but that question had nothing to do with the legal issues in *Dred Scott*.)

Thus Taney wrote:

> The powers over person and property of which we speak are not only not granted to Congress, but are in express terms denied, and they are forbidden to exercise them. And this prohibition . . . extend[s] to the whole territory over which the Constitution gives it power to legislate . . . . It is a total absence of power everywhere within the dominion of the United States and places the citizens of a Territory, so far as these rights are concerned, on the same footing with citizens of the States, and guards them as firmly and plainly against any inroads which the General Government might attempt, under the plea of implied or incidental powers. And if Congress itself cannot do this—if it is beyond the powers conferred on the Federal government—it will be admitted, we presume, that it could not authorize a Territorial Government to exercise them. It could confer no power on any local Government, established by its authority, to violate the provisions of the Constitution.[25]

The most crucial step in this process of reasoning was the proposition that a master who lost his slave by bringing the slave into a territory where slavery was prohibited had been "deprived" by Congress of his property without due process of law—even though the law forbidding slavery there was well-known in advance, and even though all American courts (including the U.S. Supreme Court in *Prigg v. Pennsylvania*) and the law of nations gave at least grudging recognition to the *Somerset* principle of emancipation by residence on free soil. (As explained in *Prigg*,[26] *Somerset* taught that slavery could exist only where supported by positive local law. Thus, under *Somerset*, the government did not "deprive" the master of his slave when the master brought the slave to live in a free state; rather, the slave simply became free because the free state's law did not affirmatively authorize his continued bondage.) For this remarkable and seemingly crucial proposition—that the Constitutional guarantee of due process of law was violated by the *Somerset* principle that a slave brought to live on free soil became free—Taney gave *no* authority, other than his own very brief say-so.

Even more disturbingly, Taney's Opinion did not set forth the limits, if any, that applied to this new theory. Certainly, Taney at least appeared to suggest that the Fifth Amendment was violated when the master lost his slave by coming into a free *territory*; but was Taney also suggesting that would be true if the master brought his slave into a free *state*? In the aftermath of *Dred Scott*, there were both critics and supporters of the Taney Opinion who thought that might indeed be what Taney was saying. This was one source of the Republican charge that *Dred Scott* was merely a step along the way to making slavery a national institution.

In connection with his argument that the doctrine of emancipation by residence on free soil was somehow equivalent to the deprivation of property without due process, Taney was particularly insistent that the Constitution recognized no distinction between slaves and other kinds of property:

> It seems, however, to be supposed, that there is a difference between property in a slave and other property, and that different rules may be applied to it in expounding the Constitution of the United States . . . . [T]he Constitution recognizes the right of property of the master in a slave, and makes no distinction between that description of property and other property owned by a citizen, [therefore] no tribunal, acting under the authority of the United States, whether it be legislative, executive or judicial, has a right to draw such a distinction, or deny to it the benefit of the provisions and guarantees which have been provided for the protection of private property against the encroachments of the government.[27]

Next, as he approached the climactic paragraph in his opinion—containing the declaration that the Missouri Compromise was unconstitutional—Taney paused to review what (he believed) he had already demonstrated, namely: a) the Constitution—by virtue of its Fugitive Slave Clause and its twenty-year ban on prohibiting the African Slave Trade—expressly blessed slavery; and b) the only power conferred by the Constitution upon Congress with regard to slavery was the power to protect slaveholders' rights. Thus Taney wrote:

> [T]he right of property in a slave is distinctly and expressly affirmed in the Constitution. The right to traffic in it, like an ordinary article of merchandise and property, was guarantied to the citizens of the United States . . . for twenty years. And the Government in express terms is pledged to protect it in all future time, if the slave escapes from his owner. . . . [N]o word can be found in the Constitution which gives Congress a

> greater power over slave property, or which entitles property of that kind to less protection that property of any other description. *The only power conferred is the power coupled with the duty of guarding and protecting the owner in his rights.* (Emphasis added.)

And then, with all this analytical heavy lifting behind him, and having proceeded roughly fifty pages into his Opinion, Taney finally came to the conclusion he had been determined all along to reach:

> Upon these considerations, it is the opinion of the Court that the act of Congress which prohibited a citizen from holding and owning property of this kind in the territory . . . is not warranted by the Constitution, and is therefore void; and that neither Dred Scott himself, nor any of his family, were made free by being carried into this territory, even if they had been carried there by the owner, with the intention of becoming a permanent resident . . . .[28]

In other words, the Missouri Compromise was unconstitutional and void, and Dred Scott's residence in the Wisconsin Territory therefore could not free him.

This conclusion was not only controversial. It was also remarkably vague and confusing. What did Taney mean by "Upon these considerations"? Which considerations? Why precisely was the Missouri Compromise unconstitutional? Was the Compromise unconstitutional simply because the Constitution nowhere granted to Congress any power to make laws concerning slavery for the territories? Was the Compromise instead unconstitutional because it violated the Fifth Amendment's requirement that no one be deprived of property without due process of law?[29] Or was Taney's brief and cryptic discussion of the Fifth Amendment a mere secondary "throw-in" point that was not essential to striking down the Compromise? Taney's Opinion did not say. (The structure of Taney's Opinion certainly seemed to point to the conclusion that the Fifth Amendment point was a mere "aside"; Taney devoted nearly twenty-five pages to the question of Congressional authority over the territories, but barely half a page to the Fifth Amendment point.)

Assuming that the Fifth Amendment point was indeed essential to Taney's Opinion, was the Fifth Amendment offended by the Missouri Compromise itself, or by the *Somerset* principle? After all, the Missouri Compromise banned slavery in certain territories, but it was not the Missouri Compromise that mandated that masters must *lose* their slave property. Emancipation of a slave brought to live on free soil was instead a consequence of the common law *Somerset* principle.

Would the Fifth Amendment have been satisfied in Taney's view if the Missouri Compromise's slavery restrictions were retained, but the *Somerset* principle were dropped? Suppose, for example, that pursuant to the Missouri Compromise a master like Dr. Emerson were simply forbidden to bring a slave like Dred Scott into the Wisconsin Territory in the first place, with the consequence that the issue of emancipation by residence on free soil would never come up. Would that have satisfied the Fifth Amendment in Taney's view?

Again, Taney's Opinion, long and labored as it was, simply did not say. These omissions were all the more remarkable since both Taney and everyone else involved clearly recognized that his Opinion—the first in American history to strike down a substantive federal law as unconstitutional—was of such great importance.

D) Strengths of Taney's Argument: The Colonial Analogy

Most historians and legal thinkers have focused on the weaknesses of the arguments advanced by Taney in order to invalidate the Missouri Compromise, and with good reason.

Yet it is useful to note that buried within Taney's lengthy and less than persuasive prose there is at least the kernel of an idea that does have some appeal, even to the modern mind. It is an idea that at the same time also harkens back to the ideology of the American Revolution. That idea, strangely enough, is the equality of all citizens—or, at least, of all *white* citizens.

Taney insisted that the people of the territories and of the new states that were created out of the territories must be treated as American citizens, with the same rights as citizens of the original states. It would be wrong, he said, for Congress to treat the people of the territories in the way that the British Empire had treated the American colonists prior to the Revolution—as second-class citizens, to be governed by laws that they did not make or agree to.

Under the Constitution, each of the original states was free to decide for itself whether to permit or prohibit slavery. Congress did not presume to dictate to the original states on the subject of slavery.

Thus Taney and his pro-slavery colleagues had questions that were hard for their opponents to answer. Why shouldn't the citizens of the territories and new states have the same right as the citizens of the old states to decide for themselves whether to permit slavery? By what right did Congress make laws about slavery for Americans in the West that they did not agree to? Was that really democracy? Didn't that contradict the purpose of the American Revolution?

Such questions could become particularly pointed in view of the requirement of both the Northwest Ordinance and the Missouri Compromise that the territories reserved for freedom therein must remain *forever* free. This meant that slavery would be barred there for all time, even after those territories had been transformed into new states. Thus, no matter how great a majority of voters in those new states wanted slavery, they could not have it. But why shouldn't the citizens of Indiana or Illinois, for example, have the same right as the citizens of South Carolina to choose slavery for their states?

Moreover, the Louisiana Purchase was paid for by taxes collected from both the South and North; and the Mexican War was fought and paid for by Americans from both sections. Shouldn't southern men and women be entitled to share equally in the territories that were thereby added to the Union? Why should Congress discourage southern slaveholders from settling the West by prohibiting slavery there? Was that consistent with equal treatment for all American citizens?

—The Uniqueness of Slavery—

The best answer that can be given is that under the Constitution slavery was different. It really was a "peculiar" institution. Taney was right to say that the Constitution did at least implicitly recognize slaves as property of a kind. But Taney also asserted, with great passion, that the Constitution did not distinguish between slaves and any other form of property. That was plainly *not* true. Both the Constitution and the entire body of American law prior to the Civil War did distinguish, over and over again, between slaves and other kinds of property, and between slavery and other domestic institutions.

First and foremost, under the Constitution a slave was entitled to representation (as three-fifths of a person) in the United States Congress; no other item of property was represented in Congress. Thus the decision whether slavery would be permitted in a new state affected not only that state; it also affected the very structure of the federal government and the relative strength of each state within that government.

Similarly, the Constitution expressly authorized Congress to ban the importation of slaves after 1808 so as to discourage the growth of slavery; that was not true for any other form of property.[30]

No other form of property was prohibited in most of the northern states at the time the Constitution was adopted. No other form of property was banned from the Northwest Territory by the first Congress as nearly the very first order of business after the adoption of the Constitution.

The Framers made a conscious decision not to call slavery by its name in the Constitution because they did not want to give moral sanction to slavery—and that was not true for any other kind of property.

No one thought it necessary to include in the Constitution the equivalent of the Fugitive Slave Clause for any other form of property. (That was true for two reasons. First, there was no other form of property that excited similar moral revulsion in a large part of the country. Second, no other form of property was subject to the *Somerset* principle—that ownership of a slave might be lost merely because the slave entered a free state. The Fugitive Slave Clause was thus necessary in order to prevent runaway slaves in free states from claiming their freedom under the *Somerset* rule.)

Finally, on a most fundamental level, no other form of property was human. A white man was generally free to slaughter his own livestock or chop down his own trees; but the killing of a slave by a master or overseer was (at least theoretically) punishable as the murder of a person, even in the antebellum South.[31] American law further treated a slave as a human in that slaves were regarded as responsible beings who could be prosecuted and punished for criminal offenses; animals and inanimate forms of property were obviously not subject to the criminal law.[32]

Most important, there was no such thing as manumission or emancipation for any kind of property other than slaves; and so no other kind of property could, under the law, become a free man or woman.

Taney may have wished that under the Constitution and law of the United States a slave were no different than a piece of timber, or a pig, or other ordinary item of property. He may also have wished that the institution of slavery were an ordinary domestic institution subject only to state legislation, like (as Lincoln mockingly put it) "the cranberry laws of Indiana, the oyster laws of Virginia, or the liquor laws of Maine."[33] But wishing did not make it so. The Constitution and American law did give special treatment to slavery, both favorable and unfavorable.

In the end, that was the crux of the dispute over slavery in the territories. Even Taney and his southern colleagues had to concede that slaves were different than other kinds of property in that a state could properly ban slavery. The open question truly at issue was this: During the period when the federal government administered a territory prior to statehood, could the federal government ban slavery as a state government could?

The relatively plain language of the Territory Clause indicated that the answer to this question should be "yes"—Congress *did* have the power to make *all* needful rules and regulations for the territories. The Northwest Ordinance passed by the first Congress under the Constitution dramatically demonstrated that the Framers themselves understood the Constitution to authorize Congress to ban slavery in the federal territories. The same understanding was embodied again in both the Missouri Compromise and the Compromise of 1850. Ultimately, slavery was not purely a local concern. It was dealt with and given special treatment throughout the federal Constitution. And, in particular, the U.S. Constitution *did* authorize the U.S. Congress to decide the fate of slavery in the U.S. territories.

E) Weaknesses of Taney's Missouri Compromise Argument

The weaknesses of Taney's argument for striking down the Missouri Compromise are thus readily apparent and have already been touched upon. Taney's attempt to limit the Territory Clause to the territory that existed in 1789 had no foundation in the Constitution's text, in history, or in logic. His attempts to explain away the Northwest Ordinance as evidence of the Framers' intentions were similarly unavailing. His efforts to distinguish *Atlantic Insurance Co. v. Canter* were unpersuasive. Taney's assertion that the Fifth Amendment applied to the territories was sound enough. But the novel idea that the prospective prohibition of slavery in a particular territory, in combination with the operation of the *Somerset* principle, deprived slaveholders of their property without due process of law was not warranted. Moreover, it was a most provocative and disturbing idea because it seemed to suggest that in the future the Court might hold that a slaveholder would not lose his slave even by bringing the slave to live in a free *state.*

In sum, it seems clear that Taney's two main goals in *Dred Scott* were to hold that the Missouri Compromise was unconstitutional and that African Americans could never be U.S. citizens. Taney did so hold, but the Opinion that he wrote to support those conclusions was not persuasive. It was long, full of citations, and had a maddening air of assumed infallibility about it. But most of the Opinion was devoted to largely irrelevant propositions, and on the key points Taney's arguments lacked both authority and logic.

Notes

1. In *Marbury v. Madison*, 1 Cr. (5 U.S.) 137 (1803) the Supreme Court also struck down a federal law as unconstitutional, and established the principle of judicial review. The particular law at issue, however, was a rather minor technical provision of the federal Judiciary Act dealing with a court's ability to issue certain kinds of writs.
2. *DS* at 427.
3. *DS* at 427–28.
4. That is especially true where—as in *Dred Scott*—the appellate court *affirms* the verdict of the trial court below so that there is no need to provide guidance for a retrial of the same case.
5. *DS* at 430.
6. *DS* at 430.
7. *DS* at 431.
8. *DS* at 431–32.
9. *American Ins. Co. v. Canter*, 26 U.S. 511 (1828).
10. *American Ins. Co.*, 26 U.S. 511 at 546.
11. *DS* at 436.
12. *DS* at 440.
13. *Cross v. Harrison*, 16 How.164 (1854).
14. Taney tried to distinguish away the *American Insurance* case. He correctly noted that Marshall's Opinion had left open the theoretical possibility that Congress's power over the territories might be derived from some source other than the Territory Clause. (*DS*, 442.) But Taney ignored the fact that Marshall did see the Territory Clause as the most obvious source for that authority.

Taney also deliberately ignored the fact that Marshall's discussion of the Territory Clause was about *Florida*. Florida was first acquired by the U.S. in *1819.*

It was not part of the original territory of the U.S. that existed in 1789 when the Constitution was adopted. The *American Insurance* case thus completely contradicted Taney's theory that the Territory Clause was limited to the U.S. territories that existed in *1789*.

Similarly, Taney argued that Marshall's broad language explaining that Congress had the power of both the federal and state government in legislating for a territory was, somehow, limited to Congress's power to establish territorial courts. (*DS*, 444.) It is true that the *American Insurance* case was about the establishment of a territorial maritime court at Key West, but there was nothing in Marshall's Opinion to suggest (and no reason to suppose) that his comments on the scope of Congress's powers over the territories were limited to that context.

15. Indeed, Taney's own Opinion elsewhere unintentionally undercut the notion that the power to make "regulations" is more limited than the power to make laws; in a different part of his Opinion Taney refers to the provisions of the Constitution—the fundamental law of the land—as positive and practical "regulations." *DS* at 451.

16. *DS* at 438–39.

17. *DS* at 435, 448 and 451.

18. *DS* at 434–35.

19. Each section of the original Northwest Ordinance of 1787 is prefaced by the language "Be it ordained by the United States in Congress assembled." The Ordinance concludes with the language "Done by the United States in Congress assembled the 13th day of July in the year of our Lord 1787, and of their sovereignty and independence the twelfth." The Ordinance is not signed by the states (or by anyone else) as a treaty or compact would be signed. The Ordinance was passed by a vote of eight states. Thus the Ordinance was a federal law, and not a treaty agreed to by all the states.

It is true that Section 14 of the Ordinance provides that it is ordained and declared by the authority aforesaid (that is, by the authority of Congress) that the following Articles shall be considered "as articles of compact" between the original states, on the one hand, and the people and future states of the Northwest Territory, on the other, that cannot be amended except by common consent. Article Six barred slavery in the Northwest Territory.

This "articles of compact" language may have been what Taney was thinking about when he framed his theory that the Northwest Ordinance was a compact or treaty among the original states. Nevertheless, the Ordinance by its own terms is ordained by Congress as a law; it is not a treaty agreed to among the original states, or even between the original states and the people of the Northwest Territory. The apparent significance of the provision that the anti-slavery provision of the Ordinance should be considered as an "article of compact" was merely to require *unanimous* consent to amend that provision.

20. *DS* at 435.

21. This was a noble idea. But it was not necessarily mandated by the Statehood Clause that Taney purported to rely on. The Statehood Clause says that new states *may* be admitted; it does not say they *must* be admitted. Thus it is possible under the Constitution that some territories will remain territories indefinitely, and that their residents will remain something less than full citizens of the United States.

22. *DS* at 447–48.

23. *DS* at 450.

24. *DS* at 450.

25. *DS* at 450–51.

26. *Prigg v. Pennsylvania*, 16 Peters at 611–12.

27. *DS* at 451.

28. *DS* at 452.

29. Taney's choice of words in declaring his conclusion that the Missouri Compromise was "not warranted" by the Constitution seemed to suggest that Taney was relying on the absence of Congressional authority over the territories. If Taney were instead relying on the Fifth Amendment argument, it would have been more logical for him to say that the Missouri Compromise was "forbidden" or "barred" by the Constitution or Fifth Amendment.

30. Congress did ban the importation of slaves beginning in 1808, and further provided that any slave illegally imported became free. That federal law was the basis of the 1837 *Garronne* case concerning the slave Priscilla, discussed in Chapter 8 earlier. Notably, in his *Garronne* Opinion, Chief Justice Taney did not perceive that mandatory forfeiture of illegally imported slaves constituted deprivation of property without due process of law. It is thus difficult to reconcile Taney's *Garronne* Opinion with his discussion of the Fifth Amendment in his *Dred Scott* Opinion.

31. David B. Davis, *Inhuman Bondage: The Rise and Fall of Slavery in the New World* (New York: Oxford U. Press, 2006) 193–204.

32. Thus Madison wrote in *Federalist* Number 54 that slaves were:

> considered by our laws, in some respects, as persons, and in other respects as property. In being compelled to labor, not for himself, but for a master; in being vendible by one master to another master; and in being subject at all times to be restrained in his liberty and chastised in his body, by the capricious will of his owner, the slave may appear to be degraded from the human rank, and classed with those irrational animals which fall under the legal denomination of property. In being protected, on the other hand, in his life and in his limbs, against the violence of all others, even the master of his labor and his liberty; and in being punishable himself for all violence committed against others; the slave is no less evidently regarded by the law as a member of the society, not as a part of the irrational creation; as a moral person, not as a mere article of property.

33. Abraham Lincoln, Speech at Chicago, Illinois, July 10, 1858, reprinted in *Lincoln, Speeches, Letters etc.*, (Library of America, 1989), Vol. I, 449.

Chapter 12
The Road Not Taken: Taney on Choice of Law and *Res Judicata*

—Choice of Law—

Having slogged at a painfully slow pace through more than fifty pages to get to the desired conclusion that the Missouri Compromise was void, Taney then virtually raced through two other points that, as a matter of logic, were far more important to the decision in *Dred Scott*.

First, Taney returned to the subject of Dred Scott's residence in the free state of Illinois. Illinois was a state, and not a territory. Illinois was not part of the area governed by the Missouri Compromise. Taney's discussion of Congressional authority over the territories and of the Missouri Compromise thus had no relevance to Illinois. Taney still needed to explain why Scott's residence in Illinois did not make Scott free.

Taney made very quick work (about three paragraph's worth) of this question—the very same question that had been the chief focus of nearly ten prior *years* of litigation in the state court case of *Dred Scott v. Emerson* and in the federal circuit court case of *Scott v. Sandford*. Taney declared:

> As Scott was a slave when taken into the State of Illinois by his owner, and was there held as such, and brought back in that character, his status, as free or slave, depended on the laws of Missouri and not of Illinois. . . . [W]e are satisfied, upon a careful examination of all the cases decided in the State Courts of Missouri referred to, that it is now firmly settled by the decisions of the highest court in the State, that Scott and his family upon their return were not free, but were, by the laws of Missouri, the property of the defendant . . . .[1]

In other words, Taney agreed with both the circuit court below and with the decision in *Scott v. Emerson* before that, that once Scott returned to Missouri, Missouri law governed Scott's status; and Missouri law provided that Scott was still a slave. Taney correctly noted that this was essentially the same position that Taney had previously taken in his Opinion of the Court in *Strader v. Graham* six years before. This was also the view expressed in greater detail by Justice Nelson in his narrow concurring Opinion in *Dred Scott*, which denied Dred and Harriet Scott their freedom without reaching the controversial issues of Negro citizenship and the Missouri Compromise's constitutionality.

The obvious question presented by Taney's assertion — that Missouri State law controlled the outcome of Dred Scott's case and provided that Scott was still a slave —was this: If the whole case could have thus been decided in the space a few paragraphs as a simple matter of Missouri law, why did Taney (and the rest of the Supreme Court) bother with 250 other pages full of discussion about the Missouri Compromise's constitutionality, Negro citizenship, the nature of the Articles of Confederation, the attitude of the British Empire toward Negro slavery, shipwrecks off the coast of Florida, laws against miscegenation, and so forth and so on?

Taney gave no answer. There was no good answer.

—*Res Judicata*—

Similarly, Taney briefly addressed as the very last item in his Opinion a point that could well have been the first and only point. Taney noted (as if this were the first time the fact had been brought to his attention):

> Moreover, the plaintiff, it appears, brought a similar action against the defendant in the State Court of Missouri, claiming the freedom of himself and his family upon the same grounds and the same evidence upon which

> he relies in the case before the court. The case [*Scott v. Emerson*] was carried before the Supreme Court of the State, was fully argued there; and that Court decided that neither the plaintiff nor his family were entitled to freedom, and were still slaves of the defendant . . . .[2]

Taney next pointed out that if Scott had believed that the decision of the Missouri Supreme Court in *Scott v. Emerson* was wrong, then the proper course would have been for Scott to appeal *that* decision directly to the U.S. Supreme Court. (Of course, Taney did not suggest that Scott was likely to win such an appeal; to the contrary, Taney indicated that the decision in *Scott v. Emerson* was in fact correct.) By bringing essentially the same claim for freedom for a second time in federal court, Scott was attempting to improperly evade the original decision of the Missouri State court and to bring an improper appeal. Accordingly, said Taney, the federal courts (including the Supreme Court) should refuse to hear Scott's federal lawsuit.[3]

A modern court would probably make essentially the same point by invoking the related doctrines of *res judicata* or collateral estoppel. These doctrines hold that once a party (like Dred Scott) has had a full and fair opportunity to litigate a claim (like the claim made by Scott in his Missouri State court suit for freedom against Mrs. Emerson that he had been emancipated by residence on free soil), the party cannot bring the same claim again in a different court. Taney's point here was a very good one. Dred Scott's federal lawsuit *did* seem like an improper end run around the Missouri State Supreme Court's decision of the very same issue.

Again, the obvious question presented was: Why didn't Taney make this seemingly dispositive point to start with, and thereby avoid all the difficulties discussed in the rest of *Dred Scott*?

Once more, Taney never discussed *that* question, because he had no good answer to give.

On this puzzling note of glaring omission, Chief Justice Taney's Opinion of the Court in *Dred Scott v. Sandford* concluded.

Notes

1. *DS* at 452–53.
2. *DS* at 453.
3. *DS* at 454.

Chapter 13
The Majority Concurs (After a Fashion)

Six Justices concurred with Chief Justice Taney that Dred Scott remained a slave. Five of those six also concurred with Taney that the Missouri Compromise was void. Each of the six concurring Justices wrote a separate Opinion. This welter of separate concurring Opinions was probably a disappointment to Taney and his pro-slavery colleagues. Justice Grier had indicated in his secret letter to President-elect Buchanan before the case was decided that Grier, Taney and Wayne were trying to persuade all the pro-slavery Justices to join in a single Opinion. Grier believed that a single Opinion would have greater persuasive power, and feared that a profusion of "clashing or inconsistent" concurring Opinions would undermine the authority of the *Dred Scott* decision.

Grier's fear was largely realized. The fact that seven Supreme Court Justices gave seven different sets of reasons for reaching the same result in the *Dred Scott* case did (and still does) encourage the suspicion that the result drove the Justices' legal reasoning, rather than the other way around.[1]

Perhaps the best way to organize an examination of the concurring Opinions in *Dred Scott* is to review them from right to left—that is, from the most extreme pro-slavery point of view to the most moderate. Viewed in this fashion, the pro-slavery Justices fell into three categories.

First, there were the "fire-eaters"—Justices Daniel, Taney and Wayne—whose Opinions demonstrated a deep and unquestionably sincere commitment to safeguarding the institution of slavery against all challenges.

Second, there were the "politicians"—Justices Campbell and Catron—who agreed with the pro-slavery result in *Dred Scott*, but appear to have had some private doubts about the legal basis for striking down the Missouri Compromise.

Third, there were the "dough-faces"—Justices Grier and Nelson. They were northern Democrats whose party loyalty in large part led them to concur with the pro-slavery result in *Dred Scott*, but whose natural preference as northerners was for a very narrow decision.

A) The Fire-Eaters

—Justice Daniel—

It is not surprising that Justice Peter Daniel[2] was the author of the most extreme pro-slavery Opinion in *Dred Scott*. Daniel has been aptly characterized as a "brooding pro-slavery fanatic."[3]

By way of background, Daniel studied law with Edmund Randolph, the first Attorney General of the United States (and Daniel also married Randolph's daughter). He rose steadily in Virginia's legal and political circles. In 1828, Daniel was a leading political supporter of the Andrew Jackson/Martin Van Buren for President/Vice President campaign ticket in Virginia. As a reward, Daniel was appointed to the federal bench by President Jackson (of Tennessee), and later appointed to the Supreme Court by President Van Buren (of New York); thus Daniel's career in politics and law was to some degree a product of the alliance between southern and northern Democrats.

But, over time, Daniel grew to hate the North. He made a solemn vow never to travel north of the Delaware River. Once, upon receiving a gift of some oranges from the South, he wondered whether the North would ever produce "anything like these oranges, or indeed anything that is good and decent."[4] Whenever the subject of anti-slavery sentiment came up in conversations with his family, Daniel would invariably cut off all discussion by simply declaring: " I fear those people are very wicked."[5]

The reason for Daniel's break with his political mentor Van Buren, and the source of his antipathy toward the North, is easy to identify. Daniel broke with Van Buren in 1847 when Van Buren gave his support to the Wilmot Proviso. The Wilmot Proviso was a controversial and ultimately unsuccessful legislative proposal that Congress prohibit slavery in all the territory to be taken from Mexico through the Mexican War.

Daniel regarded the Wilmot Proviso—or, indeed , any proposal to ban slavery from the federal territories—as a deep and profound insult to the South because it implicitly expressed the view that slave-holding was immoral. The Proviso, said Daniel, showed that the North "pretends to an insulting exclusiveness or superiority on the one hand, and denounces a degrading inequality or inferiority on the other, [it] says in effect to the Southern man, Avaunt! You are not my equal, and hence are to be excluded as carrying a moral taint with you."[6] Thus Daniel wrote to Van Buren that Daniel could never accept the Wilmot Proviso, and that Daniel saw the Proviso as the "overthrow of the great national compact; as the extreme of injury and oppression; oppression in its most galling form, because it declares to me that I am not regarded as an equal."[7]

By 1851, Daniel believed that every northern man was "an abolitionist and enemy of the South." He "hoped that the southern people would not cooperate with the northern states in the selection of any man for high office, nor in any political measure whatsoever." Nor did Daniel fear that this course might lead to secession, for in his view "the northern men, by their flagrant infractions of [the] constitution . . . dissolved the Union long ago."[8]

As a Supreme Court Justice, Daniel was single-minded in his devotion to states' rights and the interests of the agrarian South; and he was usually hostile to the growing influence of corporations and banks. He grew increasingly isolated from most of his colleagues, and wrote many bristling dissenting Opinions.

For example, in the 1844 *Letson*[9] case, the Supreme Court determined that, for purposes of federal diversity jurisdiction, a corporation would be deemed to be a citizen of the state of its incorporation. The *Letson* rule made it much easier for a corporation to either sue or be sued in a federal court, which was and is a great aid to interstate commerce.[10] Initially, Justices Daniel, Campbell and Catron dissented from the *Letson* rule. But over just a few years time, the practical need for the *Letson* doctrine and the force of the *Letson* case as binding precedent won over Campbell and Catron

Not so for Daniel. Till the end of his life (in 1860) Daniel dissented (often by himself) in every single case in which a corporation was a party to a federal court suit where jurisdiction was based on diversity of citizenship; in his last Court term in 1859 alone, Daniel dissented on this ground in six different cases. Daniel thought that to back down from his objections to the *Letson* doctrine would be a dereliction of duty, approaching sacrilege: "[A] relinquishment of those arguments or the failure to assert them on every occasion similar to that first calling them forth . . . would . . . by myself be felt as a compromise of a sacred and solemn duty."[11]

Thus, by the time *Dred Scott* was decided, it was well-known that Daniel was not a Justice who feared being branded an extremist; and Daniel's Concurring Opinion in *Dred Scott* in all likelihood did not disappoint his admirers.

Daniel Blames Scott for Decision's Scope

Like Taney and many of the pro-slavery Justices, Daniel felt it necessary at the outset of his *Dred Scott* Opinion to attempt to justify the broad scope of the decision. Daniel acknowledged that the case was the most important ever decided by an American court. The result, he said, would "control" the "faculties" and "practical operations" of the federal government; and it would also "control" the rights and powers of its "separate and independent members." (By this phrase, Daniel—an extreme states-rights advocate—meant the states.) Then Daniel made the truly remarkable claim that it was Dred Scott who was responsible for raising these issues of federal and state power because of Scott's "ambitious and far-reaching pretensions to compass these objects of vital concern."[12]

Daniel's claim was an inversion of the truth. Dred Scott did not, of course, care about the distribution of power between federal and state governments. He wanted to be free; and he wanted his wife and children to be free. Scott had begun his long legal quest for freedom more than ten years earlier by quietly bringing a garden variety "freedom suit" in Missouri state court.

Dred Scott was not the man who had first raised the great questions of national importance that Daniel now referred to. The Missouri Compromise issue was first raised by John Sanford's lawyers in their initial presentation to the U.S. Supreme Court. (Indeed, Scott's lawyer, Montgomery Blair, had not even mentioned the Missouri Compromise issue in his initial brief to the Supreme Court.) Similarly, the issue of Negro citizenship had first been raised by John Sanford's plea in abatement before the federal circuit court.

Most important, it was the pro-slavery majority on the Supreme Court (including Daniel) who reversed course and chose (in conformity with President-elect Buchanan's secret urging) to reject the narrow proposed Opinion of the Court prepared by Justice Nelson, and to instead take on all the momentous issues addressed in *Dred Scott*—even though there was plainly no need to do so.

Thus the notion expressed by Daniel that it was the powerless slave Dred Scott who had somehow forced the U.S. Supreme Court to decide those great issues was a somewhat transparent effort by Daniel to deny responsibility for his own actions and those of his pro-slavery colleagues on the Court.

Daniel Denies Negro Citizenship

Turning to the substance of the *Dred Scott* case, Daniel agreed with Taney that the jurisdictional issue was properly before the Court, and further agreed with Taney that even free Negroes could not be U.S. citizens.

A Negro slave, said Daniel, "is himself strictly property, to be used in subserviency to the . . . will of his owner." Manumission or emancipation did not change the slave's essential nature or make him a citizen; citing to ancient Roman law, Daniel argued that the private act of an individual master who gives up his slave could not compel the government to accept the freed slave as a citizen.[13]

Like Taney, Daniel's Opinion also made it clear that Daniel's real concern in connection with the citizenship issue had little to do with the nature of federal court jurisdiction, and a great deal to do with a desire to maintain the South's system of pervasive racial oppression. Specifically, like Taney, Daniel was concerned that a free Negro who was regarded as a "citizen" by a northern state might claim all the privileges and immunities of a citizen, even when visiting the South.

Thus Daniel wrote that if a master (such as Dr. Emerson) could by his own act free a slave (such as Dred Scott) and thereby convert the slave into a citizen, then the master could in effect "under color of [the Constitution's Privileges and Immunities Clause] obtrude him [the slave], and on terms of civil and political equality, upon any and every State in the Union, in defiance of all regulations or necessity or policy, ordained by those States for their internal happiness or safety." All these "revolting consequences," said Daniel, would flow from accepting the proposition that a free Negro should be regarded as a citizen for purposes of federal diversity jurisdiction.[14]

"Common Property" and Congressional Authority over the Territories

Daniel then moved from the issue of negro citizenship to the Missouri Compromise issue. Unlike Taney, Daniel did not pretend that it was legally necessary for the Court to examine the Missouri Compromise issue. Instead, Daniel frankly conceded that in view of his conclusion that the Court lacked jurisdiction (because even a free Negro could not sue in federal court), the other issues in Dred Scott's case might well be "passed by as requiring neither a particular examination, nor an adjudication directly upon them."

However, Daniel continued:

> [A]s these questions are intrinsically of primary interest and magnitude, and have been elaborately discussed in argument, and as with respect to them the opinions of a majority of the court, including my own, are perfectly coincident, to me it seems proper that they should be here fully considered and, so far as practicable for this court to accomplish such an end, finally put to rest.[15]

Thus Daniel candidly admitted that the law did not require the *Dred Scott* Court to rule on the Missouri Compromise issue, but that the Court instead chose to do so in order to try to put that issue "to rest."

Daniel's analysis of the Missouri Compromise issue was simpler and more straightforward than Taney's. Daniel subscribed to the "common property" theory (championed most prominently by John Calhoun of South Carolina). Daniel maintained that the federal territories were the common property of all U.S. citizens, both North and South, and that the territories were to be administered by the federal government as a trustee on behalf of *all* its citizens. It was not permissible for Congress to discriminate against any one group of citizens by excluding them from the territories, for to do so would be "to bestow upon a portion of the citizens of this nation that which is the common property and privilege of all."[16] The Missouri Compromise was unconstitutional because (according to Daniel) it effectively excluded the citizens of the slave-holding states from the federal territories.[17] And discrimination against slave-holders was particularly outrageous, said Daniel, because slave property was given special recognition and protection in the Constitution (by virtue of its Fugitive

Slave Clause); "no other right of property is placed by the Constitution upon the same high ground, nor shielded by a similar guaranty."[18]

Since the Constitution granted this special protected status to slave property, Daniel (somewhat overheatedly) argued, it was ridiculous to suppose that the Constitution at the same time empowered Congress to restrict the right of slaveholders to bring their slaves to live in the federal territories. "The injustice and extravagance necessarily implied in a supposition like this, cannot be rationally imputed to the patriotic or the honest, or those who were merely sane."[19]

Daniel's embrace of this "common property" theory allowed him to avoid many of the logical and legal problems that had ensnared Taney. Unlike Taney, Daniel felt no need to try to draw a dubious constitutional distinction between the anti-slavery provisions of the Northwest Ordinance and those of the Missouri Compromise. Daniel believed that *both* the Northwest Ordinance and the Missouri Compromise were unconstitutional for essentially the same reason—each attempted to restrict slaveholders' access to the federal territories, which were supposed to be the common property of *all* Americans.

Thus, according to Daniel, the Northwest Ordinance's anti-slavery provisions "never had and never could have any legitimate and binding force"[20]; and the Missouri Compromise of 1820 was likewise void.

—Justice Wayne—

James Wayne of Georgia was a three-term Congressman when President Jackson appointed Wayne to the U.S. Supreme Court in 1836. Wayne was a firm supporter of Jackson. Jackson particularly valued the support that Wayne, as a southerner, had given to Jackson in opposing the doctrine of "nullification" advanced by John Calhoun.

Wayne's gifts were probably more political than strictly legal in nature. At the time of Wayne's appointment to the Court, Senator Daniel Webster of Massachusetts (perhaps the country's leading constitutional litigator at that time) commented that Wayne might be better suited to serve as Speaker of the House. Throughout his years on the Court, Wayne was known more for his skill at working with his colleagues in conference (and for his web of valuable social and political connections) than for any purely legal or intellectual accomplishment.[21]

Fittingly, Wayne's chief contribution to the *Dred Scott* decision was his key role in the Court's conference in shaping the Court's decision. It was Wayne who proposed that the Court issue a broad Opinion (to be written by Taney) that took on the issues of the Missouri Compromise and Negro citizenship; and it was Wayne who boasted that, by persuading Taney and the Court to approve that proposal, Wayne had won a great victory for the South.

The "Peace and Harmony of the Country"

Wayne's concurring Opinion expressly adopted Taney's reasoning *in toto*. But Wayne did write a few pages of his own attempting to defend the broad scope of the *Dred Scott* decision. Wayne apparently felt the need to justify what he had wrought. His Opinion might well be placed in the category of "protesting too much."

On the one hand, Wayne appeared to acknowledge that the Court had, as a matter of discretion, chosen to issue a broad decision because the Court believed that judicial resolution of the larger issues in the *Dred Scott* case would help restore national unity. Thus Wayne wrote: "The case involves private rights of value, and constitutional principles of the highest importance, about which there had become such a difference of opinion, that the peace and harmony of the country required the settlement of them by judicial decision."[22]

On the other hand, however, Wayne repeatedly asserted in a variety of formulations that the Court was legally required to reach all the issues it did, and that the decision was therefore perfectly ordinary. Wayne declared: that no "point has been discussed and decided which was not called for by the record, or which was not necessary for the judicial disposition of it"; that "the court neither sought nor made the case"; and that the Justices had only "discharged" their "duty" as the Framers intended they should.[23]

To buttress these assertions, Wayne adopted and restated Taney's argument for moving beyond the jurisdictional issue. Like Taney, Wayne argued that the Court had the authority and the duty to review both the jurisdictional issue and the merits of the case.

However, Wayne ignored the obvious and more troubling question as to the scope of the *Dred Scott* decision: Even assuming that the Court could review the merits of the case, why was it necessary for the Court to reach the Missouri Compromise issue? After all, as to the merits of the case, Chief Justice Taney agreed with Justice Nelson (and with the circuit court below) that Missouri law governed Dred Scott's status and provided that

Scott was still a slave; and Wayne now agreed with Taney. It was perfectly appropriate to deny Dred Scott his freedom on that basis alone. Why, then, in Wayne's view was it "necessary for the judicial disposition" of Dred Scott's case for the Supreme Court to go on and also rule on the constitutionality of the Missouri Compromise?

Wayne gave no real answer because, in truth, as a legal matter—Wayne's protestations notwithstanding—it was neither necessary nor ordinary for the Court to reach that grave constitutional issue. The only intellectually honest justification that could be offered for the scope of the *Dred Scott* decision was Wayne's assertion that a broad decision was necessary in order to restore "the peace and harmony of the country."

B) The Politicians

—Justice Campbell—

Of all the Justices on the *Dred Scott* Court, John Campbell was the one who had given the most serious study to slavery as an institution, and to its future.

Prior to his appointment to the bench, Campbell wrote a series of articles concerning the future of slavery. In those articles, Campbell maintained that immediate emancipation in the United States would be a disaster, as Campbell asserted it had been in Santo Domingo and in the British West Indies. Campbell believed that American slavery was destined to expire, but that the process should be gradual, extending over several generations. In the meanwhile, Campbell argued, it was the obligation of slaveholders to begin to prepare their slaves for freedom. Campbell favored a series of proposals that—for the South of his day—were regarded as quite liberal. He believed that Negro slaves should be educated in schools, encouraged to worship in church, and taught useful trades; and Campbell thought it essential that slave families be kept intact.[24]

For these reasons, Campbell considered himself to be a moderate on the slavery issue. In the period immediately preceding the Civil War, Campbell made a series of efforts to act as a go-between—talking both to the Lincoln administration and to Jefferson Davis' Confederate government, and trying to work out an agreement that would head off the war. Upon the failure of those efforts, Campbell resigned from the Court and served as an Assistant

Secretary of War for the Confederacy. Toward the end of the Civil War, Campbell again made a number of unsuccessful efforts to broker a peace agreement between North and South.

Campbell's Private Views on Slavery and the Territories

By way of background, prior to his appointment to the Supreme Court, Campbell practiced law in Montgomery and then in Mobile, Alabama. He gained something of a hero's reputation for "ending" an uprising of Creek Indians[25] in 1836. (In truth, Campbell did little more than accept the surrender of a bedraggled band of desperate Creeks; however, Campbell did deserve credit for speaking with the Creeks, and for publicizing how they were being routinely cheated out of their treaty rights.[26]) Campbell served in Alabama's state legislature and became active in Democratic politics. Campbell's father was friendly with John Calhoun, and Campbell sometimes corresponded with Calhoun about political matters. (Calhoun had assisted Campbell in securing an appointment to West Point after Campbell had graduated from the University of Georgia at the age of fourteen.)

In particular, Campbell corresponded at length with Calhoun about the consequences of the Mexican War. Campbell feared that the territories to be taken from Mexico would naturally become free states, and that the roughly even balance of power in Congress between the free and slave states would therefore be destroyed.[27] For this reason, Campbell thought that the South should oppose taking any territory from Mexico; but, failing that, Campbell favored legislation guaranteeing slaveholders' rights in the territories to be acquired from Mexico.

In an 1848 letter, Campbell flatly told Calhoun that he believed that Congress did possess the power to ban slavery in the territories, if it chose to do so:

> I think Congress has the power to organize inhabitants of a territory of the U.S. into a body politic, and to determine in what manner they shall be governed. As incident to this power, I think that Congress may decide what shall be held and enjoyed as property in that territory and that persons should not be held as property . . . . There is nothing about Slave property that I know of that takes it from the sway of legislative authority."

Moreover, Campbell pointed out to Calhoun that this view was supported by consistent practice, including "the repeated sanctions to the [Northwest] Ordinance of 1787 by Congress; the implied sanction in the compacts of Georgia and North Carolina ceding territories and stipulating for the extension of the [Northwest] Ordinance except in one particular [the anti-slavery restriction]; the Missouri Compromise; [and] the admission of Texas with a restriction."[28]

In all of this, Campbell sounded a good deal like Montgomery Blair or George Curtis would when they argued for Dred Scott before the Supreme Court in 1856—that is, Campbell was setting forth the traditional view that Congress did possess and had routinely exercised the power to decide which federal territories would be free and which would have slavery.

As a Supreme Court Justice, however, Campbell took exactly the opposite view in *Dred Scott*; he joined the pro-slavery majority in denying that Congress possessed the power to ban slavery in the territories.

Campbell's Public Stand

Nevertheless, Campbell's stance in *Dred Scott* was not surprising. Campbell never made public the views he expressed in his private 1848 correspondence with Calhoun. Rather, as the public and Congressional debate that ultimately led to the Compromise of 1850 heated up, Campbell decided to cast his lot with the southern "fire-eaters" who declared that Congress had no right to ban slavery in the territories and who broadly hinted that the South might soon secede from the Union.

Campbell was elected to serve as one of Alabama's delegates to the Nashville Convention, a quasi-official 1850 gathering of representatives from the southern states, whose purpose was to formulate a unified southern response to the sectional conflict surrounding the Compromise of 1850. There, Campbell argued in a series of speeches and resolutions that neither Congress nor any territorial legislature had the power to restrict slavery in the territories; Campbell asserted that unless and until a newly formed state chose to ban slavery, there was a right to hold slaves in a federal territory that was protected by the federal Constitution. Campbell further hinted (employing some rather hot rhetoric) that the South was both willing and legally entitled to secede from the Union unless the rights of slaveholders in the territories were recognized.[29]

In an 1851 essay titled "The Rights of the Slave States," Campbell expanded on these themes, decrying the "pervading evil of antislavery agitation" and speaking of the uncertain future of a Union that included eleven "subjugated" slave States.[30] Campbell declared that the southern states must unite "for their common defense." He noted that the North's population and economic power were growing far more rapidly than those of the South. Thus, he wrote, it was best that the struggle between North and South over the future of slavery in the territories be conducted now, before the South was rendered politically and economically impotent.[31]

Thus, by the time the newly elected President Franklin Pierce appointed Campbell to the Supreme Court in 1853, all concerned clearly understood where Campbell stood on the issue of slavery in the territories; Campbell, like Pierce, denied that Congress possessed the power to restrict slavery in the territories, and he further believed that the issue was the key to keeping the South from leaving the Union. Indeed, Campbell's views on the territorial slavery question were likely a crucial consideration in his selection. The outgoing President Millard Fillmore had previously nominated Senator George Badger of North Carolina for the same seat on the Court, but Badger's nomination had been rejected in important part because of Badger's record of support for the Wilmot Proviso.

Campbell on Choice of Law in *Dred Scott*

Campbell's *Dred Scott* Opinion demonstrated that he had done a great deal of scholarly research. But Campbell's central argument meandered in a somewhat confusing way through a large volume of citations and quotations.

To begin with, Campbell clearly agreed with all the other pro-slavery Justices on the *Dred Scott* Court that Missouri law governed Dred Scott's status and provided that Scott was still a slave. But the basis for Campbell's agreement was remarkably unclear.

Campbell characterized the question presented as whether the removal of a slave to a free jurisdiction "where neither the master nor slave discloses a purpose to remain permanently" emancipated the slave.[32] Moreover, Campbell went out of his way to assert that he did not intend to "impugn the authority" of those prior slave state court decisions holding that a slave brought to live in a free state by a master who intended to reside there *did* become free.[33]

Yet Dred Scott claimed that he was free because Dr. Emerson *had* indeed disclosed a purpose to reside permanently on free soil, first in Illinois and later in the Wisconsin Territory; and the central, hotly contested holding of the circuit court in *Dred Scott v. Sanford* (and of the Missouri Supreme Court in *Scott v. Emerson* before that) was that once Dred Scott returned to Missouri he would be treated as a slave once again *even if* Emerson had established a permanent domicile in Illinois or

Wisconsin. Campbell thus appeared to either completely misunderstand or deliberately confuse the central issue in the entire *Dred Scott* case.

Campbell's Revisionist History

Campbell then moved into a long historical discussion on the subject of Congressional authority over the territories. In a sense, that discussion was a mirror image of Campbell's prior private correspondence with John Calhoun—Campbell addressed the same points, in almost the same order, but took the reverse position on each.

For example, Campbell had written to Calhoun that Congress certainly possessed the power to organize the territories, and that implicit within that power was the power to pass legislation for the territories—including legislation on the subject of slavery. But in *Dred Scott* Campbell wrote that the "recognition of a plenary power . . . to organize a Government over it [a Territory], does not imply a corresponding authority to determine the internal polity, or to adjust the domestic relations [of the Territory]."[34] Rather, Campbell appeared to argue, the power to legislate for a territory belonged to the territory's own legislature.

Campbell next tried to distinguish away all the same historical precedents that he had earlier argued to Calhoun supported the proposition that Congress could restrict slavery in the territories. The Northwest Ordinance of 1787 and the assertion of Congressional authority over the Georgia and North Carolina cessions, said Campbell, were of questionable constitutional validity, and were justified only by their unique historical circumstances and the doctrine of "necessity."[35]

Campbell turned next to the Louisiana Purchase (of 1803) and Missouri Compromise (of 1820). At the outset, Campbell questioned whether the original law passed by Congress providing for the government of the Louisiana Territory (which called for Presidential appointment of a Governor, Judges and Legislative Council) had been constitutional. For Campbell, this arrangement resembled an imperial form of government—like England's rule over the American colonies prior to the Revolution—and conflicted with the constitutional principle that the people of the territories were Americans who were entitled to govern themselves.[36]

As to the Missouri Compromise, Campbell blithely dismissed it as precedent by asserting that the Compromise "was not seriously debated, nor were its Constitutional aspects severely scrutinized by Congress."[37] This was truly revisionist history at its worst; the Congressional debate over slavery in the territories that led to the Missouri Compromise of 1820 had been probably the most divisive in American history (until it was succeeded by the debates concerning the Compromise of 1850 and the Kansas-Nebraska Act of 1854). Everyone concerned, both inside and outside Congress, had recognized that the future of the Union was at stake and that constitutional questions were at the heart of the debate.[38]

Moreover, the extraordinary breadth of Campbell's pro-slavery radicalism became increasingly evident here. In the space of just a few paragraphs, Campbell had seriously questioned not only the constitutionality of the Missouri Compromise's anti-slavery restriction, but also the constitutionality of a) the Northwest Ordinance; b) the cession by North Carolina and Georgia of the territory that ultimately became the states of Tennessee, Alabama and Mississippi; and c) the government of the vast western territory that was acquired by the U.S. through the Louisiana Purchase. Had Campbell's somewhat theoretical arguments here been taken seriously, they would have called into question the legitimacy of virtually every act undertaken by government in the original American West from 1789 forward.

Campbell Declares the Missouri Compromise Void

Campbell then reached the heart of his argument—attempting to demonstrate that Congress had no authority to enact the Missouri Compromise. Campbell took a very different tack than Taney. Campbell did not try to argue that the Constitution's Territory Clause applied only to the territory of the U.S. that already existed in 1789.

Instead, Campbell adopted the argument advanced by John Sanford's lawyers, and asserted that the Territory Clause merely empowered Congress to deal with and sell public lands owned by the United States, wherever situated. That is, Campbell argued, Congressional power under the Territory Clause was limited to "such administrative and conservatory acts as are needful for the preservation of the public domain, and its preparation for sale and disposition."[39]

To support his argument, Campbell somewhat melodramatically and at great length invoked the history of the American Revolution. Campbell asserted that the key principle for which the Revolution was fought was the right of the American colonists to govern themselves. Campbell maintained that it therefore made no sense to suppose that the Framers intended by the Territory Clause to confer upon the United States Congress a broad power to govern the people of the territories from afar. According to Campbell, such a reading of the Territory Clause necessarily meant that George

Washington and all the heroes of the Revolutionary era had casually surrendered the precious principle of self-government[40] for which they had sacrificed so much during the Revolutionary War.[41]

Campbell concluded that neither the Territory Clause (nor any other provision of the Constitution) empowered Congress to restrict slavery in the federal territories, and the Missouri Compromise was therefore void.

Campbell's Confusing Coda

At the very end of his long concurring Opinion, Campbell circled back in somewhat confusing fashion to the same choice-of-law issue with which he began.

Campbell stated: a) that Dred Scott's domicile had always been in Missouri; b) that Scott's travels with Dr. Emerson (for six years) on free soil were a mere "temporary elocation"; c) that the circuit court's legal instructions (stating that Missouri law governed Scott's status and provided that he was still a slave) were therefore correct; and d) that the jury's verdict declaring that Scott was still a slave was therefore also correct. "[T]he Opinion of the Circuit Court was correct upon all the claims involved in those issues, and the verdict of the jury was justified . . . ." Accordingly, said Campbell, Dred Scott was a slave, and not a "citizen" of Missouri; and, as a consequence, Scott was not entitled to bring a federal court suit in which jurisdiction was based on diversity of citizenship. Thus, according to Campbell, Dred Scott's case should be dismissed for lack of jurisdiction.[42]

In other words, Campbell agreed with the verdict of the Circuit Court below and with the reasons given for that verdict.

Campbell left unanswered the obvious question posed by this confusing coda: If the verdict of the circuit court were correct, why not simply affirm that verdict? Why was it necessary for Campbell to go on and analyze the constitutionality of the Missouri Compromise? Campbell—like most of his pro-slavery colleagues on the *Dred Scott* Court—refused to grapple with (or even acknowledge) that central question.

—Justice Catron—

John Catron was born in Pennsylvania during the 1780s. He grew up in Virginia and Kentucky, and then settled in Tennessee. He served in the Army and fought in the War of 1812 under General Andrew Jackson, and then entered legal practice in rural Tennessee, frequently serving as a prosecutor.

At General Jackson's suggestion, Catron moved to Nashville in 1818, and there Catron became an expert in disputed land claims. In 1824 the Tennessee Legislature appointed Catron to serve as a Justice on Tennessee's highest court (called the Court of Errors and Appeals), and he became Chief Justice of that Court in 1831. Catron gained fame as a judge in part because he took a firm stand against the practice of dueling—still common in Tennessee at the time—which Catron termed mere "honorable homicide."

Catron married into the same family as rising Tennessee politician James K. Polk. Together, Polk and Catron were active supporters of Presidential candidate Andrew Jackson. After Jackson's election in 1828, Chief Justice Catron (who was never overly concerned about separating judicial duties and political activity) provided Jackson with valuable support in Jackson's struggles with the Bank of the United States and with John Calhoun's "nullifiers."

In 1834 an anti-Jackson coalition briefly took control of Tennessee's state legislature. They voted to restructure Tennessee's highest court and thereby (not coincidentally) remove Catron from the bench. Catron went back to private practice, and he also took an active role with the pro-Jackson newspaper *The Nashville Union.*

Jackson's handpicked successor, Martin Van Buren, was elected President in 1836. In the very last days of his Presidency (before Van Buren's inauguration in March of 1837), Jackson pushed a bill through Congress reorganizing the U.S. Supreme Court and federal Circuit Courts,[43] and Jackson nominated Catron as a U.S. Supreme Court Justice. A few weeks later, Congress approved Catron's nomination.

Throughout his years on the Court, Catron kept his finger on the political pulse. He was a good friend and confidant to former President Jackson, to President Polk and to President Buchanan. As noted earlier, Catron was especially close to Buchanan. Buchanan had lived with the Catron family for a time when Buchanan served as Secretary of State, and some well-informed people regarded Catron as a "wire-puller" for Buchanan.

Catron's relationships with his fellow Justices were generally good. However, Catron's long tenure on the Court overlapped almost exactly with that of Chief Justice Taney, and Catron did not always show Taney the deference that would have been expected from a more junior member of the Court.

Catron Demolishes Taney's Opinion

Catron was certainly a loyal friend of Buchanan's, but his *Dred Scott* Opinion betrayed a degree of tension with Chief Justice Taney and with some of the other pro-slavery Justices that bordered on open contempt.

Catron gave short shrift to two arguments to which Taney had devoted many laborious pages. First, as a matter of the rules of pleading and appellate review, Catron firmly declared that John Sanford had waived the issue of Negro citizenship by failing to raise it at trial, and that the Supreme Court therefore had no authority to review it in Dred Scott's case.[44]

Second, Catron bluntly affirmed that the Territory Clause did indeed confer upon Congress a general power to legislate for the federal territories. He traced the history of the drafting of the clause at the Constitutional Convention and its relation to the Northwest Ordinance, and concluded that it was plain that the Framers intended to grant Congress the authority to govern and legislate for the federal territories.[45]

Catron then added a sarcastic note, while at the same time emphasizing the radical nature of the arguments now advanced by Taney and Campbell (and the other pro-slavery Justices who had denied federal authority over the territories). "It is asking much of a Judge," Catron wrote, "who has for nearly twenty years been exercising jurisdiction from the western Missouri line to the Rocky Mountains, and, on this understanding of the Constitution, inflicting the extreme penalty of death for crimes committed when the direct legislation of Congress was the only rule, to agree that he had been all the while acting in mistake, and as an usurper."[46]

Catron argued that Congress had in fact exercised authority over the territories for more than sixty years, and that it was therefore "now too late to call that power into question." Moreover, the notion that the Territory Clause did not confer the power to govern the territories was, said Catron, plainly contradicted by the Court's own prior decisions—including the quite recent decision in *Cross v. Harrison* (which had affirmed federal power over California under the Territory Clause).[47]

Furthermore, said Catron, those prior Supreme Court decisions confirming that the Territory Clause conferred upon the federal government the power to govern the territories were obviously correct. For Catron, it was almost ludicrous for Taney and his pro-slavery colleagues to argue that the Constitution could, on the one hand, authorize the federal government to acquire territory, and yet, on the other, fail to authorize the federal government to govern that territory. How, Catron asked, was it even possible "for the judicial mind to conceive that the United States government, created solely by the Constitution, could, by lawful treaty acquire territory over which the acquiring power had no jurisdiction to hold and govern it, by force of the instrument under whose authority the country was acquired"?[48] [49]

Catron's *Dred Scott* Decision

Having virtually demolished Taney's Opinion of the Court, Catron then set about giving his own reasons for denying Dred Scott his freedom and for invalidating the Missouri Compromise.

Catron acknowledged Congressional power over the territories, but he identified two important limitations on that power that impacted the institution of slavery.

First, Catron asserted that the power of Congress over each of the federal territories was limited by the terms under which the U.S. had first acquired each particular territory. Virginia had ceded the old Northwest Territory to the U.S. and had insisted as a term of cession that slavery be prohibited there forever; as a result, said Catron, the Northwest Ordinance's anti-slavery restriction was valid. Similarly, North Carolina's and Georgia's cession of the territory that ultimately became part of the states of Tennessee, Alabama and Mississippi, respectively, included a term providing that slavery must be permitted there; accordingly, said Catron, Congressional legislation to that effect was also altogether proper.

However, the Missouri Compromise of 1820 dealt with the territory acquired by the Louisiana Purchase in 1803; and Catron thought that this fact presented an important problem. The Treaty with France by which the U.S. made the Louisiana Purchase included a provision stating that "the inhabitants of the ceded territory shall be incorporated in the Union of the United States, and admitted as soon as possible, according to the principles of the Federal Constitution, to the enjoyment of all the rights, advantages, and immunities of the citizens of the United States; and, in the mean time, *they shall be maintained and protected in the free enjoyment of their* liberty, *property* and the religion which they profess."[50] (Emphasis added.)

Catron noted that by these words the Treaty guaranteed to the inhabitants of Louisiana[51] the free enjoyment of their property, which (for Catron) included the right to take their slaves anywhere in the Louisiana

Territory. (Moreover, Catron declared—without any effort at justification—that this right could not be "denied to the original inhabitants *and their descendants. And, if it be true that immigrants were equally protected, it must follow that they can also stand on the treaty.*")[52] (Emphasis added.) The Missouri Compromise, said Catron, violated the Treaty because it prohibited slaveholders from taking or holding slaves within the Louisiana Territory north of the Missouri line.

There were some obvious problems with Catron's logic. First, it is now well-settled that Congress' power to pass laws in essence trumps any treaty. Accordingly, as many modern commentators have pointed out, Catron was wrong to say that the Louisiana Purchase Treaty could invalidate the Missouri Compromise.[53]

Second, and probably more important, Catron's argument involved some remarkable legal alchemy. At most, the Louisiana Purchase Treaty protected the property rights of the people who already inhabited Louisiana at the time the Treaty was signed. (There were only a few thousand people scattered throughout the vast Louisiana Territory in 1803, and only some of them owned slaves.) Catron had no basis for asserting that the Treaty also protected the right of the original inhabitants' *descendants* to own slaves; and he had absolutely no basis for asserting that subsequent *immigrants* to the Louisiana Territory were also somehow protected by the 1803 Treaty.

In other words, Catron took what was essentially a transitional rule included in the treaty with France—a rule that, by its terms, was intended to protect a few French colonials who already owned slaves in Louisiana in 1803 from losing those slaves—and by his own say-so transformed it into something wholly different: namely, an unalterable national commitment to protect slavery throughout the Louisiana Purchase forever.

Nevertheless, even with this strained reading of the Louisiana Purchase Treaty, Catron still had a serious political problem. President Buchanan and the Democratic Party did not want to invalidate the Missouri Compromise alone; they wanted a general declaration that Congress could not prohibit slavery in *any* federal territory—including all the territory acquired through the Mexican War. The Louisiana Purchase Treaty—no matter how generously Catron read it—could not do all that.

Catron's "Equality of the States"

Accordingly, Catron identified a second limitation on Congressional authority over the territories. He too adopted Calhoun's "common property" doctrine, and argued that any restriction on slavery in the federal territories violated "that great fundamental condition of the Union—the equality of States." The Constitution's privileges-and-immunities clause, said Catron, guaranteed to each citizen of each state the right to enter the federal territory "in right of his State, and enjoy the common property." According to Catron, a law (like the Missouri Compromise) that prohibited slaveholders from bringing slaves into a federal territory excluded slaveholders from the nation's common property just as effectively as a law that flatly prohibited slaveholders from entering free territory, even if they left their slaves behind.

Catron therefore concluded that any federal restriction on slavery in any federal territory effectively excluded citizens of the slave states, and was unconstitutional because it violated the principle that all states were equal.[54]

The depth of Catron's commitment to this "common property/equality of the States" doctrine is questionable. In one of his private letters to Buchanan written just a few weeks before *Dred Scott* was decided, Catron set forth in capsule form (with some citations and quotations) his legal reasons for concluding that the Missouri Compromise was unconstitutional. Catron explained to Buchanan (himself a very able lawyer, twice offered a seat on the Supreme Court) Catrons's view that the Louisiana Purchase Treaty invalidated the Missouri Compromise's anti-slavery restriction. Yet Catron made no mention to Buchanan of the notion that—as a general matter—*all* restrictions on slavery in the territories somehow violated the "equality of the States." If Catron truly believed in this line of argument—which touched on the fundamental nature of the Union—it is very odd that he did not even mention it to Buchanan.

In any event, turning at last to the concrete question of Dred Scott's fate, in his concurring Opinion Catron reasoned that since the Missouri Compromise was void, Dred Scott's presence in the Wisconsin Territory did not free him.[55] As to Scott's time in Illinois, Catron briefly asserted that Dr. Emerson never became an inhabitant of Illinois (even though Emerson lived at Fort Armstrong for two years, and had no other home throughout that period). Accordingly, Catron concluded that—for the legal reasons set forth more fully by Justice Nelson—Dred Scott did not become free as a result of his time in Illinois either.[56]

Catron's Legal Flexibility

Catron's Concurring Opinion was truly remarkable. Using unusually harsh and sarcastic rhetoric, Catron virtually dismissed as nonsense the legal reasoning that had been employed by Chief Justice Taney and several of his pro-slavery colleagues. Then Catron constructed his own independent Opinion justifying the *Dred Scott* decision. The most distinctive element of that Opinion was Catron's willingness to read the Louisiana Purchase Treaty in a very, very broad fashion in order to strike down the Missouri Compromise.

Catron's unduly flexible reading of the Louisiana Purchase Treaty raises a strong suspicion that his Opinion was inspired more by political considerations than by genuine conviction. Similarly, Catron's last-minute embrace of the "common-property" doctrine (which Catron had not even mentioned in his private letters to Buchanan written just several weeks earlier) raises the suspicion that Catron was willing to adopt whatever argument he found at hand to justify a pre-determined result. Those suspicions grow stronger when one recalls that Catron—apparently without any ethical qualms—worked together in secret with President Buchanan to reach Buchanan's desired result in *Dred Scott* (and that Buchanan at the same time granted Catron's request that Aaron Brown be appointed Postmaster General).

Such suspicions are reinforced by the fact that Catron had, on at least one prior occasion, privately expressed views directly contrary to the position that he took publicly in the *Dred Scott* case. Specifically, back in 1848 Justice Catron wrote to his old Tennessee friend President James Polk in connection with a speech given by Massachusetts Congressman Julius Rockwell. Rockwell's speech advocated excluding slavery from the Oregon Territory (and also made some favorable references to Catron's Opinion in the Tennessee case of *Fisher's Negroes v. Dabbs*.[57])[58] In his private letter to Polk, Catron indicated that he agreed with Rockwell that slavery should be excluded from Oregon, and that Catron would vote for such a law if he were in Congress. Catron further indicated that he thought Congress should pass a law extending the Missouri Compromise line west through all the new territory acquired during the Mexican War, prohibiting slavery north of that line and permitting slavery to the south.[59]

Thus—much like Justice Campbell in his private correspondence with John Calhoun—in 1848 Justice Catron privately expressed the view that Congress *did* possess the power to exclude slavery from the federal territories, if it chose to do so. In his published Opinion in *Dred Scott* in

1857, however, Catron boldly asserted that such an exclusion violated the "great fundamental condition of the Union" that all states were equal.

Catron and Campbell's Shifting Views

In *Dred Scott* Justices Catron and Campbell each rejected their own previously expressed private views on slavery in the territories. Why? It is possible that both Campbell and Catron did not truly believe the positions they took in *Dred Scott*, but instead simply bowed to the political pressures of the day. On the other hand, it is, of course, instead possible that Catron and Campbell each *honestly* changed their thinking on the paramount constitutional issue of their era.

Perhaps the truth lies somewhere in between. Judges are, of course, usually lawyers to start with, and many lawyers possess the ability to convince themselves over time that their client's position is right. A lawyer may have serious doubts when first looking at a particular legal proposition as an objective matter; but the process of arguing a client's position and of seeing matters through the client's eyes will often change a lawyer's own beliefs.

Catron and Campbell were politically active Democrats. At the close of the Mexican War in 1848, when the U.S. first confronted the question what to do about slavery in the territory to be taken from Mexico, many Democrats—including President Polk and his Secretary of State James Buchanan—favored the extension of the Missouri Compromise line west to the Pacific, and did not challenge the constitutionality of Congressional restrictions on slavery in the territories.[60]

Accordingly, when Catron and Campbell in 1848 privately stated the view that Congress did possess the power to restrict slavery in the territories, they were in the political mainstream of their party. But by the time *Dred Scott* was decided in 1857, the political center of the Democratic Party had shifted significantly—Democratic Presidents Pierce and Buchanan both advocated "popular sovereignty," and denied Congressional authority over slavery in the territories. The change in Catron and Campbell's legal thinking about the Missouri Compromise thus mirrored the change in their party's political position.

The very same influences that caused so many other southerners and Democrats to move to the right on the issue of slavery during the decade that preceded the *Dred Scott* decision probably helped to change Catron's and Campbell's thinking too; and, at the same time, Campbell and Catron may well have altered their legal thinking in part out of their desire to maintain political solidarity with their fellow southerners and Democrats. Catron and Campbell themselves may not have fully understood (or even cared to consider) precisely where the process of sincere intellectual change left off, and where that of expedient political accommodation began.

In other words, by the time *Dred Scott* was decided, Justices Catron and Campbell may well have talked themselves into believing a legal position that they originally knew was wrong.

C) The Dough-Faces

—Justice Grier—

Robert Grier was born in Pennsylvania in 1794. His father was a Presbyterian minister and educator. Grier attended Dickinson College in Pennsylvania (as did President Buchanan and Chief Justice Taney) and, remarkably, earned his degree after a single year. Grier succeeded his father as headmaster of the Northumberland Academy, and at the same time studied law. He became a lawyer in 1817 and developed a successful practice in Danville, Pennsylvania. A solid supporter of Andrew Jackson, Grier was named Presiding Judge of Alleghany County's District Court in 1833. In 1846 President Polk named Grier to the U.S. Supreme Court.[61] Polk clearly understood that Grier was hostile to abolitionism. (Indeed, then Judge Benjamin Patton—Grier's close friend and regular fishing companion—while urging Polk in a private letter to select Grier, assured Polk that Grier had declared during a speech at his church that the purposes of the abolitionists were unconstitutional and seditious, and must be rejected by all good Christians.)

Grier and Slavery

Thus Grier was a "dough-face"—that is, a northern Democrat friendly to the interests of the slaveholding South; and Grier was no stranger to politically charged slave cases. Grier's circuit included his home state of Pennsylvania. Pennsylvania shared a border with the slave-holding state of Maryland, and incidents involving alleged runaway slaves were the source of increasing tension between the two states. Many Pennsylvanians rebelled against the notion that any runaway slaves should be returned to bondage, and they were especially concerned about incidents where slave-catchers attempted to capture free blacks.

Grier was thus subjected to competing pressures in the slave cases that he encountered in the course of his circuit court duties. On the one hand, the people of Grier's home state of Pennsylvania were, for the most part, hostile to the rendition of fugitive slaves. On the other, Grier's Democratic party was publicly and firmly pledged to defend slaveholders' rights.

Grier therefore treaded a delicate line. As a general matter, he was quietly careful to protect the rights of individuals alleged to be fugitive slaves or to have assisted fugitive slaves. But, at the same time, Grier went out of his way to make it known that as a general matter he was dedicated to protecting the interests of slaveholders.

The Christiana Incident

For example, in his capacity as a circuit court judge, Grier presided over the celebrated treason trial of Caster Hanway. Hanway's case grew out of an incident at Christiana, Pennsylvania, on September 11, 1851. A Maryland slave owner named Gorsuch obtained a warrant pursuant to the new federal Fugitive Slave Act. With the assistance of local officials, Gorsuch attempted to seize some runaway slaves in a pre-dawn raid at the house of fugitive slave William Parker. A confrontation developed. Many black men from the surrounding area arrived at Parker's house in order to aid the fugitives. Some white men, including Caster Hanway, also arrived. Hanway refused to be deputized or to aid the Deputy U.S. Marshal who had accompanied Gorsuch; instead Hanway declared that he believed that the Negroes had a right to defend themselves, and Hanway urged Gorsuch's party to go away.

Violence broke out. Deputy Marshal Kline—described "by all parties as the most consummate coward ever seen in battle"[62]—proved useless. When the fighting began, Kline ran into a nearby cornfield. Gorsuch was killed, and others (including Gorsuch's son who was shot) were wounded; the slaves escaped. Order was restored only when a group of about one hundred nearby railroad workers arrived and arrested the rioters.

Slaveholders, especially from Maryland, were outraged. Maryland's Governor proclaimed that Maryland might secede from the Union if the rioters were not punished, and various pro-slavery public officials competed to be included on the prosecution team. As sometimes happens with cases that have received a great deal of publicity and political attention, the prosecution overcharged the defendants; Hanway and forty other men were indicted for treason. Hanway's case was the first to go to trial

After the evidence was presented, Justice Grier properly instructed the jury that even armed violence against law enforcement officials did not constitute "treason" if it were undertaken for a private purpose (such as preventing the recapture of particular slaves); treason consisted of levying war against the United States. Thus, said Grier, a mere refusal to aid in the capture of a fugitive slave did not constitute treason. Not surprisingly, after hearing these instructions the jury properly acquitted Hanway after deliberating for about fifteen minutes.

At the same time, however, Grier's charge to the jury made it abundantly clear that Grier's sympathies were with Gorsuch and the other slave-catchers. Grier virtually apoligized to the people of Maryland for Hanway's acquittal, and Grier devoted a great deal of time to an extraneous denunciation of abolitionists and anti-slavery politicians as the true cause of the Christiana riot. For, example, Grier proclaimed:

> The guilt of this foul murder rests not alone on the deluded individuals who were its immediate perpetrators, but the blood taints with even deeper dye the skirts of those who promulgate doctrines subversive of all morality and all government. This murderous tragedy is but the necessary development of principles and the natural fruit from seed sown by others, whom the arm of the law cannot reach.[63]

Enforcing the Fugitive Slave Act

On a number of other occasions, Grier made it known that he believed all resistance to the rendition of fugitive slaves must be overcome, by force if necessary. In 1847, Pennsylvania repealed a prior law which had provided that a slave who remained in the State less than six months would be regarded as a sojourner, and passed a "personal liberty" law providing instead that a slave became free immediately upon entering the state. Grier wrote a private letter to his friend, then Secretary of State James Buchanan, arguing that the Pennsylvania Legislature must have failed to understand the "evil consequences" the new law would have—namely, that the new law would encourage Pennsylvanians to try to aid fugitive slaves. The new Pennsylvania law was "entirely unconstitutional, null and void," Grier wrote to Buchanan, and Grier reported that he had so held in at least one unpublished case.

A new federal Fugitive Slave Act became law as part of the Compromise of 1850. Grier was acutely concerned that its enforcement might be obstructed by anti-slavery Pennsylvanians hostile to its purposes. Grier presided over one of the very first proceedings brought under the Act. When the fugitive's lawyer asked for some additional time to prepare his case, Grier stated that he was reluctant to grant an adjournment. Grier explained that he had read reports of meetings at which resolutions had been adopted urging armed resistance to the Fugitive Slave Act (and, presumably, Grier was therefore worried that such resistance might be organized during any adjournment he might grant). Grier then proclaimed that the men who gave such advice were the colored people's worst enemy, and that the killing of the first officer engaged in enforcing the Act would be the signal for the extermination of the black race.

On a slightly less bloodthirsty note, a short time later, Justice Grier and his Philadelphia colleague Judge John Kane wrote to President Fillmore requesting an order authorizing the use of federal troops in order to quell any public disturbance that arose in connection with a fugitive slave proceeding.[64]

Oliver v. Weakley

Justice Grier presided over the 1853 case of *Oliver v. Weakley*[65] as part of his circuit court duties. *Weakley* bore some marked similarities to the *Dred Scott* case in that it too involved complex choice-of-law issues.

Cecilia Oliver passed through Pennsylvania on a return trip from Arkansas to Maryland in early 1847, together with slaves she had recently inherited from her father. A few months later the slaves escaped back to Pennsylvania. They were given shelter there by Stephen Weakley, among others. Ms. Oliver sued for the value of her escaped slaves. After several rounds of litigation, she prevailed at a jury trial conducted before Justice Grier, winning a judgment against Weakley for $2,800.

Justice Grier carefully instructed the jury that a defendant who merely performed acts of kindness to a runaway slave was not liable for the slave's escape; a defendant such as Weakley was liable only if he acted with the intention to prevent the master from recovering the slave.

More important, Grier found as a matter of law that Ms. Oliver's slaves were indeed slaves. The defendant Weakley had argued that he was not liable because once Ms. Oliver voluntarily brought her slaves into Pennsylvania they immediately became free under Pennsylvania's new personal liberty law. But Grier rejected that argument. Citing *Strader v. Graham*, Grier stated that—despite some "pretty things" said in the *Somerset* case—the slaves' status was controlled by Maryland law, rather than Pennsylvania law. In effect, Grier simply refused to enforce Pennsylvania's personal liberty law in federal court.

The result in *Weakley* certainly made it seem likely that in *Dred Scott* Grier would find that Missouri law controlled Scott's status, and that as a consequence Dred Scott—like Ms. Oliver's slaves—also remained a slave.

Grier's *Dred Scott* Conversion

As noted previously, Grier was the last convert among the Justices of the Supreme Court to a broad pro-slavery Opinion in *Dred Scott*. At the Court's initial February 14 conference on the case, Grier and Nelson jointly successfully urged that the Court should issue a narrow Opinion that would deny Scott his freedom solely on choice-of-law grounds. A few days later, Taney and his four southern Democratic colleagues decided to change course and issue a broad decision. But Grier and Nelson—the two northern dough-face Democrats—still held back. It was only when President-elect Buchanan personally appealed to Grier in a now-lost private letter of February 23, that Grier decided to join the pro-slavery majority in a broad decision.

What made Grier change his mind? Why did he decide to abandon the cautious approach that he had originally advocated (along with his fellow dough-face Justice Nelson)? Certainly, Grier must have been impressed by a direct request from the President of the United States for a ruling striking down the Missouri Compromise. But Grier was as knowledgeable about politics as any other Justice, and Grier knew Buchanan personally too; thus, even before receiving Buchanan's letter, Grier must have understood what kind of Opinion Buchanan wanted.

One possible factor in Grier's thinking has received relatively little attention. Grier was hard pressed to get by on his Judge's salary (which is not an uncommon circumstance). This was especially true because Grier had helped to educate and support ten younger brothers. Grier therefore asked the newly elected President Buchanan for help. Specifically, Grier requested that Buchanan give an old Democratic ally named George Plitt a new job. Grier wanted Plitt to resign Plitt's current post as Clerk of the Circuit Court in Philadelphia so that Grier could then install a relative in that same nicely paid job. At first Buchanan refused Grier's obviously improper request.

Grier then approached Plitt directly, asking Plitt to resign. Plitt refused, and noted that Buchanan had already rebuked Grier on this subject. Plitt probably felt that he was on especially firm ground because he was a long-time friend of Buchanan and had contributed to Buchanan's Presidential campaign fund.

In the end, however, Plitt was removed from his position as Circuit Court Clerk, despite a protest from many Philadelphia lawyers. (Ultimately, the clerkship went not to Grier's son-in-law, as originally contemplated, but to Benjamin Patton—Grier's fishing companion who years earlier had helped persuade President Polk to appoint Grier to the Supreme Court.) It seems unlikely that Plitt's removal came without the President's acquiescence; and it seems likely that Grier would be grateful to Buchanan for his tacit consent. Certainly, two experienced lawyers like Grier and Buchanan would never even hint (either aloud or in writing) that there had been a direct *quid pro quo* whereby Plitt's removal was traded for Grier's *Dred Scott* conversion. But the coincidence is remarkable.[66]

Grier Concurs (Timidly)

In *Dred Scott* Grier wanted to please President Buchanan and the slave-holding South; nevertheless, he still did not wish to wholly alienate his northern countrymen. So Grier hit upon a new formula. In his Concurring Opinion, Grier stated that he agreed both with Justice Nelson's narrow Concurring Opinion *and* with Chief Justice Taney's discussion of the Missouri Compromise issue.[67]

Grier may have thought that this posture represented a politically astute way to straddle or accommodate competing interests. But embracing both Nelson and Taney was not an altogether consistent position as an intellectual matter, because Taney and Nelson disagreed with each other on essential points.

To begin with, Taney contended at great length in his Opinion of the Court that the Court was *required* to rule upon the questions of Negro citizenship and the Missouri Compromise. However, in his Concurring Opinion, Nelson quietly insisted that in "the view we have taken of the case, it will not be necessary"[68] to pass upon the Negro citizenship question, and Nelson similarly declined to rule upon the Missouri Compromise's constitutionality. It is difficult to see how Justice Grier could truly agree both with Taney and with Nelson on this score.

Similarly, the heart of Nelson's Opinion was a lengthy and impressive demonstration (replete with citations to the Dutch legal scholar Huberus and to Lord Stowell, author of the English *Slave, Grace* decision) of the proposition that under choice-of-law principles derived from the law of nations, Dred Scott's case was governed by Missouri law (which provided that Scott was still a slave). Taney, however, flatly rejected the idea that such choice-of-law principles or authorities had any relevance to Dred Scott's case.[69] It is hard to see how Grier could truly agree with both Nelson and Taney on this score either.

In the end, Grier was so anxious to please Buchanan and the slaveholding South on the one hand, and so anxious not to offend northern sensibilities on the other, that his brief and somewhat contradictory Opinion wound up saying almost nothing at all, beyond the fact that (as Buchanan requested) Grier had joined the pro-slavery majority in striking down the Missouri Compromise.

And perhaps that murky state of affairs was precisely what Grier intended to achieve.

—Justice Nelson—

Samuel Nelson was born in upstate New York in 1792. His family owned slaves; indeed, it was believed that Nelson's father paid for Nelson's college education by selling a slave girl. Nelson attended Middlebury College in Vermont, and then returned to New York to practice law. He entered politics as well, and served as a postmaster for several years. He was appointed to the bench in 1823, and named a New York State Supreme Court Justice in 1831. In 1837 he was named Chief Justice of that court. In early 1845 there was an abortive movement to elect Nelson to the U.S. Senate. Just a few weeks later, the outgoing President John Tyler nominated Nelson to serve on the U.S. Supreme Court. Based on his New York record, Nelson was viewed as a careful, competent and non-controversial Judge. As anticipated, his nomination easily won Senate approval.[70]

Nelson served on the U.S. Supreme Court for many years. He retired in 1872, one year prior to his death. Nelson's career on the Court fulfilled most people's expectations for him. He did solid legal work, and drew little attention to himself. Apart from his participation in the *Dred Scott* case, the most noteworthy aspect of Nelson's long career in public service was that Nelson joined with Justice Campbell in making unsuccessful last-minute efforts to broker a peace agreement between North and South that might have averted the Civil War.

Nelson's Narrow Opinion

Like Justice Grier, Justice Nelson was a dough-face northern Democrat. His Concurring Opinion in *Dred Scott* was the narrowest and most modest written by any of the nine Justices.

Nelson began his analysis[71] by stating that, pursuant to well settled principles of the law of nations, every state and every nation possessed exclusive sovereignty within its own territory. A state, said Nelson, is not required to give effect to any other state's laws unless it voluntarily chooses to do so, either by statute or judicial rule. Accordingly, Nelson reasoned, it was up to the state of Missouri to decide whether of not to give effect within Missouri's borders to the anti-slavery laws of Illinois or of the Wisconsin Territory. Thus the question whether Dred Scott was a slave or a free man was a question to be answered by Missouri state law.[72]

Nelson then stated that Missouri's law on the subject had been fixed in Dred Scott's own previous state court case of *Scott v. Emerson*. There Missouri's highest court had declared that Missouri would no longer give effect to other states' anti-slavery laws (and Nelson noted that the same rule had been followed in two subsequent Missouri Supreme Court decisions). Nelson further noted that Missouri's rule was consistent with *Strader v. Graham* and with the general current of authority, both in the U.S. and abroad. The federal court in *Scott v. Sanford* was required to follow the Missouri rule, and it properly did so. The verdict of the federal trial court declaring Scott a slave was therefore correct, said Nelson, and should be affirmed.[73] Nelson further reasoned that in view of the foregoing it was not necessary for the Supreme Court to decide on the jurisdictional issue of Negro citizenship or on the constitutionality of the Missouri Compromise, and Nelson expressly declined to do so.[74]

Nelson thus approached the overarching question of the scope of the *Dred Scott* decision in a very dry, matter-of-fact fashion. Nelson's resolution of the choice-of-law issue made it plain that Dred Scott would remain a slave; accordingly, to Nelson it was almost self-evident that there was no need to deal with any of the more controversial issues concerning the Missouri Compromise and Negro citizenship that the pro-slavery majority had addressed. Nelson did not *expressly* criticize the majority's decision to reach those unnecessary issues; he simply let his workman-like, common sense approach speak for itself.

Ominous Hints

Nelson's Concurring Opinion was deliberately modest in scope; but it did contain some ominous hints as to what the Supreme Court might soon do in future slavery cases.

Specifically, Nelson's Opinion included a final paragraph that read:

> A question has been alluded to, on the argument, namely: the right of the master with his slave of transit into or through a free State, on business or commercial pursuits, or in the exercise of a Federal right, or the discharge of a Federal duty, being a citizen of the United States, which is not before us. This question depends upon different considerations and principles from the one in hand, and turns upon the rights and privileges secured to a common citizen of the republic under the Constitution of the United States. When that question arises, we shall be prepared to decide it.[75]

Similarly, Nelson stated earlier in his Opinion that "*except in cases where the power is restrained by the Constitution of the United States*, the law of the State is supreme over the subject of slavery within its jurisdiction."[76]

The import of these passages from Nelson's Opinion was not altogether clear; but when these two passages were read together and in context it appeared that the dough-face Nelson was suggesting that he would be friendly to certain pro-slavery arguments in future cases.

Specifically, the first-quoted passage suggested that Nelson might some-day hold that (because of the Constitution's privileges-and-immunities clause) slaveholders, at least in certain cases, possessed a constitutional right to travel with their slaves through a free state—even if that free state had a "personal liberty" law that declared that any slave who entered the state immediately became free.

The second passage was more enigmatic. It was not clear what limitation Nelson believed was imposed by the Constitution on a state's ability to legislate concerning slavery. Perhaps Nelson was again referring to the idea that slaveholders had a right to travel with their slaves through free states. Or perhaps Nelson believed that the Fifth Amendment restricted a state's ability to forbid slavery within its borders.[77] It was clear, however, that Nelson foresaw the possibility of future decisions by the Taney Court that would further protect and expand slaveholders' rights.

Nelson as Spokesman for the Majority of the Majority

Justice Nelson's Opinion was the most predictable Opinion in the *Dred Scott* case in that it was wholly consistent with existing precedent. Moreover, in at least one sense, Justice Nelson's Opinion (rather than Taney's) was the true Opinion of the Court. That is so because all of the majority Justices agreed in substance with all of the points made by Justice Nelson; that was not true for any other Opinion in the case. Accordingly, it might be said that Nelson was the spokesman for the majority of the majority; and Nelson's Opinion provides a good opportunity to sum up the positions taken by the majority Justices on the three key legal questions in *Dred Scott*, namely: a) choice-of-law; b) Negro citizenship; and c) the Missouri Compromise.

More specifically, on the choice-of-law issue all seven majority Justices agreed with Nelson's conclusion that Missouri State law controlled Dred Scott's status and provided that Scott was still a slave. Nelson was correct in asserting that this conclusion was consistent with the general trend of legal authority in recent cases (like *Strader v. Graham* and *Scott v. Emerson*) where a slave who had spent some time on free soil then sought freedom in the court of a slave state.

As to the jurisdictional issue of Negro citizenship, Nelson believed that it was not necessary to rule on this question. Justices Catron, Campbell and (somewhat less clearly) Grier agreed with Nelson. Only the three pro-slavery "fire-eaters" Justices—Taney, Daniel and Wayne—held that Negroes could not be regarded as citizens for purposes of federal diversity jurisdiction.

On the Missouri Compromise issue, Nelson expressed no opinion at all. The other six majority Justices all agreed that the Missouri Compromise was invalid, but they did not agree why.

Taney and Wayne (who wholly concurred with Taney) formed a bloc of two. In striking down the Missouri Compromise, they relied chiefly on the idea that nothing in the Constitution granted to Congress any power to regulate slavery in the territories. For good measure, Taney threw in his brief and confusing argument that slave property was legally indistinguishable from any other kind of property and was protected by the Fifth Amendment.

Daniel was a bloc of one. He relied chiefly on the Calhounist doctrine that the territories were the common property of all the states. For good measure, Daniel also argued that slave property was in fact given special protected status by the Constitution. (Here Daniel disagreed with Taney and Wayne, who had proclaimed that slave property was the same as all other property.)

Campbell too stood alone. He relied chiefly on the principle of territorial self-government, which was a somewhat more legalistic version of the political doctrine of "popular sovereignty" championed by the Democratic Party; in essence, Campbell denied the existence of any kind of Congressional authority over the territories.

Catron disagreed with Taney, Wayne and Campbell in that Catron vigorously asserted that Congress *did* possess the power to govern the territories. Catron asserted that the Missouri Compromise was invalid because it violated the Louisiana Purchase Treaty. For good measure, Catron also adopted a variation on the "common property" theory originally advocated by John Calhoun. (Catron's contribution to the common property doctrine was to identify it with the Constitution's privileges and immunities clause.)

Finally, Justice Grier performed the remarkable feat of concurring both with Nelson and Taney, who disagreed with each other. His Opinion is therefore difficult to summarize or categorize.

In other words, there was no line of reasoning for invalidating the Missouri Compromise that was adopted by more than two (or, depending on how one characterizes the ambivalent Grier, arguably three) Justices.

In short, a detailed review of the concurring Opinions in *Dred Scott* makes it apparent that *Dred Scott* is an especially fitting example of result-oriented jurisprudence; the *Dred Scott* majority agreed on almost nothing, except the actual result in the case—that Dred Scott was still a slave, and that the Missouri Compromise was invalid.

Notes

1. Professor Corwin put the same idea far more precisely and elegantly many years ago. "When, as in this case, the student finds six judges arriving at precisely the same result [voiding the Missouri Compromise] by three distinct processes of reasoning, he is naturally disposed to surmise that the result may possibly have induced the processes, rather than that the processes compelled the result . . . ." Corwin, "The Dred Scott Decision," reprinted in Kutler, Ed., *Dred Scott*, at 138.

2. John P. Frank, *Justice Daniel Dissenting: A Biography, 1784–1860* (Cambridge: Harvard U. Press, 1964) is a good biography of Daniel.

3. Fehrenbacher, *Dred Scott*, 234.

4. Frank, *Justice Daniel Dissenting*, 246.

5. Swisher, *The Taney Period*, 70 and n. 118.

6. Fehrenbacher, *Dred Scott*, 561.

7. Frank, *Justice Daniel Dissenting*, 245–46.

8. *See* Allen, *Jacksonian Jurisprudence*, 71–72, and 237, n. 10.

9. *Louisville Railway v. Letson*, 2 How. 497 (1844).

10. Previously, corporations had been regarded as "citizens" of all the states in which their shareholders resided. This made it difficult for federal courts to hear many cases involving a corporation where jurisdiction was based on diversity of citizenship. Under the old rule, if any one shareholder of a corporation came from the same state as the party involved in litigation against the corporation, then there was no diversity of citizenship and hence no federal court jurisdiction.

11. *Philadelphia Railroad v. Quigley*, 21 How. 202 at 219 (1858) (Daniel, J., dissenting); *see* Frank, *Justice Daniel Dissenting*, 217–21.

12. *DS* at 469 (Daniel, J., concurring).

13. *DS* at 472-482 (Daniel, J., concurring).

14. *DS* at 480-481 (Daniel, J., concurring).

15. *DS* at 482 (Daniel, J., concurring).

16. *DS* at 488 (Daniel, J., concurring).

17. This argument had some truth in it, but was plainly overstated.

Admittedly, a territorial ban on slavery disproportionately impacted the citizens of the slave states because it did indeed discourage slaveholders (who, of course, came largely from the slave states) from settling in a free territory.

However, a territorial ban on slavery did not "exclude" any free person. Most of the free citizens of the slave states did not own slaves; they certainly were not excluded from free territory. And slaveholders from the slave states were not "excluded" from entering free territory either; they were merely prohibited from bringing their slaves with them to live in free territory.

That same prohibition applied to all citizens from all states; no one from either the North or South could bring slaves to live in a free U.S. territory. (Notably, there were at least some slaveholders who—like John Sanford—lived in free states.)

Thus, in truth, a territorial ban on slavery did not exclude any citizen from free territory, and it operated in a uniform, non-discriminatory fashion on all citizens from all states.

18. *DS* at 490 (Daniel, J., concurring).

19. *DS* at 490 (Daniel, J., concurring).

20. *DS* at 491 (Daniel, J., concurring).

21. *See* Swisher, *The Taney Period*, 53–55.

22. *DS* at 454–55 (Wayne, J., concurring).

23. *DS* at 454–55 (Wayne, J., concurring).

24. *See* Robert Saunders, Jr., *John Archibald Campbell, Southern Moderate, 1811–1889* (Tuscaloosa: U.of Alabama Press, 1997), 57–66.

25. It was somewhat ironic that the Creeks should figure so prominently in Campbell's rise to fame. Campbell's father Duncan Greene Campbell died somewhat in disgrace because the elder Campbell had negotiated the fraudulent Treaty of Indian Springs with the Creeks. That Treaty was disavowed after Congressional investigation. The investigation disclosed that Campbell had negotiated with a Creek chieftain who Campbell knew spoke at most for only eight of the fifty-six Creek communities that the chieftain purported to represent.

When the elder Campbell died it was discovered that funds entrusted to Campbell to be distributed to the Indians had disappeared. Campbell's estate was liable for the funds. As a result, the elder Campbell's widow was forced to sell the family home, and young Campbell had to quit West Point and take up the practice of law.

26. *See* Saunders, *Campbell*, 22–29.

27. *See* Swisher, *The Taney Period*, 242–43.

28. Saunders, *Campbell*, 75–77.

29. Saunders, *Campbell*, 87–101.

30. Maltz, *Dred Scott*, 85.

31. Saunders, *Campbell*, 98–102.

32. *DS* at 494 (Campbell, J., concurring).

33. *DS* at 494–95 (Campbell, J., concurring).

34. *DS* at 501 (Campbell, J., concurring).

35. *DS* at 502–07 (Campbell, J., concurring).
36. *DS* at 507–08 (Campbell, J., concurring).
37. *DS* at 509 (Campbell, J., concurring).
38. *See* Graber, *Dred Scott*, 120–24.
39. *DS* at 514 (Campbell, J., concurring).
40. This argument had greater emotional appeal than logical force.

Admittedly, there was some tension between 1) the principle of self-government that the Revolutionary generation had championed and 2) the proposition that Congress should legislate for the federal territories.

But there were obvious and important differences between the status of the American colonies prior to the Revolution and the status of the federal territories under the Northwest Ordinance and Missouri Compromise. The chief difference was that the British Parliament intended to rule the American colonies indefinitely. The western U.S. territories were to be governed by Congress only briefly, until their population grew to the point where they joined the Union as equal and fully self-governing states.

Thus the power conferred upon Congress to govern the western territories was essentially transitional in nature and did not necessarily entail the surrender of the principle of self-government.

41. *DS* at 509–14 (Campbell, J., concurring).
42. *DS* at 517–18 (Campbell, J., concurring).
43. Throughout the pre–Civil War era, U.S. Supreme Court Justices were assigned as part of their regular duties to sit from time to time in the federal circuit courts for their respective circuits. Catron was assigned to the newly formed Eighth Circuit, which included Kentucky, Tennessee and Missouri.
44. *DS* at 518–19 (Catron, J., concurring).
45. *DS* at 521–22 (Catron, J., concurring).
46. *DS* at 522–23 (Catron, J., concurring).
47. *DS* at 523 (Catron, J., concurring).
48. *DS* at 523 (Catron, J., concurring).
49. As noted in Chapter 8 earlier, Catron had warned Buchanan in a secret letter prior to the announcement of the *Dred Scott* decision that if the Court should deny Congressional authority over the territories as a general matter, then the Court's action would "subject the Court to ridicule." Apparently, Catron decided to supply the ridicule himself.
50. *DS* at 524 (Catron, J., concurring).
51. The original Louisiana Territory included a vast area stretching from the Gulf of Mexico north to Canada. What is now the much smaller state of Louisiana was included within the Louisiana Purchase and was originally denominated the Orleans Territory.
52. *DS* at 525 (Catron, J., concurring).
53. *See* Fehrenbacher, *Dred Scott*, 402.
54. *DS* at 526–27 (Catron, J., concurring).
55. *DS* at 527 (Catron, J., concurring).

56. *DS* at 519 (Catron, J., concurring).

57. *Fisher's Negroes v. Dabbs*, 14 Tenn. 119 (1834).

58. *Fisher's Negroes* was an 1834 Tennessee decision that stood for the proposition that any manumission of a slave must be approved by the State. It included a lengthy and (for the modern reader) truly repulsive Opinion by Catron which asserted that free Negroes were a "very dangerous and objectionable population" and that the mere presence of free Negroes was necessarily an incitement to slave rebellion. Catron further contended that every free Negro was merely a degraded outcast, and his fancied freedom a delusion."

59. Swisher, *The Taney Period*, 563–64.

60. *See* Potter, *The Impending Crisis*, 56–77.

61. *See* Swisher, *The Taney Period*, 229–30.

62. Swisher, *The Taney Period*, 577.

63. *U.S. v. Hanway*, 26 Fed. Cas. 105, 122–23 (E.D. Pa. 1851). The *Hanway* case (and Grier's role in it) are described in: Swisher, *The Taney Period*, 577–81; Finkelman, *Slavery in the Courtroom*, 94–102; and Finkelman, *Imperfect Union*, 253–54.

64. Swisher, *The Taney Period*, 573–74.

65. *Oliver v. Weakley*, 18 F. Cas.657 (E.D. Pa..1853); *see* Finkelman, *An Imperfect Union*, 251–55.

66. *See* Nevins, *The Emergence of Lincoln*, 103–104; Swisher, *The Taney Period*, 230–32, 731–32 and note 69.

67. *DS* at 469 (Grier, J., concurring).

68. *DS* at 458 (Nelson, J., concurring).

69. Taney wrote:

> [T]here is no law of nations standing between the people of the United States and their Government, and interfering with their relation to each other. The powers of Government, and the rights of the citizens under it, are positive and practical regulations plainly written down . . . . And no laws or usages of other nations, or reasoning of statesmen or jurists upon the relation of master and slave, can enlarge the powers of the Government . . . .

DS at 451.

70. *See* Swisher, *The Taney Period*, 220–21.

71. Like several of his pro-slavery colleagues, Nelson appeared to gloss over the facts of Dred Scott's case as they related to the traditionally important distinction between temporary "sojourning" and permanent "domicile" on free soil.

Citing a single English case, Nelson simply declared that it was "too plain to require argument" that a military officer (like Dr. Emerson) who goes to a military post does so for an uncertain period of time and thus does not intend to establish a permanent domicile there. *DS* at 468 (Nelson, J., concurring). Nelson therefore asserted that the question presented in *Dred Scott* was whether the removal of slave to free soil "with a view to *temporary* residence" emancipated the slave. *DS* at 458 (Nelson, J., concurring). (Emphasis added.)

However, no one in *Dred Scott* disputed the proposition that *temporary* residence on free soil failed to free a slave. Rather, Dred Scott's contention was that Scott was entitled to freedom because Dr. Emerson made first Illinois and then the Wisconsin Territory his *permanent* domicile; and prior Missouri precedent, such as *Rachael v. Walker*, supported the view that military officers could establish domicile at their assigned posts. Nelson's Concurring Opinion simply ignored this crucial contention and prior Missouri law on the subject.

Similarly, Nelson simply ignored the fact that the decision in *Scott v. Emerson* was remarkable precisely because Missouri's Supreme Court had declared there that Scott would be regarded as a slave in Missouri *regardless* of whether Dr. Emerson's presence on free soil was viewed as temporary or as permanent.

72. *DS* at 459–65 (Nelson, J., concurring).

73. *DS* at 465–68 (Nelson, J., concurring).

74. *DS* at 458 (Nelson, J., concurring).

75. *DS* at 468 (Nelson, J., concurring).

76. *DS* at 459 (Nelson, J., concurring). (Emphasis added.)

77. Lincoln, for one, thought that this was Nelson's intention. In his "House Divided" speech, Lincoln argued that Nelson was signaling that there would soon be a "second *Dred Scott* decision" that would further southern efforts to in effect nationalize slavery.

Chapter 14
Two Ringing Dissents

Justices John McLean and Benjamin Curtis dissented from the decision of the Court in *Dred Scott*. Their Dissenting Opinions were republished in newspapers and in pamphlet form and widely circulated, as critics of *Dred Scott* attempted to rally public opinion against the Court's decision.

The two Dissenting Opinions were, of course, primarily works of legal analysis and writing. They were not intended to serve as campaign literature. They do not attempt to call forth an emotional response from the reader.

Yet each Dissent is memorable in its own way, and together they succeed in making plain most of the defects in the majority's position. Indeed, virtually every serious criticism of *Dred Scott* that has emerged in the legal and historical literature of the past 150 years is, at least to some degree, either stated or prefigured in the two Dissents.

McLean's Dissent is noteworthy chiefly for its scathing critique of the extent to which the majority had radically departed from precedent, and for its direct and stirring affirmation that a Negro slave is indeed human—a child of God, as much as any white man.

Curtis' Dissent is noteworthy for the painstaking historical scholarship with which Curtis demonstrated that at least some free Negroes were regarded as citizens at the time that the Constitution was adopted, and that

African Americans were therefore part of "We the People" who had established the American government. More generally, Curtis' Dissent is a work of exquisite legal craftsmanship in which Curtis coolly, but brilliantly, dismantled much of Taney's Opinion of the Court.

The primary purpose of this book is to analyze why the *Dred Scott* majority went wrong. McLean and Curtis were not part of that majority. Yet their two dissenting Opinions merit examination here because they began the process of illuminating why and how the *Dred Scott* Court had erred.

—Justice McLean—

John McLean was born in New Jersey in 1785, and moved with his family to Ohio a short time later. McLean fit the mold of the self-made American. His father fought in the Revolutionary War. McLean received little formal education. He was apprenticed to the circuit court clerk in Cincinnati and then studied law with Arthur St. Clair, Jr., the son of the governor of the Northwest Territory. McLean was admitted to practice in 1807. After a stint doing newspaper work for the Lebanon, Ohio, *Western Star*, McLean served in the U.S. House of Representatives, and was then appointed a justice of the Ohio Supreme Court in 1816. There he developed a reputation for often writing unusually long opinions that sometimes included extensive unnecessary moralizing.

President James Monroe named McLean U.S. Postmaster General in 1823. McLean served in that post through the administrations of Presidents Monroe and John Quincy Adams. In 1829, the new President Andrew Jackson nominated McLean for a seat on the U.S. Supreme Court, and McLean's nomination was confirmed by the Senate the very next day.[1]

McLean served on the Court for more than thirty years. Throughout all that time, McLean entertained the hope that he might be elected president. At various times the Democrats, Whigs, Republicans and Anti-Masons all gave serious consideration to McLean as a presidential candidate, but he never won the nomination of any party.[2]

By the time *Dred Scott* was decided in 1857, McLean was the only avowed opponent of slavery on the U.S. Supreme Court. Even before the case was decided McLean had managed to make his views known. As part of the run up to the Republican national convention of 1856 (where McLean hoped to be nominated candidate for president), McLean wrote a widely published "private" letter to retired Judge Hornblower of New Jersey in which McLean set forth his belief that Congress did possess the power to prohibit slavery in the federal territories.

—McLean's Historical Reputation—

Justice McLean's Dissenting Opinion does not enjoy the same reputation for legal excellence that Justice Curtis' Dissent does. That is so for a number of reasons. First, McLean gave his Dissent a structure that does not lend itself to the extended careful exposition of complex legal ideas. Rather, McLean's discursive Dissent for the most part consists of a series of short, pungent attacks on various aspects of the majority's position. It is in a sense the work of a very skillful and powerful legal counterpuncher. McLean's points are well made and for the most part valid, but they do appear somewhat disjointed at times.

Second, McLean was (as noted) a perennial presidential aspirant who had already proven by his 1856 "private" letter concerning the Missouri Compromise issue that he was overly anxious to curry favor with the anti-slavery forces of the Republican Party. As a result, both McLean's contemporaries and historians have harbored the suspicion that McLean's Dissent was intended to serve more as a political statement than as strictly a work of legal analysis.

Third, and most interesting, McClean's Dissent was based in important part upon moral and religious conviction.[3] With a pure and clear declaration of faith, McLean's Dissent cut like a laser through all the legal verbiage amassed by his colleagues. McLean wrote: "A slave is not a mere chattel. He bears the impress of his maker, and is amenable to the laws of God and man; and he is destined to an endless existence." McLean's moral clarity is admirable. However, the religious underpinnings of McLean's Dissent make *legal* analysts of many different persuasions quite uncomfortable.

—McLean on Congressional Authority—

In his dissent, McLean directly attacked the majority's contention that the Constitution failed to grant Congress power to govern the territories, and he gave no quarter. He challenged the majority with sarcastic questions: "Can anyone suppose that the eminent men of the Federal Convention could have overlooked or neglected a matter so vitally important to the country . . .?"; and "If there be a right to acquire territory, there necessarily must be an implied power to govern it. When the military force of the Union shall conquer a country, may not Congress provide for the government of such country?"[4]

McLean emphasized his view that the majority's challenge to Congressional power over the territories constituted a radical departure from precedent. To that end, he belittled the majority's position by rhetorically setting the majority up in opposition to the great progress of America's westward expansion since the adoption of the Constitution:

> The judicial mind of this country, State and Federal, has agreed on no subject, within its legitimate action, with equal unanimity, as on the power of Congress to establish Territorial Governments. No court, State or Federal, no judge or statesman, is known to have had any doubts on this question for nearly sixty years after the power was exercised. Such Governments have been established from the sources of the Ohio to the Gulf of Mexico, extending to the Lakes on the north and the Pacific Ocean on the west, and from the lines of Georgia to Texas.
>
> Great interests have grown up under the Territorial laws over a country more than five times greater in extent than the original thirteen States; and these interests, corporate or otherwise, have been cherished and consolidated by a benign policy, without any one supposing the law-making power had united with the Judiciary, under the universal sanction of the whole country, to usurp a jurisdiction which did not belong to them. Such a discovery at this late date is more extraordinary than anything which has occurred in the judicial history of this or any other country.[5]

For McLean, the Missouri Compromise issue was an easy one. The Constitution, he declared, empowered Congress to either prohibit or permit slavery in a federal territory as Congress saw fit. That power had been exercised both by the Northwest Ordinance and the Missouri Compromise. (McLean also noted that the same power had been exercised without constitutional objection by the 1803 federal law that prohibited the importation into the Orleans Territory of slaves brought to the U.S. after 1798, upon penalty of freedom for the slave.)

Relying on *Prigg v. Pennsylvania*, McLean stated that slavery was emphatically a state institution. Citing to Chief Justice Marshall's Opinion in *American Insurance v. Canter*, McLean further stated that Congress exercised the combined powers of both federal and state governments in the federal territories; thus the federal government could properly prohibit slavery in the territories, just as a state government could.[6]

As to Taney's Fifth Amendment argument, McLean dismissed it with three brief (almost contemptuous) sentences: "I do not see on what ground the [Missouri Compromise] act is held to be void. It did not purport to forfeit property, or take it for public purposes. It only prohibited slavery; in doing which, it followed the [Northwest] ordinance of 1787."[7]

—"From So Dark a Ground": McLean Dismisses Taney's Argument from History—

McLean's discussion of the citizenship issue wandered a bit. He did a good job of pointing out flaws in Taney's Opinion, but McLean failed to grapple with the essential problem—that the original Constitution simply did not define what citizenship was, or who was entitled to it.

McLean refused to accept Taney's blanket assertion that Negroes could never be citizens. Whether a free Negro would be an "agreeable member of society . . . is more a matter of taste than of law," said McLean. McLean pointed out that some free states and even some slave states had at one time or another recognized free Negroes as citizens; and when the United States acquired Florida, Louisiana and territory from Mexico, said McLean "we have made citizens of all grades, combinations and colors." Thus, for McLean, the historical record made it plain that one did not need to be white in order to be a U.S. citizen.[8]

McLean had little patience for Taney's argument from history —namely, Taney's assertion that the Framers had wholeheartedly accepted slavery and therefore could never have intended that Negroes have any rights, let alone be considered "citizens." McLean admitted (as he had to) that American slavery was a historical fact. But, said McLean, it was also well known that the leaders of the Revolutionary generation, South as well as North, cherished the belief that slavery "would gradually decline, until it would become extinct."

Accordingly, McLean declared that he would prefer to construe the Constitution according to "the lights of Madison, Hamilton and Jay" (the authors of the *Federalist Papers*, all of whom acknowledged slavery as immoral and favored eventual abolition) rather than to draw unwarranted legal conclusions from the mere fact that the Framers did permit continued traffic in slaves. That traffic, McLean noted, is "now declared to be piracy, and punished with death by Christian nations." Said McLean, "I do not like to draw the sources of our domestic relations from so dark a ground."

Moreover, said McLean, Taney's argument from history proved too much, for "[I]f we are to turn our attention to the dark ages of the world, why confine our view to colored slavery? On the same principle, white men were made slaves. All slavery has its origin in power, and is against right."[9]

McLean thus flatly rejected Taney's claim that the Framers favored slavery. In one stroke he condemned Taney as a dishonest historian, a poor lawyer, and a poor Christian.

—McLean on Choice of Law—

The most difficult point for the dissenters to deal with was the choice-of-law issue; McLean and Curtis had to explain why Missouri law as set forth in *Scott v. Emerson* did not control the case and doom Dred Scott to remain a slave.

McLean approached this issue from several angles. First, he noted that Chief Jusice Taney had found that the Court had no jurisdiction over the *Dred Scott* case because a Negro, whether free or enslaved, was not a citizen entitled to bring a lawsuit in federal court. Since Taney had held the Court was without jurisdiction, said McLean, every other point made by Taney was superfluous dicta and was not binding law. Accordingly, McLean believed that it was proper to disregard—if not completely ignore —Taney's view on the choice-of-law issue: "Nothing that has been said by them, which has not a direct bearing on the jurisdiction of the court, against which they decided, can be considered as authority. I shall certainly not regard it as such."[10]

Second, McLean attempted to distinguish away the English case of *The Slave, Grace* as precedent. *The Slave, Grace* case was an 1828 English case that stood for the doctrine of "reattachment"—the idea that once a slave who had resided on free soil returned to a jurisdiction that permitted slavery, the slave's status "reattached." (This effort by McLean may have seemed an unnecessary step to some; *The Slave, Grace* case was decided long after American independence and, thus, was not part of American law. But many American courts regarded *The Slave, Grace* decision as persuasive, if non-binding, authority. McLean therefore thought it worthwhile to discuss the case.)

McLean noted that *The Slave, Grace* case involved a slave who *voluntarily* returned to the slave holding colony of Antigua from England; by way of contrast, there was nothing in the record, said McLean, to indicate that Dred Scott had *voluntarily* chosen to return to Missouri.

More generally, England and Antigua did not have the same relationship with each other that the free and slave states did in the U.S., said

McLean. In particular, many American states and territories had statutes that affirmatively prohibited slavery and expressly provided that a slave brought within the state's borders became free. England had no such law. Rather, *Somerset* had established that a slave brought to England became free because there was no law there authorizing a slave's continued bondage.[11] Thus McLean suggested that the rule of *The Slave, Grace* case for the most part did not apply in the U.S.

Third, McLean declared that the decision of Missouri's State Supreme Court in *Scott v. Emerson* was simply wrong. The majority, said McLean, had found that "a slave may be taken by his master into a Territory of the United States, the same as a horse, or any other kind of property"; but a slave, McLean proclaimed, is not a mere chattel for "he bears the impress of his maker, and is amenable to the laws of God and man; and he is destined to an endless existence."

Because a slave was human, McLean argued, Missouri law prior to *Scott v. Emerson* (and the law of many other slave states) had provided that a slave brought to live on free soil became free. McLean pointed out that the decision in *Scott v. Emerson* reversed Missouri's law on the subject of nearly thirty years' standing, and that the decision did so on the stated ground that there was an "excitement" against the institution of slavery in the free states.

McLean claimed that he too lamented the existence of such "excitement," but argued that it did not furnish a proper basis for the Missouri Supreme Court to reverse a well-settled rule of Missouri law. "Rights sanctioned for twenty-eight years ought not and cannot be repudiated, with any semblance of justice, by one or two decisions, influenced, as declared, by a determination to counteract the excitement against slavery in the free States."[12]

Moreover, if Missouri law were to change in this way, McLean asserted, the change should operate only prospectively and should not impact a case like that of Dred Scott—whose right to freedom arose from his residence on free soil nearly twenty years prior to the decision in *Scott v. Emerson*. "Such rights might be inoperative under the decision in the future; but I cannot well perceive how it can have the same effect in prior cases."[13]

McLean thus questioned whether the decision in *Scott v. Emerson* was fair to Dred Scott himself, first because the decision—contrary to McLean's Christian faith in the brotherhood of man—denied Scott's humanity, and second because the retroactive nature of the decision denied Scott a right to freedom that Scott had already won.

McLean also questioned whether the denial of freedom to a slave like Dred Scott was fair *to the free states*, and consistent with principles of federalism and interstate comity.[14] McLean contended that (especially in his own experience as a circuit court judge) the free states had honored their legal obligation to respect and give effect to the laws of the slave states—that is, by returning fugitive slaves and by imposing liability on northerners who aided slaves to escape. Yet the result in *Dred Scott*, said McLean, meant that a slaveholder like Dr. Emerson was permitted to simply flout free state law by holding Dred Scott as a slave on free soil for many years—in effect introducing the institution of slavery in a state where it was flatly prohibited by law.

> I am not able to reconcile this result with the respect due to the State of Illinois. Having the same rights of sovereignty as the State of Missouri . . . I can perceive no reason why the institutions of Illinois should not receive the same consideration as those of Missouri. . . . [T]he principle laid down will enable the people of a slave State to introduce slavery into a free State, for a longer or shorter time, as may suit their convenience; and by returning the slave to the State whence he was brought . . . the status of slavery attaches . . . and defies the sovereignty of the free State.[15]

McLean therefore rejected the rule of *Scott v. Emerson.* He further noted that, as explained in the recent Supreme Court decision in *Pease v. Peck*, the Supreme Court was not required to accept *Scott v. Emerson* as a binding and authoritative statement of Missouri law because *Scott v. Emerson* involved principles of common law (rather than a Missouri statute) and ran contrary to previously well-established Missouri precedent.[16]

For all these reasons, McLean concluded that the U.S. Supreme Court could and should reject both the decision of the federal circuit court below and that of Missouri's State Supreme Court in *Scott v. Emerson*, and declare that Dred Scott and his family were free.

—Justice Curtis—

Justice Benjamin Curtis' Dissent in *Dred Scott* made Curtis an "unlikely hero"[17] to abolitionists and antebellum Republicans. Curtis became a "hero" because his Dissent laid out in clear and elegant language the legal reasons why Chief Justice Taney and his pro-slavery colleagues were wrong. Curtis' status as a hero to the forces of anti-slavery was "unlikely" because prior to the *Dred Scott* case Curtis had been roundly denounced by abolitionists and others as a "slave-catching Judge." Indeed, Curtis' public career before *Dred Scott* was most notably marked by his stubborn insistence—notwithstanding Curtis' personal moral opposition to slavery and the fervent anti-slavery sentiments of much of Curtis' Boston community—that the legal rights of slaveholders must be honored.

Curtis' integrity and devotion to the law (together with his seemingly natural contrarian streak) ensured that his career as an anti-slavery hero would be short. During the Civil War Curtis believed that President Lincoln overstepped his powers in his conduct of the war and in suppressing dissent; Curtis therefore termed Lincoln a "dictator" and opposed the Emancipation Proclamation. After the Civil War, the so-called "Radical Republicans" in Congress impeached President Andrew Johnson in essence[18] because they believed Johnson had not done enough to protect the rights of the newly freed slaves. Curtis became Johnson's lawyer, and Curtis' masterful argument before the Senate (which strongly resembled a judge's instructions to a jury) was the decisive factor that permitted the President to secure an acquittal by the very narrowest of margins—one vote. (Prior to Curtis' two-day opening argument, all the members of President Johnson's Cabinet believed he would be convicted; afterward, all but one changed their minds. As Republican Senator William Pitt Fessenden of Maine put it, "Judge Curtis gave us the law, and we followed it.") In all of this, Curtis again incurred the wrath of the very same abolitionists and Republicans who had so gratefully received Curtis' *Dred Scott* Dissent.[19]

—Curtis' Background—

Benjamin Robbins Curtis was born near Boston, Massachusetts, in 1809. His father, Benjamin Curtis, was a sea captain, and it appears that at times the elder Curtis traded in slaves off the coast of Africa. Captain Curtis died in 1814, leaving his wife, Lois, and two sons, Benjamin and George. Lois Curtis struggled to make ends meet, but she managed to send her two sons to Harvard. The boys' uncle George Ticknor—a language professor and a leading Boston intellectual—taught there.

Curtis entered Harvard College at the age of fifteen. One of his schoolmates was Oliver Wendell Holmes, later a physician, famed author and poet, and father of United States Supreme Court Justice Oliver Wendell Holmes. Curtis' intellectual gifts were already evident; the elder Holmes subsequently celebrated Curtis in verse as the boy in the class with "a three decker brain/that could harness a team with a logical chain." In 1829 Curtis entered Harvard Law School, which was then just beginning a revival under the leadership of United States Supreme Court Justice Joseph Story.

After graduation, Curtis became a successful commercial lawyer, typically representing textile manufacturers, banks, and the like; among his most famous clients was Samuel F. B. Morse, who engaged Curtis to assist in Morse's lifelong struggle to protect his patent on the telegraph. Curtis was quickly recognized as a superb attorney. He prospered financially, and he also advanced easily into the highest ranks of Boston society, in part because of his continuing active role in Harvard's affairs.

—*Commonwealth v. Aves*—

Curtis' first significant involvement with the issue of slavery came when he represented a slaveholder in the famous 1836 Massachusetts case of *Commonwealth v. Aves*.[20] In that case a Louisiana woman visited her father in Boston, and brought with her a six-year-old slave girl named Med. Abolitionists took up Med's cause. They brought a case seeking a declaration that Med was now free because she had been brought to the free state of Massachusetts; and, in case any one missed the legal theory of Med's case, they re-dubbed Med "Maria Somerset."

In *Aves* Curtis in essence argued for the traditional American understanding of the *Somerset* rule—that a slave "domiciled" on free soil became free, but that a mere "sojourn" on free soil did not emancipate a slave. Curtis freely acknowledged that slavery was against natural law. Indeed, he declared: "If this cause, or any cause required me to maintain slavery was not a violation of the law of nature, I would abandon it."

But, said Curtis, the Constitution was a bargain freely entered into by both the free and slave states, and part of that bargain was the legal recognition of the institution of slavery. Curtis noted that the Constitution's Fugitive Slave Clause expressly required that the free states must return fugitive slaves to bondage in the South. The U.S. Constitution is the supreme law of the land and thus formed part of Massachusetts law too; accordingly, Curtis argued, although Massachusetts did not itself permit slavery, Massachusetts was bound by the Constitution to recognize the legality of slavery elsewhere in the Union.

Curtis also pointed out that slavery had become thoroughly "incorporated" into the fabric of southern society. For northern states to deny their countrymen from the South the limited right to visit the North with their slaves would therefore strike at national unity.

Ultimately, the Massachusetts Supreme Judicial Court rejected Curtis' arguments. Chief Justice Lemuel Shaw's Opinion of the Court stated that Massachusetts had abolished slavery because it was "wholly repugnant" to the state's fundamental principles. Echoing *Somerset*, Shaw declared that slavery could exist only where supported by positive local law. Since Massachusetts law did not provide for slavery, there was no law that authorized Med's continued bondage, and Med was declared free. Shaw did allow that there might be a right for slaveholders merely passing though Massachusetts to bring their slaves with them; but Med had been visiting Massachusetts for several months and was therefore emancipated.

—Curtis and the Fugitive Slave Controversy—

After *Aves*, many years passed before Curtis once again became publicly involved in a significant way with the issue of slavery. Curtis did become active in politics, and ultimately entered into public service. In 1848, Curtis was elected to the Massachusetts State Legislature where he spearheaded a successful effort to modernize the state's rules of court procedure.

Curtis was next drawn into the national controversy over slavery by the Compromise of 1850—which included a new and much tougher federal Fugitive Slave Act. Massachusetts Senator Daniel Webster—a friend of Curtis and a fellow member of the Whig Party—had supported the Compromise of 1850 in the interest of preserving the Union. Webster did so even though he had long believed slavery to be "one of the greatest evils, both moral and political." Many of Webster's anti-slavery constituents, who had previously lionized the long-time senator, felt his support for the Compromise to be a terrible betrayal. Some expressed this feeling in verse; in his poem "Ichabod," John Greenleaf Whittier likened Webster to a "fallen angel." Ralph Waldo Emerson said of Webster: "The fairest American name ends in this filthy law."

The Fugitive Slave Act deepened the split in the Massachusetts Whig Party between the "Conscience Whigs" (who opposed Webster and the Fugitive Slave Act) and the "Cotton Whigs" (who supported Webster).

(These terms were evidently the creation of the Conscience Whigs; the Conscience Whigs attributed the Cotton Whigs' support for the Fugitive Slave Act to the desire of New England's textile manufacturers to maintain their supply of cheap cotton from the South. In the Conscience Whigs' view, an unholy alliance existed between the "Lords of the Lash" and the "Lords of the Loom".[21])

Curtis firmly cast his lot with Webster and the Cotton Whigs. He furnished Boston's U.S. Marshal Charles Devens with a legal Opinion that attempted to demonstrate the constitutionality of the new Fugitive Slave Act. (Devens was trying to capture celebrated fugitive slaves William and Ellen Craft, despite much obstruction by anti-slavery Bostonians.)

The essential constitutional difficulty with the Fugitive Slave Act was that it denied the alleged fugitive slave any real opportunity to challenge his removal to a slave state. Curtis, however, asserted that this was permissible because the alleged slave was nevertheless permitted to challenge his recapture in court once he was returned to the state of his purported master in the South.

Soon after supplying Devens with his Opinion, Curtis gave a lengthy public address at Faneuil Hall in Boston (at a meeting that his brother George Curtis had helped to organize), again defending the constitutionality and merits of the Fugitive Slave Act. In that speech, Curtis acknowledged that moral duty might counsel that it was wrong to return any person to slavery; but Curtis argued that there was an overriding moral duty owed to one's country to obey its duly enacted laws—including the Fugitive Slave Act.

In 1851, Supreme Court Justice Levi Woodbury (whose circuit was comprised of the New England states) died. President Millard Fillmore consulted Webster and selected Curtis to serve on the Supreme Court in Woodbury's place. It did not take Curtis long to make a significant mark on the Court; his insightful Opinion in the 1852 case of *Cooley v. Board of Wardens*[22] completely reoriented the Court's approach to the always knotty problem of reconciling federal and state power over commerce.

Once on the Supreme Court, Curtis continued to stand for the vigorous enforcement of the Fugitive Slave Act—despite the fact that much of Boston and of New England was caught up in a movement to resist the Act, by force if necessary.

On a number of occasions Curtis (in his capacity as a circuit court judge) gave broad instructions to the grand jury concerning the definition of treason so as to permit the indictment of those who were accused of obstructing the Fugitive Slave Act's enforcement. Curtis also presided over the trials of several defendants charged with assisting fugitive slaves to escape.

Perhaps the most interesting and dramatic of these cases was that of black attorney Robert Morris. Morris was charged with helping his client the fugitive slave Shadrach Minkins to escape from custody. Minkins had been broken out of the federal courthouse by an anti-slavery mob just before he was scheduled to appear for proceedings pursuant to the new Fugitive Slave Act before the U.S. Commissioner—none other than George T. Curtis.

Justice Benjamin Curtis' final instructions to the jury in Morris' case were quite helpful to the defendant, and Morris was acquitted. But Curtis nevertheless further antagonized opponents of the Fugitive Slave Act by insisting, in a beautifully written and carefully considered Opinion, that—whatever moral reservations the jury might have concerning slavery and the Fugitive Slave Act—the jurors were required to enforce the Act, rather than follow their individual beliefs.[23] (To this day, judges and lawyers disagree among themselves as to whether jurors—acting as the conscience of the community—may effectively "nullify" a law the jurors consider unjust by acquitting a criminal defendant.)

All of these activities helped to fix an image of Curtis in the public mind as a reliable ally of slaveholders. Abolitionists could not help but admit that Curtis' defense of slaveholders' rights was always argued brilliantly; indeed, the anti-slavery *New York Tribune* lamented that they had seen "so many exhibitions of the ingenuity and adroitness of Mr. Curtis on the side of tyranny and injustice, they would like, for once at least, and just for a change if nothing else, to see him employ his ability on behalf of justice and freedom."

The *Tribune* did not and could not know that Curtis was soon to use his truly remarkable legal skills to champion the cause of Dred Scott. Of course, Curtis took up Dred Scott's cause not in order to please the *Tribune* or its anti-slavery readers, but rather out of Curtis' own stubborn sense of dedication to the requirements of the law.

—Overview of Curtis' *Dred Scott* Dissent—

Curtis' Dissent is divided into three parts of roughly equal length. First, Curtis examined the question of Negro citizenship and federal court jurisdiction. He agreed with Taney that this question was preserved for review on appeal by the U.S. Supreme Court; but Curtis then demonstrated, with a methodical and impressive show of both legal and historical research, that free Negroes could be citizens of the United States entitled to sue in federal court.

Second, Curtis examined the choice-of-law issues presented by Dred Scott's case. Curtis rejected the Missouri State Supreme Court's ruling in *Scott v. Emerson*. There, said Curtis, Missouri's highest court had decided that as a matter of policy—because the free states had purportedly abused the South and the institution of slavery—Missouri would no longer honor the laws of any free state or territory in a case where a slave claimed emancipation by residence on free soil. Curtis declared that such a policy decision could be made only by a legislature and not by judges. Curtis then offered a series of reasons why he believed the U.S. Supreme Court was not bound by *Scott v. Emerson* as an authoritative statement of Missouri law.

Third, and finally, Curtis demonstrated that the Constitution did empower Congress to regulate slavery in the federal territories. Curtis relied on the text of the Constitution itself, on the history of the relevant portions of that text, and on the fact that the existence of such power had been confirmed by consistent and uniform practice throughout the nation's history. Curtis then went further and carefully disproved each of the pro-slavery arguments that had been advanced denying the existence of such power, including Chief Justice Taney's Fifth Amendment "due process" theory.

A) Curtis on Citizenship

"Not a Fit Subject to Be Thus Reached": Curtis Confines Taney to the Jurisdictional Issue

Curtis began his lengthy Dissent with a learned (but nevertheless tedious) discussion of the formal rules of pleading and of preserving issues for appeal. Ultimately, Curtis agreed with Taney that the jurisdictional question—whether a free Negro could be a "citizen" entitled to bring a lawsuit in federal court—was indeed preserved for review by the U.S. Supreme Court.[24]

After this initial point of agreement, however, Curtis parted ways with Taney. Like his fellow dissenter McLean, Curtis argued that once Taney and his pro-slavery colleagues decided that the federal courts had no jurisdiction over Dred Scott's case (because a Negro could not be a citizen), they were obligated to stop right there. Curtis said that it was improper for Taney and the majority to then go on and consider the merits of the case. As a consequence, everything else that the majority had said—including their declaration that the Missouri Compromise was unconstitutional and void—was, according to Curtis, beyond the authority of the Supreme Court:

> I dissent . . . from what I deem their assumption of authority to examine the constitutionality of the act of Congress commonly called the Missouri Compromise . . . .
>
> I do not consider it to be within the scope of the judicial power of the majority of the court to pass upon any question respecting the plaintiff's citizenship in Missouri, save that raised by the plea to the jurisdiction; and I do not hold any opinion of this court, or any court, binding, when expressed on a question not legitimately before it. . . . The judgment of this court is, that the case is to be dismissed for want of jurisdiction, because the plaintiff was not a citizen of Missouri, as he alleged in his declaration. Into that judgment, according to the settled course of this court, nothing appearing after a plea to the merits can enter. *A great question of constitutional law, deeply affecting the peace and welfare of the country, is not, in my opinion, a fit subject to be thus reached.*[25] (Emphasis added.)

Curtis accomplished several related purposes here. To begin with, Curtis employed the legal equivalent of ju jitsu—using an overeager adversary's own strength against him. Curtis turned Taney's evident desire to settle almost every conceivable issue concerning slavery against Taney. According to Curtis, because Taney had insisted on ruling on the Negro citizenship issue, Taney had unintentionally transformed all the rest of Taney's own Opinion of the Court into improper and non-binding dicta.

At the same time, Curtis also provided those who disagreed with the *Dred Scott* decision with an elegantly stated argument, based on the traditional legal distinction between dicta and holding, for denying that *Dred Scott* was binding law.

Moreover, in the final sentence quoted above, Curtis made a broader and more profound point. Separate and apart from the somewhat formalistic question whether the majority's discussion of the Missouri Compromise constituted dicta, Curtis here suggested that the majority had failed in their role as legal statesmen. Curtis acknowledged that there existed a great question of constitutional law concerning the validity of the Missouri Compromise. But he indicated that he believed the Court should decide such a question only when it was plainly necessary for the Court to do so in order to resolve a particular case. It was not "fit," said Curtis, for the Court to reach out for such questions.

This was consistent with Curtis' generally conservative views on constitutional interpretation and on the role of the courts in deciding questions of law. Curtis was steeped in the common law[26] tradition of judges developing the law incrementally, on a case-by-case basis. He was suspicious of broad theoretical pronouncements not rooted in the factual circumstances of a particular case.

Thus, for example, in the case of *Conner v. Elliott*[27] (decided one year before *Dred Scott*), a question arose concerning marital property rights in Louisiana and the Constitution's privileges and immunities clause. Curtis declined to attempt to formulate a comprehensive definition of "privileges and immunities" there, saying that it is "safer and more in accordance with the duty of a judicial tribunal" to leave the Constitution's "meaning to be determined, in each case, upon a view of the particular rights asserted and denied therein."

Similarly, in *Dred Scott*, Curtis criticized Chief Justice Taney and the pro-slavery majority for reaching out to decide momentous, but unnecessary, issues of constitutional law.

Who Is a "Citizen"?

Like Taney, Curtis began his own analysis of the citizenship issue by asking who was regarded as a "citizen" at the time the Constitution was adopted.

He then methodically demonstrated by reference to state constitutions and state legislation that in at least five states—New Hampshire, Massachusetts, New York, New Jersey and North Carolina—*all* native-born free persons, white and black, were regarded as "citizens" at the time the Constitution was adopted; and free male Negroes were entitled to vote in each of those states. (Notably, New York, New Jersey and North Carolina were all still slave states in 1789.) The general rule in each of these five states, Curtis noted, was the same as that set out in the 1844 case of *State v. Manuel*. There, North Carolina's Supreme Court had declared that "all free persons," white or black, "born within the State are born citizens of the State," and that it was a "matter of universal notoriety" that "free persons, without regard to color" could vote.

The understanding that free Negroes from these states were also regarded as citizens of the United States, said Curtis, was illustrated by the language of the Articles of Confederation. The Articles' "privileges and immunities" clause provided that the "free inhabitants" of each state were entitled to the privileges and immunities of citizens in all other states. At first, South Carolina had proposed that this clause be limited to the "free *white* inhabitants," but that proposal was voted down. Curtis argued that the clear implication of striking the word *white* from this clause was to include African Americans within the group of people eligible for citizenship. Thus, said Curtis, at the time the Constitution was adopted there were free Negroes who were citizens of their own states, and who were further entitled to be treated as citizens wherever they went throughout the United States.

There was nothing in the Constitution, said Curtis, that gave the federal government the power to deprive free Negroes (or any one else) of their citizenship. To the contrary, by using the phrase "natural-born citizen" at different points, the Constitution assumed the general common law rule that a free person born in a particular place automatically became a citizen of that place, unless the government affirmatively took that citizenship away. Thus, Curtis finally concluded, "under the Constitution of the United States, every person born on the soil of a State, who is a citizen of that State by force of its Constitution or laws, is also a citizen of the United States."

John Sanford's "plea in abatement" had asserted that no Negro, free or slave—including Dred Scott—could be a U.S. citizen. Curtis said that this plea was wrong as a matter of constitutional law, and that the circuit court below had instead been right—free Negroes *could* be citizens entitled to sue in federal court. Since in Curtis' view the circuit court's ruling on the plea in abatement was the only jurisdictional issue that had been preserved for Supreme Court review, it was not necessary to look further into whether Dred Scott himself was in fact a citizen of Missouri. Based on the limited record presented, said Curtis, there was no reason to doubt that Scott was a citizen. Thus Curtis found that Dred Scott had the right to sue John Sanford in federal court on the ground of diversity of citizenship.[28]

Implications of Curtis' Views on Citizenship

It is important to note how narrow and conservative Curtis' legal holding on the citizenship issue was. Curtis did not hold that *all* free Negroes were U.S. citizens. To the contrary, Curtis' Dissent made it clear that each state was free to either grant or deny citizenship to free Negroes (or any one else) born within that state: "[It is] left to each State to determine what free persons, born within its limits, shall be citizens of such State, and thereby be citizens of the United States."[29]

Moreover, Curtis adopted a very narrow view of what rights "citizens" were entitled to under the Constitution. He went out of his way to reject Taney's expressed fear that under the Constitution's "privileges and immunities" clause a free Negro who was regarded as a "citizen" by his home state in the North might claim full civil rights when visiting a southern state. In Curtis' view, the "privileges and immunities" clause did not guarantee rights of citizenship that must be honored throughout the country; it merely prohibited discrimination by a state against citizens of other states. Thus, for example, according to Curtis, a southern state could deny its own free Negroes the right to vote or to congregate in public. Moreover, that same southern state would *not* be required to grant those rights to free Negroes who were visiting from northern states, even if those free Negroes enjoyed such rights in their home states. All that was required by the privileges and immunities clause (said Curtis) was that the southern state treat free Negroes from out of state no worse than the southern state treated its own, home-born, free Negroes.[30]

It thus becomes apparent that although Curtis believed that Dred Scott should be permitted to pursue his lawsuit in federal court, Curtis was no champion of the legal rights of African Americans. And yet, at least on an emotional and rhetorical level, Curtis' discussion of the citizenship issue did advance the cause of racial justice in two related and important respects.

First, as Curtis noted, Chief Justice Taney was by no means alone in asserting that the "Constitution was made exclusively by and for the white race."[31] To the contrary, the assertion that America was a white man's country was a staple of the political rhetoric of the era.[32] But Curtis' *Dred Scott* Dissent demonstrated that some free Negroes had in fact voted on the ratification of the Constitution. Thus, according to Curtis, African Americans *were* part of "We the People" who had established the American government, and that African Americans therefore were, at least as a matter of justice, entitled to share in some of its blessings.

Second, Curtis briefly set forth his own vision of the Declaration of Independence and of the Declaration's relationship both to its own historical setting and to the Constitution—a vision that did not share in Taney's evident hostility to all African Americans. In his *Dred Scott* Opinion, Taney had argued that the most famous words contained within the Declaration—proclaiming "that all men are created equal"—could not possibly have been intended to embrace Negroes, because the Framers countenanced both slavery and racial discrimination. If the Framers had intended to say that black men as well as white men were created equal, Taney argued, then the Framers would have been guilty of terrible hypocrisy.

Curtis took a very different view. He argued that the Declaration *was* indeed intended to say that *all* men, including black men, were created equal. The Framers also recognized, said Curtis, that in the real world black men were not yet treated as equals; but, said Curtis, the Framers desired that the equality of all men would someday be realized in fact. Thus Curtis wrote:

> My own opinion is, that a calm comparison of these assertions of universal abstract truths [in the Declaration], and of their [the authors of the Declaration] own individual opinions and acts, would not leave these men under any reproach of inconsistency; that the great truths they asserted on that solemn occasion, they were ready and anxious to make effectual, wherever a necessary regard to circumstances, which no statesman can disregard without producing more evil than good, would allow; and that it would not be just to them, nor true in itself, to allege that they intended to say that the Creator of all men had endowed the white race, exclusively, with the great natural rights which the Declaration of Independence asserts.[33]

B) Curtis on Choice of Law

To "Make Him a Freeman"; Curtis Disagrees with *Scott v. Emerson*

Curtis began his discussion of the choice-of-law issue by carefully examining different variations of the doctrine of emancipation by residence on free soil. Curtis made a key distinction here—between those free jurisdictions where a master could "obtain no aid from the laws to enforce his rights," and other free jurisdictions "whose laws are designed to act directly on the status of a slave, and make him a freeman."

England (under the rule of *The Slave, Grace* case) and Massachusetts (under the rule of *Commonwealth v. Aves*), said Curtis, fell into the first of these two categories. These jurisdictions held that because they had no law that affirmatively established slavery, they would neither recognize nor enforce slavery within their borders. However, with such jurisdictions it was possible that (as in *The Slave, Grace* case) once a slave returned to a slave jurisdiction, his servile status might "reattach."

In the second category of free jurisdictions, said Curtis, slavery was expressly prohibited by law, and a slave who came within the jurisdiction's borders was *permanently* emancipated—his status as a slave forever dissolved. Curtis stated that the law of the Wisconsin Territory (as embodied in the Missouri Compromise Act and in subsequent legislation that organized the territory) affirmatively prohibited slavery. Accordingly, said Curtis, when Dred Scott was brought to live at Fort Snelling within the Wisconsin Territory, he became forever free; his status as a slave could not later "reattach" because it had already been permanently dissolved.[34]

Curtis did acknowledge that a state, such as Missouri, is not necessarily required in all cases to give effect to the laws of another jurisdiction, such as the Wisconsin Territory. Missouri had adopted the common law by statute at the time of its founding. The common law, said Curtis, includes the law of nations, and the general rule of both is that foreign laws should be enforced *in the absence of a positive local law to the contrary*. Curtis therefore conceded that it might be proper for a Missouri court to refuse to enforce a foreign law in Missouri if such foreign law contravened either a local Missouri statute or principles of Missouri's common law. But, Curtis declared, it was *not* within the scope of the authority of the courts of Missouri to refuse to recognize foreign law on mere *political* grounds. A political decision not to honor a foreign jurisdiction's laws could not be made by judges; it could only be made by a political body, such as the state legislature.

More specifically, said Curtis, in *Scott v. Emerson* Missouri's Supreme Court had exceeded its authority when it refused to give effect to Wisconsin's anti-slavery laws on the stated ground that a "dark and fell spirit" concerning slavery had overtaken the North:

> [I]t is not within the province of any judicial tribunal to refuse such recognition from any political considerations, or any view it may take of the exterior political relations between the State and one or more foreign States, or any impressions it may have that a change of foreign opinion and action on the subject of slavery may afford a reason why the State should change its own action. To understand and give just effect to such considerations, and to change the action of the State in consequence of them, are functions of diplomatists and legislators, not of judges.[35]

Curtis also conceded that under international and common law it was appropriate for a state such as Missouri to distinguish between domicile and mere sojourning on free soil, and to recognize emancipation only when a slave had been domiciled on free soil. Thus, said Curtis, it would be appropriate for Missouri courts in freedom suits to question whether a slaveholder (like Dr. Emerson) had intended to make his domicile in a free jurisdiction (such as the Wisconsin Territory).

But, Curtis continued, under well-settled law, the presumption in freedom suits like Dred Scott's was that the master *did* intend to make his domicile in the free jurisdiction. Moreover, the case of Dr. Emerson and Dred Scott was a special one in that it presented two additional reasons for finding that Wisconsin law had permanently emancipated Dred Scott.

First, Dr. Emerson had journeyed to the Wisconsin Territory as an officer of the U.S. Army—that is, as a servant of the federal government, the very same government that prohibited slavery in that territory. In Curtis' view, this meant that Dr. Emerson certainly could not challenge the assertion that he was bound by the federal law that prohibited slavery in the Wisconsin Territory.[36]

Second, Dr. Emerson had permitted Dred Scott to enter into a legal marriage with Harriet Scott in the Wisconsin Territory. As a general matter, slaves were not allowed to marry because they were not competent to enter into any contract. Accordingly, by permitting Dred Scott to marry, Curtis argued, Dr. Emerson had recognized that Scott had become a free man under the laws of the Wisconsin Territory. For Missouri to later refuse to recognize Scott's freedom, Curtis argued further, would be to impair the obligations of the Scotts' valid marriage contract[37] and to reduce their children to bastards:

> [T]he consent of the master that his slave, residing in a country which does not tolerate slavery, may enter into a lawful contract of marriage . . . is an effectual act of emancipation. And the law does not enable Dr. Emerson, or any one claiming under him, to assert a title to the married persons as slaves, and thus destroy the obligation of the contract of marriage, and bastardize their issue, and reduce them to slavery.[38]

Scott v. Emerson Not Binding on the U.S. Supreme Court

Curtis gave all these reasons to show why the decision in *Scott v. Emerson* was wrong. But he still had to demonstrate why the U.S. Supreme Court was not nevertheless bound by *Scott v. Emerson* as an authoritative statement of Missouri law by Missouri's highest court.

Curtis began this demonstration by conceding that had *Scott v. Emerson* been decided on the basis that Dr. Emerson had merely "sojourned" on free soil, the decision then might have been binding on the U.S. Supreme Court.

However, Curtis again noted that *Scott v. Emerson* was not based on a finding that Dr. Emerson had merely sojourned outside Missouri. The decision was instead based on the Missouri Supreme Court's assertion that as a matter of policy it would no longer honor the laws of the free states. And, said Curtis (relying on the rule of *Swift v. Tyson*[39]): "Upon such a question, not depending on any statute or local usage, but on principles of universal jurisprudence, this Court has repeatedly asserted it could not hold itself bound by the decisions of State courts, however great respect might be felt for their learning, ability, and impartiality."[40] Moreover, said Curtis, the import of *Scott v. Emerson* was to deny the effect of a federal law (the Missouri Compromise) in the Wisconsin Territory, and to impair the obligation of the Scotts' contract of marriage. These were questions of constitutional and federal law, concerning which the U.S. Supreme Court had authority superior to Missouri's state courts.

Curtis therefore concluded that *Scott v. Emerson* was wrong, that Dred Scott had indeed been emancipated by his residence in the Wisconsin Territory (and by his marriage there), and that the U.S. Supreme Court did have authority to in effect overrule *Scott v. Emerson*. Or, as Curtis much more cooly and drily concluded this portion of his Dissent: "Sitting here to administer the law between these parties, I do not feel at liberty to surrender my own convictions of what the law requires, to the authority of the [*Scott v. Emerson*] decision in 15 Missouri Reports."[41]

C) Curtis on the Missouri Compromise

Congressional Authority over the Territories in General

Curtis began his discussion of the Missouri Compromise by presenting two alternative hypotheses for examination. The first was that (as Dred Scott's lawyers had argued) the Constitution's Territory Clause did confer upon Congress the power to legislate for the federal territories. The second was that (as Taney and the pro-slavery majority had argued) the Constitution did not expressly grant any such power.

Curtis pointed out that the future of America's western lands was an important political consideration in 1787, and that the Framers were, of course, well aware that the United States already possessed the Old Northwest Territory (governed by the original Northwest Ordinance of

1787) and certain other territories yet to be legally organized; and the Framers similarly had a "confident expectation," said Curtis, that North Carolina and Georgia would cede additional western lands to the federal government in the very near future.

More broadly, Curtis continued, the Founding Fathers at the Constitutional Convention understood that they were creating a "frame of government" for the United States with the expectation that the country would become "a great and powerful nation, possessing the power to make war and to conclude treaties, and thus to acquire territory."

Curtis pointed out that the authors of the *Federalist Papers* (in Nos. 38 and 43) had expressed a concern that Congress under the Articles of Confederation might not possess the authority to pass a law like the original Northwest Ordinance of 1787, and had argued that one reason to support ratification of the Constitution was that the Constitution expressly conferred this important and necessary authority upon Congress. Curtis also summarized the discussions at the Constitutional Convention concerning the Statehood and Territory Clauses, including James Madison's suggestion that these clauses include language authorizing the federal government to institute temporary governments for the territories.

In short, Curtis demonstrated that the Framers were keenly aware of the need to provide government for a) the Old Northwest Territory, b) existing unorganized territories, and c) territories to be acquired in both the near and more distant future. Curtis argued that it was therefore logical to conclude that the Territory Clause was indeed intended to meet that need by conferring upon Congress a general power to govern the territories. It made little sense, said Curtis, to instead suppose that (as Taney, Campbell and their pro-slavery colleagues had argued) the Framers had chosen to silently pass this urgent subject by.[42]

Similarly, said Curtis, there was little reason to credit Taney's painfully elaborate theory that the Framers had intended that a carefully limited Congressional power over the territories should somehow be deduced by implication from Congress's power to declare war and approve treaties. Thus Curtis wrote:

> That Congress has some power to institute temporary Governments over the territory, I believe all agree; and, if it be admitted that the necessity of some power to govern the territory of the United States could not and did not escape the attention of the Convention and the people, and that the necessity is so great, that, in the absence of any express grant, it is strong enough to raise an implication of the existence of that power, it would

> seem to follow that it is also strong enough to afford material aid in construing an express grant of power respecting that territory; and that they who maintain the existence of the power, without finding any words at all in which it is conveyed, should be willing to receive a reasonable interpretation of language of the Constitution, manifestly intended to relate to the territory, and to convey to Congress some authority concerning it.
>
> It would seem, also, that when we find the subject-matter of the growth and formation and admission of new States, and the disposal of the territory for these ends, were under consideration, and that some provision therefor was expressly made, it is improbable that it would be, in its terms, a grossly inadequate provision; and that an indispensably necessary power to institute temporary Governments, and to legislate for the inhabitants of the territory, was passed silently by, and left to be deduced from the necessity of the case.[43]

Curtis then made quick work of a number of secondary arguments advanced by the pro-slavery majority. As to the notion that the power to make "rules and regulations" did not include a power to make laws, Curtis pointed to the substantial body of *laws* passed by Congress pursuant to its power to "regulate" commerce, laws that governed the conduct of U.S. citizens both at home and in ports as far away as China.[44]

Similarly, Curtis quickly dismissed Taney's notion that the Territory Clause was somehow silently limited to the territory that existed in 1789; that notion, Curtis declared, was inconsistent with both the words of that clause, and with the very nature of the Constitution:

> There was to be established by the Constitution a frame of government, under which the people of the United States and their posterity were to continue indefinitely. To take one of its provisions, the language of which is broad enough to extend throughout the existence of the Government, and embrace all territory belonging to the United States throughout all time, and the purposes and objects of which apply to all territory of the United States, and narrow it down to territory belonging to the United States when the Constitution was framed, while at the same time it is admitted that the Constitution contemplated and authorized the acquisition, from time to time, of other and foreign territory, seems to me to be an interpretation as inconsistent with the nature and purposes of the instrument, as it is with its language, and I can have no hesitation in rejecting it.[45]

The Power to Legislate Concerning Slavery

Having demonstrated that as a general matter Congress did have the power to govern and legislate for the federal territories, Curtis now approached the heart of the matter: Did that power to legislate extend to the subject of slavery?

The Territory Clause grants Congress the power to make "*all* needful rules and regulations" for the U.S. territories. Accordingly, said Curtis, the burden was on Sanford's lawyers to show that "all" did not mean "all," and that the subject of slavery was somehow excepted from the legislative power conferred by the Territory Clause:

> The assertion is, though the Constitution says all, it does not mean all—though it says all, without qualification, it means all except such as allow or prohibit slavery. It cannot be doubted that it is incumbent on those who would thus introduce an exception not found in the language of the instrument, to exhibit some solid and satisfactory reason . . . showing that the words . . . are not to be understood according to their clear, plain, and natural signification.[46]

Curtis also pointed out that at the time the Constitution was adopted the question whether slavery would be permitted or instead prohibited was universally recognized as a subject for municipal legislation, and that every state in the Union had in some measure already acted on that subject. The purpose of the Territory Clause was to enable Congress to provide a body of municipal law for the government of the settlers in the territories; thus the natural and logical way to read the Territory Clause, said Curtis, was to suppose that it included the power to legislate concerning slavery.

Curtis next reviewed in considerable detail the history of congressional legislation concerning slavery in the territories. (Here Curtis borrowed liberally from Montgomery Blair's second brief for Dred Scott and from Curtis' brother George's oral argument before the Supreme Court.) Justice Curtis enumerated eight different instances (beginning with the Northwest Ordinance of 1789, passed just a few weeks after the adoption of the Constitution) in which Congress had passed laws that prohibited slavery in various federal territories; and Curtis enumerated six instances in which Congress had passed laws that permitted slavery in other federal territories. Curtis pointed out that many of the Framers of the Constitution had themselves personally participated in passing these laws as members of Congress. Moreover, Curtis noted that the first seven presidents of the United States—all of whom were already in public life when the Constitution was written and adopted—signed such Acts of Congress into law; and among these presidents was George Washington (who had served as the President of the Constitutional Convention). For Curtis, all this was exceptionally persuasive evidence that the Framers had intended and understood that Congress would have the power to choose whether to permit or prohibit slavery in the federal territories:

> If the practical construction of the Constitution contemporaneously with its going into effect, by men intimately acquainted with its history from their personal participation in framing and adopting it, and continued by them through a long series of acts of the gravest importance, be entitled to weight in the judicial mind on a question of construction, it would seem to be difficult to resist the force of the acts above adverted to.[47]

Rejecting Political Arguments Limiting the Territory Clause

Next, Curtis acknowledged that—in spite of the apparently clear language of the Territory Clause, and in spite of the long history of Congressional legislation concerning slavery in the Territories—there were now many people who contended that Congress did *not* possess the power to decide which territories would be free and which would have slavery. Curtis identified three very different schools of thought, all of which agreed that Congress's power over slavery in the territories was somehow limited.

First, said Curtis, there were those who contended that Congress could prohibit, but could not permit, slavery in a federal territory. (This was the view, for example, of anti-slavery Republican Governor Salmon Chase of Ohio, later Chief Justice of the U.S. Supreme Court.) This point of view, said Curtis, was based on general anti-slavery principles of natural law, rather than on any particular clause of the Constitution.

Second, there were people who contended that Congress could neither establish nor prohibit slavery in a territory, but that the people of a territory themselves could do so once organized into a political body. (This was akin to the view expressed by Justice Campbell in his Concurring Opinion.) According to Curtis, this point of view was founded upon general considerations concerning the right of self-government and the very nature of the federal Union; it was not based on any particular provision of the Constitution.

Third, there were people who contended that the Constitution granted to every slaveholder an "indefeasible" right to carry and hold their slaves in any federal territory. (This was close to the view expressed by Justices Daniel and Catron.) According to Curtis, this point of view was grounded in the common-property theory of the equality of the states, which argued that a territorial ban on slavery constituted an "unjust discrimination" against the citizens of the slave states; this "discrimination" theory was also not founded on any particular language in the Constitution.

Curtis then argued that all three of these schools of thought shared the same fatal weakness that disqualified them as the basis for a *legal* argument—they were not based upon any express provision of the Constitution.[48] The principles of natural law, territorial self-government and of the equality of states, were all *political* principles, said Curtis. It would be proper for a legislature, if it wished to do so, to look to such political principles as a guide to formulating legislation. But these political principles were *not* stated in, or mandated by, the Constitution. Thus, they could not (said Curtis) serve as a basis to find that the power expressly granted to Congress by the Constitution to make "all" needful rules for the territories was subject to a silent exception for rules concerning slavery.[49]

Curtis sternly warned that it would be a dangerous step to find that mere political principles "are sufficient to authorize this Court to insert into this [the Territory] clause of the Constitution an exception of the exclusion or allowance of slavery, not found therein, nor in any other part of that instrument." In Curtis' view, such an approach undermined the very nature of government under a written constitution, because it permitted the U.S. Constitution's meaning to shift with the political sentiments of any given day. Thus Curtis wrote:

> To engraft on any instrument a substantive exception not found in it, must be admitted to be a matter attended with great difficulty. And the difficulty increases with the importance of the instrument, and the magnitude and complexity of the interests involved in its construction. To allow this to be done with the Constitution, upon reasons purely political, renders its judicial interpretation impossible—because judicial tribunals, as such, cannot decide upon political considerations. Political reasons have not the requisite certainty to afford rules of juridical interpretation. They are different in different men. They are different in the same men at different times. And when a strict interpretation of the Constitution, according to the fixed rules which govern the interpretation of laws, is abandoned, and the theoretical opinions of individuals are allowed to control its meaning, we have no longer a Constitution; we are under the government of individual men, who for the time being have power to declare what the Constitution is, according to their own views of what it ought to mean. When such a method of interpretation of the Constitution obtains, in place of a republican Government, with limited and defined powers, we have a

> Government which is merely an exponent of the will of Congress; or what, in my opinion, would not be preferable, an exponent of the individual political opinions of the members of this Court.[50]

Curtis on "Due Process"

Finally, Curtis turned to Justice Taney's suggestion that the slavery restriction of the Missouri Compromise somehow violated the Fifth Amendment's requirement that no person be deprived of property without due process of law.

At the outset, Curtis pointed out that the notion that slaveholders had a right to bring slaves into any federal territory would lead to exceedingly confusing, if not wholly illogical, results. As a preface to this point, Curtis restated the traditional view (elaborated in *Prigg v. Pennsylvania*) that slavery was contrary to natural law, and therefore was created by municipal law. Moreover, all the rights and obligations of slaveholders must be fixed by municipal law. Thus, Curtis explained by way of example, each slave state had developed its own (and sometimes quite different) rules that governed liability for crimes or torts committed by slaves, the sale of slaves, the manumission of slaves, the inheritance of slaves, and so forth.

Curtis then asked that if (as Chief Justice Taney had asserted) a slave holder had an indefeasible right to carry slaves into any federal territory, what law would govern the legal relation between master and slave there? Would it be the law of the slaveholder's home state? Did that mean that the courts of each federal territory would be required to apply the slavery codes of all the many states from which the territory's many slaveholders had come? And what did this mean for a slaveholder from a *free* state (such as John Sanford of New York)? What state's slave code could a court in a federal territory apply to such a slaveholder?

For Curtis, it made little sense to suppose that the Framers intended such a confusing state of affairs, in which a single territory would be governed by many states' different laws; it was far more logical to find that the Framers intended that Congress could either directly regulate or completely ban slavery in a federal territory, as Congress saw fit:

> Is it conceivable that the Constitution has conferred the right on every citizen to become a resident on the territory of the United States with his slaves, and there to hold them as such, but has neither made nor provided for any municipal regulations which are essential to the existence of slavery?
>
> Is it not more rational to conclude that they who framed and adopted the constitution were aware that persons held to service under the laws of

> a State are property only to the extent and under the conditions fixed by those laws; that they must cease to be available as property, when their owners voluntarily place them permanently within another jurisdiction, where no municipal laws on the subject of slavery exist; and that, being aware of these principles, and having said nothing to interfere with or displace them, or to compel Congress to legislate in any particular manner on the subject, and having empowered Congress to make all needful rules and regulations respecting the territory of the United States, it was their intention to leave to the discretion of Congress what regulations, if any, should be made concerning slavery therein?[51]

"Due Process" and Magna Charta

More important, Curtis also found that the proposition that a territorial ban on slavery constituted deprivation of property without due process of law to be meritless. After all, slaves were property "only to the extent and under the conditions" fixed by local law. A territorial ban on slavery thus did not deprive any one of "property"; rather a slave simply ceased to be an item of "property" once he entered a free territory. Indeed, for Curtis this issue seemed so simple that he devoted only a few paragraphs[52] to it; and he thought it largely sufficient to simply point out that Taney's notion ran contrary to the whole American system of regulating slavery.

The Fifth Amendment's due process clause was not new, said Curtis. It was derived in principle from the Magna Charta, and that principle was part of every state constitution at the time the Constitution was adopted. No one, said Curtis, had contended that the territorial slavery restriction of the Northwest Ordinance of 1787 somehow violated this fundamental principle; similarly, no one had perceived any violation of due process when the first Congress re-enacted the Northwest Ordinance in 1789, or when Congress passed the Missouri Compromise of 1820.

Moreover, the Constitution itself expressly permitted Congress to prohibit the importation of slaves into the United States beginning in 1808. Congress did in fact exercise that power, and had further provided that slaves illegally imported immediately become free. (This was the law that was the basis for the *Garronne* case.) Curtis noted that no one had ever contended that the federal law prohibiting the importation of slaves into America, and requiring the forfeiture of an illegally imported slave, somehow violated the Due Process clause.

Similarly, many slave states had laws that prohibited the importation of slaves from elsewhere in the Union, and further provided that illegally imported slaves became free. Again, said Curtis, such laws had never been viewed as a violation of the principle of due process:

> [I]f a prohibition of slavery in a Territory in 1820 violated this principle of *Magna Charta*, the Ordinance of 1787 also violated it . . . . I think I may at least say, if the Congress did then violate *Magna Charta* by the Ordinance, no one discovered that violation. Besides, if the prohibition upon all persons, citizens as well as others, to bring slaves into a Territory, and a declaration that if brought they shall be free, deprives citizens of their property without due process of law, what shall we say of the legislation of many of the slaveholding States which have enacted the same prohibition? . . . . A citizen of the United States owns slaves in Cuba, and brings them to the United States, where they are set free by the legislation of Congress. Does this legislation deprive him of his property without due process of law? If so, what becomes of the laws prohibiting the slave trade? If not, how can similar regulation respecting a Territory violate the Fifth Amendment of the Constitution?[53]

* * *

This concluded Curtis' *Dred Scott* Dissent. Together, the dissenting Opinions of Justices McLean and Curtis had dismantled virtually every serious argument put forward by the pro-slavery majority in *Dred Scott.* McLean's dissent was less well organized and researched, but it was more direct, and at times more powerful. Curtis' Dissent was quite long and employed an elevated and refined legal diction that somewhat blunted the emotional impact of Curtis' arguments; and at times Curtis' Dissent nearly buckled under the weight of Curtis' remarkably long rhetorical questions. Yet, in the end, the thorough quality of Curtis' legal scholarship, together with the restrained yet unrelenting manner in which Curtis drove home his points, made Curtis' Dissent all the more persuasive and powerful. As Justice Benjamin Cardozo—who was himself perhaps the most able writer in American judicial history—commented many years later, Curtis' *Dred Scott* Opinion was one of the "great dissents" in the history of American law, a classic example of a judge who "speaks to the future."[54]

That is not to say that every point made by Curtis and McLean in *Dred Scott* was equally valid. The choice-of-law issue was a much closer one than either Curtis or McLean acknowledged, and Curtis' reliance on the legal significance of the Scotts' marriage was a bit of a stretch. Curtis' treatment of the citizenship issue was impressive in its use of previously overlooked historical sources; but neither Curtis nor McLean acknowledged that were a number of legal precedents that pointed to a conclusion contrary to theirs on this issue.

Not surprisingly, McLean and Curtis were most impressive when they stood on the firmest legal ground. They each made it abundantly plain that the Missouri Compromise was constitutional, and that the pro-slavery majority's denial of Congressional authority over slavery in the territories had no valid basis.

Notes

1. McLean was not one of Jackson's political supporters. In later years, McLean attributed his selection by Jackson in part to the fact that Jackson understood that if McLean continued as Postmaster General he would not cooperate with Jackson's plans to distribute patronage according to the political "spoils" system.
2. Swisher, *The Taney Period*, 46–48; Hopkins, *Dred Scott's Case*, 78–79. Francis P. Weisenburger, *The Life of John McLean* (Columbus: Ohio State Press, 1937) is a useful biography of McLean.
3. McLean's reliance on his faith was not surprising. He proudly held the view that a "Chrisitian morality is the only basis of rational liberty" and that a free government must be sustained on the "basis of morality which is only found in the Bible, and maintained by Christian instrumentalities." *See* Austin Allen, *Origins of the Dred Scott Case: Jacksonian Jurisprudence and the Supreme Court 1837–1857* (Athens: U. Press. 2006), 32.
4. *DS* at 540 and 543 (McLean, J., dissenting).
5. *DS* at 545 (McLean, J., dissenting).
6. *DS* at 545 (McLean, J., dissenting).
7. *DS* at 547 (McLean, J., dissenting).
8. *DS* at 531–33 (McLean, J., dissenting).
9. *DS* at 537–38 (McLean, J., dissenting).
10. *DS* at 549–50 (McLean, J., dissenting).
11. *DS* at 549–50 (McLean, J., dissenting).
12 *DS* at 555–56 (McLean, J., dissenting).
13. *DS* at 556 (McLean, J., dissenting).
14. In a sense, McLean viewed the humanity of slaves and the power of each state to exclude slavery as corollary principles. In McLean's Concurring Opinion in the 1841 case of *Groves v. Slaughter* (which dealt with the interpretation of an

1832 Mississippi state constitutional ban on the importation of slaves from out of state) McLean noted that Ohio flatly prohibited the importation of slaves. According to McLean, if Ohio had attempted to ban the importation of an ordinary item of commerce—such as cotton, for example—that would have been a violation of the Constitution's Commerce Clause. (The Constitution's Commerce Clause gives Congress the exclusive power to regulate "commerce" between the states.) But, said McLean, Ohio's ban on slavery was constitutional because the Constitution—while tolerating slavery—nevertheless referred to and treated slaves as "persons," and not as mere objects of "commerce."

Indeed, said McLean, "The right to exercise this power [to exclude slaves], by a State, is higher and deeper than the Constitution. The evil [of slavery] involves the prosperity, and may endanger the existence of a State. Its power to guard against, or to remedy the evil, rests upon the law of self-preservation . . . ." *Groves v. Slaughter*, 15 U.S. 449, 508 (1841) (McLean, J. concurring).

15. *DS* at 559 (McLean, J., dissenting).

16. *DS* at 555 and 563 (McLean, J., dissenting).

17. The phrase "unlikely hero" is borrowed from the excellent essay Earl M. Maltz, "The Unlikely Hero of Dred Scott: Benjamin Robbins Curtis and the Constitutional Law of Slavery," 17 *Cardozo L. Rev.* 1995 (May, 1996).

18. The event that immediately precipitated Johnson's impeachment was his effort to dismiss Edwin Stanton as Secretary of War. *See* William H. Rehnquist, *Grand Inquests: The Historic Impeachments of Justice Samuel Chase and President Andrew Johnson* (New York: William Morow, 1992).

19. Streichler, *Justice Curtis* at 151–71 discusses Curtis's opposition to Lincoln's conduct of the war and to the Emancipation Proclamation; and Curtis' role at Johnson's impeachment trial is discussed at 172–97.

20. *Commonwealth v. Aves*, 18 Pick. 193 (Mass. 1836). The case is discussed at length in Streichler, *Justice Curtis*, 25–34, and Finkelman, *Imperfect Union*, 103–14. Curtis' argument in *Aves* is reprinted in full in B.R. Curtis, Ed., *A Memoir of Benjamin Robbins Curtis* (Boston: Little, Brown & Co., 1879), Vol.II, 69–92.

21. The terms "Conscience Whigs" and "Cotton Whigs" grew out of a famous speech given by Conscience Whig Ebeneezer Rockwood Hoar, later U.S. Attorney General. Similarly, the phrase "Lords of the Lash and Loom" came from a celebrated speech by abolitionist Charles Sumner, later U.S. senator from Massachusetts.

22. *Cooley v. Wardens*, 53 U.S. 299 (1852).

23. *See* Streichler, *Justice Curtis* at 38–65, and *U.S. v. Morris,* 26 F. Cas. 1323 (C.C.D.Mass. 1851). *See also Memoir of Curtis,* Vol. II, 172–91.

24. *DS* at 564–68 (Curtis, J., dissenting).

25. *DS* at 588–90 (Curtis, J., dissenting) (emphasis added).

26. The "common law" is an important, if somewhat imprecise, legal term. In the broadest sense, the common law is a body of substantive rules slowly developed by judges in the course of deciding individual cases. "Common law" is usually

contrasted with legislation; most English and early American law comes from common law; the modern trend has been to codify laws in statutes written by legislatures.

27. *Conner v. Elliott*, 59 U.S. 591, 593 (1856).

28. *DS* at 571–89 (Curtis, J., dissenting).

29. *DS* at 577 (Curtis, J., dissenting).

30. *DS* at 580–84 (Curtis, J., dissenting).

31. *DS* at 582 (Curtis, J., dissenting).

32. Thus, for example, Stephen Douglas declared: "I hold that a negro is not and never ought to be a citizen of the United States. I hold that this government was made on the white basis, by white men, for the benefit of white men and their posterity forever. . . . I do not believe that the Almighty made the negro capable of self-government. . . . [T]he signers of the Declaration had no reference to the negro whatever when they declared all men to be created equal." Stephen A. Douglas, Speech at Jonesboro, Illinois, Sept. 15, 1858, reprinted in *Lincoln: Speeches Letters, Miscellaneous Writings, The Lincoln Douglas Debates* (New York: Library of America, 1989) at 598.

33. *DS* at 574–75 (Curtis, J., dissenting).

34. *DS* at 590–94 (Curtis, J., dissenting).

35. *DS* at 594–95 (Curtis, J., dissenting).

36. *DS* at 595–601 (Curtis, J., dissenting).

37. The Constitution forbids any state to pass a law that impairs the obligation of contract. This was a creative (and not altogether persuasive argument) by Curtis. Previously, this constitutional provision was thought to relate chiefly to state legislation that attempted to give relief to debtors.

38. *DS* at 601 (Curtis, J., dissenting).

39. *Swift v. Tyson*, 41 U.S. 1 (1842).

40. *DS* at 603 (Curtis, J., dissenting).

41. *DS* at 604 (Curtis, J., dissenting).

42. *DS* at 604–609 (Curtis, J., dissenting).

43. *DS* at 609– 10 (Curtis, J., dissenting).

44. *DS* at 614 (Curtis, J., dissenting).

45. *DS* at 613 (Curtis, J., dissenting).

46. *DS* at 615 (Curtis, J., dissenting).

47. *DS* at 619 (Curtis, J., dissenting).

48. Curtis' argument was somewhat overstated here. Many of those who denied Congressional authority over slavery in the territories at least tried to point to some constitutional language to support their position. For example, Catron weakly attempted to equate his "equality-of-the-states"theory with the Constitution's privileges and immunities clause.

Similarly, anti-slavery thinkers like Chase argued that the federal government could not legislate slavery into a federal territory because the Fifth Amendment prohibited the federal government from depriving any person of liberty without due process of law.

Thus, it would probably have been more accurate for Curtis to say that there was no *valid* basis in the constitutional text for any of these schools of thought.

49. *DS* at 619–21 (Curtis, J., dissenting).

50. *DS* at 620–21 (Curtis, J., dissenting).

51. *DS* at 625 (Curtis, J., dissenting).

52. Apparently, Curtis took Justice Catron's arguments concerning the Louisiana Purchase Treaty far more seriously than he did Taney's comments about the Fifth Amendment. Curtis devoted several pages to dissecting Catron's argument.

In brief, Curtis conceded that a treaty became part of American law. But Curtis also pointed out that a treaty (or a provision thereof) can be modified or repealed by subsequent legislation—just like any other law. Thus the Louisiana Purchase Treaty of 1803 could not invalidate the *subsequent* Missouri Compromise of 1820. To the extent there was a conflict between the two, the later law modified the earlier treaty.

Moreover, said Curtis, there was in truth no conflict between the Louisiana Purchase Treaty and the Missouri Compromise. The Compromise prohibited slavery prospectively forever. At most, the Treaty protected the right of a few French colonials who held slaves in Louisiana in 1803 (when the Treaty was signed) to retain those same slaves during their lifetimes. *DS* at 629–34 (Curtis, J., dissenting).

53. *DS* at 627 (Curtis, J., dissenting).

54. Streichler, *Justice Curtis*, 206.

Chapter 15
Reaction and the Way to Civil War

—Reaction—

The reaction of the country to the *Dred Scott* decision was explosive. The *New York Tribune*'s editorial of March 7 caught the angry and unusually disrespectful tone of the response of northern Republicans to *Dred Scott*:

> This decision, we need hardly say, is entitled to just so much moral weight as would be the judgment of a majority of those congregated in any Washington bar-room. It is a dictum prescribed by the stump to the bench-the Bowie knife sticking in the stump ready for instant use if needed.[1]

The *Chicago Tribune* almost sputtered with outrage: "We scarcely know how to express our detestation of [*Dred Scott's*] inhuman dicta, or to fathom the wicked consequences which may flow from it."[2]

Many Democrats, on the other hand, used the *Dred Scott* decision as the occasion to associate their support for slavery with respect for the Supreme Court, for the Constitution, and for all that was good and pure. The *New York Journal of Commerce* editorial of March 11 was typical:

> [B]y the great masses of the people who prefer truth to error, light to darkness, upon important political questions, the decision will be respected and honored, and . . . will be accepted as a permanent record stamped with the absolute authenticity of the Constitution itself.[3]

The *New York Herald* was even more emphatic: "[D]isobedience [of the *Dred Scott* decision] is rebellion, treason and revolution."[4]

Critics of *Dred Scott* expressed special concern that the decision foreshadowed the possibility that in the near future the Supreme Court might decide that a slaveholder would not lose a slave even by bringing the slave into a free *state*—thus, in effect, nationalizing slavery. They focused on the possible implications of Taney's discussion of the Fifth Amendment. Thus the New York *Daily Times* of March 9 opined:

> This is the fundamental position which the Supreme Court has just asserted, and upon which all its decisions in the case rest. Congress cannot exclude slavery from Federal territory, because the *right* to slaves is the right to *property*, and cannot be divested. For the same reason the People of the Territory cannot exclude Slavery from their own domain: – and when the time for that next step comes, we shall have it in the logical sequence, that *no State government has a right to deprive any citizen of property which the Constitution protects him in holding*. . . . Slavery is no longer local; it is national.[5] (Emphasis in original.)

This fear may have been somewhat overstated.[6] The Fifth Amendment was a restriction that operated against the *federal* government only; thus even Taney might have had difficulty arguing that the Fifth Amendment was violated by a *state* law barring slavery.[7]

But the concern that the *Dred Scott* rule might be extended to strike down *state* laws barring slavery was nevertheless very real, and it was not limited to editorialists. To the contrary, this concern was a theme of serious Republican legal thinkers such as Lincoln and Salmon P. Chase of Ohio (who was later Taney's successor as Chief Justice of the Supreme Court). Chase predicted in an 1859 speech that if the Democrats won the Presidency in 1860, there would then be a new Supreme Court decision allowing slavery in the North "just as after the election of Mr. Buchanan the *Dred Scott* case was decided in favor of the claim to carry slavery into the territories."[8]

Similarly, a Joint Committee of the New York State Legislature issued a report on the *Dred Scott* decision which declared:

> It follows as a direct consequence of this [*Dred Scott*] doctrine, that a master may take his slave into a free State without dissolving the relation of master and slave; and your committee cannot but be alarmed and shocked at the apprehension that some future decision of the pro-slavery majority of the Supreme Court will authorize a slave driver, as threatened by the devotees of slavery, to call the roll of his manacled gang at the foot of the monument on Bunker Hill, reared and consecrated to freedom.[9]

Dred Scott became a common and heated topic of political debate. In the 1858 Illinois senatorial campaign Democratic incumbent Stephen Douglas (a former judge) and Republican challenger Abraham Lincoln (a practicing lawyer) each discoursed at length about *Dred Scott* in the course of their famous series of debates.[10]

In his "House Divided" speech delivered at the outset of that senatorial campaign, Lincoln elaborated on his own version of the popular Republican theory that *Dred Scott* was part of a conspiracy to nationalize slavery, a conspiracy that would soon culminate in a new Supreme Court decision that extended slavery to all the states. Lincoln acknowledged that there was no proof of an express agreement among the alleged pro-slavery conspirators. But Lincoln argued that the course of events had shown that, among others, Chief Justice (Roger) Taney, Senator (Stephen) Douglas, former President (Franklin) Pierce, and President (James) Buchanan, were in fact acting together toward that goal. Lincoln likened these conspirators to workmen putting up a house, presumably pursuant to a common plan:

> We cannot absolutely know that all these exact adaptations are the result of preconcert. But when we see a lot of framed timbers, different portions of which we know have been gotten out at different times and places by different workmen—Stephen, Franklin, Roger, and James, for instance—and when we see those timbers joined together . . . in such a case we find it impossible to not believe that Stephen and Franklin and Roger and James all understood one another from the beginning, and all worked upon a common plan or draft drawn up before the first lick was struck
> . . . .
>
> Such a [Supreme Court] decision is all that slavery now lacks of being

> alike lawful in all the States. Welcome or unwelcome, such a decision is probably coming . . . .
>
> We shall lie down pleasantly dreaming that the people of Missouri are on the verge of making their State free, and we shall awake to the reality, instead, that the Supreme Court has made Illinois a slave State.[11]

In 1860, the Democrats (after a struggle described below) nominated Senator Douglas as their candidate for President. Lincoln was far less well-known nationally, and began 1860 as something of a dark-horse candidate. It was Lincoln's great speech given at Cooper Union in New York City in February of 1860 that first made Lincoln a serious contender for the Presidency.[12]

The central thrust of Lincoln's Cooper Union Address was a methodical and (especially for a political speech) remarkably well-documented and scholarly demonstration that the Framers of the Constitution believed that slavery was an evil that should be banned from the federal territories as a first step on the road leading to slavery's ultimate extinction. (The chief evidence cited by Lincoln for this proposition was the Framers' approval of the Northwest Ordinance.) Lincoln then proclaimed that the constitutional doctrine of the Republican party of 1860 and that of the Founding Fathers was essentially one and the same—opposition to the expansion of slavery into the territories.

Taney's *Dred Scott* Opinion—and, in particular, Taney's assertion that it was the "fixed and universal" view of the Revolutionary generation that slavery was a just institution—and Lincoln's Cooper Union Address should be read side by side. Together, they show that the political debate in pre–Civil War America over slavery in the territories was, in a sense, an intellectual struggle between slavery's supporters and slavery's opponents for the mantle of the Founding Fathers.

In particular, Lincoln argued in his Cooper Union Address that the *Dred Scott* decision—tenuous as it was, according to Lincoln, given the division among the various Justices' views and the uncertainty as to how much of *Dred Scott* was mere dicta—should and would soon be reversed. Lincoln asserted that a reversal would be forthcoming because the *Dred Scott* decision was based in important part by an "obvious mistake" in Taney's Opinion[13]: namely, Taney's assertion that the right to hold slaves as property is "distinctly and expressly affirmed in the Constitution."[14]

Lincoln pointed out that the Constitution does not "expressly" affirm any "right" to hold slaves. Slavery is not even directly mentioned anywhere in the Constitution. To the contrary, Lincoln noted, the Framers consciously decided never to use the words *slave* or *slavery* in the Constitution because they did not wish "to admit the idea that there could be property in men."[15]

Dred Scott thus helped to put Lincoln and Chief Justice Taney (along with Douglas, who was already there) at the very center of American politics and of the great struggle over slavery that preceded the Civil War.

The parties to the *Dred Scott* case themselves remained largely obscure, however, and they came to a quick and sad end. In May of 1857, just two months after the *Dred Scott* decision was announced, John Sanford died in an insane asylum.

The particulars of what happened to Dred Scott are a little murky, but it is clear that ownership of Scott quickly passed from Sanford to Taylor Blow. Taylor Blow was one of the sons of Peter Blow, Dred Scott's first owner. Taylor Blow thus knew Scott from the time Taylor was a boy. (Scott himself once referred to Taylor Blow as one of "them boys" he had been "raised" with.[16]) Taylor Blow and his family had provided financial support for Dred Scott's legal suit. Once the Supreme Court made its decision and John Sanford died, it appears that Taylor Blow purchased Dred Scott and his family, presumably from Sanford's estate. (Irene Emerson Chaffee's new husband Dr. Calvin Chaffee—a Republican politician—was embarrassed by her connection to Dred Scott and slavery; Mrs. Emerson Chaffee therefore executed a quit claim deed renouncing any ownership interest she might have in the Scotts following the death of her brother John Sanford.[17]) Then, on May 26, 1857, Taylor Blow formally manumitted Dred and Harriet Scott and their children in St. Louis.

Dred Scott was free at last. Despite the fame of the *Dred Scott* case, Dred and Harriet Scott lived quietly. Dred Scott worked as a porter in a St. Louis hotel, and Harriet Scott continued to take in laundry. (The hotel was owned by Theron Barnum, a cousin of the famous circus promoter, P.T. Barnum; many hotel guests were curious to see Dred Scott, whose case had drawn so much attention.) When one intrepid (white) newspaperman came around the Scotts' home looking to write a story about the Scotts, Harriet was initially fearful that Dred Scott might somehow be taken from her and enslaved once again. Once the newsman assured the Scotts that he had no such intentions, the Scotts agreed to be interviewed and to have their pictures taken. Much of what we know about Dred and Harriet Scott comes from that interview and newspaper story, and Dred Scott's oft-reproduced portrait now sits in the Missouri Historical Society in St. Louis.

Sadly, Dred Scott's freedom was short lived. In September of 1858,

Dred Scott died of tuberculosis. Harriet Scott stayed on in St. Louis. According to some accounts, she passed away just a few years later, in 1862. If so, she lived to see the Civil War, but not the end of American slavery. However, some historians believe that Harriet lived until the year 1876.

Harriet Scott helped set in motion what is perhaps the most famous case in American history. But even so, we know very little about her; indeed, no one can even say with any certainty when she was born or when she died.[18] Dred and Harriet Scott were American slaves. Their freedom was stolen from them at birth, and much of their life story has been lost forever.

The Way to Civil War

—Taney's Unexpected Gift and Its Unintended Consequences—

Taney's *Dred Scott* Opinion presented pro-slavery Democrats with an unusual problem—it gave them more than they could reasonably have hoped for.

Democrats both North and South were happy with Taney's declaration that *Congress* could not prohibit slavery in any federal territory. But (as noted above) Taney's *Dred Scott* Opinion also included a very brief aside in which Taney asserted that a *territorial legislature* (like Congress) was also powerless to prohibit slavery during the pre-statehood period.

The *Dred Scott* case had nothing to do with any act of any territorial legislature. Taney's comment about the limited nature of the power of a territorial legislature over slavery thus clearly constituted superfluous dicta. Moreover, it was not at all clear whether any other Justice—either pro-slavery or anti-slavery—agreed with Taney on this very narrow point. Thus while it was plain that Taney and five other Justices all agreed in *Dred Scott* that the Missouri Compromise was unconstitutional, Taney was the *only* Justice to comment in *Dred Scott* on the power of a territorial legislature over slavery.

If Taney's brief comment about a territorial legislature were nevertheless accepted as good law, however, then the doctrine of "popular sovereignty"—which had been the official platform of the Democratic Party—

appeared to be in serious trouble. According to the view expressed by Taney in *Dred Scott*, even if every single settler of a federal territory (and every member of that territory's legislature) wanted to prohibit slavery prior to statehood, a territorial legislature still did not possess the power to prohibit slavery.

The most ardent friend of slavery could not have asked for more from Justice Taney. Under Taney's reading of the Constitution, neither the federal government nor a territorial government could exclude slavery from any federal territory prior to statehood. As a matter of past experience, every state that had been formed from a slave territory had ultimately joined the Union as a slave state. Taney's ruling therefore appeared to promise that going forward every new state to join the Union would also be a slave state.

Taney's gratuitous declaration in *Dred Scott* that a territorial legislature could not prohibit slavery was thus an unexpected and very generous gift to slaveholders. But it had unintended and far-reaching consequences. Through a strange series of twists and turns (outlined below), the issue of territorial legislative power over slavery played a continuing and decisive role in dividing both the Democratic Party, and the entire country, between North and South.

Buchanan and Douglas Part Ways

That process of aggravating the conflict between the two sections began with the President. As noted in Chapter 7, in his Inaugural Address Buchanan had made the seemingly strange prediction that the *Dred Scott* case would soon settle the question whether a territorial legislature could prohibit slavery prior to statehood. The prediction seemed strange at the time because that precise issue had never been raised or argued in the *Dred Scott* case. However, Buchanan's prediction in fact proved correct— Chief Justice Taney *did* opine that a territorial legislature could not prohibit slavery. In retrospect, the accuracy of Buchanan's strange prediction thus strongly suggests that Buchanan and Taney were secretly acting in concert—much as we now know that Buchanan also had secret advance communications about the *Dred Scott* case with Justices Catron and Grier.

It is therefore not surprising that once the Court issued its *Dred Scott* decision, Buchanan seized upon Taney's very brief comment about the limited power of a territorial legislature and then whole-heartedly accepted it as binding law. In Buchanan's view there was *no* question that the *Dred Scott* case stood for the proposition that a territorial legislature could not prohibit slavery—even though only Justice Taney had made that precise point, and Taney had done so only in passing. Accordingly, in Buchanan's Third Annual Message to Congress, Buchanan declared in no uncertain terms:

> The right has been established of every citizen to take his property of any kind, including slaves, into the common Territories belonging equally to all the States of the Confederacy, and to have it protected there under the Federal Constitution. *Neither Congress nor a Territorial legislature nor any human power has any authority to annul or impair this vested right* . . . .
>
> Thus has the status of a Territory during the intermediate period from its first settlement until it shall become a State been irrevocably fixed by the final decision of the Supreme Court.[19]

Other Democrats, chiefly from the North, took a very different view of *Dred Scott*, however. They wanted to hold on to some vestige of their campaign platform of "popular sovereignty"—the idea that a Territory's settlers should be allowed to choose between slavery and freedom.

Stephen Douglas was chief among these northern Democrats. Douglas proclaimed that he too whole-heartedly accepted the *Dred Scott* decision. (Indeed, Douglas repeatedly, and somewhat pompously, castigated Lincoln, among others, for daring to criticize the *Dred Scott* decision).[20] But Douglas—mindful that many of his Illinois constituents were troubled by *Dred Scott* and the advance of slavery—nevertheless refused to concede that Taney's *Dred Scott* Opinion had dealt Douglas' doctrine of territorial popular sovereignty a mortal blow.

Douglas did admit that *Dred Scott* had declared that slaveholders had a *theoretical* right to bring their slaves into any federal territory. But, said Douglas:

> It necessarily remains a barren and worthless right, unless sustained, protected and enforced by appropriate police regulation and local legislation. . . . These regulations and remedies must necessarily depend entirely upon the will and wishes of the people of the Territory. . . . Hence the great principle of popular sovereignty and self-government is sustained and firmly established by the authority of this [*Dred Scott*] decision.[21]

Douglas thus labored mightily to reconcile *Dred Scott* with popular sovereignty; he asserted that although a territorial legislature could not directly prohibit slavery, it could nevertheless *effectively* exclude slavery from a territory by refusing to enact a slave code that included all the regulations that customarily governed the institution of slavery. Over the next few years, Douglas repeated and elaborated on this theme in many speeches and in an extended essay in *Harper's*[22] magazine. (Douglas' position was sometimes referred to as the "Freeport Doctrine" because Douglas explained it at some length during a debate with Lincoln at Freeport, Illinois in 1858.)

Over time, the split between Douglas and Buchanan, and between southern and northern Democrats, concerning the proper interpretation of *Dred Scott* became more and more pronounced; in particular, that split became dramatically evident during the course of the continuing struggle over the future of slavery in Kansas.

Lecompton

In President Buchanan's view, *Dred Scott* should have settled the controversy over "Bleeding Kansas" once and for all. Buchanan believed that by virtue of *Dred Scott* it was plain that slavery was now legal in Kansas, and that neither Congress nor the Kansas territorial legislature could exclude slavery; all that remained was for Kansas voters to decide between slavery and freedom at the time that Kansas drafted a state constitution and applied for admission to the Union as a state. Thus, in a Special Message to Congress Buchanan proclaimed (in words that echoed those of Justices Daniel and Catron, among others):

> Kansas is therefore at this moment as much a slave State as Georgia and South Carolina. Without this, the equality of the sovereign States composing the Union would be violated, and the use and enjoyment of a territory acquired by the common treasure of all the States would be closed against the people and property of nearly one-half the members of the confederacy.[23]

In October of 1857, Kansas' pro-slavery Lecompton legislature drafted a proposed state constitution that provided for slavery. A complex series of maneuvers followed. The proposed constitution was put to a popular vote in Kansas, but the referendum was structured so that—regardless of the outcome—slavery would remain in force in Kansas until Kansas achieved statehood. This approach to the referendum seemed unfair to many Kansans; but it was consistent with President Buchanan's view that—based on Taney's brief aside in *Dred Scott*—no territorial legislature could prohibit slavery.

Anti-slavery settlers now constituted an overwhelming majority in Kansas.[24] They boycotted the Lecompton referendum. The pro-slavery Lecompton Constitution was therefore approved in the referendum organized by the Lecompton legislature. But a few weeks later, Kansans voted down the Lecompton Constitution (by a vote of 10,266 to 162) in a referendum organized by the competing anti-slavery Topeka legislature.

Robert Walker was the territorial governor of Kansas. He had been hand-picked for that politically sensitive job by Buchanan. Walker declared that the Lecompton-sponsored referendum had been a fraud and a travesty, and he urged Buchanan to start the state constitutional drafting and ratification process all over again.[25] Stephen Douglas was the chairman of the Senate Committee on the Territories (and the foremost advocate of "popular sovereignty"). Douglas also believed that the Lecompton Constitution did not reflect the will of the people of Kansas, and he too urged Buchanan to reject it. But Buchanan stubbornly chose to support the Lecompton Constitution and the admission of Kansas as a slave state.

In December of 1857, Buchanan and Douglas had a private meeting about Kansas and the Lecompton controversy. The meeting went very badly. No agreement was reached, and each man reportedly promised to ruin the other's political future. A lengthy and heated Congressional battle over the Lecompton Constitution followed. The Democratic Party was divided in two. Southern Democrats almost unanimously followed Buchanan and favored the Lecompton Constitution. Many northern Democrats followed Douglas and opposed Lecompton.

Finally, after many months of acrimony and debate, a compromise of sorts was reached. The Lecompton Constitution was resubmitted to Kansas voters in August of 1858, where it was voted down in a fair election by a vote of more than six to one against. (Kansas was ultimately admitted to the Union as a free state in 1861.)

Buchanan's decision to back the Lecompton Constitution cost him dearly. To begin with, Kansas became free, despite his best efforts; the result exposed Buchanan as an ineffective, indeed almost powerless, leader. Moreover, Buchanan's southern supporters felt cheated, and many came to hate Douglas with a special fury. (For example, one Mississippi editor wrote that Douglas had placed himself at the head of "the Black column," and had been "stained with dishonor of treachery without a parallel in the political history of the country."[26]) Most important, as a result of the Lecompton controversy, Buchanan's party was now split between its southern and northern wings; and, unless that breach was quickly repaired, it seemed likely that the Republicans—whom Buchanan regarded as a mortal danger to the Union—might soon take control of the federal government.

John Brown

Separate and apart from *Dred Scott* and the related dispute over the Lecompton Constitution, a number of other events pulled the country closer to Civil War. Most important, in October of 1859, John Brown shocked the nation by leading a ragtag "army" of about two dozen men in an armed raid on a U.S. Army arsenal at Harper's Ferry in Virginia.[27]

By all accounts, John Brown was a strange, dramatic, and sometimes violent man. Brown had failed in numerous business ventures throughout his adult life, and he appeared destined for anonymity. But in his mid-fifties Brown took up the cause of anti-slavery with fanatic religious zeal. He played a prominent part in the violence in Kansas that followed the passage of the Kansas-Nebraska Act; it was Brown who was responsible for the 1856 Potawatomie Massacre, in which several pro-slavery settlers were pulled from their homes and murdered.

With the secret support of a number of leading New England intellectuals and philanthropists—who were impressed with Brown as a charismatic anti-slavery "fighting man"—Brown formulated a murky plan to strike a blow for freedom at Harper's Ferry. Brown's precise purpose was somewhat unclear. At times, Brown appeared to claim that he intended only to liberate a small number of slaves in the vicinity of Harper's Ferry and to then help them escape to freedom in the North. On the other occasions, however, Brown indicated that the had a far grander vision: Brown hoped that his raid on Harper's Ferry would inspire slaves throughout Virginia (and, ultimately, throughout the entire South) to take up arms, liberate themselves, and rally to Brown's side.

In the event, Brown's men initially encountered virtually no resistance. They quickly took the arsenal at Harper's Ferry, and Brown's men also captured two local slaveholders, along with their slaves.

However, the very next day, a small force under the command of U.S. Army Lieutenant Robert E. Lee retook the arsenal, killing several of Brown's men (including two of his sons) in a brief fight. Within the space of the next two months, John Brown was tried and then hanged for treason.

Brown remained both defiant and eloquent to the end. He invoked the

Bible, declaring that God's law demanded that slavery must come to an end, and that all good men must resist evil laws that enforced slavery. When sentenced to die, Brown proclaimed:

> Now, if it is deemed necessary that I should forfeit my life for the furtherance of the ends of justice, and mingle my blood further with the blood of my children and the blood of millions in this slave country whose rights are disregarded by wicked, cruel, and unjust enactments, I say, let it be done.[28]

John Brown's raid at Harper's Ferry had no immediate practical significance. No slaves rose up in rebellion or to join John Brown. (Of course, Brown never thought to actually communicate with any slaves.) The authority of the Army was quickly re-established. Yet Brown's raid had a profound impact on popular feeling, both North and South.

In the North, many people regarded Brown as a hero and a martyr. Louisa May Alcott (later the author of *Little Women*) wrote a poem for Brown that rhapsodized: "Living, he made life beautiful / Dying, made death divine." Henry David Thoreau termed Brown an "angel of light," and likened Brown to Jesus Christ. Admittedly, some more conservative Republicans (like Lincoln) condemned Brown's raid. But all across the North Brown's death was mourned in public meetings, church services, speeches, newspapers, and pamphlets.[29]

The South, for its part, was horrified by Brown's raid and disgusted by the North's outpouring of sympathy for the lawless Brown. For example, South Carolina State Legislator C.G. Memminger (later Confederate Secretary of the Treasury) wrote: "Every village bell which tolled its solemn note at the execution of John Brown proclaims to the South the approbation of that village of insurrection and servile war." A *Baltimore Sun* editorial similarly declared that the South could no longer afford to live "under a government, the majority of whose subjects or citizens regard John Brown as a martyr and a Christian hero."[30]

The South Demands Congressional Protection for Territorial Slavery

John Brown's raid set the stage for the presidential election year of 1860. Stephen Douglas appeared to be the leading candidate for the Democratic Party's nomination, and Senator William Seward of New York the leading Republican candidate.

Just four years earlier, at the Democratic National Convention of 1856 in Cincinnati, southern Democrats had been among Douglas' warmest supporters. (Six southern state delegations had cast all their votes for

Douglas for President during the first few ballots at the Cincinnati Convention.) They were grateful that Douglas had pushed the Kansas-Nebraska Act of 1854 (with its partial repeal of the anti-slavery provisions of the Missouri Compromise) to passage.

But by 1860 everything had changed. Southern Democrats and other supporters of slavery now reviled Douglas as a traitor to their cause, chiefly because Douglas had opposed the pro-slavery Lecompton Constitution. President Buchanan remained furious at Douglas; and Buchanan used all the political influence and patronage powers at his disposal to punish Douglas and Douglas' supporters. (Some of Buchanan's anti-Douglas tactics—especially his distribution of government contracts—were so heavy-handed that Buchanan's Administration was dogged by one of the first major investigations undertaken by a Congressional Committee, chaired by Congressman "Honest John" Covode of Pennsylvania.)

The Lecompton question had been settled, at least for the time being. Southern Democrats and other anti-Douglas men therefore cast about for a new issue that would highlight their differences with Douglas. They found it in *Dred Scott*, in Douglas' response to *Dred Scott* as embodied in Douglas' Freeport Doctrine, and in a new notion—namely, that Congress should now enact a slave code for the federal territories.

As noted, during his 1858 Freeport debate[31] with Lincoln (and on many other occasions) Douglas had maintained that—*Dred Scott* notwithstanding—territorial settlers could still effectively exclude slavery by refusing to pass friendly local legislation (such as a slave code) that would implement and enforce slavery as a matter of day-to-day practice.

Accordingly, beginning in 1859, and with renewed vigor in 1860, southern Democrats responded by demanding that the United States Congress pass a slave code for the federal territories. Senators Jefferson Davis and Albert Brown of Mississippi led the way. On February 23, 1859, Brown took to the Senate floor and called for federal legislation protecting slavery in the territories.

In his speech, Brown asserted that *Dred Scott* had decided that slaveholders had a right to carry their slave property into any federal territory, and that the Chief Justice had further declared "that the whole duty of this Government towards slave property was to protect it." Brown argued that Douglas had deliberately undercut the *Dred Scott* decision by arguing that a territorial legislature could nevertheless effectively exclude slavery by refusing to pass local legislation friendly to slavery; Brown then challenged the Senate to do its duty and to affirmatively protect slavery in the territories:

> If the Territorial Legislature refuses to act, will you act? If it pass unfriendly laws, will you pass friendly? If it pass laws hostile to slavery, will you annul them, and substitute laws favoring slavery in their stead? . . . We have a right of protection for our slave property in the Territories. The Constitution, as expounded by the Supreme Court, guards it. We demand it; and we mean to have it.[32]

Brown's speech led to a day of debate on the Senate floor—in which Douglas, among others, took issue with Brown. (Douglas' Democratic colleague, Senator George Pugh of Ohio, agreed with Douglas that *Dred Scott* did not mean the end of territorial popular sovereignty; and, as to Brown's demand for a federal slave code, Pugh hotly responded: "Never; while I live, never."[33]) No further action resulted.

However, a year later, in February of 1860, Jefferson Davis took up Brown's idea again. Davis proposed to the Senate a series of resolutions that appeared aimed directly at Douglas and Douglas' Freeport Doctrine. Davis' resolutions stated that neither Congress nor a "Territorial Legislature, whether by direct legislation or legislation of an indirect and unfriendly character, possesses power to annul or impair the constitutional right of any citizen of the United States to take his slave property into common Territories, and then hold and enjoy the same while the territorial condition remains." Davis' resolutions further asserted that if a territorial legislature should fail to provide adequate protection for slave property, then "it will be the duty of Congress to supply such deficiency."[34] (Senator Brown quickly followed up on Davis' resolutions by introducing a bill to punish offenses against slave property in the Kansas Territory.) In other words, Davis and Brown now proposed that Congress pass a federal slave code for the U.S. territories.

President Buchanan and the Senate Democratic Caucus (which was dominated by southern Democrats) endorsed the Davis resolutions. The resolutions were debated by the Senate as a whole for many months. As the 1860 Democratic National Convention (scheduled for late April 1860 in Charleston, South Carolina) approached, a number of southern state Democratic conventions also endorsed the Davis resolutions.

Accordingly, as the Democrats gathered in South Carolina to choose their presidential candidate, the *Dred Scott* decision loomed large. On the one hand, Buchanan and the southern Democrats insisted on the doctrine that—as Chief Justice Taney had asserted in passing in *Dred Scott*—a territorial legislature could not prohibit slavery, and (at least as a matter of political rhetoric) the South therefore called on Congress to pass legislation that affirmatively protected slavery in the territories. On the other hand, Douglas and many northern Democrats paid lip service to *Dred Scott*, but nevertheless insisted that *Dred Scott* had not killed off the Democratic Party's doctrine of territorial popular sovereignty and Congressional non-intervention. The Douglas Democrats insisted that a territorial legislature could still effectively exclude slavery, and they rejected all demands for a federal slave code.

Thus, by the time the Charleston Convention began, Taney's unexpected gift to slaveholders in *Dred Scott* had split the Democratic Party—historically, the most valuable political stronghold of the institution of slavery—right in two.

The Election of 1860

The Democrats convened in Charleston beginning on April 23, 1860. Southern Democrats controlled the party's Platform Committee. That Committee therefore recommended a platform that echoed Davis' Senate resolutions. However, Douglas' supporters constituted a bare majority of the Convention as a whole. Accordingly, in a floor vote the Convention rejected the Platform Committee's recommendation and instead adopted a plank that—like the 1856 Democratic Platform—vaguely endorsed the idea of popular sovereignty.

In response, the delegations from eight southern states angrily walked out of the Convention. After a few more days and many more ballots, it became apparent that neither Douglas nor any other candidate could win the two-thirds vote necessary for a Presidential nomination. The Convention therefore agreed to adjourn and to reassemble in Baltimore in June.

The delay did not bring unity to the Democrats. The Senate debate over Davis' resolutions continued. Southern Democrats repeatedly sounded the same themes: first, that *Dred Scott* had decided that a territorial legislature could not prohibit slavery; and second, that the Douglas Democrats (together with the "Black Republicans") were trying to cheat the South of its victory in *Dred Scott*. Georgia Congressman Robert Toombs argued that the Douglas Democrats' doctrine of territorial popular sovereignty rendered the Court's *Dred Scott* decision almost meaningless; Douglas' approach, said Toombs, was akin to: "Heads we win, tails you lose." And, like many other men of the South, Toombs threatened that seccession might come if Congress failed to protect slavery in the territories: "If the dissolution of the

Union be the cost of protection, I say, let it come, and the sooner the better."[35]

When the Democrats reconvened in Baltimore, the southern state delegations walked out even more quickly than they had at Charleston. The remaining Democrats nominated Douglas for President. The southern Democrats moved across town, declared themselves to be the real Democratic Party, and nominated Vice President John Breckenridge as their Presidential candidate.

There was in fact not much difference between Douglas and Breckenridge politically, except for the conclusions that each drew from the *Dred Scott* case. Breckenridge followed Jefferson Davis[36] and the South —he asserted that *Dred Scott* protected slavery in the territories against both Congressional and territorial legislation, and Breckenridge called for a federal slave code. (President Buchanan, of course, cited *Dred Scott* and endorsed both Breckenridge and southern demands for a slave code, all in the course of a flowery speech delivered from the portico of the White House shortly after the Baltimore Convention.) For his part, Douglas continued to insist that *Dred Scott* did not put an end to territorial popular sovereignty.

Two other candidates rounded out the Presidential field of 1860. The Republicans surprised most political observers (and themselves) by choosing Abraham Lincoln over William Seward as their candidate for the Presidency. John Bell of Tennessee was nominated by the newly formed Constitutional Union Party. (This new party was made up chiefly of former Whigs and Know-Nothings from the border and southern states, and it also attracted a number of moderate southern Democrats.) Lincoln was firmly committed to prohibiting slavery in the federal territories and had criticized the *Dred Scott* decision at length. Bell ran on a vague platform that endorsed the Constitution and the Union. The four way race was made even more complex because in some states anti-Lincoln "fusion" tickets were formed.

In the end, the election went to Lincoln and the Republicans. Lincoln received about 1.8 million votes, a little under 40 percent of the total cast. Lincoln's strength was concentrated in the North, where he carried every state and thus collected virtually every northern vote in the electoral college. Douglas finished second in the popular vote tally, receiving about 1.3 million votes (depending on how one counted "fusion" votes); but Douglas carried only the state of Missouri. Bell carried the border states of Virginia, Kentucky, and Tennessee, and Breckenridge swept the rest of the

South.

The two Democrats (Douglas and Breckenridge) together outpolled Lincoln by four hundred thousand popular votes. Clearly, the Democratic Party's chances in the election of 1860 were dealt a severe blow by the division in the party's ranks over *Dred Scott* and the related southern demand for a federal slave code. There is, of course, no way to know whether a united Democratic Party could have prevented Lincoln's election; but it is certain that the divided Democrats could not. (In particular, Lincoln's victory was made possible because Pennsylvania and Illinois—the home states of Douglas and Buchanan, whose feud had helped divide the Democrats—switched from the Democratic column in 1856 to the Republican column in 1860.)

The key role that the *Dred Scott* decision played in dividing the Democrats in 1860 is the reason why Supreme Court historian Charles Warren once observed (in words that might well have caused Roger Taney to roll over in his grave): "It may fairly be said that Chief Justice Taney elected Abraham Lincoln to the Presidency."[37]

Warren's observation that Taney (and *Dred Scott*) elected Lincoln as President may be somewhat oversimplified, but it is essentially correct. It is even plainer that Lincoln's election in turn caused the southern states (within the space of a few months) to secede from the Union. And the Civil War came.

Notes

1. Finkelman, *Dred Scott*, 145.
2. Fehrenbacher, *Dred Scott*, 419.
3. Finkelman, *Dred Scott*, 138.
4. Fehrenbacher, *Dred Scott*, 420.
5. Finkelman, *Dred Scott*, 146.
6. The expressed fear that State laws prohibiting slavery would be voided altogether by a Supreme Court decision was not very likely to be realized, because the Taney Court placed a high value on protecting states' rights.

However (as Justice Nelson's *Dred Scott* Concurring Opinion, in particular, broadly hinted) there was ample reason to suspect that a future Court decision might recognize some sort of federal constitutional right for a slaveholder to *travel through* a free state with his slaves—in spite of any state "personal liberty" law that declared slaves in such a situation to be immediately emancipated.

Many observers thought that such a decision might come in the case of

Lemmon v. New York; but the Civil War then intervened and made that case moot. *See* Paul Finkelman, *An Imperfect Union: Slavery, Federalism and Comity* (Chapel Hill: U.N.C. Press, 1981), 285–339.

7. On the other hand, however, many state constitutions did contain due process clauses similar to the Fifth Amendment's.

8. Finkelman, *Dred Scott*, 48.

9. Fehrenbacher, *Dred Scott*, 437–38.

10. Relevant excerpts are reprinted in Finkelman, *Dred Scott*, 182–200.

11. Abraham Lincoln, Speech at Springfield, Illinois, June 16, 1858 (The "House Divided" Speech), *Lincoln Speeches*, Vol I, 431–32.

12. The enormous impact of Lincoln's Cooper Union Speech is the subject of the book Harold Holzer, *Lincoln at Cooper Union: The Speech That Made Abraham Lincoln President*, (New York: Simon & Schuster, 2004). The speech is reprinted therein at 249–84.

13. Holzer, *Lincoln at Cooper Union*, 277–80.

14. *DS* at 451.

15. Holzer, *Lincoln at Cooper Union*, 278–79, n. 34.

16. Ehrlich, *They Have No Rights*, 11.

17. However, Mrs. Emerson Chaffee did insist that she collect all the money that the Scotts had earned by being "hired out" while their case was pending over the preceding seven years. In this regard, Mrs. Emerson Chaffee appears to have followed the example her late father—the pro-slavery activist Colonel Sanford—rather than the teachings of her abolitionist husband, Congressman Chaffee.

18. Thus, for example, Kauffman, *Dred Scott's Advocate*, 228, places Harriet Scott's death in or about the year 1862; but Christin Elley, *Missouri's Dred Scott Case 1846–1857*, On Line/Missouri Secretary of State (2002) places Harriet's death in the year 1876.

It is not clear what became of Dred and Harriet Scott's older daughter, Eliza. Their younger daughter, Lizzy, married a man named Henry Madison. Henry and Lizzy Madison's great-granddaughter (that is, Dred and Harriet Scott's great-great-granddaughter) Lynn Madison Jackson lives in the St. Louis area today (and is actively involved in the Dred Scott Heritage Foundation).

Lynn Madison Jackson's father, John A. Madison, Jr., contributed a brief introduction to the quasi-fictional Shelia P. Moses, *I, Dred Scott* (New York: McElderry Books, 2005). Lynn Jackson and her connection to the Scotts are the subject of Cheryl Walker, "The Legacy Lives," *Mound City News* (Supplement to the *St. Louis Daily Record*), Nov. 2006, 5MC.

19. Fehrenbacher, *Dred Scott*, 524–25.

20. Thus, for example, Douglas stated:

> I respect the decisions of that august tribunal [the Supreme Court]; I shall always bow in deference to them. I am a law-abiding man. I will sustain the Constitution of my country as our fathers have made it. . . . Mr. Lincoln goes for a warfare upon the Supreme Court of the United States, because of their judicial decision in

> the Dred Scott case. I yield obedience to the decisions in that court—to the final determination of the highest judicial tribunal known to our Constitution.

Stephen Douglas, Speech at Chicago, Illinois, July 9, 1858.

21. Stephen Douglas, Speech at Springfield, Illinois, June 12, 1857, quoted in Fehrenbacher, *Dred Scott,* 456. The speech is reprinted in full in Stephen A. Douglas, *Remarks of the Hon. Stephen A. Douglas on Kansas, Utah and the Dred Scott Decision* (Chicago: Daily Times Book and Job Office, 1857).

22. Douglas' *Harper's* article is reprinted in H. Jaffa and R. Johannsen (Eds.), *In the Name of the People: Speeches and Writings of Lincoln and Douglas in the Ohio Campaign of 1859* (Columbus: Ohio State University Press, 1959).

23. Baker, *James Buchanan*, 102–03.

24. Kansas Territorial Governor Robert Walker estimated that there were about 17,000 anti-slavery Kansans and about 7,000 pro-slavery Kansans. Potter, *Impending Crisis*, 299. Chapter 12 of *Impending Crisis* is an excellent short history of the Lecompton controversy.

25. There were other problems with the Lecompton Constitution apart from its treatment of slavery during the territorial period. There were well-documented and significant abuses in the elections that led to the formation of the legislature that drafted the document. Moreover, the popular referendum did not allow the voters to reject the Lecompton Constitution altogether; it simply allowed the voters to choose between the Constitution with slavery and without slavery. *See* Stampp, *America in 1857*, 266–294.

26. Fehrenbacher, *Dred Scott*, 450.

27. Chapter 12 ("Harper's Ferry: A Revolution that Failed") in Potter, *Impending Crisis*, is a good short treatment of the Harper's Ferry raid. Stephen B. Oates, *To Purge this Land with Blood: A Biography of John Brown* (Reprint) (Amherst: U. Mass. Press, 1984) is a good biography.

28. Potter, *Impending Crisis*, 377. Brown's speech is reprinted in full in William Safire (Ed.), *Lend Me Your Ears: Great Speeches in History* (New York: W.W. Norton, 1992), 366–68.

29. Potter, *Impending Crisis*, 378–9.

30. Potter, *Impending Crisis*, 383.

31. At Freeport, Douglas stated: "[T]he people have the lawful means to introduce it or exclude it [slavery] as they please, for the reason that slavery cannot exist a day or an hour anywhere, unless it is supported by police regulations . . . no matter what the decision of the Supreme Court may be on the abstract question, still the right of the people to make a slave Territory or a free Territory is perfect and complete . . . ."

32. Reprinted in Kutler, *Dred Scott Decision*, 80–84.

33. Pugh's speech is reprinted in Kutler, *Dred Scott Decision*, 85–89.

34. Fehrenbacher, *Dred Scott*, 531.

35. Fehrenbacher, *Dred Scott*, 536–537.

36. Breckenridge later followed Davis in a more literal sense. Although Breckenridge's home state of Kentucky remained loyal to the Union, Breckenridge became a Confederate general, and later Confederate Secretary of War.

37. Historian Don Fehrenbacher takes limited issue with this thesis in his masterful *Dred Scott.* In particular, Fehrenbacher points out that it was the Lecompton controversy, more than *Dred Scott*, that divided the Democrats between Buchanan and Douglas (and their respective followers).

Fehrenbacher is correct to note that the Lecompton controversy was the immediate cause of the schism between the Buchanan and Douglas Democrats. However, this argument does not give adequate weight to the observation that the Lecompton controversy, in a very important sense, grew directly out of *Dred Scott.*

Specifically, perhaps the most controversial aspect of the proposed Lecompton Constitution was its requirement that slavery be permitted in Kansas until statehood was achieved. (This was the main reason why anti-slavery Kansans boycotted the Lecompton-sponsored referendum on the proposed Constitution.)

Buchanan supported the Lecompton Constitution and welcomed this requirement that slavery continue until statehood was achieved because, for Buchanan, the most important part of the *Dred Scott* decision was Taney's assertion that no one (including a *territorial* legislature) could prohibit territorial slavery prior to statehood.

In other words, the Lecompton controversy was itself an echo of the *Dred Scott* controversy; and thus in truth it was these *two* issues that, taken *together*, irreparably split the Democratic Party.

ANALYSIS

Chapter 16
The Use and Misuse of History

History has been harsh to the *Dred Scott* decision. Historians, legal scholars, judges and politicians of all stripes have been nearly[1] unanimous in criticizing *Dred Scott*, though often for very different reasons. The *Oxford Companion to the Supreme Court* neatly sums up the judgment of history on *Dred Scott*: "American legal and constitutional scholars consider the *Dred Scott* decision to be the worst ever by the Supreme Court."[2] Scholars who are ordinarily quite restrained (sometimes to the point of tedium) in expressing their judgments have described *Dred Scott* by using such dramatic and stirring words as "disastrous," "odious," "atrocity," and "abomination."[3] Even the late Chief Justice Charles Evans Hughes—an eminently sober man, not given to hyperbole—described the decision as a "self-inflicted wound" that almost destroyed the Supreme Court.[4]

The *Dred Scott* decision did not even fulfill the hopes of its authors. In his Concurring Opinion, Justice James Wayne expressed the view that the *Dred Scott* decision was necessary in order to settle the national controversy about slavery once and for all, and thereby restore and preserve "the peace and harmony of the country."[5] The *Dred Scott* decision clearly failed to restore national harmony. Instead, *Dred Scott* became something of a byword among Republicans and many other Americans as a sort of shorthand for what they saw as, at best, Southern aggression, and, at worst, a vast conspiracy to expand and perhaps nationalize slavery. Many Republicans, including Lincoln, campaigned on a platform of criticism of and lawful resistance to *Dred Scott*. When Lincoln was elected President in 1860, the southern states quickly began to leave the Union, prompting the Civil War.

The War and its aftermath rendered *Dred Scott* meaningless as a legal matter. Constitutional amendments passed at the close of the war abolished slavery throughout the country and promised full citizenship to African Americans. Thus within roughly ten years of the *Dred Scott* decision slavery was destroyed, and the two most controversial holdings set out in Taney's Opinion—denying Negro citizenship and striking down the Missouri Compromise's ban on slavery—were brought to nothing.

In this respect the majestic words of the great abolitionist and former slave Frederick Douglass were indeed prophetic, in the truest biblical sense of that word. Douglass declared in a speech he gave just a few months after the *Dred Scott* decision was announced:

> The Supreme Court of the United States is not the only power in this world. It is very great, but the Supreme Court of the Almighty is greater. Judge Taney can do many things, but he cannot perform impossibilities. He cannot bale out the ocean, annihilate this firm old earth, or pluck the silvery star of liberty from our Northern sky. He may decide, and decide again; but he can not reverse the decision of the Most High; he cannot change the essential nature of things-making evil good, and good, evil . . . .
>
> In one point of view, we the abolitionists and colored people, should meet this decision, unlooked for and monstrous as it appears, in a cheerful spirit. This very attempt to blot out forever the hopes of an enslaved people may be one necessary link in the chain of events preparatory to the downfall and complete overthrow of the whole slave system . . . .
>
> Come what will, I hold it to be morally certain that, sooner or later, by fair means or foul, in quiet or in tumult, in peace or in blood, in judgment or in mercy, slavery is doomed to cease out of this otherwise goodly land, and liberty is destined to become the settled law of this Republic.[6]

Once slavery was abolished, Taney's Opinion of the Court in *Dred Scott* became a relic of a bygone era of American law. The Opinion was not forgotten, however. To the contrary, the reputation of the Supreme Court fell dramatically because of *Dred Scott*, and, in most observers' view, it did not begin to recover for more than a generation. Even today, well over a century later, most Americans who know almost nothing about *Dred Scott* do know two essential things: the decision favored slavery, and the decision was very wrong. That summary view of *Dred Scott* is essentially accurate.

What did go wrong?

Some of the answers given by modern observers are not very illuminating. There is a tendency among many pundits to view *Dred Scott* through the prism of contemporary disputes about how the Constitution should be interpreted today. As one review of the modern literature aptly puts it:

> Each school of contemporary constitutional thought claims *Dred Scott* embarasses rival theories. Proponents of judicial restraint maintain that Chief Justice Roger Taney's opinion demonstrates the evils that result when federal judges prevent the elected branches of government from resolving major social disputes. Originalists maintain that the Taney opinion demonstrates the evils that result when constitutional authorities fail to be tethered by precedent or the original meaning of the Constitution. Aspirational[7] theorists maintain that the Taney opinion demonstrates the evils that result when constitutional authorities are too tethered by precedent or the original meaning of the Constitution.[8]

In particular, there is a tendency to view *Dred Scott* in relation to *Roe v. Wade*, the modern (1973) Supreme Court case recognizing a constitutional right to obtain an abortion. Many critics of *Roe* assert that *Roe* was like *Dred Scott* in that each case attempts to decide what they see as an essentially moral and political issue as a matter of constitutional law; and some critics of *Roe* argue that the constitutional right to privacy and reproductive freedom guaranteed by *Roe* is no more valid than the supposed "right" to carry slaves into a federal territory protected by *Dred Scott*.

Thus former federal Judge Robert Bork, for one, declares "Who says *Roe*, must say . . . *Scott*." Similarly, noted conservative legal thinker Bruce Fein recently wrote "The Supreme Court's decision in *Roe* is first cousin to *Dred Scott* . . . [in that it] removed the anguished and anguishing moral debate over abortion from the political agenda."[9]

Supreme Court Justice Antonin Scalia expresses a kindred view in a beautifully written—indeed, almost poetic—passage at the close of his dissenting Opinion in the 1992 decision in *Planned Parenthood v. Casey*. Scalia invokes a portrait of Taney that was painted shortly after *Dred Scott* was decided and shortly before the Civil War began. He sees in Taney's face and deepset eyes an expression of "profound sadness and disillusionment." Scalia attributes Taney's sadness to the realization that the misguided effort Taney had made in *Dred Scott* to settle by judicial decision that era's great national moral controversy over slavery was already doomed to bloody failure. Scalia then urges today's Supreme Court to refuse to repeat Taney's error; Scalia argues that the Court should not attempt to decide today's great national moral controversy over abortion.[10]

Pro-*Roe* observers like Professor Christopher Eisgruber, on the other hand, claim that *Roe*'s critics such as Judge Bork "adhere . . . to a professional credo that mimics Taney's indifference to injustice." Eisgruber argues that Taney went wrong by adhering to a "dogmatic originalism" that looked only to the understandings of the past without regard to their injustice.[11] Professor Alan Dershowitz goes one step further along this road and argues that *Dred Scott* was the inevitable result of the "originalist" methodology advocated by many modern conservatives, including, for example, Justice Scalia.[12]

"Aspirationalists" and "originalists" (and friends and foes of the right to abortion) are not the only ones to invoke *Dred Scott* in debates about modern-day legal issues. Some commentators, for example, have argued that Taney's *Dred Scott* Opinion—with its brusque rejection of all arguments based on international jurisprudence—is an illustration of American "exceptionalism" gone wrong, and that *Dred Scott* should therefore encourage today's U.S. Supreme Court to draw on the decisions of courts in other countries.[13] Similarly, other scholars have argued that *Dred Scott* exemplifies the danger of treating the judiciary as the sole arbiter of questions of constitutional law, and that the negative example provided by *Dred Scott* should encourage the executive and legislative branches to take a more assertive role in deciding what the Constitution means today.[14] Still other writers contend *Dred Scott* was wrong because it refused to recognize "a new kind of freedom, a freedom of family continuity, cohesion, autonomy and privacy."[15]

Somewhat surprisingly, *Dred Scott* emerged from history books and very briefly re-entered the world of active politics during the 2004 Presidential election. In his second debate with Senator Kerry, President Bush referred to the *Dred Scott* case. The President's reference was brief and somewhat telegraphic. Its meaning may therefore not have been altogether clear to those people who were not already familiar with the case and how it figures in present-day scholarly debates about constitutional interpretation. Nevertheless, it appears that the President invoked *Dred Scott* as a negative example of a decision made by judges who purportedly "legislate from the bench," rather than simply apply the law:

> Another example would be the *Dred Scott* case, which is where judges, years ago, said that the Constitution allowed slavery because of personal property rights . . . .
>
> And so I would pick people (as Supreme Court Justices) that would be strict constructionists. We've got plenty of law-makers in Washington, D.C. legislators make law; judges interpret the Constitution.[16]

All of this modern commentary about *Dred Scott* is interesting, and (as detailed below) some of the modern critiques of the *Dred Scott* do have at least some merit. But their real purpose seems to be largely rhetorical. It appears that many modern-day pundits seek to associate their political or philosophical adversaries with *Dred Scott* in the hope that the odium of slavery will somehow attach to their adversaries.[17] That sort of debating tactic does little to advance a good and informed understanding of either *Dred Scott* or the modern-day controversies in which *Dred Scott* has been invoked. *Dred Scott* is an important and complex part of our constitutional history; it is not a mere epithet.

Many of the people who have thought and written about *Dred Scott* in recent years are lawyers, and not primarily historians. Lawyers are accustomed to citing past cases as precedents as part of making a legal argument. When lawyers cite cases, they often must boil down a long, rich and carefully nuanced judicial opinion to a clear legal rule that can be stated in a brief phrase or two. So perhaps we should not be too surprised that some modern lawyers have attempted to cite the *Dred Scott* case as precedent in a very simplistic manner, hoping that the mere mention of *Dred Scott* can serve as a very blunt instrument with which to batter their adversaries in today's controversies about the proper direction of the law.

Similarly, many of the people who have thought and written about *Dred Scott* in recent years are interested in modern politics, either as political journalists or as politicians themselves. Political pundits often look to the past for material to use in support of arguments about present-day policy issues. But pundits often see only what they want to see in the past; and they sometimes ignore richer and more complex truths, both of history and of present-day reality. Thus, for example, for some political thinkers *any* unpopular foreign military involvement, whatever its merits, automatically must be defended by reference to "Munich" and the "appeasement" of the Nazis; while for other political thinkers the words "Vietnam" and "quagmire" come to mind just as reflexively.

Neither historical analogy does much to illuminate today's world. There are, of course, lessons that can cautiously be drawn from history, and that includes the *Dred Scott* case. But we must always be mindful of the glaring particularity of history. For the reasons detailed in the next few chapters, modern-day commentary about *Dred Scott* is, for the most part, so concerned with scoring debating points in *contemporary* disputes about law and social policy that it misses the real point of *Dred Scott*. To understand *Dred Scott* correctly, one must take the case chiefly on its own terms, and in the unique legal and historical context in which it arose.

Notes

1. There is one recent and very notable exception. Mark A. Graber, *Dred Scott and the Problem of Constitutional Evil* (New York: Cambridge U. Press, 2006) takes on the daunting task of (in the author's words) "Rehabilitating Dred Scott." Professor Graber (who long ago was a classmate of mine at Columbia Law School) does not, of course, condone slavery or racism. The theme of his book is that the Constitution was saturated with concessions to the evil institution of slavery, and that the arguments made by Taney and the majority for striking down the Missouri Compromise were as "plausible" as those made by the other side. Similarly, Graber argues that in most highly charged debates about issues in constitutional law—such as those concerning abortion and the death penalty—each side can make plausible arguments.

Professor Graber's work is brilliant in many respects. For one thing, Graber's survey of the literature concerning *Dred Scott* is encyclopedic. The book makes for dense reading because virtually every paragraph is packed with provocative insights, and because it is heavily indebted to "historical institutionalism." Historical institutionalism is a scholarly discipline that attempts to meld history and law (with which I am familiar) with political science (a field I do not feel at home in).

In the end, however, Graber's central argument is less than persuasive. It is true that in any serious litigation both sides can make "plausible" legal arguments that have at least some basis in some respectable legal text; and Supreme Court Justices almost never take positions that are *wholly* "implausible."

Nevertheless, the essence of any judge's task is (appropriately enough) to exercise good judgment and to choose wisely from among competing arguments—*all* of which pass the threshold test of mere "plausibility"—that interpretation of the law which is best. It is an easy task to identify and reject "implausible" arguments. A judge's more difficult responsibility is to first discern and then firmly reject seemingly plausible, but ultimately meritless, arguments.

In the case of *Dred Scott*, Taney and his pro-slavery colleagues did make arguments that were for the most part "plausible" and respectable. Nevertheless, for all the reasons set forth by nearly countless authors over the years—beginning with

Justices Curtis and McLean—the *Dred Scott* majority was plainly *wrong* on the law, and the dissenters were right.

2. Walter Ehrlich, "Scott v. Sanford," in Kermit L. Hall, Ed., *The Oxford Companion to the Supreme Court of the United States* (New York: Oxford U. Press, 1971), 761.

3. "Disastrous" Robert G. McCloskey, *The American Supreme Court* (4th Ed) (rev. by Sanford Levinson) (Chicago: U. Of Chicago Press, 2005), 62; "Odious" Gary J. Jacobsohn, *The Supreme Court and the Decline of Constitutional Aspiration* (Totowa, N.J.: Rowman & Littlefield, 1986), 44; "Atrocity" Christopher L. Eisgruber, "Dred Again: Originalism's Forgotten Past," 10 *Constitutional Commentary* 37, 41 (1993); "Abomination" Cass. R. Sunstein, "Dred Scott v. Sanford and its Legacy," in Robert P. George, Ed., *Great Cases in Constitutional Law* (Princeton: Princeton U. Press, 2002), 86.

4. Charles E. Hughes, *The Supreme Court of the United States: Its Foundation, Methods and Achievements* (New York: Columbia U. Press, 1928), 50.

Mark Graber, "Desperately Ducking Slavery: Dred Scott and Contemporary Constitutional Theory," 14 *Const. Commentary* 271 (1997) nicely surveys the modern critical literature about *Dred Scott*. That survey is updated in his more recent book, *Dred Scott and the Problem of Constitutional Evil* noted above.

5. *DS* at 455 (Wayne, J., concurring).

6. Frederick Douglass, Speech, May 11, 1857, reprinted in Finkelman, *Dred Scott*, 174–75.

7. The split between "aspirationalist" and "originalist" critiques of *Dred Scott* has also been characterized as one between "fundamental values" jurisprudence on the one hand and "originalism" on the other. The split has been nicely summarized in this way:

> Proponents of an approach that looks on constitutional interpretation as having the basic purpose of protecting certain fundamental rights typically contend that *Dred Scott* shows the perils of an originalist approach, that is approaching constitutional interpretation as if the basic goal were to divine what what the founding generation intended or understood the document's words to mean. Advocates of originalism, by contrast, commonly claim that *Dred Scott* illustrates the dangers of an interpretive approach of protecting fundamental rights.

W. Murphy, J. Fleming, S. Barber, and S. Macedo, *American Constitutional Interpretation* (3d Ed.) (New York: Foundation Press, 2003), 218.

8. Graber, "Desperately Ducking Slavery," 273.

9. Robert H. Bork, *The Tempting of America: The Political Seduction of the Law* (New York: The Free Press, 1990), 28–34. Bruce Fein, "Pack the Supreme Court," *DC Bar*, Feb. 2005.

10. *Planned Parenthood v. Casey*, 505 U.S. 833 at 1001–1002 (1992) (Scalia, J., dissenting).

11. Christopher Eisgruber, "Dred Again: Originalism's Forgotten Past," 10 *Constitutional Commentary* 37, 64 (1993). This article is updated in Eisgruber, "The Story of Dred Scott: Originalism's Forgotten Past" in Michael C. Dorf, Ed., *Constitutional Law Stories* (New York: Foundation Press, 2004), 151–81.

12. Alan M. Dershowitz, *America on Trial*, 117–22.

13. *See* Mark W. Janis, "Dred Scott and International Law," 43 *Columbia Journal of Transnational Law* 763 (2005): "Dred Scott reminds us that American exceptionalism in international law and politics helped persuade some on the Supreme Court to protect our then so-called peculiar institution slavery, and to disregard the progressive developments of international and foreign law."

The question of the degree to which the U.S. Supreme Court should consult decisions of foreign courts has become more controversial in the wake of *Roper v. Simmons*, 543 U.S. 551 (2005) where the Court referred to such decisions in holding that the execution of juveniles constitutes cruel and unusual punishment.

Sarah H. Cleveland, "Foreign Authority, American Exceptionalism and the *Dred Scott* Case," 82 *Chicago-Kent L. Rev.* 1, 393 (2007) further examines the degree to which all nine *Dred Scott* Justices consulted foreign law.

14. *See e.g.* Keith Whittington, "The Road Not Taken: Dred Scott, Judicial Authority and Political Questions," 63 *Journal of Politics* 365 (2001).

15. VanderVelde and Subramanian, "Mrs. Dred Scott," 1036.

16. Quoted in Timothy Nash, "Why Bush Opposes *Dred Scott*: It's Code for *Roe v. Wade*," *Slate* (onlinemagazine), Oct. 11, 2004. A transcript of the October 8, 2004 Presidential Debate is available online at www. debates.org./pages/trans2004c.html.

17. Because *Dred Scott* is almost universally condemned today, it is extremely unusual for any court to cite *Dred Scott* in a positive manner. One rare exception to this general rule can, however, be found in the 2007 D.C. Circuit Court case of *Parker v. District of Columbia*, 478 F.3d 370 (D.C. Cir. 2007). The Court there held that the right to bear arms is a *personal* right rather than a right limited to the context of militia service. In that connection, the D.C. Circuit court noted that Chief Justice Taney's Opinion in *Dred Scott* included a passing comment that seemed to point to the same conclusion.

Chapter 17
The Aspirationalist Critique—"Indifference to Injustice"

(A) Defining Terms

There is a subtext to much of the modern commentary about *Dred Scott*, and that subtext is often less than subtle. Many modern commentators discuss the seemingly distant historical issues involved in *Dred Scott* because they want to make certain points about one of the central conflicts in *modern* constitutional law—the conflict between "originalism" and "asprationalism." More specifically, many modern pundits have written about *Dred Scott* as a means to discuss three modern controversial doctrines that are closely linked to the question of originalism versus aspirationalism. Those three doctrines are: a) "substantive due process"; b) the "right to privacy"; and c) the right to obtain an abortion.

The Constitution is, of course, the fundamental law of our land. The proper interpretation of the Constitution is therefore a matter of great importance to all Americans. Judges, legal scholars and historians have devoted many years of study and careful thought to different theories about how the Constitution should be interpreted and applied. It is probably not much of an exaggeration to say that there are almost as many theories and schools of constitutional interpretation as there are law schools.

There are a number of wonderful full-length books that introduce the often complex philosophies of the various leading schools of constitutional interpretation (and the sometimes quite fine distinctions that can be drawn between various philosophies). The best of these books include essays, judicial opinions and other materials that explain and exemplify various philosophies.[1] It is not possible in the space available here to even begin to summarize in any meaningful way the central ideas that are the subject of that rich and important field of study.

Nevertheless, because so much of the modern commentary about *Dred Scott* appears to be at least in part concerned with modern-day debates about theories of constitutional interpretation—including originalism, aspirationalism and the associated doctrines of substantive due process and the right to privacy—it is useful and important to (fairly) quickly acquaint the reader in a general way with those terms and concepts. The quick introduction provided here should help the reader to better understand and evaluate the modern literature concerning *Dred Scott*. (Moreover, I hope it inspires some students to undertake further study of these issues.)

—Originalism—

Originalism is a term used to describe a number of closely related approaches to constitutional interpretation. Generally speaking, an originalist judge (or other legal thinker) is one who, when confronted with a problem of constitutional law, looks chiefly to the constitutional text and then tries to discern its "original" meaning—that is , the meaning that the Framers of the Constitution intended and that their contemporaries (especially those who voted to ratify the Constitution) understood. (Most originalists are, of course, willing to consider certain historical materials—such as the records of the Constitutional Convention and the Federalist Papers—as an aid to the process of discerning the Constitution's original meaning.)

Originalists stoutly resist both the doctrine that the meaning of the Constitution can evolve over time, and the idea that the Constitution's meaning can in part be determined by reference to intentions or philosophical ideals (such as "natural law") that are not expressly stated in the Constitution itself.[2]

The chief arguments usually advanced in favor of originalism are that an originalist interpretation of the Constitution is consistent with democracy and restrains judges from trying to exercise unwarranted discretion and power. The Framers' intentions and understandings, says the originalist, were expressed in the text of the Constitution and then ratified in a democratic process at the time the Constitution (and its Amendments) were adopted; judges (who are not elected by popular vote, by and large) should not be permitted to substitute their own subjective and often changing sense of what the Constitution ought to mean for the objective original intention of the Framers.[3]

The originalist believes that if there is a need to alter the Constitution to meet the changing needs of American society, the *only* proper way to meet that need is through the democratic and orderly process of amending the Constitution; the notion that the Court should instead interpret the original Constitution in new ways invites judges to usurp powers properly reserved to the people. Thus, for example, Justice Hugo Black once wrote (in a blistering dissenting Opinion):

> The Court's justification for consulting its own notions rather than following the original meaning of the Constitution, as I would, apparently is based on the belief of the majority of the Court that for this Court to be bound by the original meaning of the Constitution is an intolerable and debilitating evil; that our Constitution should not be 'shackled to the political theory of a particular era,' and that to save the country from the original Constitution the Court must have constant power to renew it and keep it abreast of this Court's more enlightened theories of what is best for our society. . . . [T]his is an attack not only on the great values of our Constitution itself but also on the concept of a written constitution which is to survive through the years as originally written unless changed through the amendment process which the Framers wisely provided. Moreover, when a 'political theory' embodied in our Constitution becomes outdated, it seems to me that a majority of the nine members of this Court are not only without constitutional power but are far less qualified to choose a new constitutional political theory than the people of this country proceeding in the manner provided by Article V.[4]

—Aspirationalism—

The term "aspirationalism" is, if anything, even broader and more amorphous than the term originalism. There are many legal thinkers who proudly call themselves originalists. By way of contrast, very few judges (or other legal thinkers) call themselves aspirationalists. The term aspirationalism is instead better understood as a descriptive term that applies to a manner of thinking about constitutional interpretation that is shared (to a lesser or greater extent) by many legal thinkers.

The common thread shared by aspirationalists is the belief that courts should, in a proper case, interpret the Constitution in new ways to meet changing times; generally speaking, the aspirationalist thinker rejects the originalist notion that the Constitution's original meaning can never vary or evolve. Thus many aspirationalists embrace the concept of a "Living Constitution" that—like a living creature—can grow and change.

As the word *aspirationalism* itself suggests, most aspirational thinkers give great emphasis to the noble overarching aspirations that are embodied in the text of the Constitution. Thus, for example, the late Supreme Court Justice William J. Brennan, Jr., once wrote that the "Constitution embodies the aspiration to social justice, brotherhood, and human dignity that brought this nation into being. The Declaration of Independence, the Constitution, and the Bill of Rights solemnly committed the United States to be a country where the dignity and rights of all persons were equal before all authority."[5]

Most aspirationalists do not take issue with the idea that the Framers' intentions are a very important consideration in interpreting the constitutional text. But many aspirationalists point out that for a number of reasons it is often difficult, if not impossible, to ascertain the "original meaning" of the Constitution. To begin with, the historical sources are quite limited. There are questions as to precisely *whose* original understanding should control the interpretation of the Constitution. Should it be the understanding of Framers themselves? Or should it be that of those people who participated in the state ratification process? Moreover, today's courts are often confronted with issues that were not (and, indeed, could not have been) foreseen in 1789. (For example, the Framers did not anticipate the development of telephones, and therefore never considered whether wiretapping without a search warrant constitutes an unconstitutional "search" or "seizure.") Thus, as one aspirationalist aptly put it: "[O]riginalism requires us to determine what long dead drafters would think about questions they did not consider occurring in a world they could not have imagined."[6] Perhaps most troubling of all (the aspirationalist argues), a close study of the historical sources reveals that there was no original *common* understanding of certain constitutional provisions; rather, the Constitution sometimes employs broad generalities precisely because the Framers were trying to mask, or paper over, profound disagreements among themselves as to what the Constitution should mean.

Aspirationalist thinkers champion the idea that as our nation grows, and as our government and society change, the Constitution must be interpreted in *new* ways. They emphatically reject the notion that Constitution's meaning is fixed—either by the "original understanding" of the founding generation, or otherwise. As Justice Brennan wrote:

> We current Justices read the Constitution in the only way we can: as Twentieth-Century Americans. We look to the history of the time of framing and to the intervening history of interpretation. But the ultimate question must be, what do the words of the text mean in our time? For the genius of the Constitution rests not in any static meaning it might have had in a world that is dead and gone, but in the adaptability of its great principles to cope with current problems. . . . Interpretation must account for the transformative purpose of the text. Our Constitution was not intended to preserve a pre-existing society, but to make a new one, to put in place new principles that the prior political community had not sufficiently recognized.[7]

Aspirationalist thinkers generally do acknowledge that there are many relatively straightforward and concrete provisions in the Constitution that leave little, if any, room for interpretation. However, aspirationalists also typically point out that in other parts of the Constitution the Framers themselves deliberately chose to use broad, open-ended language—such as the Constitution's guarantees of "liberty" and "due process of law." The Framers (says the aspirationalist) thus intended to call upon *future* generations to work out the meaning and application of such broad declarations of principle:

> The Constitution is replete with clauses that call on the Courts to apply norms to ever changing political and social circumstances. Consistent with the notion of the Constitution as a living document, definitions and applications of terms like "due process," . . . evolve over time.[8]

—Originalism and Aspirationalism Contrasted in Action: Substantive Due Process, Privacy and Abortion—

The Fifth Amendment to the Constitution provides in substance that the federal government shall not deprive any person of "life, liberty or property without due process of law." The Fourteenth Amendment (passed after the

Civil War, in part in response to *Dred Scott*'s denial of Negro citizenship) similarly provides that no state government may deprive any person of life, liberty or property without due process of law.

There is a broad divide between originalists and aspirationalists as to what the Due Process Clause means. Almost all originalists tend to read these guarantees far more narrowly than do aspirationalists.

Even among originalist thinkers, however, there is some division of opinion about how to interpret and apply the Due Process Clause. There are at least four identifiable schools of originalist thought on this subject. Some originalists argue that "liberty" means only freedom from physical restraint (that is, ordinarily, being placed in jail); thus, in their view, the Due Process Clause is solely a limitation on the government's ability to put people in jail without a fair trial.

Other originalists view the Fifth and Fourteenth Amendments solely as guarantees of *procedural* fairness. They argue that, according to the plain import of the constitutional language, *with* due process the government *can* deprive people of life, liberty and property; these originalists further assert that the Due Process Clause merely requires that when the government takes someone's life, liberty or property, the government must a) operate under a previously established known law, and b) must afford that person a fair opportunity to challenge the deprivation—usually a hearing, or trial, or similar "process." These originalists mock the idea that the Due Process Clause places any *substantive* limitation on what kinds of activities the government may prohibit or regulate; in the words of Professor John Hart Ely the idea of "substantive due process" is an oxymoron, sort of like "a green pastel redness."[9]

A third group of originalists argues that the Due Process Clause *does* limit what kinds of conduct the government may prohibit or regulate. But these originalists further maintain that the Due Process Clause is nevertheless not a free-floating mandate for courts to invalidate *any* sort of legislation that judges may think is unwise or unjust. Rather, say these originalist thinkers, the Fifth and Fourteenth Amendment forbid both the federal and state government from passing any law that invades any of that limited list of rights (such as freedom of speech and religion) that are *expressly* set out elsewhere in the Bill of Rights.

A fourth group of originalists adopts a somewhat broader conception of due process. They maintain that the Due Process Clause does set an important *substantive* limit on government power. In their view the Due Process Clause bars the government from passing laws that conflict with those traditions of liberty that are so deeply rooted in the Anglo-American legal tradition that they are fundamental to a concept of ordered liberty; these traditions include, but are *not* limited to, the freedoms that are expressly guaranteed in the Bill of Rights.

This last school of originalism is the most liberal kind of originalism; indeed, in a sense it begins to veer quite close to the aspirationalist end of the spectrum of constitutional interpretation. Nevetheless, it is defended by some originalists on the ground that it still looks to the fixed historical "original" understanding of the Framers, and does *not* give courts free rein to recognize new or "evolving" definitions of liberty.

Aspirationalists view the Due Process Clause very differently. They argue that the Due Process Clause is not merely a guarantee of *procedural* fairness; rather, it sets a limit on the *substance* of what the government can prohibit or regulate. Aspirationalists maintain that the Due Process Clause forbids the arbitary invasion of liberty by the government; and the definition of "liberty" may evolve over time as the courts encounter new situations. The classic statement of this position was made by Justice John Marshall Harlan in the 1961 case of *Poe v. Ullman*[10] (which involved a Connecticut law that prohibited the sale and use of contraceptives):

> [D]ue process is a discrete concept which subsists as an independent guaranty of liberty and procedural fairness, more general and inclusive than the specific prohibitions [of the Bill of Rights].
>
> Due process has not been reduced to any formula; its content cannot be determined by reference to any code. The best that can be said is that through the course of this Court's decisions it has represented the balance which our Nation, built upon postulates of respect for the liberty of the individual, has struck between that liberty and the demands of organized society. . . .
>
> It is a rational continuum which, broadly speaking, includes a freedom from all substantial arbitrary impositions and purposeless restraints, and which also recognizes, what a reasonable and sensitive judgment must, that certain interests require particularly careful scrutiny of the state needs asserted to justify their abridgment.[11]

The aspirationalist view of the Due Process Clause expressed by Justice Harlan in his *Poe* dissent has become recognized as law, despite great opposition, in some of the most controversial Supreme Court decisions of the last half-century. In the 1965 case of *Griswold v. Connecticut* the Court held that a Connecticut law that prohibited the use of contraceptives, even by married couples, was unconstitutional because it violated the Due Process Clause. The liberty protected by the Due Process Clause, said the *Griswold* Court, embraced a right to privacy that Connecticut's anti-contraceptive law improperly invaded.

Building in part on *Griswold*, in 1973 the Court held in *Roe v. Wade*[12] that as part of her liberty under the Due Process Clause, a woman had a right to choose to have an abortion, although that right was not absolute. Accordingly, *Roe* in substance declared that state laws that prohibited abortions early on in a woman's pregnancy were unconstitutional, but that state laws which prohibited late-term abortions were constitutionally permissible.

In the 1993 case of *Planned Parenthood v. Casey*[13] the Rehnquist Court upheld *Roe v. Wade* and again affirmed the doctrine of substantive due process. More recently, in the 2003 case of *Lawrence v. Texas*[14]—while striking down a Texas anti-sodomy statute as a violation of the Due Process Clause—the Court (in Justice Kennedy's words) summarized its current view of the Due Process Clause:

> [O]ur laws and tradition afford constitutional protection to personal decisions relating to marriage, procreation, contraception, family relationships, child rearing, and education. . . . "These matters, involving the most intimate and personal choices a person may make in a lifetime, choices central to personal dignity and autonomy, are central to the liberty protected by the Fourteenth Amendment." . . .
>
> Had those who drew and ratified the Due Process Clauses of the Fifth Amendment or the Fourteenth Amendment known the components of liberty in its manifold possibilities, they might have been more specific. They did not presume to have this insight. They knew times can blind us to certain truths and later generations can see that laws once thought necessary and proper in fact serve only to oppress. As the Constitution endures, persons in every generation can invoke its principles in their own search for greater freedom.[15]

This is an essentially aspirationalist conception of due process. The Court does not look solely to the Framers' *original* understanding of the words *liberty* and *due process* as used in the Due Process Clause. Rather, in cases like *Roe v. Wade* and *Lawrence v. Texas*, the Court has taken the view that the protections afforded by the Due Process Clause can evolve and expand over time, and that the Court can therefore in essence recognize *new* rights—such as the right to privacy, the right to obtain an abortion, and the right to engage in gay sex—that are not expressly enumerated in the Constitution.

Originalists and conservatives decry this development in the law. The notion of substantive due process and of unenumerated rights strikes originalists as a form of judicial usurpation. Originalists complain that there are no principles or fixed rules that guide aspirationalist judges in determining what sort of "liberty" is protected by the Due Process Clause, and that decisions like *Griswold* and *Lawrence* are nothing more than thinly disguised efforts by the Supreme Court to substitute it own value judgments for that of the people (as expressed by their duly elected legislators). *Roe v. Wade* is the special *bete noir* of most originalist thinkers—it is, in their view, *the* extreme example of asprirationalism run amok, creating a constitutional "right" to abortion that has no basis in the text of the Constitution and that results in the wholesale slaughter of innocent unborn life.

All of these current legal issues—concerning substantive due process, privacy, abortion, and gay sex—appear to have very little relation to the issues explored in *Dred Scott*. Yet, as one reviews the modern commentary about *Dred Scott*, it becomes clear that many modern legal thinkers have chosen to talk about *Dred Scott* as a means to score points in the modern-day debate between originalists and aspirationalists concerning the proper interpretation of the Constitution; and, in particular, it seems that *Roe v. Wade* looms large in the minds of many pundits who write about *Dred Scott* today. In a sense, *Roe v. Wade* has hijacked *Dred Scott*'s historical significance. *Dred Scott* was, in truth, chiefly about slavery. But for many modern writers, *Dred Scott* is merely a proxy in today's great legal and political controversy over abortion.

(B) The Aspirationalist Critique of Dred Scott

—Overview—

In recent years a number of aspirational legal thinkers have taken aim at *Dred Scott*. With varying degrees of sophistication, they hold the *Dred Scott* decision up as a negative example—that is, as an illustration of originalism gone terribly wrong. One recent law review article (written by Sol Wachtler, former Chief Judge of New York State's highest court) is typical; it describes *Dred Scott* as a "nightmare for originalists," and contends at length that the "inarguable" truth is that *Dred Scott* was "decided the way it was because . . . Taney stubbornly insisted on sticking to an originalist analysis that anchored him to the time and mind-set of the Framers of the Constitution."[16] Similarly, another law review article describes *Dred Scott* as a "riot of originalism,"[17] and still another terms *Dred Scott* a case of "strict constructionism run amok."[18] The effort to equate *Dred Scott* with the philosophy of the more conservative Justices who serve on today's Supreme Court approaches its rhetorical apex in such statements as: "*Dred Scott* [is the] poster boy for the originalists' view of the Constitution"[19]; and "A contemporary Roger Taney could be nominated today to the Supreme Court."[20]

Some aspirationalists have taken special pains to liken Taney's *Dred Scott* Opinion to the philosophy of constitutional interpretation embraced by Justice Antonin Scalia (and other modern-day champions of originalism). For example, in the 2003 case of *Lawrence v. Texas*[21] the Supreme Court struck down as unconstitutional a state law that prohibited sodomy. Justice Scalia vigorously dissented, and his dissent argued that the Framers never even imagined that there might be a constitutional right to engage in gay sex.

In response, a number of aspirationalist thinkers argued that Scalia's *Lawrence* dissent echoed Taney's approach in *Dred Scott* in that each focused exclusively on the Framers' original understanding. Thus one aspirationalist academic commented that: "Scalia's dissent [in *Lawrence*] is very reminiscent of *Dred Scott*, in that it embraces Taney's cramped notion of history and the law. Scalia, like Taney, has a view that the only liberty traditions are the ones we've had [all along] since the Constitution was written."[22]

Professor Alan Dershowitz has staked out somewhat broader ground; he has argued that *Dred Scott* fully embodies the originalist methodology embraced by Justice Scalia and his fellow conservatives today. Dershowitz further contends that if Scalia and his conservative colleagues were intellectually consistent, then they would have been compelled to decide the *Dred Scott* case in the same way that Taney did. Thus Dershowitz pointedly observes: "I have yet to hear a persuasive explanantion of how honest 'originalists' could have wiggled their way out of the majority conclusion in *Dred Scott* . . . ."[23]

—"Indifference to Injustice": Elaborating the Aspirationalist Critique—

Perhaps the two fullest and most interesting statements of the aspirationalist critique of *Dred Scott* are those written by Professor Dershowitz and by

Professor Christopher Eisgruber. Each correctly points out that Taney's *Dred Scott* Opinion contains a stirring statement of Taney's faith in originalism, and each (with slightly different points of emphasis) goes on to argue that much of what is wrong in *Dred Scott* grows out of Taney's view that the Court was strictly bound by the original understanding of the Constitution.

Professor Dershowitz's critique of *Dred Scott* directs the reader primarily to Chief Justice Taney's denial of Negro citizenship. Dershowitz summarizes Taney's argument from history—namely, that the Framers countenanced both extensive racial discrimination and African slavery, and that it was therefore plain that the Framers could not possibly have regarded Negroes as citizens. Dershowitz then gives special emphasis to two particular passages from Taney's Opinion. In those passages Taney asserted with great force that even if his own generation's attitude toward African Americans had grown more liberal than that of the Framers, the Court was nevertheless bound by the Framers' original understanding of the Constitution—which (according to Taney) was that Negroes were barred from citizenship.

The two passages from Taney's Opinion highlighted by Dershowitz do indeed contain ringing declarations of Taney's faith in his own brand of originalism. In the first, Taney wrote:

> It is not the province of the court to decide upon the justice or injustice, the policy or impolicy, of these laws. The decision of that question belonged to the political or law-making power; to those who formed the sovereignty and framed the Constitution. The duty of the court is, to interpret the instrument they have framed, with the best lights we can obtain on the subject, and to administer it as we find it, according to its true intent and meaning when it was adopted.[24]

And in the second, Taney even more dramatically declared:

> No one, we presume, supposes that any change in public opinion or feeling, in relation to this unfortunate race . . . should induce the court to give to the words of the Constitution a more liberal construction in their favor than they were intended to bear when the instrument was framed and adopted. Such an argument would be altogether inadmissible in any tribunal called on to interpret it. If any of its provisions are deemed unjust, there is a mode prescribed in the instrument itself by which it may be amended; but while it remains unaltered, it must be construed now as it was understood at the time of its adoption. . . . [The Constitution] speaks not only in the same words, but with the same meaning and intent with which it spoke when it

> came from the hands of its framers, and was voted on and adopted by the people of the United States. Any other rule of construction would abrogate the judicial character of this court, and make it the mere reflex of the popular opinion or passion of the day. This court was not created by the Constitution for such purposes. Higher and graver trusts have been confided to it, and it must not falter in the path of duty.[25]

Professor Dershowitz goes on to argue that this originalist philosophy of constitutional interpretation articulated and employed by Taney in *Dred Scott* is essentially the same as that embraced by the conservative Justices on today's Supreme Court. Thus Dershowitz writes:

> The *Constitutional methodology* by which the Supreme Court reached its decision in 1856 [sic]—a rigid and static focus on the original intent or understanding of the Constitutional framers—bears a striking similarity to the methodology currently espoused by several members of the Supreme Court. Indeed it is fair to say that at least three of our current Justices—if they were to remain true to their professed philosophy of constitutional interpretation—would have to have joined Chief Justice Taney's majority ruling that the Framers of the U.S. Constitution intended to disqualify freed African slaves from U.S. citizenship, even if a State awarded them full citizenship. Ironically, one of them [Justice Thomas] would have been disqualified for membership on the Supreme Court by his own logic.[26]

Professor Christopher Eisgruber has expressed a view somewhat like Professor Dershowitz's. Eisgruber describes Taney's Opinion of the Court in *Dred Scott* as a "riot of originalism," and he characterizes Taney's declaration that the Constitution speaks "with the same meaning and intent" as when it came from the hands of the Framers as "a credo to warm the hearts of originalists."[27]

Like Dershowitz, Eisgruber sees a marked similarity between Taney's *Dred Scott* Opinion and the philosophy of modern legal conservatives such as Justice Scalia and Judge Bork; their originalist "credo," says Eisgruber, "mimics Taney's indifference to injustice." For Eisgruber, Taney's "errors are evidence of how originalism can contribute to injustice."[28]

Professors Dershowitz and Eisgruber do differ to some degree in their criticism of Taney's originalism. For Dershowitz, the chief flaw in Taney's approach is Taney's refusal to recognize that the Framers deliberately employed "open-textured language" in the Constitution that left room for the Court to interpret the Constitution in new ways over the course of time.[29]

For Eisgruber, Taney's brand of originalism was flawed because "Taney maintained that the Framers' words should be measured by the Framers' actions, rather than by their aspirations." In denying Negro citizenship, Taney relied on the fact that the Framers maintained slavery and pervasive racial discrimination; and Taney claimed not to care whether this state of affairs was just or unjust. The central defect of Taney's Opinion, according to Eisgruber, is this "indifference to injustice." Thus Professor Eisgruber declares:

> An originalism more contemptuous of fundamental values is scarcely imaginable. Taney found no cause for concern in the possibility that originalist interpretation would render the Constitution unjust. He also refused to assume that the Framers wanted their constitutional principles to transcend the shortcomings of their own conduct. Had Taney adopted such an assumption, it would have favored construing the Framers' intentions, and hence the Constitution, in a way consistent with justice.[30]

Other aspirationalist critics of *Dred Scott* echo the concerns expressed by Professors Dershowitz and Eisgruber. For example, much like Professor Dershowitz, William Wiecek criticizes Taney's view that the Constitution's meaning never changes—that the Constitution is a "rigid, static, concrete instrument, rather than a plastic, fluid growing one."[31] And Sanford Levinson has written that Taney sounds "altogether like Robert Bork, who pronounced original intent the only legitimate modality of constitutional interpretation."[32] Like Professor Eisgruber, Gary Jacobsohn criticizes Taney for failing to "acknowledge the moral dimensions of American constitutionalism"[33]; and Milner Ball tasks Taney for "refusing the responsibility to create with us a future of human flourishing."[34] Historian David Potter has melded these two related lines of criticism, asserting that *Dred Scott* was a failure "because the justices followed a narrow legalism which led them into the untenable position of pitting the Constitution against basic American values, although the Constitution in fact derives its strength from its embodiment of American values."[35]

(C) Flaws in the Aspirationalist Critique

Today's aspirationalist thinkers are certainly correct when they point out that Taney and his pro-slavery colleagues employed an originalist constitutional philosophy in *Dred Scott*; but that is really only half the story.

There are two additional—and more doubtful—propositions that run throughout the aspirationalist critique of *Dred Scott*. First, aspirationalists suggest that the *only* possible result of applying an originalist approach to the *Dred Scott* case was to rule for slavery and against Dred Scott, as the Taney Court did. (Thus, for example, Professor Dershowitz argues that no "honest" originalist can quarrel with the result in *Dred Scott*.) Second, aspirationalists further suggest that if the *Dred Scott* Court had instead employed an aspirationalist approach, then the Court would have found for freedom and Dred Scott. (Thus Professor Eisgruber argues that had Taney and his colleagues adopted an aspirational approach "it would have favored construing the Framers' intentions, and hence the Constitution, in a way consistent with justice.")

Neither of these propositions stands up under examination. Rather, for the reasons set out more fully below, it was in fact quite possible for an honest originalist to disagree with the *Dred Scott* decision; moreover, there is little reason to think that the *Dred Scott* case would have come out very differently even if Taney and his colleagues had adopted an aspirationalist approach. Ultimately, the *Dred Scott* case was not about constitutional "methodology," or philosophies of constitutional interpretation. The *Dred Scott* case was chiefly about slavery and about how far the Justices of the Taney Court were willing to go in order to protect slavery.

—Curtis and McLean: Originalists for Freedom—

It is in truth quite easy to envision an "honest" originalist disagreeing with the result in *Dred Scott*. That is so because Justices Curtis and McLean each dissented in *Dred Scott*, and each did so on essentially originalist grounds.

More specifically, the two key holdings in *Dred Scott* concerned Negro citizenship and the constitutionality of the Missouri Compromise. On the question of Negro citizenship, Justice Curtis made a painstaking historical demonstration that at the time the Constitution was adopted free Negroes *were* regarded as citizens in many states. Based on those historical facts, Curtis concluded that the Framers' original intention was that free Negroes would be included among those people who were eligible for U.S. citizenship.

Similarly, both Curtis and McLean came to the crucial conclusion that the Framers originally intended that Congress would possess the power to ban (or permit) slavery in the federal territories. They came to this conclusion by looking to the text of the Territory Clause, to the record of the proceedings of the Constitutional Convention, and to the history of the adoption of the Northwest Ordinance of 1789 by the very first Congress operating under the Constitution. (In the same vein, Curtis also pointed out that many of the Framers concurred in subsequent federal legislation regulating slavery in the territories.) This *originalist* analysis—that is, looking for the Framers' original intention based on the text of the Constitution as amplified by historical materials—was the central basis for Curtis and McLean's key finding that the Missouri Compromise was indeed constitutional.

Moreover, it should be recalled that—in rejecting the idea that the Territory Clause was subject to an unspoken exception that denied Congress the power to regulate slavery in the territories—Curtis sounded a note that is very pleasing to the ear of the modern originalist, and that at the same time clashes to a degree with the aspirationalist notion that judges should enjoy broad discretion in interpreting the Constitution. Curtis wrote:

> [W]hen a strict interpretation of the Constitution, according to the fixed rules which govern the interpretation of laws, is abandoned, and the theoretical opinions of individuals are allowed to control its meaning, we have no longer a Constitution; we are under the government of individual men, who for the time being have power to declare what the Constitution is, according to their own views of what it ought to mean.[36]

In short, Justices Curtis and McLean—like Taney—were in essence originalists. McLean and Curtis did not quarrel with Taney's "originalist" methodology; rather, they dissented in *Dred Scott* because they disagreed with Taney as to what the Framers' "original" intentions in fact were. Indeed, *all* the members of the *Dred Scott* Court invoked the Framers' original understanding to a greater or lesser degree. None were aspirationalists in anything resembling the modern sense of that term. That is hardly surprising, because "aspirationalism"—the open profession of the belief that the Constitution's meaning should evolve to meet changing circumstances—is essentially a twentieth-century development.

If anything, to the modern reader the most striking feature of the *Dred Scott* Court's "methodology" of constitutional interpretation might be the *personal*—almost emotional—nature of the Justices' originalism. Scattered here and there throughout the nine separate Opinions written in *Dred Scott* are expressions of reverence for the sacrifices and achievements the Founding Fathers, and the accompanying suggestion that deviating from the

Framers' intentions is not only unwarranted as a legal matter, but also a desecration of the Framers' memory.

For example, Taney—in rejecting the proposition that the authors of the Declaration of Independence truly meant to say that "all" men (including Negroes) were created equal—proclaimed that "the men who framed the Declaration were great men. . . high in their sense of honor, and incapable of asserting principles inconsistent with those on which they were acting."[37] For his part, Curtis took the opposite tack, arguing that authors of the Declaration *did* mean what they said, and that the Founding Fathers hoped that one day *all* men would be treated as equal. As if called upon to defend the honor of the founding generation, Curtis further asserted that a "calm comparison" of the Framers' "individual opinions and acts" would demonstrate that the authors of the Declaration could not be faulted for any inconsistency; but Curtis then stopped short, declaring: "[T]his is not the place to vindicate their memory."[38] Thus, for both Curtis and Taney, deciding the *Dred Scott* case was in part a matter of laying claim to the legacy of the great men who founded the American republic.[39]

The members of the *Dred Scott* Court thus shared in a form of originalism notable for its personal devotion to the Framers—a desire to honor the Founding Fathers by implementing their intentions for the American form of government.

That desire is understandable. For modern originalists, the era of the Revolution and of the framing of the Constitution is crucial as a legal matter because it is in that historical context that they seek the Constitution's "original" meaning. Nevertheless, for the modern originalist the era of the founding is now a matter of distant history, more than two centuries old.

By way of contrast, the *Dred Scott* decision issued in 1857—less than seventy years after the adoption of the Constitution. The members of the *Dred Scott* Court were therefore still connected to the Founding Fathers by a chain of *living* memory. For example, John McLean's father fought in the American Revolution. Peter Daniel's father-in-law (Edmund Randolph) served in the Continental Congress during the Revolution, and was an important participant in the Constitutional Convention. Roger Taney argued cases before John Marshall (Taney's predecessor as Chief Justice), and Marshall gave valuable support to Taney's nomination to the Court; Marshall, in turn, fought in the Revolution and endured the freezing winter of 1778 with Washington at Valley Forge. The personal sacrifices and political legacy of the founding generation were thus still very close and very real to the members of the Taney Court. Taney and his colleagues were therefore originalists not only in the modern intellectual sense, but also on a more fundamental, almost visceral, level.[40]

To sum up, the *Dred Scott* decision was indeed rendered by Justices who followed an essentially originalist philosophy. But the *dissenting* Justices in *Dred Scott* also embraced originalism. The majority and the dissenters in *Dred Scott* did not disagree over constitutional methodology. The real difficulty was that the Framers' "original" legacy concerning slavery was itself ambivalent and divided; the Framers proclaimed liberty, but maintained slavery. The *Dred Scott* majority and dissenters disagreed with each other chiefly because they drew different lessons from the Framers' ambivalent legacy.

—Imagining an Aspirationalist *Dred Scott* Decision—

Aspirationalists also argue that the *Dred Scott* majority went wrong because it was "indifferent to injustice," and they suggest that an aspirationalist "justice-seeking" approach would have led the *Dred Scott* Court to a better result.

Certainly, no court should ever be indifferent to injustice. Nevertheless, the members of the *Dred Scott* Court were not free to substitute their own moral sense of what justice demanded for the requirements of the Constitution. And, in the case of *Dred Scott*, that was plainly a *good* thing—because the Justices who made up the *Dred Scott* majority were in fact personally more militantly *pro*-slavery than the Framers had been. In the warped view of Taney and his pro-slavery colleagues, justice was on the side of the slaveholder, not the slave.

Slavery was, of course, a terrible evil. But it was an evil to which the original Constitution (through the Fugitive Slave Clause and Three-Fifths Clause, among other provisions) plainly gave sanction, albeit in limited form. Thus—even if the *Dred Scott* majority had possessed the good moral sense to see that slavery was an intolerable injustice of the greatest magnitude—the Court was still not free on that basis alone to either emancipate Dred Scott or uphold the Missouri Compromise as constitutional.

Most serious aspirationalist legal thinkers do not state their argument in such simple and exaggerated terms. They do not advance the bald assertion that the Court should have freed Dred Scott simply because slavery was wrong. Rather, the thrust of the aspirationalist critique of *Dred Scott* is that the Court's reading of the Constitution's text should always be informed by considerations of justice, but that the *Dred Scott* majority ignored such considerations and instead focused solely on the original understanding of the Framers.

More generally, (as noted above) many aspirationalists take the view that the Court should distinguish between two different kinds of constitutional provisions. They observe that some constitutional provisions embody fairly plain and concrete directives, concerning which there is little room for argument or the exercise of judicial discretion. (For example, the constitutional directive that each state shall have two United States senators leaves little room for interpretation.)

However, aspirationalists further argue that there are other constitutional provisions that deliberately employ language that is broader, more abstract and more open-ended, and that these broader provisions embody the Constitution's most noble aspirations. (Professor Lawrence Tribe has neatly characterized this distinction as one that differentiates between a) those concrete constitutional provisions that merely put in place constitutional "architecture," and b) other, broader provisions of the Constitution that proclaim open-ended "principles" which courts are bound to elaborate over time.[41]) One example of an open-ended "aspirational" provision of the Constitution is the Fifth Amendment's guarantee that no person be deprived of "liberty" without due process of law. Most aspirationalist thinkers argue that by using such open-ended language the Framers intended to leave room for future courts to stake out a broad and evolving concept of liberty.

In the context of pre–Civil War cases involving slavery, like the *Dred Scott* case, the aspirationalist theorist would therefore probably not quarrel with the implementation of a concrete constitutional directive such as the Three-Fifths Clause (counting slaves as three-fifths of a person for purposes of representation in Congress)—even though the unmistakable effect of that "architectual" directive was to augment the power of the slave states and thereby reinforce the institution of slavery.

However, that same aspirationalist thinker would likely argue as follows: first, that the Constitution (and especially the Fifth Amendment) embodies the broad and noble aspiration that all men be free; and second, accordingly, in a case like *Dred Scott*—where no specific concrete constitutional directive expressly mandated any particular result—the Court should have read the Constitution in a way that favored human freedom.[42]

This line of thinking does have some appeal. For one thing, it is probably an accurate description of how many judges in fact approach knotty legal questions. When a judge must choose between two arguments that are—as a matter of legal precedent and logic—roughly equally persuasive, most of the time the judge will choose the line of argument that yields a result that accords with the judge's own moral sense of what is right. The judge may not always acknowledge—even to himself or herself—that moral intuition, rather than strict legal logic, was a decisive factor in the judge's thinking; but—like any other person—most judges try to do the right thing.

Nevertheless, there are some very serious problems with the notion that the *Dred Scott* Court erred because it refused to follow an aspirationalist approach. Those problems become apparent when one considers what sort of Opinion Justice Taney and his pro-slavery colleagues would have written had they adopted an avowedly aspirational approach—that is, an analysis that kept in mind constitutional aspirations and considerations of justice in interpreting the constitutional text.

It is of course true that (as modern aspirationalists point out) the Constitution embodies a broad and noble aspiration to secure human freedom. That aspiration is given expression throughout the Bill of Rights. Yet the Constitution also embodies other, and sometimes competing, aspirations; and some of those aspirations—at least in the eyes of the *Dred Scott* majority—pointed to a *pro*-slavery result in *Dred Scott*.

For example, the Constitution embodies the noble aspiration that people be secure in holding and enjoying the fruits of their own labor—that is, their property. That aspiration is given expression, among other places, in the Fifth Amendment's guarantee that no person be deprived of property without due process of law. Moreover, the original Constitution gave special recognition and protection to *slave* property by virtue of its Fugitive Slave Clause. Thus a pro-slavery aspirationalist Justice on the *Dred Scott* Court might well have argued that the *Dred Scott* decision furthered the constitutional aspiration that private property, and especially slave property, be safeguarded.

Similarly, the Constitution also embodies the broad and noble aspiration that law and order and "domestic tranquility" be maintained, so that people need not lead their lives in fear of violence. Taney, and his pro-slavery colleagues (like President Buchanan and much of the slave-holding South) strongly believed that the mere presence of free Negroes in any significant numbers was an incitement to servile rebellion, and they further believed that the mere possibility of abolition or emancipation threatened widespread race war and terrible violence (along the lines of what had occurred in Santo Domingo). Thus a pro-slavery aspirationalist Justice on the *Dred Scott* Court might well have argued that the *Dred Scott* decision advanced the constitutional aspiration to promote domestic tranquility.

In other words, the Constitution embodies at least three different noble aspirations that at least some of the Justices might have viewed as relevant to the *Dred Scott* case: namely, a) to protect human freedom; b) to protect private property (including slave property); and c) to protect public order.[43] The aspiration to protect freedom pointed to a decision *for* the slave Dred Scott; but the pro-slavery Justices might have argued that the constitutional aspiration to protect both private property and public order pointed to a decision *against* Dred Scott.

If—as today's aspirational thinkers suggest—constitutional aspirations should have controlled the result in *Dred Scott*, who was to say which of these three arguably competing constitutional aspirations was the most important? Should the choice among these aspirations have been made by Chief Justice Taney—who believed that few, if any, Negroes were fit for freedom, and who feared that Lincoln's election would herald an American re-enactment of the "horrors of Santo Domingo"? Should it have been made by Justice Daniel—who firmly believed that all abolitionists were "very wicked"? Should it have been made by Justice Catron—who believed that free Negroes were necessarily a "very dangerous and objectionable population"? Should it have been made by Justice Grier—who contemplated with apparent equanimity the prospect that the killing of a single officer engaged in enforcing the Fugitive Slave Act would signal the extermination of the entire black race?

Given these pro-slavery Justices' warped and racist conception of "justice," it seems very likely that had the *Dred Scott* Court decided the great questions of constitutional law raised by the case utilizing an aspirationalist "justice-seeking" approach, the result would still have been pretty much the same as it actually was—the *Dred Scott* Court would still have denied Dred Scott his freedom and invalidated the anti-slavery provisions of the Missouri Compromise.

* * *

The aspirationalist critique of *Dred Scott* certainly provides one very valuable insight. The aspirationalists are on the mark when they highlight how Justice Taney—especially in his treatment of the issue of Negro citizenship—insisted upon a narrow, history-driven "originalist" conception of constitutional interpretation. Taney looked to the undeniable pervasive racism practiced by the founding generation, and on that basis Taney concluded that the Framers could not have intended to confer citizenship upon African Americans.

The other arguments concerning *Dred Scott* commonly put forward by modern aspirationalists, however, are far more doubtful. Despite a great deal of (sometimes overheated) argument from today's aspirationalist thinkers, it seems clear that: a) originalism did not *inevitably* lead to the result reached in *Dred Scott*; and b) an aspirationalist approach would not necessarily have avoided that result.

Aspirationalists may, or may not, be right in contending that a rigid "originalism" is a flawed philosophy of constitutional interpretation. But, in *either* case, the real fault in *Dred Scott* lies elsewhere.

Notes

1. *See* for example J. Garvey, T. Alenikoff, and D. Farber, *Modern Constitutional Theory: A Reader* (5th Ed.) (St. Paul: West Publishing, 2004); W. Murphy, J. Fleming, S. Barber, and S. Macedo, *American Constitutional Interpretation* (3d Ed.) (New York: Foundation Press, 2003); Antonin Scalia, *A Matter of Interpretation: Federal Courts and the Law* (Princeton: Princeton U. Press, 1997).

2. Perhaps the quickest way to explain and give substance to the term originalism is to provide a common example of originalist thinking in action: namely, the originalist view of the death penalty.

Most modern-day originalist thinkers quickly dismiss the idea that the death penalty might be regarded as an unconstitutional "cruel and unusual" form of punishment. The originalist thinker typically notes that the text of the Constitution itself contemplates that the death penalty may be imposed; for example, the Fifth Amendment requires that a grand jury indictment must be obtained in any "capital" (that is, death penalty) case. It is therefore plain (says the originalist) that the Framers themselves did not intend that the death penalty be viewed as "cruel and unusual" punishment.

Moreover, the originalist thinker will typically insist that we should read the Constitution today *in the same way* that its authors originally intended, so that modern courts should therefore continue to regard the death penalty as a constitutionally permissible penalty. Originalists reject the idea that the definition of "cruel and unusual" punishment can evolve over time in order to reflect society's changing conception of what constitutes "cruelty." *See e.g.* Antonin Scalia, *A Matter of Interpretation: Federal Courts and the Law* (Princeton: Princeton U. Press, 1997), 46.

3. *See e.g.* Antonon Scalia, "Originalism: The Lesser Evil," 57 *U. Cinn. L. Rev.* 849 (1989).

4. *Harper v. Virginia State Board of Elections*, 383 U.S. 663 at 677–78 (1965) (Black, J., dissenting).

5. William J. Brennan, Jr., "The Constitution of the United States: Contemporary Ratification," (Lecture, Oct. 12, 1985), reprinted in Murphy, et al., *American Constitutional Interpretation*, 249.

6. Cass R. Sunstein, "Five Theses on Originalism," 19 *Harv. J. L. & Pub. Policy* 311, 312 (1996).

7. Brennan, "Contemporary Ratification," 252.

8. *See* Lawrence C. Marshall, "Contempt of Congress: A Reply to the Critics of an Absolute Rule of Statutory Stare Decisis," 88 *Mich. L. Rev.* 2467, 2478 (1990).

9. John Hart Ely, *Democracy and Distrust* (Cambridge: Harvard University Press, 1980), 18.

10. *Poe v. Ullman*, 367 US 497 (1961).

11. *Poe v. Ullman*, 367 US 497, 542–43 (1961) (Harlan, J., dissenting).

12. *Roe v. Wade*, 410 US 959 (1973).

13. *Planned Parenthood v. Casey*, 505 US 833 (1993).

14. *Lawrence v. Texas*, 539 US 558 (2003).

15. *Lawrence*, 539 US at 574–79 (quoting *Casey*).

16. Judge Wachtler's "Dred Scott: A Nightmare for the Originalists," 22 *Touro L. Rev.* 575 (2006) appears to be one of the more recent (and strident) full-length expositions of the aspirationalist critique of *Dred Scott*.

17. Eisgruber, "Dred Again," 46.

18. Slater, "Two Men Before the Storm," 2.

19. Sol Wachtler, "Dred Scott: A Nightmare for Originalists," 22 *Touro L. Rev.* 575, 593 (2006).

20. Dershowitz, *America on Trial*, 119.

21. *Lawrence v. Texas*, 539 U.S. 558 (2003).

22. Stephen Henderson, "Anti-Sodomy Dissent Mirrors Slavery Reasoning, Scholars Say," *Knight-Ridder Newspaper*, July 18, 2003.

23. Dershowitz, *America on Trial*, 122.

24. *DS* at 405.

25 *DS* at 426.

26. Dershowitz, *America on Trial*, 118.

27. Christopher Eisgruber, "The Story of Dred Scott: Originalism's Forgotten Past" in Michael C. Dorf, Ed., *Constitutional Law Stories* (New York: Foundation Press, 2004), 161–62. Eisgruber's "Story of Dred Scott," is a modified version of his earlier article "Dred Again: Originalism's Forgotten Past," 10 *Constitutional Commentary* 37 (1993).

28. Eisgruber, "Dred Again", 64 and 48.

29. Dershowitz, *America on Trial*, 120–21.

30. Eisgruber, "Story of Dred Scott," 161, 162.

31. William M. Wiecek, *The Sources of Antislavery Constitutionalism in America* (Ithaca: Cornell U. Press, 1977), 247.

32. Sanford Levinson, "Slavery in the Canon of Constitutional Law," 68 *Chicago Kent L. Rev.* 1087, 1107 (1993).

33. Gary S. Jacobsohn, *The Supreme Court and the Decline of Constitutional Aspiration* (Totowa, N.J.: Rowman and Littlefield, 1986), 8.

34. Milner S. Ball, "A Letter to Professor Burt," 42 *Washington & Lee Law Rev.* 27, 35 (1985).

35. Potter, *The Impending Crisis*, 292.

36. *DS* at 420–21 (Curtis, J., dissenting).

37. *DS* at 410.

38. *DS* at 414–15 (Curtis, J., dissenting).

39. In a similar vein, Justice Campbell extolled the heroism of the revolutionary generation—as he rejected the idea that the Territory Clause conferred upon Congress a broad power to legislate for the territories—by posing the rhetorical question: "Could it have been the purpose of Washington and his illustrious associates . . . to reestablish in the Constitution of their country that fort which had been prostrated amid the toils and with the sufferings and sacrifices of seven years of war?" *DS* at 510–11 (Campbell, J., concurring).

Daniel's *Dred Scott* Opinion similarly invoked the "sages and patriots by whom the Constitution was framed." *DS* at 490 (Daniel, J. concurring). Along the same lines, Catron's Opinion noted that the original western territories had been wrested from England during the Revolution "by the blood and treasure of all the States." *DS* at 520 (Catron, J. concurring). And John McLean's *Dred Scott* Opinion struck a similar chord of reverence for the Framers by noting that James Madison, "that great and good man," took care to see to it that the Constitution never blessed slavery by name. *DS* at 537 (McLean, J. dissenting).

40. Robert E. Mensel, "Originalism and Ancestor-Worship in the Post-Heroic Era: The Dred Scott Opinions," 17 *Widener Law Journal* 29 (2007) elaborates an interesting theory derived from cultural history tying both Taney's and Curtis' originalism to a general tendency among Americans born during the generation after the Revolution to "Ancestor Worship."

41. *See e.g.* Lawrence Tribe, "Comment," in Scalia, *A Matter of Interpretation*, 67–68 and 93–94.

42. Thus, for example, Professor Eisgruber lauds Justice McLean's *Dred Scott* dissent because McLean insisted "that we should interpret the Framers' intentions in the way most consistent with justice." Christopher Eisgruber, "Dred Again: Originalism's Forgotten Past" 10 *Const. Commentary* 37, at 49 (1993).

Similarly, Professor Sotirios Barber condemns Taney's Opinion because it "furthered the degradation of both law and the community by denying that the Constitution is what it says it is: an instrument of justice;" according to Barber, because "the Constitution had put slavery in the course of ultimate extinction . . .

asking the Court to overrule *Dred Scott* can be construed as asking the Court to play its part in achieving a constitutional aspiration to rise above conditions responsible for the initial protection of slavery." Sotirios Barber, "Whither Moral Realism in Constitutional Theory?: A Reply to Professor McConnell," 64 *Chicago-Kent L. Review* 111 at 118 and 127 (1988).

43. Similarly, it might be argued that the Constitution embodies an "aspiration" that all Americans be treated as equals, and that all Americans are entitled to govern themselves. In the minds of some members of the *Dred Scott* majority, these aspirations would also point to a *pro*-slavery result in *Dred Scott*.

For example, Justice Campbell pointed out that there was some tension between the principle of *local* self-government on the one hand, and a *Congressional* ban on slavery in a federal territory on the other; and Justice Catron pointed out that a ban on slavery in the federal territories did have a discriminatory impact on white people from the South who wanted to settle in the territories.

Thus, had Campbell or Catron adopted an "aspirationalist" approach, they might well have argued that these constitutional aspirations required a *pro*-slavery result in *Dred Scott*.

Chapter 18
The Originalist Critique—
"First Cousin" to *Roe*

—Overview—

Aspirationalists criticize the *Dred Scott*'s decision's fidelity to originalism. Many originalist thinkers have returned the favor. They argue that *Dred Scott* exemplifies aspirationalism gone wrong; thus Supreme Court Justice William Rehnquist once wrote that *Dred Scott* is "the apogee of the living Constitution doctrine in the nineteenth century."[1] In particular, many originalists argue that *Dred Scott* and *Roe v. Wade*—the modern (1973) Supreme Court cases recognizing a right to abortion—are very much alike in that in each case the Court substituted its own subjective notions of justice for the objective intention of the Framers. *Roe v. Wade*, according to many originalists, is "The *Dred Scott* of Our Time."[2]

The originalist critique of *Dred Scott*, with its analogy between *Dred Scott* and *Roe v. Wade*, has been repeated with great frequency by conservative legal thinkers in books, essays and speeches. (Even President Bush appeared to make reference to it during a 2004 Presidential debate with Senator John Kerry.[3]) Indeed, the originalist charge that *Roe v. Wade* is an echo of *Dred Scott* has become so common that Professor Christopher Eisgruber has dubbed it the "Dred Again Theory."[4]

There are at least two common variations on the Dred Again Theory; for ease of reference, they can be thought of as the "Moral Issue" and "Substantive Due Process" Variations, respectively.

First—as to the Moral Issue Variation—many originalists (including, most prominently, Justice Scalia in his eloquent dissent in *Planned Parenthood v. Casey*) liken *Dred Scott* to *Roe v. Wade*; they argue that each decision improperly reached out to decide what was essentially a moral question as a matter of constitutional law. Noted conservative legal thinker Bruce Fein has expressed this idea in crisp and memorable fashion, stating: "The Supreme Court's decision in *Roe* is first cousin to *Dred Scott* . . . [in that] it removed the anguished and anguishing moral debate over abortion from the national agenda."[5]

Second, on a related but distinct note, many originalists (including, most prominently, former federal judge and unsuccessful Supreme Court nominee Robert Bork) contend that Taney's *Dred Scott* Opinion marks the beginning of what they view as the Supreme Court's mistaken "substantive due process" and "privacy" jurisprudence—a jurisprudence that ultimately led to *Roe v. Wade*.

Thus Judge Bork has written: "Who says *Roe* must say . . . *Scott*," and contends that the doctrine of substantive due process "originated in the judicial desire to protect slavery."[6] Similarly, Senator Orrin Hatch (for many years a ranking Republican on the Senate Judiciary Committee) has stated: "[I]n my view it's impossible to distinguish *Dred Scott v. Sandford* from the Court's due process privacy cases like *Roe v. Wade*."[7]

The Dred Again Theory—in both its Moral Issue and Substantive Due Process Variations—is certainly thought provoking; but, for the reasons outlined below, it is ultimately less than persuasive.

As to the Substantive Due Process Variation, the effort made by Judge Bork (among many others) to equate both Taney and *Dred Scott* with aspirationalism and with modern substantive due process jurisprudence is a very doubtful one. To begin with, Taney's *Dred Scott* Opinion itself indicates that Taney was an avowed and determined *originalist*. He believed that the Constitution "speaks not only in the same words, but with the same meaning and intent with which it spoke when it came from the hands of its framers . . . ."[8]

With regard to the notion that Taney embraced substantive due process, it is true that in *Dred Scott* Taney very briefly invoked the Fifth Amendment's Due Process Clause in a way that was (and remains) controversial. However, upon close examination it does not appear that Taney's brief and somewhat confusing discussion of the Fifth Amendment was essential to Taney's own Opinion; the better view is that Taney's mention of the Due Process Clause was something of a rhetorical aside. (The main thrust of Taney's argument for invalidating the Missouri Compromise was that neither the Territory Clause nor any other provision of the Constitution authorized Congress to pass laws regulating slavery in the territories; that line of argument did not refer to or rely on the Fifth Amendment.)

Moreover, it is plain that Taney's short and somewhat cryptic discussion of the Fifth Amendment was not specifically adopted by any other Justice on the *Dred Scott* Court, and has never been favorably cited by any subsequent Supreme Court Opinion—either in support of a theory of substantive due process, or otherwise.

Thus, the most that can be said is that Taney's *Dred Scott* Opinion contains a nineteenth-century feint in somewhat the same direction as the modern doctrine of substantive due process—a doctrine that was developed in the twentieth century by a very different line of thinking for very different reasons.

As to the Moral Issue Variation, the originalist argument (best stated by Justice Scalia) that *Dred Scott* represented an effort to convert a moral question into a question of constitutional law has greater weight. Taney and his pro-slavery colleagues did indeed strain mightily in *Dred Scott* to settle by judicial fiat their era's great national controversy about slavery; and that controversy plainly had important moral and political aspects.

Yet the question whether Congress possessed the authority to ban slavery in the federal territories was a genuine *legal* question, and that question could *only* be answered by reference to the Constitution. Thus—whatever one thinks of *Roe v. Wade*—the *Dred Scott* Court cannot fairly be faulted merely for looking to the Constitution in order to decide the genuine question of constitutional law presented by the *Dred Scott* case.

(A) Elaborating the Originalist Critique

—The Substantive Due Process Variation—

The most famous and most eloquent statement of the originalist critique of *Dred Scott* is that written by former federal Judge Robert Bork in his book *The Tempting of America*. That book is remarkably ambitious in its scope. In the space of a single volume, Judge Bork: a) sets forth his judicial philosophy, one that calls on the Supreme Court to look for the "Original Understanding" of the Constitution; b) outlines the entire history of the U.S. Supreme Court, with a view to tracing the Court's various departures from the philosophy of the Original Understanding; c) summarizes (and then discounts) all the major competing philosophies of constitutional interpretation; and d) tells the story of how the U.S. Senate, amid great controversy, rejected Judge Bork's own 1987 nomination to serve on the U.S. Supreme Court (a story that Judge Bork—somewhat understandably—overdramatizes as "the Bloody Crossroads"). With extraordinary skill and compression, Judge Bork's book manages to discuss all these subjects in real depth, with grace and elegance.

Judge Bork abhors the doctrine of substantive due process, and Bork traces the doctrine's roots back directly to Chief Justice Taney and *Dred Scott*:

> Substantive due process, though it originated in the judicial desire to protect slavery, had now been validated as constitutional doctrine. Perhaps "doctrine" implies too much of rationality and intellectual rigor. Since the clause was designed only to require fair procedures in implementing laws, there is no original understanding that gives it any substantive content. Thus, a judge who insists upon giving the due process clause such content must make it up. That's why substantive due process, whenever it appears, is never more than a pretense that the judge's views are in the Constitution. That has been true from *Dred Scott* to today.[9]

Like many other originalists, Bork believes that the Due Process Clause is merely "a requirement that government not do certain things to people without fair procedures, not a statement of what things may not be done."[10] Accordingly, Bork argues that we must "condemn the hundreds of cases stretching from *Dred Scott* to today, in which the courts have given the Due Process Clause substantive content in order to read their own notions of policy into the Constitution." And it appears that, for Bork, the worst of these cases is *Roe v. Wade*, which he terms "the greatest example and symbol of the judicial usurpation of democratic prerogatives in the twentieth century."[11]

Bork argues that in *Dred Scott*, "Taney employed, and probably invented, substantive due process."[12] He explains that:

> Chief Justice Roger Taney began the misuse of due process in *Dred Scott* to invent a substantive right to own slaves, and the Court has never looked back. Taney found his power in the word property. *Roe* . . . claim[s] authority from the liberty mentioned in the clause. Neither word has any substantive meaning other than what the Court chooses to give it. The power assumed proved too seductive for a satisfaction so arid as sticking to the principles of the Constitution.[13]

Bork's analysis of *Dred Scott* zeroes in on a few (and, in Bork's view, crucial) sentences toward the end of Taney's Opinion of the Court. Indeed, these few sentences seem to be the *only* important aspect of the *Dred Scott* case for Bork. Thus Bork makes no mention of any of the concurring Opinions in *Dred Scott*, and Bork disregards all the rest of Taney's Opinion too. In particular, Judge Bork completely ignores Taney's long (and somewhat tortured) effort to demonstrate that the Constitution's Territory Clause somehow failed to confer upon Congress the power to legislate for the territories—even though that effort takes up the lion's share of Taney's discussion of the Missouri Compromise's constitutionality. Bork similarly ignore Taney's long and labored effort to demonstrate that no other provision of the Constitution empowered Congress to regulate slavery in the territories.

Rather, for Bork, the entire *Dred Scott* case essentially boils down to those two sentences from Taney's Opinion in which Taney declared:

> [T]he rights of property are united with the rights of person, and placed on the same ground by the fifth amendment to the Constitution, which provides that no person shall be deprived of life, liberty, and property, without due process of law. And an act of Congress, which deprives a citizen of the United States of his

> liberty or property, merely because he came himself or brought his property into a particular Territory of the United States, and who had committed no offense against the laws, could hardly be dignified with the name of due process of law.[14]

Bork views these two sentences as the very heart of the *Dred Scott* decision. Here, says Bork, Justice Taney declared that the Missouri Compromise Act violated the Fifth Amendment's Due Process Clause. (Bork thus ignores—or glosses over as too simple to require discussion—a complex question that has long divided serious *Dred Scott* scholars: namely, in coming to the conclusion that the Missouri Compromise was unconstitutional, did Taney rely on the affirmative prohibitions of the Fifth Amendment, or did Taney instead rely on the absence of any express grant of authority in the Constitution for Congress to legislate concerning slavery in the territories?)

Moreover, according to Bork, the second sentence quoted above contains Taney's key error. It was here, says Bork, that Taney transformed the Due Process Clause from a mere guarantee of *procedural* fairness into "a rule about the allowable *substance* of a statute . . . . Though [Taney's] transformation of the due process clause from a procedural to a substantive requirement was an obvious sham, it was a momentous sham, for this was the first appearance in American constitutional law of the concept of 'substantive due process,' and that concept has been used countless times since by judges who want to write their personal beliefs into a document that, most inconveniently, does not contain those beliefs."[15]

Bork contends that because the *Dred Scott* decision invented "substantive due process," *Dred Scott* is *Roe v. Wade*'s "very ugly ancestor." In Bork's view, both cases are part of a pattern in which unelected judges have improperly substituted their own political and moral beliefs for the original understanding of the Constitution. "[O]nce it is conceded that a judge may give due process substantive content," Bork contends, then it must also be conceded that it is legitimate for a judge to impose his "morality and politics upon you. . . . Who says *Roe* must say . . . *Scott*. This is vehemently denied by today's proponents of judicial policymaking, but the denial is hollow and merely means that they like the policies now being made."[16]

Many other originalist thinkers have echoed Judge Bork's analysis. For example, then Attorney General Richard Thornburgh opined that Taney "applied substantive due proocess—for the first time in the history of the

Court—to find that the Fifth Amendment protected a slave owner's property right in another human being."[17] Senator Hatch has similarly declared: "As you know, the first substantive due process case was the *Dred Scott* case in 1857. That is where the Supreme Court held that the liberty clause of the Due Process Clause prevented Congress from forbidding slavery in the territories."[18] Then professor (and now federal judge) Michael McConnell, writing in a more scholarly vein, has argued along the same lines, asserting:

> Chief Justice Taney . . . invoked a constitutional principle that was as unprecedented at the time as it is notorious today: substantive due process. *Dred Scott* was the very first Supreme Court case to take the view that a statute can be unconstitutional because it violates unenumerated rights."[19]

Justice Scalia has also appeared to endorse Judge Bork's characterization of *Dred Scott* as the fount of substantive due process. At a recent forum, a questioner suggested that *Dred Scott* had been the first originalist decision. Justice Scalia retorted: "*Dred Scott* was the first originalist case? You know what *Dred Scott* was? *Dred Scott* was the first case to use the horrid term substantive due process which has been the . . . source of all the inventiveness of the Supreme Court in developing an evolving standard of decency"[20]

—The Moral Issue Variation—

The Substantive Due Process variation on the Originalist Critique of *Dred Scott* is often joined up with a related, but distinct, line of argument—that *Dred Scott* was wrong because it attempted to settle by judicial decision what was in truth a moral and political dispute about slavery. This criticism of *Dred Scott* is often voiced by modern originalists, and many of those originalists see further parallels between *Dred Scott* on the one hand, and two modern Supreme Court cases that recognize a woman's right to obtain an abortion on the other—that is, *Roe v. Wade* and *Planned Parenthood v. Casey*.

The most dramatic and best expression of the Moral Issue Variation on the Dred Again Theory is that written by Justice Scalia in his dissent in *Planned Parenthood v. Casey*. Scalia's dissent evidences his familiarity both with *Dred Scott* itself and with the history that surrounded the *Dred*

Scott decision—including President Buchanan's role. For Scalia, *Dred Scott* exemplifies the folly of believing—as Taney and Buchanan apparently did—that a judicial decision can ever settle a fundamental disputed question of right and wrong. In Scalia's view, *Roe v. Wade* repeats *Dred Scott*'s error; Scalia believes that *Roe v. Wade* has inflamed, rather than quieted, our national debate about abortion. Thus Scalia wrote:

> There is a poignant aspect to today's opinion. Its length, and what might be called its epic tone, suggest that its authors believe they are bringing to an end a troublesome era in the history of our Nation and of our Court. "It is the dimension" of authority, they say, to "cal[l] the contending sides of national controversy to end their national division by accepting a common mandate rooted in the Constitution."
>
> There comes vividly to mind a portrait by Emanuel Leutze that hangs in the Harvard Law School: Roger Brooke Taney, painted in 1859, the 82d year of his life, the 24th of his Chief Justiceship, the second after his opinion in *Dred Scott*. He is all in black, sitting in a shadowed red armchair, left hand resting upon a pad of paper in his lap, right hand hanging limply, almost lifelessly, beside the inner arm of the chair. He sits facing the viewer and staring straight out. There seems to be on his face, and in his deep-set eyes, an expression of profound sadness and disillusionment. Perhaps he always looked that way, even when dwelling upon the happiest of thoughts. But those of us who know how the luster of his great Chief Justiceship came to be eclipsed by *Dred Scott* cannot help believing that he had that case-its already apparent consequences—for the Court and its soon-to-be-played-out consequences for the Nation—burning on his mind. I expect that two years earlier he, too, had thought himself "call[ing] the contending sides of national controversy to end their national division by accepting a common mandate rooted in the Constitution."
>
> It is no more realistic for us in this litigation, than it was for him in that, to think that an issue of the sort they both involved—an issue involving life and death, freedom and subjugation—can be "speedily and finally settled" by the Supreme Court, as President James Buchanan in his inaugural address said the issue of slavery in the territories would be. . . . Quite to the contrary, by foreclosing all democratic outlet for the deep passions this issue arouses, by banishing the issue from the political forum that gives all participants, even the losers, the satisfaction of a fair hearing and an honest fight, by continuing the imposition of a rigid national rule instead of allowing for regional differences, the Court merely prolongs and intensifies the anguish.
>
> We should get out of this area, where we have no right to be, and where we do neither ourselves nor the country any good by remaining.[21]

The theme sounded by Justice Scalia[22] here was not an altogether new one. Long before *Dred Scott* became a proxy in the national debate about abortion rights under the Constitution, *Dred Scott* was, on occasion, cited as a case where the Supreme Court had overstepped its bounds by attempting to resolve a political issue. The tendency to view *Dred Scott* in such a light has usually been most prominent in those periods of American history where there has been widespread concern that the Supreme Court has been unduly assertive.

Thus, in the aftermath of the struggle between President Franklin Roosevelt and a Supreme Court that had struck down many early pieces of New Deal legislation, Supreme Court Justice Robert Jackson reflected that the *Dred Scott* decision was wrong because it foreclosed "hope that American forbearance and statesmanship would prove equal to finding some compromise between the angry forces that were being aroused by the slave issue."[23] Similarly, Alexander Bickel (writing in the midst of controversy over the Warren Court's activism during the 1950s and 1960s) termed *Dred Scott* a "futile and misguided effort, by way of a legalism . . . to resolve the controversy over the spread of slavery."[24]

Constitutional law scholars Robert McCloskey and Cass Sunstein have more recently expressed kindred views, arguing that *Dred Scott*'s fundamental error was to decide a political question as a matter of law. McCloskey contended that the *Dred Scott* Court erred by "imagining that a flaming political issue could be quenched by calling it a 'legal' issue and deciding it judicially."[25] And Professor Sunstein contends that *Dred Scott* at least strongly "suggest[s] that . . . the Supreme Court should . . . leave Great Questions to politics."[26]

(B) Flaws in the Originalist Critique

—"Aspirationalism" Absent from *Dred Scott*—

The effort by modern conservatives to equate *Dred Scott* with aspirationalism and the modern doctrine of substantive due process seems misguided.

To begin with, it is plain that Chief Justice Taney and all the other Justices on the *Dred Scott* Court (both concurring *and* dissenting) were essentially originalists. All the Justices' Opinions—including Taney's—were framed in terms of discerning and implementing the Framers' original intentions. In particular, the *Dred Scott* Court's common embrace of originalism was the reason why Taney struggled so hard (if not very persuasively) to distinguish away the Northwest Ordinance (barring slavery in the original Northwest Territory) as precedent; as both Curtis and McLean argued, the Northwest Ordinance of 1789 certainly appeared to demonstrate that the Framers themselves believed that the Constitution empowered Congress to prohibit slavery in the territories if Congress saw fit.

Moreover (as any number of modern-day aspirationalists have happily pointed out), Justice Taney's Opinion of the Court includes at least two separate express (and quite eloquent) assertions of Taney's faith in originalism. Justice Taney believed that the Constitution spoke "not only in the same words, but with the same meaning and intent with which it spoke when it came from the hands of the framers,"[27] and Taney insisted that the Court must administer the Constitution "according to its true intent and meaning when it was adopted"[28] and never "falter in the path of duty."[29]

Thus the effort by modern-day originalists and conservatives to paint Chief Justice Taney and his pro-slavery colleagues on the *Dred Scott* Court as aspirationalists has very little (if any) merit. It amounts to a form of legal name-calling, and not much more.

—Scholarly Disagreement Over the Role of Due Process in Dred Scott—

The contention that *Dred Scott* marks the beginning of substantive due process, however, presents more complex and substantial issues.

Scholars have long disagreed[30] as to whether Taney's very brief discussion in *Dred Scott* of the Fifth Amendment's Due Process Clause was essential to Taney's Opinion.[31]

One group of scholars has concluded that the Due Process Clause was *not* a necessary link in the argument made by Taney against the constitutionality of the Missouri Compromise. These scholars point out that Taney devoted over twenty pages in his Opinion to the Missouri Compromise, but only two sentences to the Due Process Clause. They argue that the main thrust of Taney's argument was that: a) the Territory Clause did not confer upon Congress the power to regulate slavery in the territories (because it applied only to the territory that existed in 1789); and b) no other provision of the Constitution conferred any such power. For these scholars, the chief reason given by Taney for voiding the Missouri Compromise was that (as Taney stated in the words that immediately preceded his declaration that the Compromise was void): "The only power conferred [by the Constitution on Congress] is the power coupled with the duty of guarding and protecting the [slave] owner in his rights."[32]

According to this view, Taney's *Dred Scott* Opinion was essentially the work of a "strict constuctionist," in the original sense of that term. Taney voided the Missouri Compromise because he believed that the powers conferred by the Constitution on the federal government should be strictly (that is, narrowly) construed. The federal government, said Taney in *Dred Scott*, could "exercise no power . . . beyond what that instrument [the Constitution] confers, nor lawfully deny any right which it has reserved."[33] (This was essentially the same approach that led Taney, at the outset of his national political career, to join President Jackson in questioning whether Congress possessed the implied power to charter a national bank.) Since the Constitution did not *expressly* authorize Congress to forbid slavery in the territories, Taney believed that Congress could not do so and that the Missouri Compromise was therefore unconstitutional.

Other scholars take a very different view. They believe that Taney's discussion of the Fifth Amendment's Due Process Clause *was* essential to Taney's *Dred Scott* Opinion; that is, they believe that Taney held that the Missouri Compromise was unconstitutional because it violated the Fifth Amendment. (These scholars correctly note that Taney's contemporaries certainly did not regard his discussion of the Fifth Amendment as mere surplusage; to the contrary, both Taney's critics and supporters gave a great deal of attention to his discussion of due process.) This group of scholars points out that—although Taney denied that the Territory Clause authorized Congress to legislate for the territories—Taney *did* contend that the Constitution's Statehood Clause, by implication, granted Congress a limited power to legislate for the territories in order to prepare them for statehood. Thus, logically speaking (these scholars argue), Taney must have been relying on the Fifth Amendment when he asserted that this limited implied power to legislate for the territories somehow did not include a power to legislate against slavery.[34]

This disagreement among scholars as to precisely *why* Taney held that the Missouri Compromise was unconstitutional reflects the fact that Taney's writing and thinking were quite confused on this crucial point. After twenty pages of analysis, Taney finally declared that "upon these considerations" the Missouri Compromise was not "warranted by the

Constitution and is therefore void."[35] But he never made clear what "considerations" he intended to refer to. Was the anti-slavery restriction of the Missouri Compromise "not warranted" by the Constitution because the Constitution did not expressly confer upon Congress the power to prohibit slavery in the territories (or anywhere else)? Or was the Missouri Compromise's anti-slavery proviso instead unconstitutional because it deprived a slave owner of property without due process of law? Or was Taney perhaps relying on some combination of these two lines of argument? Because Taney's Opinion was so poorly reasoned and written, there is no undeniably correct answer to these complex questions.

—Due Process Not Essential to Dred Scott—

Judge Bork and the Dred Again theorists, however, largely gloss over all this complexity. They believe that Taney's own words make it plain that Taney did rely on the Fifth Amendment and on substantive due process in striking down the Missouri Compromise. In particular, they point to the following passage from Taney's Opinion of the Court, which includes (in two brief sentences) Taney's entire discussion of the Due Process Clause:

> [N]o one, we presume, will contend that Congress can make any law in a Territory respecting the establishment of religion, or the free exercise thereof, or abridging the freedom of speech or of the press, or the right of the people of the Territory peaceably to assemble, and to petition the Government for the redress of grievances.
>
> Nor can Congress deny to the people the right to keep and bear arms, nor the right to trial by jury, nor compel any one to be a witness against himself in a criminal proceeding.
>
> These powers, and others, in relation to rights of person, which it is not necessary here to enumerate, are, in express and positive terms, denied to the General Government; and the rights of private property have been guarded with equal care. Thus the rights of property are united with the rights of person, and placed on the same ground by the fifth amendment to the Constitution, which provides that no person shall be deprived of life, liberty, and property, without due process of law. *And an act of Congress which deprives a citizen of the United States of his liberty or property, merely because he came himself or brought his property*

> *into a particular Territory of the United States, and who had committed no offence against the laws, could hardly be dignified with the name of due process of law.*
>
> So, too, it will hardly be contended that Congress could by law quarter a soldier in a house in a Territory without the consent of the owner, in time of peace; nor in time of war, but in a manner prescribed by law.[36] (Emphasis added.)

Judge Bork and the other Dred Again theorists have assumed that the long phrase (highlighted directly above) in Taney's Opinion that begins with the words "an act of Congress" was intended by Taney to describe the Missouri Compromise. (That assumption has also been made by many other readers over the years.) Thus the Dred Again theorists go on to argue that in this passage Taney intended to say in substance that: a) the Missouri Compromise could not be "dignified with the name of due process of law"; and b) accordingly, the Court must strike down the Missouri Compromise as a violation of the Fifth Amendment's Due Process Clause.

But is that the right way to read Taney? And, in particular, is it correct to assume that Taney meant to describe the Missouri Compromise by the long phrase beginning with the words, "an act of Congress"?

The answer is less than clear because Taney's logic and writing are so muddled. However, based on a close reading of Taney's words, the answer is: probably not. It seems unlikely that Taney intended to describe the Missouri Compromise in this passage. That is the case because if Taney did intend to describe the Missouri Compromise here, then his description would have been wrong in at least four fairly obvious respects.

First, the Missouri Compromise clearly prohibited slavery in certain federal territories. Thus, if a slaveholder nevertheless brought a slave to live in such a free territory, then it was equally clear that the slaveholder had violated the law. Yet in this passage Taney speaks of "an act of Congress" that adversely impacted a citizen "who had committed *no* offence against the laws." (Emphasis added.) Accordingly, Taney's words do not sound like a description of the Missouri Compromise.[37]

Second, Taney's words describe "an act of Congress" that deprives a citizen of his "*liberty* or property" (emphasis added). No one ever contended that the Missouri Compromise deprived a slaveholder (or any other citizen) of his *liberty*. Thus, once again, it does not seem that Taney intended to describe the Missouri Compromise by these words.

Third, Taney refers to an act that deprived a citizen of his liberty or property because he "*came himself*" into a free territory. But no one contended that the Missouri Compromise had any effect on any slaveholder who merely "came himself" into a free territory; its only impact was on slaveholders who *brought slaves* into a free territory. Again, Taney's words here do not sound like a description of the Missouri Compromise.

Fourth, (as noted), the Missouri Compromise did ban slavery in certain federal territories. But the Missouri Compromise legislation did not specify what should happen if somebody disobeyed its anti-slavery provisions; and, in particular, the Missouri Compromise did *not* itself empower any court to free a slave who had been brought to live in a free territory. (If a court did choose to free a slave in such a case, it did so by applying the common-law *Somerset* principle, and not pursuant to any power granted by the Missouri Compromise.) Thus the Missouri Compromise did not itself "deprive" anyone of property; it merely prohibited bringing a slave into a free territory. Accordingly, once again, it does not seem that the "act of Congress" referred to by Taney here was the Missouri Compromise.

Taney was many things, but he was not stupid. Yet if the passage written by Taney beginning with the phrase "an act of Congress" were intended by Taney to serve as a description of the Missouri Compromise, then Taney would have described the Missouri Compromise in a grossly inaccurate and very stupid way.

As noted, Judge Bork and other Dred Again theorists have *assumed* that when Taney spoke here of an "act of Congress" that could hardly be "dignified" by the name of "due process of law": a) Taney was talking about the Missouri Compromise, and b) Taney therefore intended to say that the Missouri Compromise violated the Fifth Amendment's Due Process Clause. Based on a close reading of Taney's actual words, however, that two-fold assumption seems wrong; Taney was *not* talking about the Missouri Compromise when he spoke here of an "act of Congress," because his description of that "act" did not come close to matching the actual Missouri Compromise.

What was Taney saying, then, when he spoke of an "act of Congress" that could not be dignified with the name "due process of law"? The surrounding context—that is, the sentences that come before and after this highlighted passage—makes Taney's true intentions somewhat clearer. Taney was making a general point here: namely, that Congress, in governing the territories, was bound by the Constitution and all the restrictions in it. To illustrate that point, Taney rattled off a series of *hypothetical* unconstitutional laws that Congress could not properly pass for the territories. In governing the territories, said Taney, Congress could not: establish a religion; restrict freedom of speech or of the press; do away with jury trials; or require citizens to quarter soldiers during peacetime. None of these were *actual* laws passed by Congress. They were merely *hypothetical* illustrations of laws that (Taney said) Congress could not pass for the territories.

Taney's description of "an act of Congress" that deprives a citizen of liberty or property without due process of law, appears right in the middle of this long list of *hypothetical* unconstitutional laws. Thus, when read in context, it becomes relatively clear that Taney's reference to an "act of Congress" that could hardly be dignified with the name "due process of law" was *not* intended to be a description of the Missouri Compromise (or of any other *actual* law); it was instead intended by Taney to serve as a description of one in a series of *hypothetical* unconstitutional laws, and nothing more. (Moreover, as my high school grammar teacher could doubtless have explained more ably, Taney's use of the subjunctive construction—"could hardly be dignified"—supports the conclusion that Taney was speaking of a *hypothetical* law.)

Read in this way, Taney's description of a *hypothetical* law that would violate the Fifth Amendment makes perfect sense. But if we follow the Dred Again theorists and instead read Taney's words as an effort to describe the *actual* Missouri Compromise, then Taney's words make almost no sense at all.

In short, a very close reading of Taney's discussion in *Dred Scott* of the Fifth Amendment's Due Process Clause does *not* bear out the assertion that Taney struck down the Missouri Compromise because it violated the Due Process Clause. Admittedly, Taney did briefly invoke the Fifth Amendment in a very loose way in an effort to dress up what was an inherently weak and flawed argument for invalidating the Missouri Compromise. But Taney's two-sentence reference to the Fifth Amendment was essentially a mere rhetorical fillip. Taney did *not* rely on Due Process—substantive, procedural or otherwise—in declaring the Missouri Compromise unconstitutional.

Moreover, in assessing the Dred Again theorists' contention that *Dred Scott* was the first decision to embrace substantive due process, it is useful to recall that only two Justices (Wayne and, arguably, Grier) concurred with Taney's Opinion of the Court concerning the Missouri Compromise. Thus six of the Justices in *Dred Scott* plainly did not accept Taney's analysis; and it is a stretch to assume that even the two Justices who did concur with Taney necessarily agreed with Taney's brief and passing reference to the Fifth Amendment. Accordingly, even if the due process point was essential to Chief Justice Taney's thinking, it was not essential to the *Dred Scott* decision taken as a whole.

Even more important, it does not appear that any subsequent Supreme Court Justice ever adopted (or even favorably referred to) Justice Taney's comments in *Dred Scott* about the Due Process Clause. Thus—even if one accepts for argument's sake the very doubtful proposition that Taney's *Dred Scott* Opinion represented an attempt by Taney to apply the doctrine of substantive due process—it is nevertheless plain that *Dred Scott* has played no part in the intellectual development of that doctrine.

It is thus difficult to credit Judge Bork's claim that *Dred Scott* is *Roe v. Wade*'s "very ugly ancestor." Since no subsequent Supreme Court decision ever drew on Taney's Fifth Amendment analysis, Judge Bork (if forced to choose a colorful genealogical metaphor) might have more accurately likened *Dred Scott* to an evolutionary "dead-end" such as the neanderthal man—an early human-like species that began to grow away from the apes much as man did, but then died out without descendants.[38]

In point of fact, the doctrine of substantive due process (which had a few scattered antecedents, chiefly in State Court decisions, prior to *Dred Scott*[39]) was not first fully articulated and developed till long after the *Dred Scott* was decided—that is, not until the twentieth century in the series of Supreme Court cases that led up to *Roe v. Wade*. The main concern expressed in those twentieth-century cases has been (to paraphrase Justice Harlan) to provide an "independent guaranty of liberty . . . more general and inclusive than the specific prohibitions [of the Bill of Rights]" and to thereby safeguard our "freedom from all substantial arbitrary impositions and purposeless restraints."[40] The decisions that have developed the modern doctrine of substantive due process do not, of course, rely on or refer to *Dred Scott*, and they have nothing at all to do with safeguarding slavery or with the extent of Congressional power over the territories.

In sum—without regard to whether one accepts or rejects the doctrine of substantive due process, or whether one approves or decries the decision in *Roe v. Wade*—it should be plain that: a) the *Dred Scott* decision did *not* rely on the Due Process Clause; b) the Supreme Court decisions that many years later developed the doctrine of substantive due process did not draw on *Dred Scott* in any way; and c) the concerns and logic that underlie the modern doctrine of substantive due process bear little or no resemblance to those that were involved in the *Dred Scott* decision.

Thus the very most that can reasonably be claimed is that Chief Justice Taney's *Dred Scott* Opinion includes a suggested reading of the Fifth Amendment that vaguely points in somewhat the same direction as the twentieth-century doctrine of substantive due process—and even that modest claim is difficult to defend after a close examination of Taney's actual words.

—*Dred Scott* and Judicial Resolution of Moral Issues—

The originalist effort to equate *Dred Scott* with *Roe v. Wade* by holding *Dred Scott* up as the forerunner of modern substantive due process thus seems misguided. However, some originalists also argue that *Dred Scott* and *Roe v. Wade* are alike in that in each case the Court attempted to decide a deeply divisive moral and political issue as a matter of constitutional law. Courts should not attempt to decide such issues, originalists argue, and when the Supreme Court attempts to do so (in Justice Scalia's phrase) it merely "prolongs and intensifies the anguish."[41]

This argument has some weight. Even those who believe that *Roe v. Wade* was correctly decided should concede that there is at least some similarity between *Dred Scott* and *Roe v. Wade* in that in each case the Court attempted to resolve a deeply divisive moral issue that was the subject of intense political debate.

And yet this facile comparison between *Dred Scott* and *Roe v. Wade* misses the main point. Justice Scalia and other critics of *Roe* are of course right to say that as a general matter the Court should not look to the Constitution in order to decide *purely* moral or political questions that are not in truth addressed by that instrument. But the real and more complex problem that often confronts the Supreme Court in difficult cases is whether the Constitution truly speaks to a particular issue—regardless of whether that issue also has a significant political or moral component.

For example, at the time *Brown v. Board of Education*[42] was decided in 1954 the practice of "separate but equal" legally enforced racial segregation was the subject of intense political debate—and that debate had a significant moral component in that (at least in many people's view) racism and racial segregation are a great moral evil. Nevertheless, few people now doubt that it was appropriate for the Court to rule on the constitutionality of public school segregation in *Brown*.

Why? Because it is plain that the post–Civil War Amendments to the Constitution *do* speak directly to race relations and the issue of government-enforced segregation. In particular, the Fourteenth Amendment was deliberately intended to restructure the relationship between state governments and racial minorities; thus no one can fairly fault the Supreme Court for looking to the Fourteenth Amendment in order to decide the issues presented in *Brown*.

Thus—as *Brown* demonstrates—it *is* appropriate in *some* cases for the Court to decide a great moral and political issue as a matter of constitutional law, *provided* that the Constitution clearly speaks to the issue in question.

Roe v. Wade is a difficult case precisely because reasonable people strongly disagree as to whether the Constitution in truth addresses the issue of abortion. *Roe*'s supporters argue that a woman's right to control her own body (and hence to obtain an abortion) is implicitly protected by the Fifth Amendment's guarantee of "liberty." However, *Roe*'s critics argue that there is nothing in the Fifth Amendment (or elsewhere in the Constitution) that compels the conclusion that a woman's liberty includes her right to obtain an abortion; *Roe* is illegitimate, its critics argue, because the Constitution is in truth silent on the subject of abortion.

Justice Scalia (among many others) may complain that when the Court decides a hotly disputed political issue it forecloses "all democratic outlet for the deep passions this issue arouses . . ."[43] And yet it might well be argued that one of the central purposes of a written Constitution and of the institution of judicial review is to remove certain highly charged issues from the realm of legitimate political debate.

For example, American history (and the history of other democracies) has shown that during time of war there often arises widespread popular sentiment in favor of suppressing dissent or persecuting citizens with certain ethnic backgrounds. Nevertheless, the Bill of Rights, properly interpreted, should operate to prevent such sentiment from being translated into law; it firmly and finally places the principle of freedom of expression and of equal protection of the laws beyond the reach of any political or legislative majority—just as the Fourteenth Amendment, as interpreted by *Brown v. Board of Education* (and its progeny), ultimately forced a reluctant American public to accept the unpopular principle that legally enforced segregation in public education was unconstitutional.

In short, there is and should be no general rule that the Court cannot decide a case that has important political or moral aspects. As Justice

Brennan explained in the landmark "reapportionment" case of *Baker v. Carr*, the Court must avoid purely "political questions"; but the Court *can* properly decide some "political cases." The Court *should* decide a case with important political implications *if* (and only if) the case turns on a genuine question of constitutional law; and, on the other hand, if the case does not turn on a such a genuine legal question, then the Court should not attempt to decide the case as a matter of constitutional law.

What about *Dred Scott*? Does the Constitution in truth speak to the issues decided in *Dred Scott*?

The answer—regardless of whether one agrees or disagrees with *Roe v. Wade*—is plainly yes. The key issue that emerged in *Dred Scott* was whether Congress possessed the authority to prohibit slavery in the federal territories as it had done in the Missouri Compromise Act. That was a genuine question of constitutional *law*—even though that question was tied up with urgent moral concerns over slavery, and even though that question was also the subject of intense (indeed, almost all-consuming) political debate during the years that led up to the Civil War.

Indeed, the nature of the U.S. territories, the rights of the territories' inhabitants, the extent of Congessional power over the territories, and the limits on such power, were all legal questions that could *only* be answered by reference to the Constitution. Thus the *Dred Scott* Court can not fairly be faulted merely because the Justices looked to the Constitution in order to decide the question whether the Missouri Compromise was valid. Rather, the *Dred Scott* Court's chief error was that—because of its bias in favor of slavery—it drew a clearly *wrong* answer to that question from the Constitution.

* * *

The assertion that *Roe v. Wade* is "first cousin" to *Dred Scott* has become a staple of modern conservative political and legal rhetoric, but it does not hold up well after close analysis.

Roe v. Wade is, of course, both a very important and very controversial decision. It may or may not be correctly decided. But—in *either* case—*Roe* has very little to do with *Dred Scott*. In particular, it seems clear that: a) *Dred Scott* was not an aspirationalist decision; b) *Dred Scott* did not rely on or inspire the doctrine of substantive due process; and c) *Dred Scott* had nothing to do with the right to privacy, or with the profound question when human life begins.

The only real point of similarity between *Dred Scott* and *Roe v. Wade* is that each case dealt with a deeply divisive moral and political issue. But that is also true of many other important Supreme Court decisions throughout American history, both good and bad.

Accordingly, drawing parallels between *Roe v. Wade* and *Dred Scott* does little to advance our understanding of either case. The repeated invocation of *Dred Scott* in modern-day debates about unrelated issues of constitutional law serves only to suggest that the level of our national discourse about law and society can and should be raised.

Notes

1. William H. Rehnquist, "The Notion of a Living Constitution," 54 *Tex. L. Rev.* 693, 700 (1976).
2. Richard J. Neuhaus, "The Dred Scott of Our Time," *Wall Street Journal*, July 2, 1992, A8.
3. Nash, "Why Bush Opposes Dred Scott."
4. Eisgruber, "Dred Again."
5. Fein, "Pack the Supreme Court."
6. Bork, *Tempting of America*, 32, 43.
7. Fed. News Service (Lexis, Fed. Legislation Library), Comments of Sen. Hatch, Senate Confirmation Hearings for Ruth Bader Ginsberg, July 22, 1993.
8. *DS* at 426.
9. Bork, *Tempting of America*, 43.
10. Bork, *Tempting of America*, 181.
11. Bork, *Tempting of America*, 116.
12. Bork, *Tempting of America*, 301.
13. Robert H. Bork, "Again, a Struggle for the Soul of the Court," *New York Times*, July 8, 1992, A19.
14. *DS*, at 450, quoted in Bork, *Tempting of America*, 31.
15. Bork, *Tempting of America*, 31.
16. Bork, *Tempting of America*, 32.
17. Remarks of Attorney General Richard Thornburgh on Supreme Court Choices, Legal Forum Luncheon of the Lincoln Legal Foundation, Aug. 20, 1970.
18. Fed. News Service (Lexis, Fed. Legislation Library), Transcript of Confirmation Hearings, Clarence Thomas, Sept. 16, 1991, Comments of Sen. Hatch.

Senator Hatch makes at least two obvious mistakes here. Clearly, Taney relied on the "property" aspect of the Due Process Clause, not the "liberty" aspect. Second, Hatch completely glosses over any distinction that might be drawn between Taney's Opinion of the Court and what the "Supreme Court held" in *Dred Scott*.

19. Michael W. McConnell, "A Moral Realist Defense of Constitutional Democracy," 64 *Chicago-Kent L. Rev.* 89, 101 (1988). Earl M. Maltz, "Roe v. Wade and Dred Scott," 17 *Widener Law Journal* 55, 62 (2007) comes to a similar conclusion.

20. Association of Constitutional Law Discussion: "Constitutional Relevance of Foreign Law Decisions," with Justices Breyer and Scalia, Fed News Service, Jan. 13, 2005.

Many legal thinkers disagree with Justice Scalia on numerous issues, but he is (almost) universally recognized and admired as perhaps the most brilliant legal mind and legal writer of our era.

Nevertheless, Justice Scalia's comment here exemplifies the very worst of the distressing tendency for even sophisticated legal theorists (such as Justice Scalia) to invoke *Dred Scott* with little care or caution in today's running debate between aspirationalists and originalists.

In his comment Scalia claims that *Dred Scott* was the first case ever to use the "horrid term substantive due process." That is plainly untrue. The *Dred Scott* decision never used the term "substantive due process," or anything like it. Indeed, it appears that the term "substantive due process" was not used in any Supreme Court Opinion until 1948 in the case of *Republic National Gas v. Oklahoma*, 334 US 62, 90 (Rutledge, J., dissenting).

Moreover, Justice Scalia seems to lose track of his own train of thought here. "Substantive due process" first emerged in its current form in the Supreme Court's privacy jurisprudence that led to *Roe v. Wade*. By way of contrast, the phrase "evolving standard of decency" referred to by Scalia here is usually associated with the Supreme Court's modern Eighth Amendment "cruel and unusual " punishment jurisprudence, a jurisprudence that begins with *Trop v. Dulles*, 366 US 86, 101 (1958).

Scalia deplores both the Court's substantive due process cases like *Roe v. Wade*, and its Eighth Amendment "cruel and unusual" punishment decisions (which have restricted the use of the death penalty). But, in this quoted comment, Scalia appears to be mixing up "substantive due process" decisions with "cruel and unusual punishment" decisions, and somehow associating *Dred Scott* with both. *Dred Scott*, however, had absolutely *nothing* to do with cruel and unusual punishment," "evolving standards of decency," or the Eighth Amendment.

Justice Scalia has also expressed agreement with the Substantive Due Process variation on the Originalist Critique of *Dred Scott* in a more measured and thoughtful way in his dissent in *Planned Parenthood v. Casey*. There Scalia noted: "*Dred Scott* . . . rested upon the concept of 'substantive due process' that the Court praises and employs today." *Planned Parenthood*, 505 US 833 at 998, (Scalia, J., dissenting).

21. *Planned Parenthood of Southeastern Pa. v. Casey*, 505 US 833, 1001–1002 (1992), (Scalia, J., dissenting).

22. Justice Scalia attributes the sadness apparent in Leutze's portrait of Taney to a recognition by Taney that the *Dred Scott* decision was a failure. In all likelihood, Justice Scalia intended these observations largely as a literary conceit.

In point of fact, it appears that in the wake of *Dred Scott* Taney's predominant emotions were anger at his critics, and frustration that he could not publicly respond to those critics; and Taney certainly never admitted that the *Dred Scott* decision was wrong in any way.

Thus in late 1858 Taney drafted a lengthy "Supplement" to his *Dred Scott* Opinion. The Supplement was never published. (It appears that Taney hoped to incorporate this Supplement into an Opinion in a future case.) In his Supplement, Taney marshaled additional authorities in support of his *Dred Scott* Opinion and fulminated against his critics.

Taney dismissed all the scholarly and legal commentary that had questioned *Dred Scott* as founded upon mere "misrepresentations and perversions of the points described by the Court. . . . They cannot mislead any one who is in search of truth, and will read the opinion." Tyler, *Memoir of Taney*, 578–608; Fehrenbacher, *Dred Scott*, 445–48.

23. Robert H. Jackson, *The Struggle for Judicial Supremacy: A Study of a Crisis in American Power Politics* (New York: Vintage, 1941), 327.

24. Alexander M. Bickel, *The Morality of Consent* (New Haven: Yale U. Press, 1975), 37.

25. McCloskey, *American Supreme Court*, 63.

26. Sunstein, "Dred Scott and Its Legacy," 66.

27. *DS* at 426.

28. *DS* at 405.

29. *DS* at 426.

30. *See* Currie, *The Constitution*, 271 and Note 261.

31. *See* David P. Currie, *The Constitution in the Supreme Court: The First Hundred Years, 1789–1888* (Chicago: U of Chicago Press, 1985), 271 and note 261.

For example, Carl Swisher—Taney's biographer, and official Supreme Court historian—took the view that Taney's discussion of the Due Process Clause was merely a "suggestion, rather than . . . a necessary link in his argument." Swisher, *Roger B. Taney*, 508. Don E. Fehrenbacher—author of the Pulitzer Prize–winning study *The Dred Scott Case: Its Significance in American Law and Politics* (at 377–84)—similarly concludes that Taney did *not* rely on the Due Process Clause in *Dred Scott.*

On the other hand, both the eminent historian David Potter and Edward S. Corwin—perhaps the leading scholar in American constitutional law of the early twentieth century—expressed the view that Taney's discussion of the Due Process Clause *was* central to Taney's Opinion in *Dred Scott*. *See* Potter *The Impending Crisis*, 276; and Edward S. Corwin, "The Dred Scott Decision in Light of Contemporary Legal Doctrines," reprinted in Kutler, Ed., *The Dred Scott Decision*,

132 ("Such then is the basis of the Chief Justice's decision: 'the due process of law' clause of the Fifth Amendment.")

32. *DS* at 452.

33. *DS*, at 449–50.

34. *See e.g.*, Currie, Note 261 at 271–72.

35. *DS* at 452.

36. *DS*, at 450.

37. Taney's comment about a citizen who has committed no offense against the laws also undercuts in a different way the argument of Judge Bork (and others) that *Dred Scott* involved *substantive* due process.

Taney does not even attempt to lay out a fully considered theory of the Due Process Clause in this brief passage. But—to the limited extent that Taney does identify a due process issue here—he appears to be speaking of a *procedural* (rather than substantive) due process violation.

That is so because procedural due process has long been understood to require that the government can only act against a citizen pursuant to previously established laws concerning which the citizen has had fair notice. *See Lambert v. California*, 355 U.S. 225 (1957). Yet here Taney posits a hypothetical situation in which the government takes property from a citizen who has violated no law; such conduct by the government would constitute a violation of *procedural* due process.

38. *See* H. Mayell, "Neanderthals Not Our Ancestors, DNA Study Suggests," *National Geographic News*, May 14, 2003.

39. *See* Corwin, "The Dred Scott Decision," 133–34; Streichler, *Justice Curtis*, 98–118.

40. *Poe v. Ullman*, 367 U.S. 497, 542–43 (1961).

41. *Planned Parenthood v. Casey*, 505 U.S. at 1002 (Scalia, J., dissenting.)

42. *Brown v. Board of Education*, 347 U.S. 483 (1954).

43. *Planned Parenthood v. Casey*, 505 U.S. at 1002 (Scalia, J., dissenting.)

Chapter 19
The Traditional "Judicial Restraint" Critique

—"The Fallibility of Human Judgment"—

Long before *Dred Scott* became something of a proxy for *Roe v. Wade* in political and scholarly debate about the proper interpretation of the Constitution and the right to privacy, it was customary for proponents of "judicial restraint" to hold *Dred Scott* up as an example of unduly "activist" Court in action. The focus of this line of criticism was not so much that the *Dred Scott* Court tried to resolve an essentially political or moral issue; rather, the thrust of this critique was that the *Dred Scott* Court took up legal issues that were not necessary to resolve the case before the Court.

Traditional advocates of judicial restraint argue that a wise Supreme Court should always be mindful that any court is, after all, fallible. The Court may make mistakes and should therefore act with great caution—says the advocate of judicial restraint—before deciding any fundamental issue of constitutional law; and if the Court can reasonably avoid such fundamental issues in any particular case, it should.

Supreme Court Justice Felix Frankfurter best expressed this view in his Opinion in the case of *United States v. International Union AFL-CIO*, written almost exactly 100 years after the *Dred Scott* decision. Justice Frankfurter wrote there:

> The impressive lesson of history confirms the wisdom of the repeated enunciation, the variously expressed admonition, of self-imposed inhibition against passing on the validity of an Act of Congress 'unless absolutely necessary to a decision of the case.'. . . Observance of this principle makes for the minimum tension within our democratic political system where 'Scarcely any question arises which does not become, sooner or later, a subject of judicial debate.'. . . The wisdom of refraining from avoidable constitutional pronouncements has been most vividly demonstrated on the rare occasions when the Court, forgetting 'the fallibility of the human judgment,' has departed from its own practice. The Court's failure in *Dred Scott v. Sandford* . . . 'to take the smooth handle for the sake of repose' by disposing of the case solely upon 'the outside issue' and the effects of its attempt 'to settle the agitation' are familiar history.[1]

Justice Frankfurter's view was not new. Indeed, the same essential idea appears in a not too different form in the *Dred Scott* case itself, in the two dissenting opinions—and especially in Justice Curtis' Dissent. There Curtis took Taney to task for reaching the question of the constitutionality of the Missouri Compromise. In that connection, Curtis argued that once Taney had decided that the Court lacked jurisdiction over Dred Scott's case (because free Negroes could not sue in federal court), Taney was without any authority to go on and consider any other issue; and Curtis directly challenged Taney's decision to nevertheless strike down the Missouri Compromise, saying "A great question of constitutional law, deeply affecting the peace and welfare of the country, is not, in my opinion, a fit subject to be thus reached."[2]

In the immediate aftermath of the *Dred Scott* decision, Taney's critics took up Curtis' theme; many charged that the Court's decision to void the Missouri Compromise was superfluous (and therefore non-binding) "obiter dicta." Indeed, even after emancipation had rendered the *Dred Scott* decision almost entirely moot as a legal matter, scholarly criticism of the *Dred Scott* decision for many years still largely focused on the charge that Taney and his colleagues had improperly decided unnecessary issues—including, most important, the constitutionality of the Missouri Compromise. The underlying theme of this criticism was this: the central flaw in the *Dred Scott* decision was Taney's abandonment of appropriate judicial restraint.

—Strengths of the "Judicial Restraint" Critique—

The traditional "judicial restraint" critique of *Dred Scott* articulated by Justice Frankfurter and others has considerable merit. What was and is probably most troubling (especially from a judge's point of view) about the *Dred Scott* decision is the *range* of issues that Taney took on. There were so many ways that Taney could have fashioned a narrower decision for Sanford and against Scott. He could have relied on the jurisdictional ground of Negro citizenship alone. Like Justice Nelson and the circuit court below, he could have relied on Missouri state law as elaborated in *Scott v. Emerson* alone. He could have relied on the principles set forth in *Strader v. Graham* alone. He could have relied on principle of *res judicata* alone.

But Taney refused to do so. He insisted on deciding *all* those questions, and then further insisted on reaching out to rule on the constitutionality of the Missouri Compromise. Then Taney went even further, declaring—in a statement that had absolutely *no* relevance to the case at hand, but was a matter of active political dispute in connection with the Kansas controversy—that a *territorial legislature* was also powerless to prohibit slavery. Further still, Taney's novel and imprecise discussion of the Fifth Amendment at least seemed to suggest that slave masters might not lose their slaves even by bringing them to live in a free *state*.

In other words, Taney reached out over and over again in order to rule on questions about slavery that were not necessary to the resolution of the *Dred Scott* case, and that had never been raised before or considered by the court below. And Taney staked out the most extreme pro-slavery positions on *every single one* of these questions. It is thus evident that Taney's true purpose was not to decide the case before him fairly on the law; his true purpose was (in the words of historian Don Fehrenbacher) "to launch a sweeping counter attack on the anti-slavery movement and to reinforce the bastions of slavery at every rampart and parapet."[3]

To put the same idea far more bluntly, Taney's Opinion demonstrated that he was bound and determined to keep the black man down. Taney made it clear in every way he could that there was no hope for African Americans and no hope for compromise on the issue of slavery: Slaves in the South would, of course, always remain slaves; free Negroes were not citizens and must be systematically oppressed in order to make sure that they did not foment trouble among the slaves; neither the federal government nor a territorial legislature could keep slavery out of any U.S. territory; slaves would not become free when their masters brought them to live on free soil; the Constitution protected the institution of slavery as sacred; the federal government was duty-bound to make sure that fugitive slaves were returned to bondage; slaves were mere property, and nothing more; and free Negroes were hardly better off than slaves.

As is often the case, Lincoln said it best when he summed up the import of *Dred Scott* in this way:

> All the powers of earth seem rapidly combining against [the black slave] . . . . They have him in his prison house; they have searched his person, and left no prying instrument with him. One after another they have closed the heavy iron doors against him, and now they have him, as it were, bolted in with a lock of a hundred keys, which can never be unlocked without the concurrence of every key; the keys in the hands of a hundred different men, and they scattered to a hundred different and distant places; and they stand musing as to what invention, in all the dominions of mind and matter, can be produced to make the impossibility of his escape more complete than it is.[4]

Taney's powerful bias against African Americans and for slavery was thus revealed as much by the *number* of issues he took on, as it was by the manner in which he resolved each of those issues.

To put these matters in a more mundane, everyday context, many lawyers think it is a good idea to offer up every conceivable argument in a client's behalf in the hope that at least one argument will find favor with a judge or jury. Other (and, in my view, wiser) lawyers try to be more selective. They pick out the one or two best arguments they can, and then they stick largely to those arguments; they correctly fear that their credibility will be lost if they push *every* possible argument, no matter how thin.

Taney was, of course, not an advocate but a judge. Moreover, he was a judge on the highest court in the land, from which there is no appeal. He did not need to discuss and adopt *every* possible theory for denying Scott his freedom; one would have sufficed. Nor did Taney need to answer *every* critic of slavery on virtually *every* point in the ongoing national debate about slavery. But he tried to do so, and he and the Supreme Court did indeed suffer a terrible "self-inflicted wound" to their reputation as a result.

In particular, Taney's decision—made in conformity with the secret and improper urging of the incoming President Buchanan—to decide on the constitutionality of the Missouri Compromise was a very bad one. *Dred Scott* was the very first instance in which the Supreme Court struck down a substantive federal law as unconstitutional. That was no accident. Judicial review of federal statutes is, of course, proper. But both simple wisdom and a proper understanding of where the power of judicial review comes from dictate that it is a power to be used very, very sparingly.

Judges make law all the time, at least in the limited sense that their written opinions explicate and apply the law in new or complex situations where the meaning and proper application of the law might not be immediately clear. That is true for all courts, and especially true for appellate courts. The Supreme Court is the highest appellate court in the land, and we all properly look to the Supreme Court to resolve the most important and difficult questions of law that affect the nation. As Chief Justice John Marshall memorably declared in *Marbury v. Madison*, it is emphatically the province of the courts to say what the law is.

But judges do not have a free-roving commission to go about making pronouncements about whatever legal questions may seem important or interesting to them. (If judges feel an urgent need to express themselves on a particular subject, the less modest among them can always write a book, like this one.) The power of a judge to make law is a consequence of, and is limited to, the power of the judge's court to decide a particular case that is before it. The judge's power and primary responsibility is to decide *the case that is presently before the court* fairly. The judge's power to explicate, or make, law is limited to what is necessary to fulfill that primary responsibility.

The restriction on a judge's authority to make law to those issues that are necessary to the case at hand is particularly important when a court is presented with the claim that a federal statute is unconstitutional. The judiciary and Congress (along with the executive branch) are co-equal branches of the federal government. A court is not authorized to set aside a statute passed by Congress and signed into law by the President as unconstitutional merely because the court thinks the statute is unwise, or even because there is good reason to believe that the statute may be unconstitutional as a general matter. A court only has the power to declare a statute unconstitutional if that declaration is necessary for the court to do its job—to decide the particular case before the court fairly.[5]

As a consequence of these principles, the Supreme Court has over the years developed a number of self-imposed "rules" that require the Court to avoid deciding constitutional issues, unless decision of those issues is truly necessary in a particular case. The classic statement of these rules was written in 1936 by Justice Louis Brandeis in the case of *Ashwander v. Tennessee Valley Authority.*[6] Justice Brandeis summarized seven interrelated rules of judicial avoidance, at least two of which have direct relevance to *Dred Scott*.

Brandeis wrote:

> The court has developed for its own governance in the cases confessedly within its jurisdiction, a series of rules under which it has avoided passing upon a large part of all the constitutional questions pressed upon it for decision. They are . . . .
>
> 2. The Court will not anticipate a question of constitutional law in advance of the necessity of deciding it . . . . It is not the habit of the Court to decide questions of a constitutional nature unless absolutely necessary to a decision of the case . . . .
>
> 4. The Court will not pass upon a constitutional question although properly presented by the record, if there is also present some other ground upon which the case can be disposed of . . . . Thus if a case can be decided on either of two grounds, one involving a constitutional question, the other a question of statutory construction or general law, the Court will decide only the latter . . . . (Citations omitted.)

The first rule thus provides that the Court will not decide on the constitutionality of a statute unless a particular case before the Court absolutely requires such a decision. The second and corollary rule further provides that, whenever possible, the Court should decide cases as a matter of general law, rather than constitutional law.

The decision by Taney and the concurring Justices to address the Missouri Compromise issue in *Dred Scott* violated both these rules. Taney's own Opinion demonstrates that there were at least three or four completely sufficient and independent bases for Taney to deny Scott his freedom without ever going near the issue of the Missouri Compromise. Thus, to paraphrase *Ashwander*, it was quite possible (and, indeed, far more natural) for the Court to decide *Dred Scott* as a "question of . . . general law"; it was wrong for the Court to force the constitutional question into the picture. Moreover, Taney's decision to address the Missouri Compromise issue also violated the rule that an appellate court should normally only take up issues that were raised before the court below.

In Taney's partial defense, it should be noted that Brandeis's "rules" of avoidance were not yet fully formulated back in 1857. But the principle that a court's power to make law is restricted to deciding the case before it certainly existed when *Dred Scott* was written; it is a fundamental of the American legal system.[7]

In the final analysis, it was the willingness—indeed, the palpable desire —of Taney and his colleagues to reach the issue of the Missouri Compromise when it was plainly not necessary to do so that, more than anything else, left the stench of injustice and judicial overreaching about the *Dred Scott* decision.

—Weakness of the "Judicial Restraint" Critique—

And yet—having given due recognition to the wisdom of Justice Curtis, Justice Frankfurter, and many others, who have properly faulted the *Dred Scott* Court for unnecessarily passing upon the constitutionality of the Missouri Compromise—the traditional "judicial restraint" critique does not by itself satisfactorily or fully explain why *Dred Scott* was wrong.

Admittedly, the *Dred Scott* Court reached out over and over again to decide unnecessary and overbroad questions of constitutional law. Still, one suspects that if the Court had decided those questions *correctly*, then *Dred Scott* would not enjoy its current infamous reputation as the worst Supreme Court decision ever.

In particular, consider how the *Dred Scott* decision would have been viewed had the Court followed precedent and found that the Missouri Compromise *was* constitutional. Such a decision would simply have left American law where it had stood since 1787— with the understanding that it was up to Congress to decide whether or not to permit slavery in the territories. In other words, such a *Dred Scott* decision would have been largely a non-event. The sectional crisis would likely have continued unabated, and might well have resulted in Civil War anyway; but the Supreme Court would not have loomed so large in the deterioration of relations between North and South.

Accordingly, Justice Frankfurter and other advocates of judicial restraint do make a good point when they say that the *Dred Scott* Court should not have reached the issue of the Missouri Compromise; but the decision to reach the Missouri Compromise issue was *not* the chief reason why *Dred Scott* was wrong. Rather, the *Dred Scott* decision was wrong chiefly because the Court decided the Missouri Compromise issue in the *wrong* way: Specifically, *Dred Scott* is a monument of legal error because Taney and his colleagues deliberately misread both law and history in order to support slavery by striking down the Missouri Compromise.

And so, once again, upon analysis it becomes plain that the *Dred Scott* case was not really about judicial philosophy, or about schools of constitutional interpretation; *Dred Scott* was not about originalism, or aspirationalism, or judicial activism, or judicial restraint. The *Dred Scott* case was chiefly about African American slavery, and about how very far the Justices of the U.S. Supreme Court were willing to go in order to protect slavery.

Notes

1. *United States v. International Union AFL-CIO*, 352 US 567, 590–91 (1957).

2. Fehrenbacher, *Dred Scott*, p. 341.

In a thought-provoking article, Mark Graber has attempted to argue that *Dred Scott* was in truth a "centrist" decision, rather than a completely one-sided victory for the supporters of slavery. See Mark Graber, "Dred Scott as a Centrist Decision," 83 *N.C.L Rev.* 1229 (June 2005).

This is a very doubtful argument. Professor Graber tries to characterize *Dred Scott* as "centrist" by pointing out that there were some extreme pro-slavery politicians who favored both reviving the slave trade and conquering new lands (such as Cuba) where slavery would likely flourish. Since *Dred Scott* did not endorse such a program, Graber suggests, it occupied a centrist, rather than an extremist, position.

However, the question of Cuba and the slave trade were not even remotely relevant to the *Dred Scott* case. It was therefore hardly a sign of moderation or "centrism" that the *Dred Scott* decision said nothing about those subjects.

In point of fact—as the 1860 Presidential election demonstrated—*Dred Scott* was not close to America's political center. Taney's Opinion of the Court in *Dred Scott* rejected both the Lincoln/Republican view that Congress could and should restrict slavery in the territories, and the Douglas/Democrat platform that advocated territorial popular sovereignty. The Lincoln and Douglas camps together won *60* percent of the popular vote in the 1860 Presidential election. (John Bell's Union Party—whose platform was hopelessly vague—took 10 percent of the vote.)

John Breckenridge—the only candidate who wholeheartedly agreed with Taney's *Dred Scott* Opinion—took only 30 percent of the popular vote. Moreover, the Breckenridge/*Dred Scott* camp took only 3 percent of the popular vote in the free North, and under 50 percent of the popular vote even in the slave South. The *Dred*

Scott doctrine was thus supported only in the South, and even there it was rejected by a small majority. Plainly, then, *Dred Scott* was *not* a "centrist" decision.

Louise Weinberg "Dred Scott and the Crisis of 1860," 82 *Chicago Kent L. Rev.* I, 97 (2007) disagrees at length with Graber's notion of *Dred Scott* as a "centrist" decision.

Graber also argues (like some other notable scholars of the past) that Congress had by legislation virtually invited the Supreme Court to rule on the constitutionality of the Missouri Compromise. *See also* Wallace Mendelsohn, "Dred Scott's Case—Revisited," 38 *Minn. L. Rev.* 16 (Dec. 1953).

This point also seems mistaken. The Compromise of 1850 and the Kansas-Nebraska Act did expressly contemplate that the Court might review questions regarding the status of slavery in a territory where popular sovereignty was the rule—like Kansas or Nevada. But those statutes did *not* contemplate that the Court would review or revisit Congress's authority to pass laws like the Missouri Compromise and the Northwest Ordinance that barred slavery outright in certain territories.

3. *DS* at 590 (Curtis, J., dissenting).

4. Abraham Lincoln, Speech at Springfield, Illinois, June 20, 1857, reprinted in *Lincoln, Speeches*, Vol. 1, 396–97.

5. *See Adkins v. Children's Hospital*, 261 U.S. 525, 544 (1923):

> The judicial duty of passing upon the constitutionality of an act of Congress is one of great gravity and delicacy. The statute here in question has successfully borne the scrutiny of the legislative branch of the government, which, by enacting it, has affirmed its validity; and that determination must be given great weight. This Court, by an unbroken line of decisions from Chief Justice Marshall to the present day has steadily adhered to the rule that every possible presumption is in favor of the validity of an act of Congress until overcome beyond rational doubt. But if by clear and indubitable demonstration a statute be opposed to the Constitution we have no choice but to say so. The Constitution, by its own terms, is the supreme law of the land, emanating from the people, the repository of ultimate sovereignty under our form of government. A congressional statute, on the other hand, is the act of an agency of this sovereign authority and if it conflict with the Constitution it must fall; for that which is not supreme must yield to that which is. To hold it invalid (if it be invalid) is a plain exercise of the judicial power—that power vested in courts to enable them to administer justice according to law. From the authority to ascertain and determine the law in a given case, there necessarily results, in case of conflict, the duty to declare and enforce the rule of the supreme law and reject that of an inferior act of legislation which, transcending the Constitution, is of no effect and binding on no one. This is not the exercise of a

substantive power to review and nullify acts of Congress, for no such substantive power exists. It is simply a necessary concomitant of the power to hear and dispose of a case or controversy properly before the court, to the determination of which must be brought the test and measure of the law.

6. *Ashwander v. Tennessee Valley Authority*, 297 U.S. 288 (1936).
7. *See Muskrat v. United States*, 219 U.S. 346 (1911).

Chapter 20
Dred Scott and the Dangers of a Political Court

A review of the modern-day commentary about the *Dred Scott* case by politicians and constitutional scholars teaches us very little about *Dred Scott*. Too much of what has been written and said about *Dred Scott* in recent years appears to be more concerned with *Roe v. Wade*, and with related disputes in modern constitutional law, than with *Dred Scott* itself. The effort to equate *Dred Scott* with modern-day schools of constitutional interpretation obscures, rather than advances, our understanding of the *Dred Scott* case

But—having set aside most of the recent literature about *Dred Scott*—we come back to certain fundamental questions: What did go wrong in *Dred Scott*? Why was this landmark case so poorly decided?

There were at least three major sources of error in *Dred Scott*. The first was the very nature of the original Constitution—a document that embodied and entrenched the Framers' (somewhat reluctant) acceptance of the institution of human slavery.

The second was the pervasive racism of antebellum America—a widely held belief that people of African descent were not fully human. That belief enabled judges, lawyers and other legal thinkers to in effect read African Americans out of the Constitution and its guarantees of human liberty and equality.

In fairness, these first two sources of error were largely external and cannot be blamed in whole, or even in large part, on Chief Justice Taney and his colleagues.

However, the third major source of error in *Dred Scott* (and the most important for present purposes) came from within the Court itself. Specifically, the *Dred Scott* Court became so absorbed in the pursuit of the political agenda of the slaveholding South—an agenda that the pro-slavery Justices considered noble and worthwhile—that the Court compromised its intellectual integrity. In the view of the *Dred Scott* majority, protecting slavery was the highest form of patriotism—because the majority believed that it was anti-slavery sentiment and "agitation" that threatened the integrity of the Union. The *Dred Scott* Court therefore intentionally misread the law, and it did so in order to safeguard slavery and the South's way of life.

Dred Scott was in essence a political, and not a legal, decision; and insightful observers—both pro and anti-slavery—understood this point at the time the decision was rendered. Thus Justice Wayne privately boasted—on the very day the Court adopted his proposal to issue a broad pro-slavery Opinion in *Dred Scott*—that the *Dred Scott* Court's purpose was to deliver "a triumph for the southern section of the country . . . by . . . put[ing] an end to all further agitation on the subject of slavery in the territories." And Horace Greeley's anti-slavery *New York Tribune* declared, in a sharply critical editorial written just one day after the decision was announced, that "[t]he decision . . . is a dictum prescribed by the stump to the bench—the Bowie knife striking in the stump ready for instant use if needed." (Indeed, the *Tribune*'s observation was remarkably prescient, for Greeley and his contemporaries did not yet know anything about how President Buchanan had secretly and effectively lobbied Justices Catron, Taney, Grier, and Wayne concerning the *Dred Scott* decision.)

In particular, contemporary observers understood that the authors of the *Dred Scott* decision wanted to strike a death blow on behalf of President Buchanan's pro-slavery Democratic Party against the rising anti-slavery Republican Party. Thus the quasi-official Democratic newspaper the *Washington Union* crowed that *Dred Scott* had "shivered" the platform of the "late great" Republican Party into "atoms." And former long-time Missouri Senator Thomas Hart Benton (who was so angered by the partisan nature of *Dred Scott* that he devoted the final months of his battle with fatal cancer to writing a book denouncing the decision) asserted that *Dred Scott* was "both child and champion of party, and itself a touchstone of party."

The *Dred Scott* decision was a terrible mistake for many reasons. But, for those who wish to draw a valuable lesson from history, the real importance of the *Dred Scott* case is that it exemplifies the dangers of a *political* court.

—External Sources of Error—

We are accustomed to praising the Constitution as the foundation of American freedom and American greatness, and properly so. But it cannot be denied that the original Constitution was fundamentally flawed in that—through the Fugitive Slave Clause, the Three-Fifths Clause and the protection of the African slave trade through the year 1808—the Constitution countenanced and protected African slavery on a massive scale in the United States.[1] Taney and his colleagues were therefore interpreting a document that was, in important part, an instrument of racism and oppression. That they read the Constitution as approving further racism and oppression at the margins of the United States—that is, in the territories added to the Union after the adoption of the Constitution—was thus not completely implausible. So, part of what went wrong in *Dred Scott* is that the original Constitution itself was wrong.

Second, and somewhat similarly, Taney, his fellow Justices, advocates of slavery, and even a large majority of white opponents of slavery, all shared in certain fundamental racist beliefs. In 1857, many white people opposed slavery, or at least opposed its expansion. But virtually every leading white American of that day—from the abolitionists at one end of the spectrum, to the hottest "fire-eating" defenders of slavery at the other—believed in varying degrees that Negroes were inferior and should be treated as such.[2]

In both the "free" North and the slave South, the assumption that Negroes were inferior and subject to systematic persecution was part of the fabric of American law. Four northern states prohibited Negroes from even entering their territory. Only five northern states granted Negroes the right to vote. Even there, the overwhelming majority of African American could expect a life characterized by pervasive segregation, menial labor and grinding poverty. DeTocqueville summarized the plight of free Negroes in the United States prior to the Civil War by declaring that the "Negro is free, but he can share neither the rights, nor the labor, nor the afflictions, nor the tomb of him whose equal he has been declared to be; and he cannot meet him upon fair terms in life or in death."[3] John Quincy Adams similarly observed that free Negroes in antebellum America were "doomed by their complexion to drudge in the lowest offices of society, excluded by their color from all the refined enjoyments of life accessible to others, excluded from the benefits of a liberal education, from the bed, from the table, and from all the social comforts of domestic life."[4]

Taney was, of course, a product of antebellum society; and, although Taney attempted to couch his *Dred Scott* Opinion in disinterested legal language, the Opinion nevertheless reveals that Taney himself was a racist. For example, in his Opinion's discussion of what was for Taney the purely theoretical possibility that free Negroes might be entitled to equal treatment with whites, Taney's indignation and disgust almost jump off the page. Similarly, Taney's prose unintentionally becomes almost gleeful when he summarizes what he (falsely) characterized as the universal view of the Framers' era that Negroes had no rights that a white man was bound to respect.

Taney was by no means unique among the members of the *Dred Scott* Court in his racism and in his fear of African Americans. For example, Justice Daniel's Concurring Opinion expressed similar anxieties about all the "revolting consequences" that might flow if free Negroes were treated as citizens.[5] Prior to joining the Court, Justice Campbell had expounded at length in "scholarly" articles his view that it would take generations to begin to prepare Negroes for freedom and thereby avoid a repetition of the horrors of Santo Domingo.[6] Justice Catron had declared in the *Fisher's Negroes* case that every free Negro was merely "a degraded outcast, and his fancied freedom a delusion."[7] And President Buchanan—who, along with Catron, helped to create the coalition of Justices who chose to issue a broad pro-slavery decision in *Dred Scott*—was at times nearly consumed with the fear that abolition would lead to the "massacre" of the "chivalrous race of the men of the South."[8]

The almost universal racism of the pre–Civil War era pervades the *Dred Scott* decision, and infects virtually every pronouncement within it. Part of what went wrong in the *Dred Scott* case, then, is that racism and race hatred distorted the judgment of the Supreme Court. That is sad, but not really surprising; judges are only human and, despite their best efforts, they do not often rise far above the general prejudices of their time and place.

—*Dred Scott* as Bad Law—

Looking solely at the legal merits of Taney's two chief holdings—regarding Negro citizenship and the Missouri Compromise—Taney probably gets a grade of around C-minus or D-plus. (And, as my students will attest, I am a "soft" grader.)

The original Constitution made no effort to define who is a citizen, and was not at all clear as to whether free Negroes should be regarded as citizens. (Charles Pickney—who claimed authorship of the Constitution's privileges and immunities clause, which promised no discrimination by any state against "citizens" of other states—for one declared that it was impossible to even think of such a thing "as a black or colored citizen.") In practice, free blacks were subject to extensive legally sanctioned discrimination throughout the antebellum era in both the North and the South. Thus Taney's finding that the Framers did not regard Negroes as citizens for purposes of federal diversity jurisdiction was at least defensible. It was also consistent with the small body of prior pre–Civil War law on the question whether free Negroes should be regarded as citizens.[9]

On the other hand, Taney's efforts a) to discount the Territory Clause as a basis for Congressional authority over the territories, b) to discount the Northwest Ordinance as illustrative of the Framers' intent that Congress would possess the power to ban slavery in the territories, c) to dismiss the *American Insurance* case as relevant precedent, and d) to at least suggest that the *Somerset* principle somehow violated the Fifth Amendment, were all *very* weak indeed. The conclusion that Congress had no authority to pass the Missouri Compromise was just plain *wrong*, even under the law of Taney's day, regardless of what school of constitutional interpretation one adheres to.

Indeed, some of the points argued by Taney and his colleagues were so obviously faulty that it is difficult to believe that even their own authors were sincere in putting them forward. Did Taney truly believe that the Territory Clause was somehow intended to apply only to the U.S. territory that existed in 1789? Did he really see any conflict between the *Somerset* principle (which he appeared to have no problem with in the *Garronne* case) and the Due Process Clause? Was Campbell truly serious when he questioned the validity of the form of territorial government that had been exercised over the Louisiana Purchase? Did Campbell and Catron sincerely come to reject their own prior (privately expressed) conviction that Congress *did* possess the power to ban slavery in a territory? Was Catron actually convinced that the Louisiana Purchase Treaty somehow invalidated the subsequent Missouri Compromise, or that it protected slavery in perpetuity?

The answer to all these questions is: probably, no. The *Dred Scott* majority repeatedly took positions that strained credulity. The published Opinions in the *Dred Scott* case by themselves make it apparent that the pro-slavery Justices were willing to use whatever flimsy arguments they could find at hand in order to achieve their pre-determined goal—to strike down the Missouri Compromise, and to thereby protect slavery.

Separate and apart from the flaws in the arguments advanced by Taney and his colleagues for finding the Missouri Compromise unconstitutional was the overarching issue of the Taney Court's very decision to decide. As already detailed at great length herein, there was no valid legal justification for the *Dred Scott* Court to even consider the Missouri Compromise issue. That the Court nevertheless reached out to strike down the Missouri Compromise revealed its true purposes.

Moreover, the decision to issue a broad pro-slavery Opinion in *Dred Scott* was of a piece with the Court's willingness to abandon for this one special case so many of the Court's ordinary and sound practices. The Justices of the U.S. Supreme Court handled *Dred Scott* like no other case: They ignored the traditional rule that constitutional questions should be avoided; they disregarded the usual rule that appellate courts should consider only those issues raised before the trial court below; they leaked details about their confidential discussions of the case to the press and to politicians; they plotted in secret with the President-elect about both the *Dred Scott* decision, and about its impact on the President-elect's Inaugural Address; and, for one of the few times in the entire history of the Court prior to the Civil War, each Justice thought it necessary to write his own separate Opinion, and thus preserve for posterity (and, probably more to the point, for the contemporary press) his own individual views on *Dred Scott*. None of this was normal, and none of it was wise.

—*Dred Scott* as a Political Decision—

The most unusual and the most distressing aspect of the Court's approach to the *Dred Scott* case was the Court's powerful concern with politics—specifically, with the politics of slavery. The *Dred Scott* Court's decision to abandon Nelson's narrow Opinion, and to instead adopt Taney's broad Opinion striking down the Missouri Compromise, did not come about in a vacuum; and it was not a choice motivated by a mere abstract intellectual interest in the issue of the extent of Congressional power over the territories. Rather, the Court reached out to decide on the constitutionality of the Missouri Compromise with the conscious purpose of trying to settle the red-hot political conflict between North and South over slavery once and for all—and to do so in favor of slavery and the South.

President Buchanan played an important and improper part in politicizing *Dred Scott*. His role was almost like that of a secret tenth Justice—and a Justice with the unusual ability to dispense political favors (such as the appointment of Justice Catron's candidate as U.S. Postmaster General) at that. Buchanan worked closely with Justice Catron to slowly and discreetly assemble a majority coalition of Justices willing to issue a broad pro-slavery Opinion. Catron and Buchanan's privately acknowledged purpose was to settle the political controversy over slavery that (as Catron secretly wrote to Buchanan) "had so long and seriously agitated the country."

Buchanan and Catron ultimately succeeded. Together with Wayne, they persuaded Taney (and later Grier) to join the coalition favoring a broad pro-slavery Opinion. Indeed, on the same day that Taney cast his decisive vote in favor of a broad Opinion, Justice Wayne exulted in a conversation with Senator Yulee of Florida that he had "gained a triumph for the southern section of the country, by persuading the Chief Justice that the Court could put an end to all further agitation on the subject of slavery in the territories."[10]

Taney and his colleagues resented what they saw as self-righteous Northern attacks upon slavery and the South's system of race relations. As Justice Daniel put it, they believed that the North, with its dedication to excluding slavery from the territories, "pretended to an insulting exclusiveness or superiority . . . [that] says in effect to the Southern man, Avaunt, you are not my equal, and hence are to be excluded as carrying a moral taint with you."[11]

Taney and his colleagues further believed that Northern attacks on slavery threatened national unity and safety; they feared that anti-slavery "agitation" might foment slave rebellion and race war. As Taney put it, they believed that the "knife of assassin" was at the throat of the South, and that nothing but firm united action could check "Northern insult and Northern aggression."[12]

Taney and Wayne and their colleagues in the *Dred Scott* majority thus believed that they were acting in the best interests of the nation when they reached out to decide the question of slavery in the territories—a question that was threatening to tear the country apart. To use a phrase from Wayne's Concurring Opinion, they believed they were acting in order to restore "the peace and harmony of the country."

But they were wrong. It was not the Court's proper role to deliver a political triumph for one section of the country over the other. It was not the Court's proper role to try to quell political "agitation" of the slavery issue. Simply speaking, Taney and his colleagues should have stuck to doing their own jobs in the usual way: to decide those constitutional and legal issues that were fairly and squarely presented by the case before them, but to decide *only* those issues, and to do so in a manner consistent with precedent and logic.

—The Dangers of a Political Court—

Supreme Court Justice Oliver Wendell Holmes once wrote:

> Great cases . . . make bad law. For great cases are called great, not by reason of their real importance in shaping the law of the future, but because of some accident of immediate overwhelming interest which appeals to the feelings and distorts the judgment. These immediate interests exercise a kind of hydraulic pressure which makes what previously was clear seem doubtful, and before which even well settled principles of law will bend.[13]

Justice Holmes was right. Every once in a long while—perhaps once in a generation— a "great" case comes before the U.S. Supreme Court that grabs the attention of much of the country, that arouses intense emotions, that has the potential to reshape an important part of American life—and that comes out terribly wrong. Certain Supreme Court cases—*Dred Scott, Plessy v. Ferguson*[14] and *Korematsu*[15] come immediately to mind—stand out as monuments of legal error. (Some observers might add *Bush v. Gore*,[16] and a very different group might add *Roe v. Wade*, to this list; but there is , as yet, no general consensus as to those cases.)

Dred Scott is probably the very worst of these "great" cases. Holmes' description fits *Dred Scott* all too well. The "accident of immediate overwhelming interest" was the fear shared by Taney and his pro-slavery colleagues of the emerging Republican Party and of the ascendency of the free northern states—the fear that the "knife of the assassin" was at the throat of the South. That fear exerted a "hydraulic pressure" that distorted the *Dred Scott* Court's judgment, and caused the Court to abandon well-settled principles of constitutional law.

That fear had a solid basis in reality. By 1857 it was apparent to Taney and to most intelligent observers that the American South was fighting something of a rearguard action in defense of slavery. In 1776 slavery had been present in virtually every New World colony, from Canada to Chile. By 1857, however, most of the Western European colonial powers (as well as Mexico) had prohibited slavery in their New World possessions. By 1888 (when Brazil enacted emancipation) slavery had largely disappeared throughout the Western Hemisphere. Within the United States, the tide of history was also clearly in favor of freedom. The population and economic power of the free North were growing at a much faster rate than those of the South. As a result, the forces of freedom seemed poised to win the competition with those of slavery for the American West; slavery had so far failed to take hold even in those western territories (like Kansas and Nebraska) where "popular sovereignty" was the rule. Taney and his colleagues thus correctly understood that the South's system of slavery was, at best, destined to a long and lonely struggle for survival.

Justice Taney and his colleagues were therefore intent on safeguarding the slave South by insuring that the territories (and thus the future states to be formed from those territories) would institute slavery. In an effort to achieve those political goals, Taney and his pro-slavery colleagues misread the Constitution, ignored legal precedent, distorted history, and reached out over and over again to decide issues concerning slavery and race relations that were not properly before the Court; and Taney took the extreme pro-slavery position on every one of those issues.

The *Dred Scott* Court thus gave in to temptation. It abandoned intellectually honest legal reasoning and the disinterested application of neutral principles of law because the Court wished to pursue what it believed to be noble and important political goals.

That is a temptation that calls to "originalists" and "aspirationalists" alike. It arises whenever a case of great moral and political importance comes before the Court. It has led to some of the worst decisions in the history of the Court, with *Dred Scott* being the worst of all.

For example, in *Plessy v. Ferguson* the Court blessed "separate-but-equal" legally enforced racial segregation as constitutional, because the Court wanted to facilitate a full reconciliation between North and South following the Civil War (even at the expense of the rights of black citizens). In *Korematsu* the Court approved the large-scale imprisonment of Japanese-Americans who had never performed any disloyal act (or even harbored a disloyal thought); the Court did so because it wanted to help America to win World War II over the Nazis and the Japanese Empire, and to safeguard against espionage and sabotage. In *Bush v. Gore*, the Court stepped in to decide a Presidential election by embracing legal principles that the majority Justices had otherwise consistently rejected; the Court did so in order to insure a swift and orderly Presidential succession in a world full of dangerous enemies and nuclear weapons.

In each case the Court succumbed to the temptation to subordinate law to politics—to sacrifice intellectual integrity in order to accomplish what it considered to be important and noble political goals. And—given the overly political nature of legal discourse today—that is a temptation that is nearly as strong in twenty-first-century America as it was during the era leading up to the Civil War. *Dred Scott* should therefore serve as a constant reminder that the Court should not decide legal questions based on political considerations.

Historians disagree as to whether *Dred Scott* truly helped to cause the Civil War. In one sense, *Dred Scott*'s finding that the Missouri Compromise was unconstitutional should not have been that important. The Kansas-Nebraska Act of 1854 had already in effect repealed the Missouri Compromise for the Kansas and Nebraska Territories, and allowed the people of those territories to decide for themselves whether to permit slavery. The Kansas and Nebraska Territories made up the lion's share of the area governed by the Missouri Compromise's restriction on slavery in the territories. So the decision in *Dred Scott* to invalidate the Missouri Compromise had limited significance as a practical matter.

But, in a larger sense, the decision to invalidate the Missouri Compromise was most important and most destructive. The *Dred Scott* decision set aside a national understanding that had prevailed since 1787 that the U.S. Congress did possess the power to decide the fate of slavery in the territories, and thus in the states to be added to the Union; and the *Dred Scott* decision also essentially outlawed the Republican Party's core principle of opposition to the expansion of slavery in the territories.

The *Dred Scott* decision therefore radicalized large numbers of northern Republicans. It encouraged them to believe that there was a vast southern conspiracy afoot to expand and even nationalize slavery.

Republican attacks on *Dred Scott* and on this suspected southern conspiracy in turn further embittered and radicalized the South. Right or wrong, many southerners felt especially threatened by a seemingly lawless Republican Party that simply would not accept what the South felt should have been the Supreme Court's authoritative statement of the law of slavery. As one Virginia editorialist put it "[t]he refusal of the majority [in the North] to recognize the decision of the Supreme Court in Dred Scott as law . . . proves the inefficiency of legal, judicial or constitutional defenses against the encroachments of majorities who hold physical power."[17]

At the same time, many southerners became furious with their former ally Stephen Douglas, and with other Northern Democrats, who tried to argue that Taney's *Dred Scott* Opinion had not quite put an end to the doctrine of territorial "popular sovereignty" and who insisted on the possibility that at least some U.S. territories might remain free.

Given the mutual distrust between North and South that was reflected and magnified by the reaction to *Dred Scott*, it was not surprising that when the Republican Lincoln was elected in 1860, southern states began to leave the Union. The Civil War followed, and hundreds of thousands of American men and boys, white and black, died in battle against each other.

Dred Scott did not by itself cause all that. But by taking, without valid constitutional justification, the most controversial issue of the day—slavery in the territories—out of the hands of Congress, *Dred Scott* contributed to a series of events that made it seem impossible for the country to resolve the sectional differences between North and South through the ordinary democratic process of party politics, elections, debate and compromise. *Dred Scott* thus made conflict and war—if not irrepressible—much more likely. *Dred Scott* was a great case that made bad law; and because *Dred Scott* came at a crucial juncture in our history, it helped lead to great destruction and human suffering.

Notes

1. Thus President Bush's description of *Dred Scott* as a case where judges mistakenly declared that the "Constitution allowed slavery because of personal property rights" is off the mark. (*See* Chapter 18.) The fact of the matter is that the

original Constitution—and especially its Fugitive Slave Clause—*did* indeed allow and protect slavery because of personal property rights.

Similarly, the President's suggestion that "strict constructionist"judges —who refrain from trying to act as "law-makers"—were what was needed in *Dred Scott,* appears mistaken. The original Constitution was in fact biased in favor of slavery in that the Fugitive Slave Clause compelled citizens of the free states to honor the property rights of slaveholders from the slave states.

For that reason, Dred Scott's chief hope for freedom was based on the *Somerset* principle—a creature of *judge-made* common law that was developed by American courts in order to mitigate the original Constitution's pro-slavery bias.

It was John Sanford and his pro-slavery judicial ally Roger Taney who—like President Bush—invoked strict construction and resisted judicial "law-making."

2. Leon F. Litwack, *North of Slavery: The Negro in the Free States* (Chicago: U. of Chicago Press, 1961) is the classic study of the pervasive oppression of free African Americans in the North prior to the Civil War. Eric Foner, *Free Soil, Free Labor, Free Men* (New York: Oxford U. Press, 1970) chronicles in detail how anti-slavery forces in the North prior to the Civil War in large measure shared in the racism of slavery's supporters.

3. Alexis DeTocqueville, *Democracy in America*, P. Bradley, Ed. (New York: Oxford U. Press, 1945) Vol. I, 373.

4. Litwack, *North of Slavery*, 35.

5. *See* Chapter 13.

6. *See* Chapter 13.

7. *See* Chapter 13.

8. *See* Chapter 7.

9. Graber, *Dred Scott and the Problem of Constitutional Evil*, 28–30 and notes 83–86 collects various judicial opinions, and other legal sources, from the pre–Civil War era that concluded in a variety of contexts that free blacks were not "citizens." Pickney's comment is quoted in Davis, *Inhuman Bondage*, 279.

10. *See* Chapter 7.

11. *See* Chapter 13.

12. *See* Chapter 8.

13. *Northern Securities Co. v. United States*, 193 U.S. 197, 400–401 (1904).

14. *Plessy v. Ferguson*, 163 U.S. 537 (1896).

15. *Korematsu v. United States*, 323 U.S. 214 (1944).

16. *Bush v. Gore*, 531 U.S. 98 (2000).

17. *Richmond Semi-Weekly Examiner*, Jan. 6, 1860.

Select Bibliography

- Books -

Allen, Austin. *Origins of the Dred Scott Case: Jacksonian Jurisprudence and the Supreme Court 1837–1857*. Athens: U. Of Ga. Press, 2006.

Baker, Jean. *James Buchanan*. New York: Times Books, 2004.

Benton, Thomas Hart. *Historical and Legal Examination of that Part of the Decision of the Supreme Court of the United States in the Dred Scott Case*. New York: D. Appleton and Co., 1859. (Reprinted by Kessinger Publishing Legacy Reprints.)

Bickel, Alexander. *The Supreme Court and the Idea of Progress*. New York: Harper & Row, 1970.

——. *The Morality of Consent*. New Haven: Yale U. Press, 1975.

Bork, Robert. *The Tempting of America: The Political Seduction of the Law*. New York: The Free Press, 1990.

Currie, David. *The Constitution in the Supreme Court: The First Hundred Years, 1789–1880*. Chicago: U. Of Chicago Press, 1985.

Curtis, Benjamin. *A Memoir of Benjamin Robbins Curtis*. Boston: Little, Brown & Co., 1879.

Davis, David Brion. *Inhuman Bondage: The Rise and Fall of Slavery in the New World*. New York: Oxford U. Press, 2006.

——. *The Problem of Slavery in the Age of Revolution*. Ithaca: Cornell Press, 1975.

Dershowitz, Alan. *America on Trial: Inside the Legal Battles That Transformed Our Nation*. New York: Warner Books, 2004.

Ehrlich, Walter. *They Have No Rights: Dred Scott's Struggle for Freedom*. Westport, Ct.: Greenwood Press, 1979.

Ellis, Joseph. *American Sphinx: The Character of Thomas Jefferson*. New York: Alfred Knopf, 1997.

——. *Founding Brothers: The Revolutionary Generation*. New York: Alfred Knopf, 2001.

Ely, John Hart. *Democracy and Distrust*. Cambridge: Harvard U. Press, 1980.

Fehrenbacher, Don. *The Dred Scott Case: Its Significance in American Law and Politics*. New York: Oxford U. Press, 1978.

Finkelman, Paul. *An Imperfect Union: Slavery, Federalism and Comity*. Chapel Hill:U.N.C. Press, 1981.

——. *Slavery in the Courtroom*. Washington, D.C.: Library of Congress, 1985.

——. *Slavery and the Founders: Race and Liberty in the Age of Jefferson*. Armonk, NY: M.E. Sharpe, 1996.

——. *Dred Scott v. Sandford: A Brief History with Documents*. Boston: Bedford/St. Martin's, 1997.

Foner, Eric. *Free Soil, Free Labor, Free Men*. New York: Oxford U. Press, 1970.

Frank, John. *Justice Daniel Dissenting: A Biography, 1784–1860*. Cambridge: Harvard U. Press, 1964.

Graber, Mark. *Dred Scott and the Problem of Constitutional Evil*. New York: Cambridge U. Press, 2006.

Holzer, Harold. *Lincoln at Cooper Union: The Speech That Made Abraham Lincoln President*. New York: Simon & Schuster, 2004.

Hopkins, Vincent. *Dred Scott's Case*. New York: Fordham U. Press, 1951.

Hughes, Charles Evans. *The Supreme Court of the United States: Its Foundations, Methods and Achievements*. New York: Columbia U. Press, 1928.

Jackson, Robert. *The Struggle for Judicial Supremacy: A Study of a Crisis in American Power Politics*. New York: Vintage Books, 1941.

Jacobsohn, Gary. *The Supreme Court and the Decline of Constitutional Aspiration*. Totowa, N.J.: Rowman & Littlefield, 1986.

Kauffman, Kenneth. *Dred Scott's Advocate: A Biography of Roswell Field*. Columbia, Mo.: U of Mo. Press, 1996.

Kurland, Philip and Gerhard Casper, Eds. *Landmark Briefs and Arguments of the Supreme Court of the United States: Constitutional Law* (Vol. 3).Washington, D.C.: University Publications of America, 1978.

Kutler, Stanley, Ed., *The Dred Scott Decision: Law or Politics?* Boston: Houghton Mifflin, 1967.

Lawson, John, Ed. *American State Trials* (17 Vols.). St. Louis: Thomas Law Books, 1914–1936.

Lewis, Walker. *Without Fear or Favor: A Biography of Chief Justice Roger Brooke Taney*. Boston: Houghton,Mifflin, 1965.

Litwack, Leon. *North of Slavery: The Negro in the Free States*. Chicago: U. of Chicago Press, 1961.

Maltz, Earl. *Dred Scott and the Politics of Slavery*. Lawrence: U. of Kansas Press, 2007.

McCloskey, Robert (Rev. By Sanford Levinson). *The American Supreme Court* (4th Ed.). Chicago: U. of Chicago Press, 2005.

Menand, Louis. *The Metaphysical Club: A Story of Ideas in America*. New York: Farrar Strauss, 2001.

Moses, Shelia. *I, Dred Scott*. New York: McEldery Books, 2005.

Nevins, Allan. *The Emergence of Lincoln*. New York: Charles Scribner's, 1950.

Potter, David. *The Impending Crisis*. New York: Harper & Row, 1976.

Rehnquist, William. *Grand Inquests: The Historic Impeachments of Justice Samuel Chase and President Andrew Johnson*. New York: William Morow, 1992.

Saunders, Jr., Robert. *John Archibald Campbell: Southern Moderate*. Tuscaloosa: U. of Alabama Press, 1997.

Scalia, Antonin. *A Matter of Interpretation: Federal Courts and the Law*. Princeton: Princeton U. Press, 1997.

Simon, James. *Lincoln and Chief Justice Taney*. New York: Simon & Schuster: 2006.

Smith, Elbert. *The Presidency of James Buchanan*. Lawrence: U. of Kansas Press, 1975.

Stampp, Kenneth. *America in 1857: A Nation on the Brink*. New York: Oxford U. Press, 1990.

Steiner, Bernard. *Life of Roger Taney*. Baltimore: Williams & Wilkins, 1922.

Streichler, Stuart. *Justice Curtis and the Civil War Era*. Charlottesville: U. Va. Press, 2005.

Swisher, Carl. *Roger B. Taney*. New York: MacMillan, 1935.

——. *The Taney Period: 1836–1864*. New York: MacMillan, 1974.

Tyler, Samuel, Ed. *Memoir of Roger Brooke Taney, LLD*. Baltimore: John Murphy & Co., 1872.

Vander Velde, Lea. *Mrs. Dred Scott*. New York: Oxford U. Press, 2009.

Wallance, Gregory. *Two Men Before the Storm: Arba Crane's Recollection of Dred Scott and the Supreme Court Case That Started the Civil War*. Austin: Greenleaf Press, 2005.

Weisenburger, Francis. *The Life of John McLean*. Columbus: Ohio State Press, 1937.

Wiencek, Henry. *An Imperfect God: George Washington, His Slaves and the Creation of America*. New York: Farrar Straus, 2003.

- Articles -

Allen, Austin. "Rethinking Dred Scott: New Context for an Old Case." 82 *Chicago Kent L. Rev.* 141 (2007).

Auchimpaugh, Phillip. "James Buchanan, the Court and the Dred Scott Case." *Tennessee Historical Magazine*, Vol. IX (1926).

Ball, Milner. "A Letter to Professor Burt." 42 *Washington & Lee L. Rev.* 27 (1985).

Bestor, Arthur. "State Sovereignty and Slavery: A Reinterpretation of Pro-Slavery Constitutional Doctrine, 1846–1860." *Journal of the Illinois State Historical Association* Vol. LIV, 148 (Summer, 1961). Reprinted in S. Kutler, Ed. *The Dred Scott Decision: Law of Politics?*

Cleveland, Sarah. "Foreign Authority, American Exceptionalism and the *Dred Scott* Case." 82 *Chicago-Kent L. Rev.* 393 (2007).

Corwin, Edgar. "The Dred Scott Decision in Light of Contemporary Legal Doctrines" (1911). Reprinted in S. Kutler, Ed. *The Dred Scott Decision: Law or Politics?*

Eisgruber, Christopher. "Dred Again: Originalism's Forgotten Past." 10 *Constitutional Commentary* 37 (1993).

Fein, Bruce. "Pack the Supreme Court." *DC Bar*, Feb. 2005.

Finkelman, Paul. "The Founders and Slavery: Little Ventured, Little Gained." 13 *Yale Journal of Law and the Humanities* 413 (2001).

Graber, Mark. "Desperately Ducking Slavery: *Dred Scott* and Contemporary Constitutional Theory." 14 *Constitutional Commentary* 271 (1997).

——. "*Dred Scott* as a Centrist Decision." 83 *N.C.L. Rev.* 1229 (2005).

Janis, Mark. "Dred Scott and International Law." 43 *Columbia Journal of Transnational Law* 763 (2005).

Levinson, Sanford. "Slavery in the Canon of Constitutional Law." 68 *Chicago-Kent L. Rev.* 1087 (1993).

Maltz, Earl. "The Unlikely Hero of *Dred Scott*: Benjamin Robbins Curtis and the Constitutional Law of Slavery." 17 *Cardozo L. Rev.* 1995 (1996).

——. "*Roe v. Wade* and *Dred Scott*." 17 *Widener Law Journal* 55 (2007).

McConnell, Michael. "A Moral Realist Defense of Constitutional Democracy." 64 *Chicago-Kent L. Rev.* 89 (1988).

Mendelsohn, Wallace. "Dred Scott's Case–Revisited." 38 *Minn. L. Rev.* 16 (1953).

Mensel, Robert. "Originalism and Ancestor-Worship in the Post-Heroic Era: The *Dred Scott* Opinions." 17 *Widener Law Journal* 29 (2007).

Nash, Timothy. "Why Bush Opposes Dred Scott: It's Code for *Roe v. Wade*." *Slate*, Oct. 11, 2004.

Rehnquist, William. "The Notion of a Living Constitution." 54 *Tex. L. Rev.* 693 (1976).

Scalia, Antonin. "Originalism: the Lesser Evil." 57 *U. Cinn. L. Rev.* 849 (1989).

Slater, Daniel. "Two Men Before the Storm; Arba Crane's Recollection of Dred Scott and the Supreme Court Case that Started the Civil War." *New York Law Journal,* March 17, 2006, 2.

Sunstein, Cass. "*Dred Scott v. Sanford* and its Legacy," in Robert P. George, Ed. *Great Cases in Constitutional Law*. Princeton: Princeton U. Press (2002).

Vander Velde, L. and S. Subramanian. "Mrs. Dred Scott." 106 *Yale L.J.* 1033 (1997).

Wachtler, Sol. "*Dred Scott*: A Nightmare for Originalists." 22 *Touro L. Rev.* 575 (2006).

Weinberg, Louise. "*Dred Scott* and the Crisis of 1860." 82 *Chicago-Kent L. Rev.* 97 (2007).

Whittington, Keith. "The Road Not Taken: *Dred Scott*, Judicial Authority and Political Questions." 63 *Journal of Politics* 365 (2001).

Index

About the Author

Ethan Greenberg is an Acting State Supreme Court Justice in the Bronx, New York. He also teaches as an adjunct professor at Fordham University Law School. Judge Greenberg was first appointed to the bench in 1997. Before becoming a judge, he was a litigation partner, first with the firm of Lord Day & Lord, Barrett Smith and later with the firm Morgan Lewis & Bockius. This is his first book.

www.ingramcontent.com/pod-product-compliance
Lightning Source LLC
LaVergne TN
LVHW102005210926
848483LV00009B/47

* 9 7 8 0 7 3 9 1 3 7 5 8 1 *